SPACE 1889

SOLDIER'S COMPANION

Heliograph Incorporated

SPACE 1889®

SOLDIER'S COMPANION

Made in the U.S.A.
Printed in the U.S.A by Lightning Source.
http://www.lightningsource.com
ISBN 1-930658-10-9.

A catalog of **Space: 1889** products is available at http://www.space1889.com, or from Heliograph. Just write and ask.

Space: 1889 is Frank Chadwick's registered trademark for his games of Victorian era space-faring.

This reprint of **Soldier' Companion** was created from a scan of the original printing. For that reason, many of the photographs in this book have not reproduced as sharply as they did in the original printing. Aside from the problem with the photos, this book is identical to the original printing by GDW in August 1989.

CREDITS

Design and Development: Frank Chadwick

Additional Research: Greg Novak and Steph Lawrence

Playtesting: Loren K. Wiseman, Greg Novak, Tom Reed, Tom Harris, Neil Lasiter, Steve Anderson, and other members of the Central Illinois Tabletop Warriors

Cover Art: Richard Hasenauer

Interior Art: Angela Bostick, Tim Bradstreet, Steve Bryant, Rick Harris, Rick Lowry, and James Colton McGonigle

Art Direction: Shea Ryan

Text Manager: Michelle Sturgeon

Text Processing: Julia Martin and Julie Amdor

HELIOGRAPH INCORPORATED
26 Porter Street
Somerville, MA 02143

http://www.heliograph.com
info@heliograph.com

Table of Contents

Introduction

The essence of **Space: 1889** is a melding of science fiction with the colonial adventurism of the Victorian Era. It was a time of heroic charges, noble rescues, and the occasional broken square. Since the military was so important to the establishment and maintenance of the empire, we felt that it deserved extensive and detailed coverage of its own.

Much of the ground covered here will be familiar to players of **Sky Galleons of Mars**, as the basic system mechanics are an elaboration on that game's mechanics and, by extension, the ship combat rules from **Space: 1889**. This was deliberate, as that system was designed to provide a solid basis for land, aerial, and aquatic combat. But our principal concern was to provide a good, solid set of colonial miniatures rules. While the rules allow for the addition of submarines, gunboats, land juggernauts, combat tripods, and aerial flyers, they are not essential to the enjoyment of the game. The system works just as well for a British column fighting its way through the passes of the Northwest Frontier against Pathan marksmen in the rugged hills, or a Camel Corps square fighting off waves of dervishes and Fuzzy Wuzzies.

This manuscript is broadly divided into four books. *Book I: The Rules Of War* constitutes the actual miniatures rules and is quite extensive. While the basic mechanics of the game are simple, a variety of special cases (such as sieges, naval warfare, aerial vessels, etc.) have to be covered. Don't worry; these are all segregated into special sections of the rules, and you needn't read and absorb them until you want to actually game out such a situation.

Book II: The Road To War provides brief campaign rules for miniatures campaigns, as well as rules for integrating the **Soldier's Companion** into your **Space: 1889** role-playing campaigns. It also includes a number of sample campaigns and several preset miniatures games.

Book III: The Sinews of War covers the wealth of military equipment available. Essays on artillery and naval vessels of the world are combined with lists of armored vehicles from the **Space: 1889** world and complete vehicle design rules for land juggernauts and combat tripods.

Book IV: Army Lists provides an extensive listing of all of the major armies of Earth, as well as a great many armies from Venus, Mars, and Luna. This section covers organizational information, unit ratings, equipment, and uniforms.

Finally, at the back of the book are a number of reference charts and data sheets. These should be photocopied for you and your players' personal use, and permission to do so is hereby specifically granted.

Now it is time to start reading *Book I: The Rules of War*. In order to present the rules in a logical sequence, they have been broken up into five parts, as shown below:

THE RULES OF WAR

Part A: Basic Rules

Part B: Unit Organizations

Part C: Mechanical Conveyances

Part D: Advanced Weapons

Part E: The Defense of Places (Siege Warfare)

Once you have read the basic rules and unit organizations, you are ready to play.

Part A: Basic Rules

A FEW BASIC concepts need to be covered before addressing the the mechanical aspects of the rules.

Dice: All dice rolled in the game are simple six-sided dice numbered from one to six.

Scale: Range and distance measurements are frequently given in scale inches on the gaming surface or table. These are not actual inches.

Figures: The rules are intended for use with 25mm figures. Each figure should be mounted on its own square or round base. Infantry figures should be mounted on 3/4" bases. Cavalry figures should be mounted on 1 1/2" bases. Square balsa wood or metal bases are acceptable, but round steel washers are recommended.

These are inexpensive, uniform in size, and, for some reason, seem to have a more natural look than square bases.

Units: The rules will repeatedly refer to units. The basic unit in the game is the 20-man company or war band. Sometimes an army will have smaller units (such as platoons of infantry, troops of cavalry, or individual gun sections). The unit organization section in Part B of *The Rules of War* elaborates on this.

FORMATIONS AND FACING

TROOPS MOVE and fight in formations, and different formations have different effects on a unit's ability to move, fire, and melee. Regular troops have been extensively trained and drilled and can assume a variety of precision formations. Irregulars are not professional soldiers at all; they may be hastily mustered civilians or warrior nomads, but in either case they are not trained to move in exact formations.

Regular troops may be in column, line, square, or open order. Irregulars may be in mass or open order. Both types of troops may find themselves in disorder, which is treated as a formation for game purposes, but is actually the complete lack of one.

Artillery may be limbered or unlimbered. In both cases the gun crews are treated as if in open order.

A unit may not change formation the same turn in which it charges. Any noncharging unit can change its formation during its movement phase. (Note that only units on the side with the initiative can change formation during a turn.) The unit may make the change either at the beginning or the end of its movement phase. If it changes at the beginning of the phase, then its movement rate for the turn is based on its new formation; if it changes at the end, then its movement rate for the turn is based on its original formation.

The figures in a unit must be arranged according to the following descriptions of the specific formations.

Line

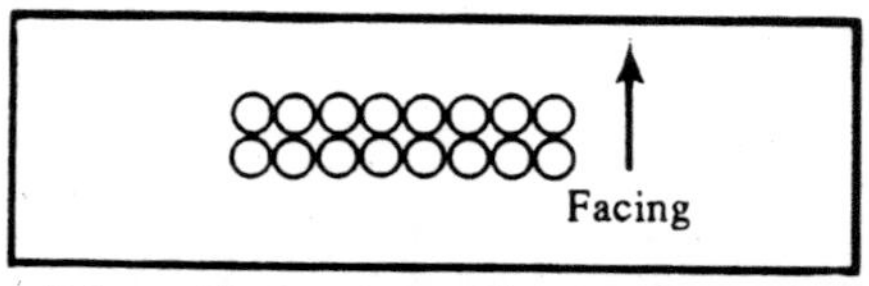

Line: One or two figures deep and as wide as desired. All bases touching.

Column

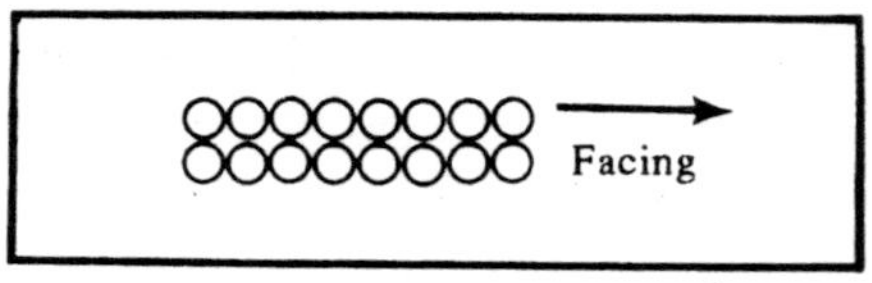

Column: Two to four figures wide, and more figures deep than wide. All bases touching.

Square

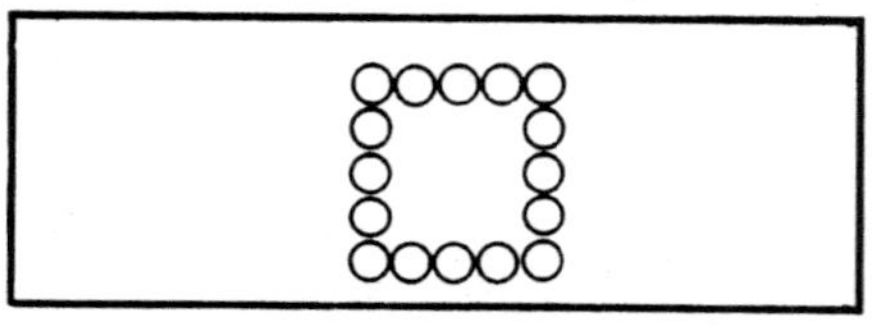

Square: Four lines forming a hollow box and facing outward.

Mass

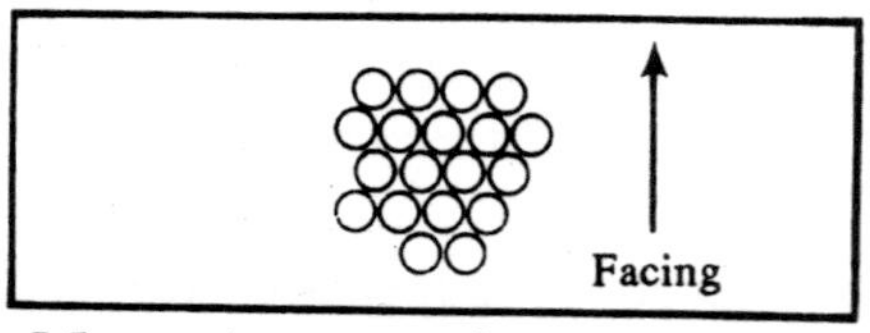

Mass: As many figures wide as deep. All figures touching.

Open Order

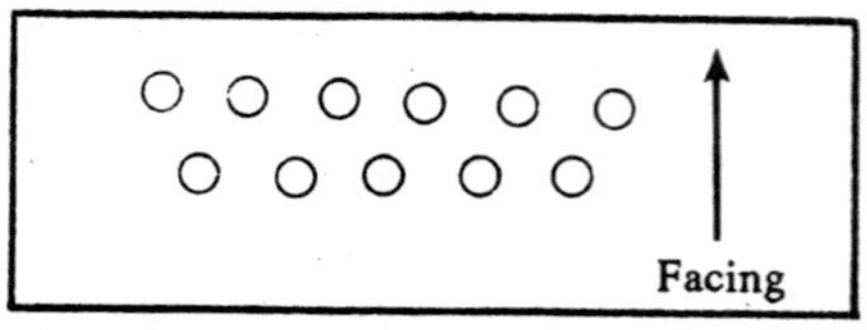

Open Order: One or two figures deep and with at least one base-width separating each figure.

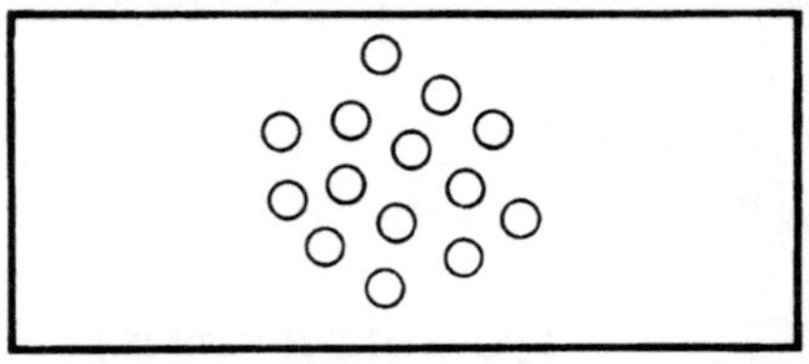

Disorder

Disorder: As many figures wide as deep and with at least one base-width separating each figure.

Formed Troops: At various times, the rules will refer to formed troops. Formed troops include all units except those in open order or disorder. In order for a unit to assume one of the formations included in the category "formed troops," it must have at least six soldiers in it. *Units with fewer than six figures may only be in open order or disorder.*

SEQUENCE OF PLAY

EACH GAME TURN has seven phases:

- Initiative Phase (both players)
- Charge Declaration Phase (moving)
- Offensive Fire Phase (moving)
- Movement Phase (moving)
- Defensive Fire Phase (nonmoving)
- Held Fire Phase (moving)
- Melee Phase (both)

In the initiative phase, players roll dice to determine who has the initiative for that turn. The player who wins the initiative roll is the moving player for the turn, and he first declares which of his units will charge during the movement phase. He then has as many of his units as he wishes fire (provided they are not committed to a charge). Next, he may move any unit which did not fire. He *must* move all units which he declared as charging. Note that each unit of the moving player may either fire or move, but may not do both.

Once the moving player has finished moving his units, the nonmoving player may have all of his units fire (the defensive fire phase). Following this, the moving player may have any units which held fire (did not move or fire previously) fire. This enables the moving player to fire at units which were concealed at the beginning of the turn but which were revealed by his movement or their fire.

Once all defensive fires and held fires are resolved, all melee attacks are resolved (the melee phase).

When a *friendly* movement phase or fire phase is mentioned in these rules, this means the next phase in which the side to whom the rule is referring could legally perform the action of moving or firing. This may mean several game turns of wait if initiative is lost repeatedly in the case of movement. Units of the moving side which perform a fire action in the offensive movement phase (including trying to clear a jam, etc.) may not perform another such action in the held fire phase.

INITIATIVE

IN THE INITIATIVE PHASE, the players determine which side has the initiative for this turn. To determine the initiative, the player representing the supreme commander for each side rolls two dice and makes any additions to the die roll as called for below. The high die roll wins the initiative, and that side is referred to as the moving player during the turn. The side which lost the initiative is referred to as the nonmoving player.

The initiative die roll is modified by several factors. These are explained below and summarized on the Initiative Table to the right.

Leadership: Every general has a leadership rating. If the supreme commander of one side has a higher leadership rating than the supreme commander of the other, he adds one to his die roll.

Regulars vs. Irregulars: If a regular army is fighting an irregular army, the regular army adds one to its die roll. In the case of armies made up of both regulars and irregulars, the majority troop type in the army determines its composition for this rule.

Frenzied Troops: If a player has one or more bodies of frenzied troops, he adds one to his initiative roll.

Isolated Leader: If the figure representing the supreme commander for one side is unable to see or address orders to a majority of the units in his army, he is considered isolated. The usual circumstances which bring this about are a majority of the army hidden by intervening terrain obstacles or out of the range of visibility of the commander at night, in a dust storm, or some other condition of limited visibility. If the commander is involved in melee combat during a turn, he is automatically considered isolated for initiative purposes in the following turn.

INITIATIVE TABLE

Factor	*Modifier*
Better Leader	+1
Regulars vs. Irregulars	+1
Frenzied Troops	+1
Isolated Leader	–1

Exceptions to Initiative: Under the following circumatances, no die roll for initiative is necessary.

1. If melees were fought in the previous turn, then the side which won the most melees automatically has the initiative. (A side which passes its post-melee morale test when all its opponents fail the test has won a melee.) If both sides won the same number, then roll the dice.

2. Either player may seize the initiative by declaring a charge from a hidden unit. Usually this option will be open only to one player, as the other player will be moving onto the battle area, and all of his units will be in the open.

3. If the figure representing the supreme commander of one side is killed, the opposing commander rolls one die and automatically has the initiative for that many turns.

4. A player may voluntarily choose to surrender the initiative to his opponent; his opponent then automatically has the initiative. A player with frenzied troops may not voluntarily surrender the initiative.

MOVEMENT

EACH UNIT'S movement allowance is determined by the type of movement being made, the type of unit making the move, and the formation it is in. All figures of a unit must move together in formation.

Types of Movement

THERE ARE TWO general types of movement: a normal move and a charge move.

Any unit may make a normal move. A unit making a normal move may never move more than half the distance toward a visible enemy unit.

Any unit except for artillery may charge (although shaken and demoralized, or disordered, infantry and cavalry units may not). In order for a player to declare a charge by a unit, the unit must be able to see the enemy unit it is to charge toward. The charging unit must move as directly toward the unit which it is charging as the terrain allows. The unit must move its full charge movement allowance toward the target unit, and if this is not sufficient to bring it in contact, the charging unit's formation is changed to disorder.

Types of Units

FOR PURPOSES of movement, there are eight different types of units: regular foot, irregular foot, regular light cavalry, regular heavy cavalry, irregular cavalry, limbered artillery, unlimbered artillery, and horse-drawn vehicles. Each of these types of troops has different movement allowances, and some have different allowed formations. These are summarized on the Movement Chart to the left.

Formations

A UNIT'S MOVEMENT allowance is determined by its formation. In addition, formations have specific limitations on movement associated with them.

MOVEMENT CHART

Infantry	*Formation*	*Move*	*Charge*
Regular	Column	18"	30"
	Line, Open Order, Disorder	12"	20"
	Square	6"	*
Irregular	All	3D"	5D"

*A square may not charge. One or more sides of the square may charge, however, and do so as lines.

Cavalry	*Formation*	*Move*	*Charge*
Regular Light	Column	24"	48"
	Line, Open Order, Disorder	18"	42"
Regular Heavy	Column	24"	42"
	Line, Open Order, Disorder	18"	36"
Irregular	All	4D"	8D"

ARTILLERY MOVEMENT

Type	*Limber*	*Move*	*Unlimber*	*Move*
Light	1/2	24"	Free	8"
Medium	1/2	24"	1/2	6"
Heavy	1/2	18"	Full	4"
Very Heavy	Full	18"	Full	2"
Siege	2 turns	12"	2 turns	—

Horse-drawn vehicles (such as wagons and carts) move as siege artillery.

Line: A line must move in a direct line or obliquely up to 45 degrees. It takes half its movement to change direction during a move. It may about-face at a cost of 2" of movement.

Column: A column may not move obliquely. It costs a column 2" of movement for every 45-degree turn it makes. A column may follow twists and turns in a road at no penalty, and may about-face at a cost of 2" of movement.

Square: A square may advance in the direction that any one of its sides is facing, but may not change direction during a move. It costs half a square's next move to change its facing.

Open Order: A unit in open order may move in any direction or combination of directions. It pays no penalty to change facing or direction of movement.

Mass: A unit in mass formation must move in a straight line. It costs half its movement to change its facing.

Disorder: A unit in disorder moves like a unit in mass formation, except the unit may not voluntarily move toward the enemy. (Frenzied units in disorder are still required to charge. See the morale rules for elaboration.)

Limbered or Unlimbered: Notice that artillery can be manhandled by its gun crew while unlimbered, but that it moves much more quickly when limbered.

Terrain

THE TWO GENERAL types of terrain are ground and barrier. A woods, for example, is categorized as ground, while a river ford or a steep slope is categorized as a barrier. Both types of terrain are categorized as being either easy, difficult, or impassable. One terrain will have different effects for different types of troops and different formations. A steep bank, for example, may be difficult for open order or disordered infantry and impassable for formed infantry. See the Terrain Types Chart (page 171).

Movement across difficult ground is at twice the normal cost. That is, each inch actually moved counts as 2" of movement. Movement across a difficult barrier consumes half the unit's movement for the turn.

The referee may designate some barriers as being wide barriers. A unit which attempts to cross a wide barrier must end its move halfway across the barrier. During the next turn, it may expend half of its movement to move the other half of the distance across the barrier, then move away from it with the remaining half.

Roads

ALL REGULARS in a column move at twice normal speed on a road. All limbered artillery and other vehicles move at twice normal speed on a road.

Special Types of Movement

A VARIETY OF special movement types, or special actions, are explained below.

Flee: Open order troops may flee, if charged. They flee during the enemy movement phase, move at the charge rate for a column or mass, must move directly away from the charging enemy unit, and end the move in disorder.

Limber/Unlimber: Artillery pieces may only limber or unlimber during a friendly movement phase. The amount of the gun's movement spent limbering or unlimbering depends on the weight of the gun. Light guns take half a move to limber and unlimber for free. Medium guns take half a move to limber or unlimber. Heavy guns take half a move to unlimber and a full move to limber. Very Heavy guns take a full move to limber or unlimber. Siege guns take two full moves to limber or unlimber. A gun may not limber and unlimber in the same move.

Change Formation: All regulars except for Green troops spend one-half their movement changing formation. Green regulars and all irregulars spend a full move changing formation.

Mount/Dismount: Mounting and dismounting counts as a formation change. Each figure dismounts in place, and one-fourth of the figures (round fractions down), along with all of the mounts, move 2" to the rear. The cost to remount includes movement to the mounts, provided they remain within 2" of the unit.

The requirement that one-quarter of the force be used as mount holders is ignored in the following cases:

If the unit is defending near a cattle pen or other similar enclosure, the mounts may be released into the enclosure. The required time to remount is doubled, however (as the men have to recover their mounts first).

If the unit does not care to remount, its mounts may be released and will run away.

If the unit has a Fieldcraft of 3, its mounts will remain where they have been left, and the entire unit may move 2" forward after dismounting to move clear of the mount line.

Passage of Files: One unit may pass through a friendly unit at no penalty, provided one or both of the units is in open order. If both units are formed, both units are disordered.

SMALL ARMS FIRE

SMALL ARMS FIRE includes the fire of all personal weapons as well as machineguns. Small arms fire by the moving player takes place in the fire phase and the held fire phase. Small arms fire by the nonmoving player takes place in the defensive fire phase. In each of the these phases the firing player must first declare the targets of all of his firing units. He then resolves fire in any order desired.

Procedure

TOTAL THE NUMBER of dice that the firing unit is allowed. This is a function of the weapons with which the unit is armed, its formation, number of men, and so forth. (See Rate of Fire below.) Next, determine the firing unit's hit number. All units start out with a hit number of 6, but this can be increased or decreased due to the nature of the firing unit or the target unit. (See Hit Procedure on page 11.) Roll the dice and note the number of hits scored. If the target is eligible to attempt saving throws, the player who owns the target unit makes the throws. (See Saving Throws on page 11.) Finally, subtract all casualties from the unit. (See Casualties on page 12.)

Rate of Fire

OVERALL FIREPOWER is expressed as number of dice per figure firing and is based on type of weapon used (see the Small Arms Firing Tables, page 170). For example, breechloaders have a rate of fire of 1; when a unit armed with breech-loading rifles fires, roll one die per figure. Rates of fire which are not expressed by a single-digit number indicate that the weapon is either a slow-firing weapon, a magazine weapon, or is subject to jamming.

Slow-Firing Weapons: Weapons which have a rate of fire expressed as a fraction are slow-firing weapons; in all cases their rate of fire is listed as "1/2." These weapons roll one die for every two figures firing. If a player wishes, he may have a regular unit armed with slow-firing weapons fire in massed volleys. If so, the unit fires one die per figure. The following restrictions apply:

1. The unit must be formed (in column, line, or square) and must use volley fire (see page 12).

2. The unit may only fire every other turn.

3. The unit may not have fired at all the turn prior to commencing massed volley fire.

Magazine Weapons: Some small arms weapons have two rates of fire separated by a hyphen. These weapons have high rates of fire while their magazines are full, but it takes some time to refill the magazine when emptied. These weapons include revolvers, multibarrel pistols, shotguns, scatterguns, and lever-action rifles and carbines. Lever-action rifles are fed from a long tubular magazine under the barrel. When it is empty, it must be reloaded one bullet at a time. Likewise, revolvers, shotguns, and scatterguns are fed from multiple chambers which, when empty, must be reloaded one bullet at a time.

Magazine weapons are given two rates of fire. The first is always a 1 and represents the unit's sustained rate of fire, which assumes that some men in the unit are reloading while others are firing. (For simplicity's sake, even an individual figure may fire at this rate.) The second number is the weapon's maximum rate of fire. A unit can roll this many dice per figure in any fire phase desired, but must then take a full fire phase to reload, during which time the weapon cannot fire. A moving unit may not reload. (It was common for troops to fire at the sustained rate of fire and save the rounds in their magazines to repulse a charge.)

Bolt-action rifles constitute a special case. All bolt-action rifles were equipped with a magazine cutoff that effectively converted the rifle to a breechloader. This was used at long range to conserve ammunition. When the enemy came closer, the cutoff was removed, and the rifle was fired from its magazine, which was usually a quick-loading box magazine attached to the rifle immediately in front of the trigger guard.

On the Small Arms Firing Tables (page 170), bolt-action rifles and carbines have two rates of fire separated by a colon. The first (2) is their rate of fire at close range; the second (1) is their rate of fire at long range.

Jammed Machineguns: Some machineguns have two rates of fire listed, with the second one in parentheses. They may always fire at the first rate of fire without danger of jamming. They may, instead, chose to fire at the larger parenthetical rate of fire, but have a chance of jamming if they do so. Roll a die after the gun fires; if a 5 or 6 is rolled, it jams. In each subsequent fire phase, roll a die. On a roll of 5 or 6, the jam is cleared; on any other roll it remains jammed. The machinegun may not fire again until the friendly fire phase after the one in which the jam was cleared.

Formation

A UNIT'S FORMATION determines how many troops in the unit may fire. It may also affect the number of casualties a unit will suffer from both small arms and artillery fire.

Line: All troops in a line may fire to the front of the line. Only the troops on the end may fire to the flank.

Column: The front two ranks of troops may fire to the front. Half of the troops on each side of the column may fire to its flank.

Square: All troops in a square may fire; the troops making up each face of the square may only fire in the direction that they are facing.

Open Order: All troops in open order may fire to the front. Only the troops on the sides may fire to the flanks.

Mass: The front rank of troops in mass formation may fire to the front. Half of the troops on each side of the mass may fire to its flank.

Disorder: Half of the front rank may fire to the front. No troops may fire to the flank.

Limbered/Unlimbered: Artillery may only fire if it is unlimbered.

Hit Procedure

EACH DIE ROLLED produces a hit if the number rolled is equal to or greater than the base hit number. The base hit number always starts out as 6, but is modified by the status of the firing unit and the target unit. These modifications are listed on the Small Arms Firing Tables. All modifications are applied to the the number needed to hit, not the die roll. For example, a –1 modifier would mean that a unit hits on a roll of 5 or more instead of a 6.

Range: The first number listed on the Small Arms Firing Tables is the weapon's close range; weapons fire at that number or less in inches is at close range. The second number is weapons long range; weapons fire at greater than close range up to the number listed in inches is at long range. Weapons which fire at long range suffer a penalty to hit of +2. Weapons may not fire at greater than long range.

Doubled Hits: Machineguns and infantry firing volleys double the number of hits rolled when firing on formed troops (anything but open order or disorder).

Defensive Fire: Defensive fire is resolved after the moving player has completed his movement, but may be conducted at a unit at any point along its path of movement. Thus, a unit which is not visible to the enemy at the start of its movement and is out of sight again at the end of its movement could still be fired at during defensive fire, provided it was visible at some point during its movement.

Cover: There are three categories of cover: light, medium, and hard. Any category of cover may be represented by either a barrier (such as a wall) or a structure (such as a building). Troops in any formation may take cover behind a barrier; only troops in open order may take cover in structures. Each category of cover has a separate modifier to the hit number.

Light cover consists of barriers or structures which partially obscure the unit behind them, but which offer no real resistance to bullets. Examples of light cover include rail fences, thorn barriers (zaribas), hedges, and grass huts.

Medium cover consists of barriers or structures which partially obscure the unit behind them and provide some resistance to bullets, but none to artillery. Examples of medium cover include wooden houses, mud huts, and low mud walls.

Hard cover consists of barriers and structures which both partially obscure the unit and provide substantial protection against bullets and artillery fire. Examples of hard cover include adobe or brick houses, stone walls, and earthworks.

Fieldcraft: Certain terrain types provide intermittent patches of cover. Only troops in open order benefit from this type of terrain, and the extent to which they do so is determined by their Fieldcraft rating. Open order troops receive a favorable hit modifier equal to their Fieldcraft rating when they are fired *at* in any terrain except clear or field. Open order troops which are eligible for a Fieldcraft advantage and a cover advantage receive whichever is greater, but not both.

Saving Throws

ALL MODIFIERS to the base hit number are cumulative. If the net modification is a positive number that would normally make it impossible to hit (as a 7 or higher would have to be rolled on a six-sided die), instead the base hit number remains 6, but the target unit is allowed a saving roll for each hit suffered. Roll the die once per hit; the casualty is saved if the roll is equal to or less than the cumulative hit modifier. However, the hit always produces a casualty on a roll of 6, even if the cumulative hit modifier is 6 or more.

For example, a unit is firing at long range (+2) at a unit behind hard cover (+3). This is a net modification of +5. The firing unit rolls to hit normally, but the defender rolls a saving roll for each hit, and saves on a roll of 5 or less.

Line of Fire

UNITS MAY NOT fire through intervening obstacles, such as buildings or woods, or any friendly or enemy units. Small arms fire may be delivered over the heads of intervening troops if the firing unit is on higher ground, the upper stories of a building, the parapet of a tall wall, etc.

Special Cases

THE FOLLOWING sections cover special types of fire or special firing units.

Firing From Walls: Units on a tall wall (such as a city or fortress wall) cannot fire at troops within 2" of the base of the wall and retain the cover of the wall. If they fire at troops within 2" of the base of the wall, they are treated as being in the open, with no cover advantage at all.

Volley Fire: Volley fire may only be conducted by regular troops in a column, line, or square. Units which conduct volley fire cause fewer casualties, since volley fire has a high hit modifier, but cause the the target unit to test morale at –2 (see Morale on page 19). In addition, the number of hits caused by volley fire is doubled if the target unit's troops are formed. The result is that while independent firing may knock more of the enemy down, volley fire is an effective means of breaking up a native charge or sweeping a unit out of your way.

Sharpshooters: Sharpshooters should multiply their weapon range by 1 1/2. For example, a breech-loading rifle has a normal close range of 12" and a long range of 24". A sharpshooter, however, would fire at close range out to 18" and long range out to 36".

Enfiladed Lines: A column or mass is generally an easy target for small arms fire, since bullets which miss the front ranks have a good chance of passing through and hitting soldiers deeper in the formation. A line is usually less vulnerable to this, which is why there is a favorable modifier to the hit number for column, mass, and disorder, but not for line. However, an enfiladed line (that is, one attacked on the flank) is like a column in many ways and so has a similar hit modifier.

A line is enfiladed if the center of the unit attacking it lies within a 45-degree arc to either side of its lengthwise axis.

For example, in the diagram below Unit A is enfiladed by Unit B, since Unit B's center is within a 45-degree arc of Unit A's lengthwise axis. Unit A is not enfiladed by Unit C. Unit C's center is outside of a 45-degree arc to either side of Unit A's lengthwise axis.

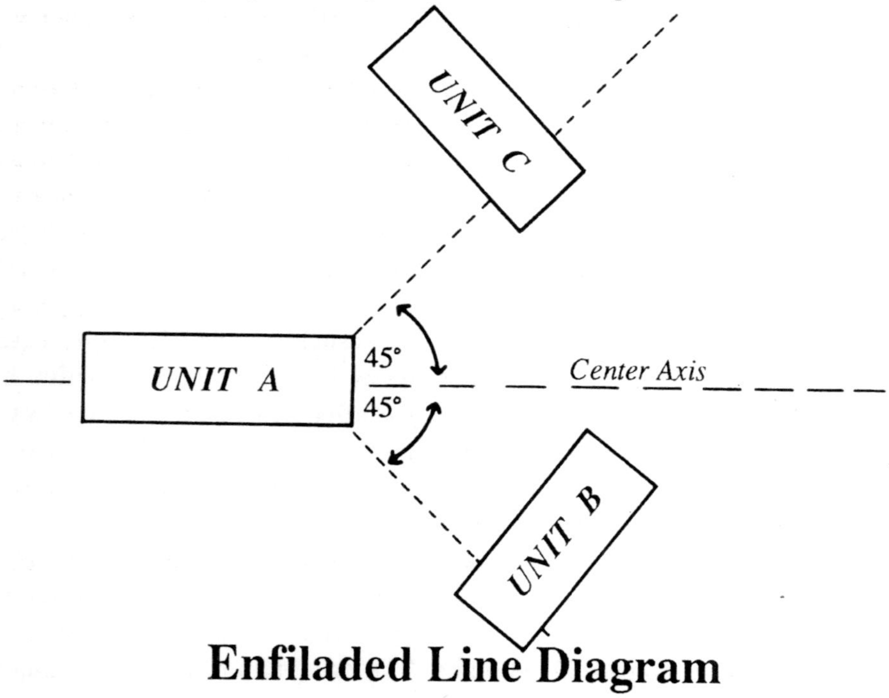

Enfiladed Line Diagram

CASUALTIES

WHENEVER CASUALTIES are taken from small arms fire or artillery fire, it is necessary to determine whether any leader figures become casualties and how many figures are wounded.

Leader Casualties: Whenever a regular unit suffers casualties in a fire phase, half of all casualties (round fractions down) are NCOs; the balance are privates. For both regulars and irregulars, roll a die. If the result is equal to or less than the number of casualties suffered by the unit, one of the casualties is an officer or leader. (In a regular unit this officer casualty is suffered *in place of* an NCO casualty if one was suffered that phase.) If the number rolled is 1 exactly, the highest ranking officer or leader in the unit is the casualty.

Artillery Gun Crews: Gun crews may be fired at as separate units if they are not formed as part of a gun section in a unit of troops. All gun crews are always in open order. A player may form a gun section up on either flank or in the middle of an infantry or cavalry unit. In this case, all small arms fire must be directed at the infantry or cavalry unit (referred to as the artillery's "supports"). All casualties inflicted are on the supports, except that half of all officer/leader casualties are gunners instead. Roll a die for each officer/leader casualty. If the result is 4-6, a gunner is lost. If the result is 1-3, an officer or leader is lost, with a roll of 1 still indicating that the highest ranking officer with the unit is a casualty.

Wounded: Two-thirds of all casualties from fire are only wounded. It is not necessary to determine which figures are wounded in an irregular band unless playing a campaign game, and even then this can be put off until after the conclusion of the battle. The same is true if two bodies of regular troops are fighting. However, if regulars are fighting irregulars, it is important to determine which regulars are wounded, since the morale of a force of regulars will decline if their wounded are left behind to irregulars.

To determine which figures are wounded, roll a die once per casualty. On a roll of 1-2, he is lightly wounded; on a 3-4, he is seriously wounded; on a 5-6, he is dead. If a unit takes many casualties, it is acceptable to count out one-third as lightly wounded, one-third as seriously wounded, and one third as dead, and roll the die only for casualties which are not evenly divisible by three.

Lightly wounded soldiers (also called walking wounded) may not fight, but may move. They move in disorder and may not move toward a visible enemy unit. Seriously wounded soldiers may not fight or move, but may be carried.

Carrying Wounded: Wounded may be carried by horses, vehicles, and other soldiers. A horse can normally carry one wounded soldier, although horses fitted with special litters can carry two wounded. Horses carrying wounded move at half their normal speed.

Each wagon can carry six wounded soldiers. Each gun limber can carry two wounded, and additional wounded may be carried on the gun carriage of a limbered gun. One wounded soldier may be carried on the carriage of a light gun, two on a medium gun, three on a heavy gun, four on a very heavy gun, and five on a siege gun. Wagons and guns move at their normal speed when carrying wounded.

Each unwounded soldier may carry one wounded soldier. Soldiers carrying wounded comrades move as if in open order, may not move toward a visible enemy unit, and may not fire. If charged, they are not allowed defensive fire, but they melee normally. If they lose the melee, the wounded troops being carried are lost to the enemy. Demoralized soldiers will not carry wounded. If soldiers carrying wounded become demoralized, they will drop the wounded and flee.

THE BOLT-ACTION MAGAZINE RIFLE

THE CONSERVATIVES asserted that with a magazine rifle the man would fire away all his cartridges. It was explained that if the fire was made to tell, as it might, with the use of proper guns, it was not half a bad idea to fire away cartridges; that, indeed, some people thought cartridges should be fired from guns, even if it soiled them with powder grime. Then it was objected that the bullet would make only a little hole in a man, and that it was much more satisfactory to literally let daylight through one's enemy than to puncture him in such a dilettante fashion....

The argument...was efficiently made in England to prove that all one really needed to do in battle, in the way of hitting an enemy, was to drop him in his tracks, and make him stop being disagreeable with his shooting, and that if one could hit him hard enough, it was just as well to do it with a fast-flying small bullet, as with a slow-going big one, while it was a much easier, surer, and simpler thing to do....

Then the conservatives had their inning. The magazine was detachable and might be lost. So it was chained to the gun....The reason for chaining the gun and magazine together is excellent, but the idea is not thoroughly carried out; if it were, all the detachable parts should be chained together: the bayonet and cleaning-rod by a couple of small chains, and the cartridges by a hundred very little ones to the gun; the gun by a stouter one to the man, and the man by a good strong one to his comrades.

(Reprinted from "The Small Arms of the European Armies," W. W. Kimball, *Scribner's Magazine*, September, 1889.)

ARTILLERY FIRE

ARTILLERY IS DIVIDED into two categories for the purposes of these rules: modern and primitive weapons. Primitive weapons include all Martian guns and all terrestrial smoothbore guns, mortars, and howitzers. Modern weapons include all the rest.

Firing Guns: Only unlimbered artillery may fire. Each type of artillery piece has a printed range. This is the weapon's close range, in feet, on the gaming table; long range is twice this.

As a general rule, artillery hits on a roll of 5 or higher at long range (from double close range to close range) and 3 or higher at close range (the close range number and less). If firing at open order troops (including all gun crews), this number is reduced to a 6 at long range, and a 5 or 6 at close range.

If a hit is scored, the round causes casualties based on the damage value (DV) of the weapon. The hit procedure and casualties inflicted vary, depending on the type of ammunition used.

Ammunition: There are four types of artillery ammunition: shot, shell, shrapnel, and grapeshot. Machine cannon may only fire shell. Modern weapons may fire shell and shrapnel. Primitive guns may fire shot and grapeshot. Primitive howitzers may fire shell and grapeshot.

Primitive mortars may only fire shell. Martian lob guns may only fire shot, but since the shot is a large stone boulder which shatters on inpact and scatters fragments, it is treated as if it were a shell.

Shell: Shell is a hollow metal artillery round filled with explosives and either a timed fuse or a contact fuse. When the round hits, it explodes. Modern weapons and machine cannon may fire shell at any range. If a hit is scored by a gun firing shell, it causes casualties equal to the damage value of the gun.

This is halved (round fractions up) if the target unit was in open order and doubled if the target was in column or mass.

Shot: Shot is a solid, round projectile, usually made of iron, but sometimes carved from stone. Primitive guns fire shot at any range. If a hit is scored by a gun firing shot, it causes casualties equal to the value of the gun against units in column, mass, or enfiladed line.

In all other cases, casualties equal half the damage value of the gun (round fractions up).

Shrapnel: Shrapnel is a a hollow projectile filled with a small bursting charge, many small bullets, and using a timed fuse. The round is fired at enemy troops and timed to detonate while overhead, showering them with bullets.

Most modern weapons may fire shrapnel at any range, but modern guns with an asterisk after their damage value (including all machine cannon) may not fire shrapnel. If a shrapnel hit is scored, roll one die. The result is the number of casualites inflicted. Halve the result (rounding fractions down) when firing at troops in open order.

Grapeshot: Grapeshot (also called canister) consists of lots of smaller round shot loaded into the muzzle of a gun or howitzer, turning it into a large shotgun. Smoothbore guns fire grapeshot and may do so at half their printed close range. Smoothbore howitzers may fire grapeshot to a range of 12" (regardless of their printed range). When firing grapeshot, add one to the chance of scoring a hit.

If a hit is scored, roll one die. The result is the number of casualties inflicted. Halve the result (rounding fractions down) when firing at troops in open order.

Casualties: All casualties suffered as a result of shot are killed. All casualties suffered from other types of artillery ammunition produce kills and wounded in the same way as small arms fire.

Rate of Fire: The artillery tables list the rate of fire (ROF) of each artillery piece. Rate of fire is the number of shots the weapon can fire each friendly fire phase. A parenthetical ROF is the number of turns the gun spends reloading between shots.

The gun charts (pages 172-175) list the required crew of each gun. For every deficiency of two gunners (one gunner if on a ship, vehicle, flyer, or fortress-mounted gun) reduce the rate of fire by one. If the rate of fire is already one or less, each reduction adds one turn to the time required to reload the gun.

For example, a 15-pounder field gun has a rate of fire of 1 and a crew of four. If the crew were reduced to two, the rate of fire would become (1), meaning it takes one turn to reload. A 7" gun has a rate of fire of (2) and a crew of six; if its crew were reduced to two, its rate of fire would become (4). If all gunners are killed, the gun may not fire. Gunner casualties may be replaced by gunners from other guns, by extra men from the artillery unit (drivers), or by any officer.

Guns which have fired and which must be reloaded should be marked by placing a cotton ball in front of the gun. This serves as an easy memory aid.

The next friendly fire phase, after all other weapons have fired, remove the cotton ball. If the weapon requires two fire phases to reload, place two cotton balls in front of the gun and remove one each friendly fire phase it reloads.

Cover: Cover has different effects on artillery than on small arms fire.

Light Cover: Light cover has no effect on artillery fire.

Medium Cover: Casualties from shrapnel and grapeshot are halved against troops behind medium cover. This is cumulative with other halvings or modifiers. Medium cover has no effect on shot or shell.

Hard Cover: Troops behind hard cover are immune to shrapnel and grapeshot. Shot and shell fired at troops behind hard cover may do less damage than normal, depending on the penetration of the gun and the armor value of the cover.

Penetration is listed on the gun charts in the Pen column (pages 172-175). The first number is the weapon's penetration at close range; the second is its penetration at long range. The armor value of a number of typical types of hard cover is also listed. If the penetration of the gun is less than the armor value of the cover, the gun has its damage value halved (round fractions up). If the penetration is less than half the armor value of the cover, the firing player rolls a die. If the result is equal to or less than the damage value of the gun, it causes damage as if with an effective damage value of 1. Otherwise it has no effect.

Line of Fire: Artillery may not fire through intervening obstacles, such as buildings or woods, or any friendly or enemy units.

Artillery may fire over the heads of intervening troops if the firing unit is on higher ground, the upper stories of a building, the parapet of a tall wall, etc. However, artillery may never fire canister (grapeshot) over the heads of friendly troops.

Artillery fired from high walls or towers, such in a city or fortress, may not fire at targets within 2" of the base of the wall.

High-Angle Fire: Howitzers, mortars, and lob guns (the Martian term for a heavy mortar) conduct high-angle fire and have several special characteristics.

Range: The printed range on the gun charts (pages 172-175) is the maximum range of the weapon. Rifled howitzers always hit on a roll of 5 or 6, regardless of how near or distant the target, provided it is within their printed range. Smoothbore mortars and howitzers, and Martian lob guns always hit on a roll of 6, regardless of how near or distant the target, provided it is within their printed range.

Indirect Fire: High-angle fire weapons may fire over intervening obstacles at hidden targets. This is allowed if an artillery officer is within 6" of the firing weapon and can see the target himself (usually the case when a mortar or howitzer is set up behind a hill or city wall, and the artillery officer is in a vantage point to direct the fire). If allowed, the fire is resolved normally.

Searching Fire: High-angle fire weapons may fire at troops behind intervening obstacles (such as hills, or woods, or inside the middle of a town) which are not visible to either the firing weapon or an observer. This is called searching fire. The normal roll to hit is made, but the referee then makes an additional "confirming" die roll.

The hit is confirmed on a roll of 5 or 6, and it misses on any other roll. The confirming roll may be made openly and the casualty visibly removed if a unit of the firing player is in a position to witness the effects. Otherwise, the confirming roll and all casualty rolls are made in secret by the referee.

A player may not engage in searching fire until he has seen at least one enemy unit somewhere in the battle area.

Firing at Fortification: Units in fortifications which are hit by high-angle shell fire receive no cover benefit from the fortification (since the shell lands behind the walls).

Counterbattery Fire: Field guns may fire at individual enemy guns, even if they are attached to an infantry unit. When firing at an enemy gun with shot or shell and a hit is achieved, roll a die. On a roll of 6, the gun is hit and destroyed; otherwise, the hit causes artillery gun crew casualties (as on pages 12–13). Remember that gun crews are treated as troops in open order for purposes of hit and casualty determination.

Spiking Guns: Only gunners may spike guns. If a gunner spends a full friendly movement phase adjacent to a gun and attempts to spike it, roll a die.

On a roll or 4, 5, or 6, it is spiked (rendered unfireable). Spiked guns may be repaired later. During a campaign game or a siege, roll once per spiked gun per day. The gun is repaired on a roll of 1 or 2.

MELEE

MELEE TAKES place when two bodies of troops are in contact at the start of the melee phase. A unit may voluntarily enter melee only as the result of a charge. It is possible for a unit to inadvertently enter a melee by walking into the position of a previously unspotted enemy unit.

Allocation: First, determine how many figures are involved in the melee. Only the parts of the two units actually in contact may fight. If part of a charging unit is stopped by coming in contact with the opposing unit, the rest of the charging unit may continue to move directly forward if this would bring it in contact with the opposing unit. In the example below, Unit A's left flank is halted by contact with Unit B. The rest of Unit A may continue forward and make contact, as illustrated.

Example: Before

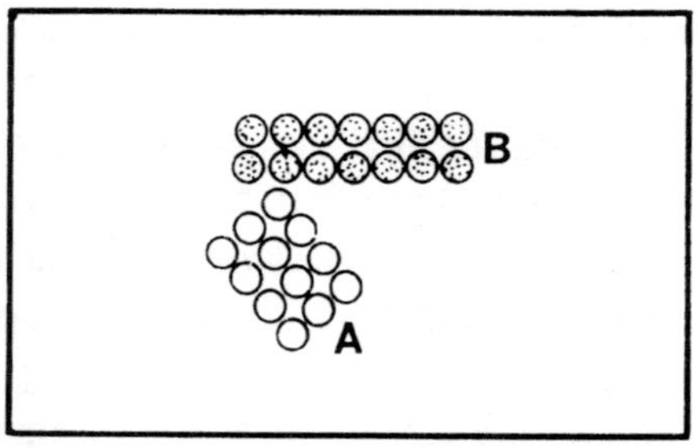

Example: After

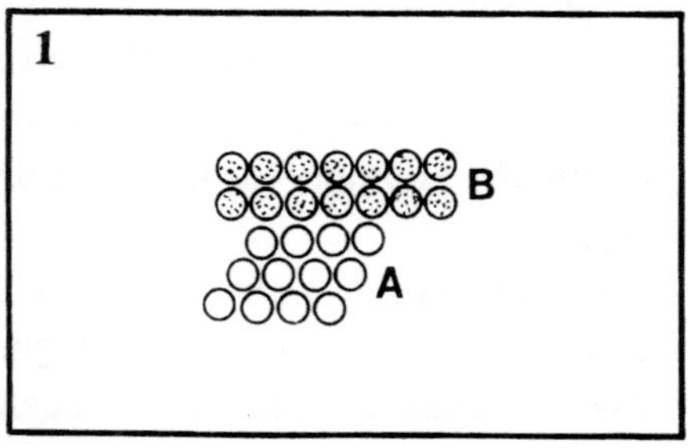

The front two ranks of a formed unit may fight. Only the first rank of a unit in open order or disorder may fight. In the example which follows, Unit A (in line) has charged Unit B (in open order). Ten figures from Unit A are involved in melee; only three figures from Unit B are involved.

Example

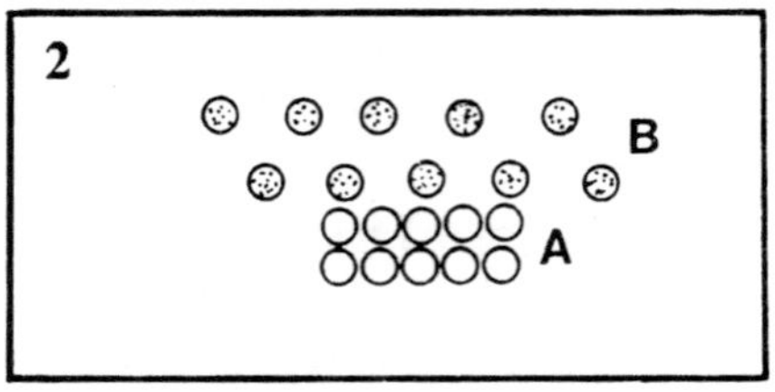

A unit attacked from the flank may only fight with one rank of troops on that flank. In the example below, Unit A (in column) has charged the flank of Unit B (in line). A total of six figures are in melee from Unit A, while only the two end figures are in melee from Unit B.

Example

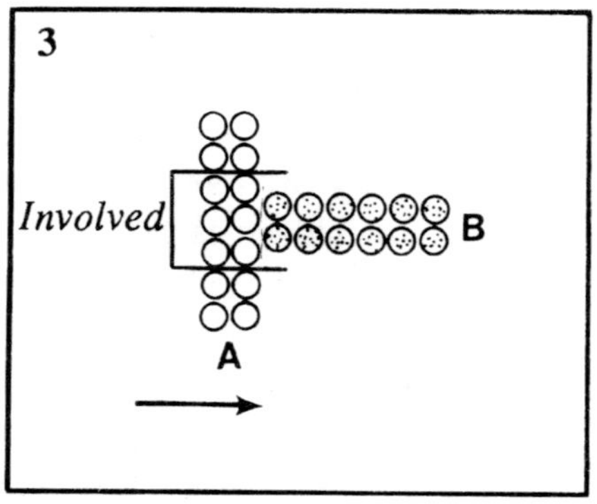

All figures involved in the melee are paired off against each other. If one side has more figures than the other, the extra figures are used to "gang up on" the other side, but must be distributed as evenly as possible. For instance, in the example above Unit A has six figures in contact to two for Unit B. Unit A would match three figures against each of Unit B's men, not five against one and one against the other.

Resolution: In each melee contest, roll one die per figure. The highest roll after modifications wins. Add to the die roll as in the Resolution Modifiers Table on page 17.

Three results are possible:

- One die roll is twice that of the other: The losing figure is killed.
- One die roll is more than the other, but less than twice as much: The losing figure loses the melee and is forced back to the rear of his unit.
- The die roll is tied: Neither figure is forced back.

If two opposing figures both have melee modifiers, they do not cancel each other out; all additions are still made. Note that while equal melee modifiers on both sides may not alter the chances of one side winning the melee, they make it more difficult to achieve twice the opponent's score. Thus, if both sides have modifiers, as, for example, in a cavalry versus cavalry melee, there will tend to be fewer casualties.

If several attackers are fighting one defender, the defender rolls one die as usual, and the attacker rolls one die per attacking soldier, applying the appropriate modifiers to each die. He then uses the single highest modified die roll for purposes of the melee. If the lone defender wins, only one attacking soldier, of the attacker's choice, is forced back to the rear of the unit. The lone defender only kills an enemy if he rolls twice the highest of the attacking die rolls, and then he only kills one attacker, of the attacker's choice.

Morale Tests: Once all of the individual melees are resolved, test morale for each unit involved in the melee, as explained in the morale rule on page 19. In most cases, one or both of the units will retreat from the melee. If both units end the turn still in contact, the melee continues the next turn.

If infantry fails the morale check while fighting cavalry and the cavalry passes their check, the infantry will run and the cavalry will immediately pursue them. The cavalry unit will move half the distance the infantry unit would have run and stop there in disorder (having caught up with the infantry and begun to saber them). The infantry unit suffers as many additional casualties as there are pursuing enemy cavalry. If any infantry survive, the unit breaks and is removed from play. (This is important only if playing a campaign game in which the number of actual survivors is important. In a scenario game, simply remove the infantry unit.)

If, due to the nature of the terrain, the owning player can demonstrate that his fleeing infantry can outdistance the pursuing enemy cavalry, then the infantry will run its full charge move, the cavalry will pursue as far as its movement and terrain allow, and both units will be disordered. (The infantry unit will not take casualties or be removed.)

Melee-Caused Disorder: Infantry in square formation which wins its melee and which avoids becoming Frenzied (see the morale rule) remains in square formation. In all other cases all troops are disordered after fighting one turn of melee. This is so whether the unit wins, loses, or remains in melee.

MELEE MODIFIERS

Factor	*Modifier*
Officer, Leader, Chief, Senior NCO**	+1
Higher Troop Quality	+ Difference
British in Square	+1
Lancers Charging	+1
Light Horse	+1
Light Cavalry (Including All Irregulars)	+2
Heavy Cavalry	+3
Gashant vs. Horse	+1 (for gashaant)
Infantry in Square vs. Cavalry	+1
(British receive this in addition to their normal square bonus.)	
Infantry Defending from Higher Ground	+1
Infantry Defending Fortification, Doorway, or Barricade	+1
Attacking From Flank	+1
Checked Adversary	+1
Disordered Adversary	+1
Weak Adversary*	+1

*Includes Moon Men, Lizard-men, Selenites, and firearm-equipped irregulars.

**A senior NCO is any NCO above the rank of sergeant. (In the British Army this includes colour sergeants and sergeant majors.) Senior musician NCOs (drum majors, pipe majors, trumpet majors) do not count as senior NCOs for melee.

A scientific party defends a ruined temple against Canal Martian infantry. Martian archers converted from RAFM elves. All other figures from GDW.

Continuing Melee: If, as result of the morale checks after the melee phase, two or more opposing units remain in contact, then the melee will continue in the melee phase of the following turn. These special conditions apply to a continuing melee:

At the start of the second melee phase both sides may spread out to their flanks if they are in a formation three or more ranks deep. Each formation may expand its frontage by 50 percent to each flank; if it is possible to expand to both flanks, then a unit could conceivably double its frontage. All figures used to spread to the flanks must be from the third rank or further back; second rank figures may not be used. If one unit is able to spread out farther than its opponent, the extra figures may curl around the opponent's flank and join the melee in that manner.

Continuing Melee

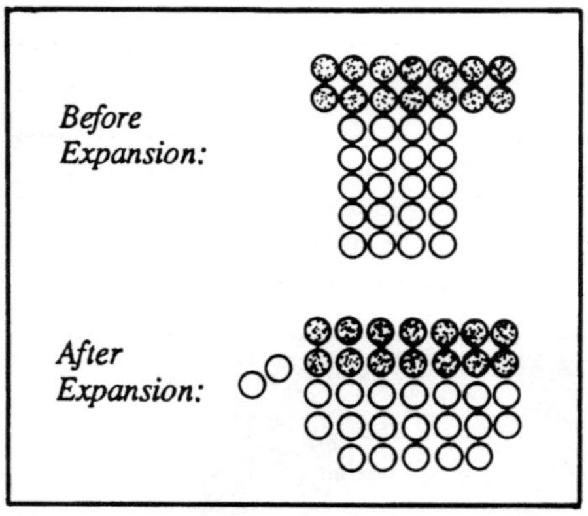

Since both sides will be disordered at the start of the second melee turn, only the figures in the front rank and actually in contact may fight.

Either side may fire into a continuing melee, but all losses are randomly assigned to the units of each side.

Special Cases: The following special cases are likely to occur fairly frequently.

Charged From the Flank: In order for an attack to count as a charge from the flank, the center of the front rank of the charging unit must be in contact with the flank of the defending unit.

In example one below, the unit is attacked in flank. In example two, the unit is not attacked in flank.

Example 1

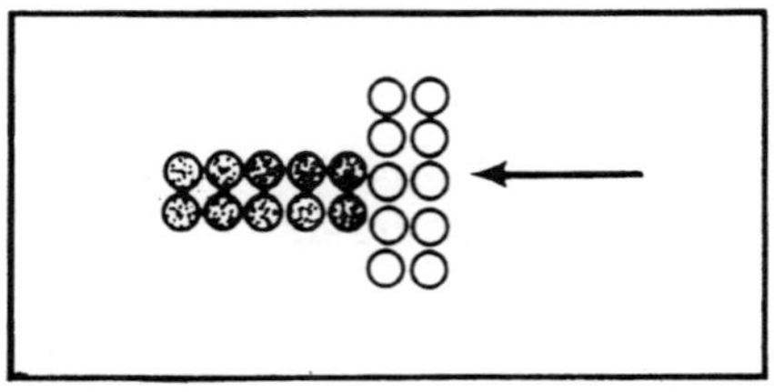

Example 2

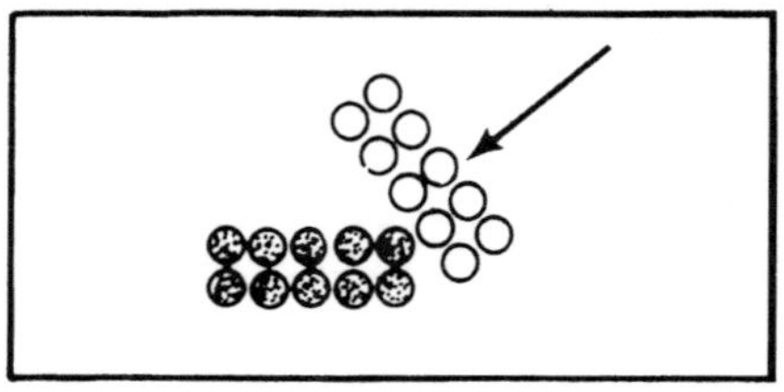

If a unit is charged from the flank, the soldiers on the contacted flank turn and fight their attackers but may not fire defensive fire.

Charged From Behind: In order for an attack to count as a charge from behind, the center of the front rank of the charging unit must be in contact with the rear of the defending unit. If a unit is charged from behind and is already locked in melee, each charging soldier who ends in contact with the unit kills the figure he is in contact with. If a unit is charged from behind and is not locked in melee, it is allowed to turn and face its attackers but is not allowed defensive fire. If a unit is charged simultaneously from the front and the rear, half the soldiers in the unit turn and face to the rear and melee, and half fire to the front and melee.

If the defender is in column or mass formation, the rear rank will turn to face the charging enemy and the front rank or ranks will be able to fire normally.

Cavalry vs. Open Order/Disorder: If a cavalry unit charges either infantry or cavalry in open order or disorder, stop the charging cavalry unit at the point of contact, but place a marker of some sort at the extent of the unit's full charge movement allowance. If the charging cavalry unit fails a morale test due to defensive fire, it will recoil to its starting position, and the marker can be removed. If the cavalry unit does not fail its test, it will automatically cut its way through the open order or disordered unit and end its move where the marker is placed. If the defending unit is infantry, kill one infantryman for every two charging cavalrymen. If the defending unit is cavalry, conduct a normal melee round. The charging cavalry figures which lose melees recoil to their starting positions and effectively become a separate unit until they manage to rejoin their parent unit.

If the charging cavalry collides with another unit before it reaches the end of its movement, it will fight another melee round. (If the second unit is also in open order or disorder, the melee will take place as described immediately above and the charging cavalry will then continue its movement.) Note that any additional units encountered during the charge will not have the opportunity to conduct defensive fire against the charging unit. (They didn't expect it to get this far.)

MORALE

BATTLES ARE SELDOM fought to the last man; instead, victory goes to the army whose morale best survives the shock of combat.

Morale States: Each regular unit is in one of the following morale states at all times:

- Frenzied
- Steady
- Shaken
- Demoralized
- Broken

Irregular units are in one of the same morale states, except that irregulars have no Shaken morale state; they go directly from Steady to Demoralized.

As a general rule, all units begin the game Steady. The referee may, however, begin units in any morale state desired. A unit's morale state may change due to either fire combat or melee.

The effects of the different morale states are as follows:

Frenzied: The unit must pursue a retreating enemy beaten in melee. If no such unit is visible, it must charge the closest enemy unit. Even units in disorder are required to charge. Frenzied units move or charge in their friendly movement phase.

Steady: The unit performs normally.

Shaken: Irregulars are never shaken. A shaken regular unit will not advance toward the enemy. When firing, the unit fires half the number of dice normally allowed. In addition, on the turn the unit suffers the shaken result it will do the following:

If stationary behind cover, the unit will go completely behind cover. All saving rolls for hits on the unit the next turn are automatically made, but the unit may not fire at all. This applies only to morale checks caused by fire combat. If the Shaken state is caused by melee, the unit falls back a half move.

If the unit is charging, it recoils to its starting position.

If the unit is stationary in the open, it falls back a full charge move.

Demoralized: A demoralized unit will retreat at its charge movement rate away from the closest visible enemy, and will continue to do so until it is in some form of cover. All demoralized units are in disorder and may not assume any other formation so long as they remain demoralized.

Broken: A broken unit will either permanently leave the field or, if that is not possible, will surrender to the closest enemy unit. In either case, the unit is permanently removed from play. (The distinction is only important when playing campaign games, where any broken troops which escape will later rejoin the army.)

Troop Quality: Troop quality is a measure of the training, experience, and esprit de corps of a unit. There are five levels of troop quality, ranging from Green to Elite. Each level of troop quality has an associated morale number. This number is the amount of punishment that a unit can take before having to check morale. The various troop qualities and morale numbers are:

MORALE NUMBERS

Quality	*Morale*
Green	7
Trained	8
Experienced	9
Veteran	10
Elite	12

Morale Modifiers: A unit's morale number can be modified up or down for a variety of circumstances (see the Morale Modifiers Chart, page 171). Most of these are self-explanatory.

Superior officer present means that the officer is physically present with and part of the unit or detachment, not merely visible to it. A superior offi-

Venusian schutztruppen chase an English couple into the swamps. Lizard-men converted from RAFM Reptiliades.

cer may only be present with one unit or detachment at a time.

Banner, flag, or musician advancing (or retiring) in sight means that a unit receives a morale modificiation if a friendly banner, flag, or musician is advancing (or retiring) in sight.

Defending at night does not refer to the overall role of a side in a scenario but instead specifically refers to the player who does not have the initiative in the current turn. (Night actions are very confusing, and actually getting your troops to undertake some purposeful movement is good for their spirits and frightening to the enemy.)

Own (regular) wounded left to irregular enemy means that a regular force's morale will suffer if their wounded are allowed to fall into the hands of irregulars. This modification is permanent for the rest of the battle. The first time this happens in a battle, it will affect the morale of the unit or units to which the wounded men belong. The second time it happens it will affect the entire army. A third occurrence has no additional effects.

Firearm irregulars charging or charged refers to an irregular unit armed entirely (with the possible exception of leaders) with firearms. Irregulars armed with firearms are generally reluctant to close with the enemy and this morale modifier reflects that. This modifier is also in effect for any morale tests made by the unit as a result of melee.

Under cover means that the unit is in a position to receive a favorable modifier from either cover or Fieldcraft when fired upon. Troops in brush, for example, are considered under cover if in open order, but not if formed.

Attacked from flank means that the unit was enfiladed during fire combat by either small arms fire or artillery fire (see page 12 for the definition of enfilade), or attacked from the flank during melee combat. In order for a melee attack to count as a flank attack, the center of the front rank of the attacking unit must be in contact with the flank of the defending unit.

Decreasing Morale State: A unit's morale state may decline either due to fire, melee, or fear of impact. In all cases, the unit will be called upon to test morale. A unit may be required to test once per phase but never more than once per phase. A unit tests morale by rolling two dice and adding the results together. If the total is equal to or less than the unit's current morale, the unit passes. If the result is one or two greater than the current morale, the unit suffers a *check*. If the result is three or more greater than the unit's current morale, the unit's morale declines one morale state.

Checked: If a unit suffers a check, it may not advance toward the enemy and fires at half its normal rate of fire. Small arms units fire half their normal number of dice (round fractions down). Artillery units fire (or reload) half their guns; solitary gun sections roll a die and fire (or reload) on a roll of 1-3. A charging unit which suffers a check stops halfway to the object of its charge. The effects of a check last for the rest of the turn in which it was suffered and for all of the next turn. In addition to the above effects, any Frenzied unit which suffers a check has its morale state reduced to Steady.

Fire Combat: If a unit is fired at in a fire phase, it must test morale. Its current morale number is reduced by one for every hit suffered during the fire phase. Note that a hit which does not produce a casualty due to a successful saving roll still counts against morale. So, for example, a unit which suffered six hits but made four successful saving throws would only suffer two actual casualties but would test morale at –6 for hits (in addition to any other modifiers). Each casualty suffered due to artillery fire is treated as a small arms hit.

Melee Combat: If a unit is involved in melee combat, it must test morale at the end of the turn. Its current morale number is reduced by one for every soldier forced to the rear of the unit due to losing a melee and is reduced by two for every man killed in melee.

If both units in a melee pass their morale tests or suffer only checked results, they will remain locked in melee for another turn. At the end of the next turn, only men forced to the rear or killed in that turn are counted for morale purposes (even though the men forced back in the first turn may not rejoin the fight).

For example, a unit loses five melees in a turn, of which three result in a forced back soldier and two result in kills. The unit tests morale a –7. It passes its morale test and fights again next turn, in which it loses three more melees: two men forced back and one killed. It now tests morale at –4.

Fear of Impact: Whenever a unit is charged, it must test morale at the end of the movement phase in which the charge took place.

Detachments: A detachment, for purposes of morale, is any group with 10 or fewer figures. A unit may be reduced to the status of a detachment by casualties, or it may begin the game that way (as, for example, a separate gun section or detached platoon). Detachments check morale normally, except that all negative morale modifiers due to fire combat hits, lost melees, and casualties are doubled. A detachment of Veterans and a unit of Veterans, for example, both normally tests for an 11. If both of them take two hits in fire combat, however, the unit would test for a 9 while the detachment tested for a 7.

Increasing Morale State: A unit's morale state may increase due to rallying, witnessing a victory, or winning a melee.

Rallying: If a demoralized or shaken unit belonging to a moving player spends one friendly movement phase stationary with a superior officer or leader (other than the officers or leaders of the unit itself) and is not fired upon or engaged in melee, it increases one morale state (but it never goes higher than Steady).

Witness to Victory: If a Shaken or Demoralized regular unit (other than a Green or Trained regular unit, for which see below) sees an enemy unit retire due to a failed morale test, roll a morale test for the witnessing unit. If the unit passes the test, its morale state becomes Steady; if it fails, there is no effect.

If a Green or Trained regular unit, or any irregular unit at any morale state sees an enemy unit retire due to a failed morale test, roll a morale test for the witnessing unit. If it passes, its morale becomes (or remains) Steady; if it fails the test, its morale state becomes Frenzied.

No unit involved in melee ever makes a witness-to-victory test, as its attention is otherwise occupied. Note that all units conducting a witness-to-victory test do so with a –2 morale modifier. This serves to make them more likely to become Frenzied.

Victorious in Melee: All irregular units, and all Green and Trained regulars which win a melee immediately become Frenzied. If an Experienced, Veteran, or Elite regular unit wins a melee (passes its morale test while its opponent fails its test and retreats), test its morale again. If it passes the test, its morale state becomes (or remains) Steady; if it fails the test, its morale state becomes Frenzied. (Note that this allows regulars who began the turn Frenzied to be brought back under control if they win a melee.)

German infantry advances in support of a combat tripod. Figures by Wargames Foundry.

LEADERSHIP

ALL UNITS BEGIN with several officers or leaders. Over the course of the game officers and leaders will become casualties, and a unit may find itself without any officers or leaders present, which affects the unit as follows:

A regular unit without an officer present may not advance toward the enemy and suffers a –1 morale modifier, providing there is still at least one NCO present with the unit.

If there are no NCOs present, the unit is immediately lowered to a morale state of demoralized. Any other officer may serve as the officer of a regular unit if the unit's own officers have been killed, provided the officer is physically present with the unit.

An irregular band which has lost all of its leaders will flee from the field or, if that is not practical, surrender to the closest enemy unit. In either case, it is eliminated from play.

In addition to the above, each army has one or more senior officers who command groups of units rather than a single unit or detachment. Each of these officers has a leadership rating of from 0 to 3. (Roll a die and divide by two, rounding fractions down.) The supreme commander's leadership affects the morale and initiative of the army.

The leadership of each senior officer affects the morale of any unit or detachment to which the officer attaches himself.

A unit or detachment only receives a morale bonus from the highest-ranking officer attached to it, not from all officers attached to it. A senior officer may only be attached to one unit at a time.

HIDDEN UNITS

USUALLY, ONLY one side will have hidden units at the start of the game, although a referee may generate a battle in which both sides have units hidden from view. Units may start the game hidden by being behind a blocking feature or in concealing terrain.

Concealing terrain includes any area of sharply uneven ground (such as hills, gullies, and boulder fields), tall patches of vegetation (such as brush, woods, or very tall grass), or structures (such as villages, camps, and farmsteads).

Blocking features include hills, settlements, walls, woods, and forests. A unit may see over a blocking feature if it is on even higher ground. However, a blocking feature has a 3" "shadow" behind it within which units are hidden from view even from higher ground. A unit may be concealed on the edge of a forest or woods. A unit fully inside a forest or woods may not be seen and may not see out. If two units are both inside the same forest or woods, they see each other if they are within 2" of each other.

A unit behind a blocking feature may not be seen until an enemy unit has an unobstructed line of sight to it. A unit in concealing terrain may be seen as soon as an enemy unit enters its detection range. Detection range in inches for hidden units is the Fieldcraft of the spotting unit times five. For example, a unit with a Fieldcraft of 3 spots enemy units in concealing terrain at a distance of 15". Units with a Fieldcraft of 0 do not spot hidden units until they come into physical contact. A unit in concealing terrain is also spotted as soon as it fires.

Spotting of concealed units takes place at the end of movement and in whatever fire phase a unit fires.

Units with a Fieldcraft of 0 may not be hidden in concealing terrain, but they may be hidden behind blocking terrain.

MOUNTED INFANTRY AND LIGHT HORSE

MANY ARMIES deployed mounted infantry or light horsemen due to the strategic mobility it offered. Mounted infantry units were just that: infantrymen mounted on horseback. They were not cavalrymen and were not trained to fight mounted. Light horsemen, on the other hand, were experienced horsemen trained to fight dismounted.

Mounted infantrymen may not fire while mounted. They may charge while mounted, but do not receive any melee bonus for being cavalry. Mounted infantry move at the regular heavy cavalry rate.

Light horsemen may fire while mounted. They may charge while mounted and receive the light horseman melee bonus of +1. Light horsemen move at the regular light cavalry rate. The Australian Light Horse is a good example of light horsemen, as opposed to mounted infantry.

LIGHT PACK GUNS

CERTAIN LIGHT FIELD GUNS and machineguns were designed to be broken down for transportation by animals in difficult terrain. Pack artillery includes the 2-pounder gun, the 6-pounder gun, and the 7-pounder mountain howitzer. Pack machineguns include the Maxim, the Gardner, and the .50-caliber Gatling.

Pack weapons can be manhandled

more easily than regular artillery. When unlimbered, they treat all ground and barriers as one difficulty level less. Impassable barriers become difficult; difficult becomes open. (Open remains open.) When limbered, they move normally.

Instead of limbering, a pack weapon may be broken down into loads and strapped to pack animals. Pack animals move at the rate of infantry in column but treat terrain the same as open order cavalry. It takes one complete turn to disassemble a pack weapon and load it onto pack animals. To reassemble the weapon, roll a die and halve the result (rounding fractions up). It takes that many friendly movement phases to reassemble the gun.

NIGHT

The main effects of night are on visibility and morale.

Visibility and Detection: Visibility at night is mostly a function of ambient light, which is due to moonlight and starlight, and is affected by cloud cover.

Maximum visibility in inches on Mars and Earth at night is equal to the roll of two dice. Maximum visibility on Venus at night is equal to the roll of one die.

It is possible to detect the approach of units at night as far away as 20" by sound. To do so, roll a die and subtract one for each moving enemy unit within 20" in excess of one. If the result is equal to or less than the detecting unit's Fieldcraft, the enemy units are detected. Detected enemy units which have not yet been seen may be fired at by small arms or artillery, but only if they are within close range. The fire is resolved as if it were at long range. (Bolt-action rifles may only fire one die per figure, not two.)

A fire will illuminate part of the battlefield. A small fire (such as a camp fire) will illuminate everything within 2".

A large fire (such as a burning vehicle or building) will illuminate everything within 6". Both sorts of fires will illuminate any unit "backlit" by them. A unit is backlit if it passes directly between the fire and a spotting enemy unit *and* the line of sight from the spotting unit to the fire passes through the spotted unit, not over it.

Morale: Darkness and confusion that attends combat in it are particularly destructive to unit morale and cohesion.

In addition to the negative modifier listed on the Morale Modifiers Chart (page 171), units may never rally at night. A unit's morale state may only go up at night due to winning a melee or witnessing victory.

SMOKE

Any burning building or vehicle will generate smoke, which will drift downwind and dissipate. The rule on fire indicates the length of the smoke trail of a burning building. (See page 63.) A vehicle has a smoke trail of 12". Units may not see through a smoke trail, although aerial vessels and units two elevations higher than the smoke may see over it.

Moving through a smoke trail counts as crossing a difficult barrier. Cavalry and horse-drawn vehicle units must make a morale test before entering a smoke barrier, with failure indicating that the animals are spooked and refuse to enter the smoke that turn.

RAIN

Rain reduces visibility and the ability of certain units to fire.

Visibility: Rainstorms generally have alternating periods of high and low intensity.

To take this into account, roll a die at the start of each initiative phase. The result, referred to as the rain intensity, is the maximum visibility in inches×12 for that turn. Enemy units may not be detected beyond visibility range in the rain. When determining the range for spotting concealed enemy units, multiply the spotting unit's Fieldcraft by the number rolled in the initiative phase (but never by more than 5).

For example, a 3 is rolled for rain intensity.

The maximum visibility on the table for that turn is 36". Units with a Fieldcraft of 2 will spot concealed enemy units at a range of 6", while those with a Fieldcraft of 3 will spot them at 9".

If a 6 for rain intensity is rolled for three successive turns, the rainstorm is over.

Fire Combat: Units with smoothbore muskets, rifle muskets, or bows must roll each time they fire, to determine if their powder has become wet or if their bowstrings have lost tension.

Powder or bowstrings become wet if the number rolled is less than the rain intensity for that turn. Once either powder or bowstrings are wet, units using them may only fire using half the number of dice normally rolled.

If a second powder/bowstring wet roll is missed later by the unit, then it may not fire again for the rest of the game.

GROUND CONDITION

GROUND CONDITIONS affect movement, particularly movement of vehicles. Ground conditions will be specified for the scenario in advance by the referee. In rare cases the ground condition may change during a scenario (such as the ground becoming muddy from a long and particularly intense rainstorm).

Mud: Mud is an impediment to movement. There are two possible mud conditions: light mud and heavy mud. Vehicles, including artillery and horse-drawn vehicles, pay double cost when moving through both light and heavy mud. In addition, vehicles must roll each movement phase in which they move through heavy mud to see if they become bogged down. They do so whenever they roll a 6.

Infantry and cavalry are unaffected by light mud and pay double when moving through heavy mud.

Ice: Ice is also an impediment to movement. All units and vehicles have their movement halved. All slopes become impassable barriers to vehicles, including tripods. Unlimbered artillery may be manhandled up a gentle slope by three times the normal number of gun crew figures. Infantry and cavalry may cross frozen rivers and lakes (if the referee declares them to be frozen to a sufficient thickness) but large animals (elephants and ruumet breehrs), vehicles, and artillery may not.

ARMY MORALE (OPTIONAL)

THIS RULE is not necessary when fighting battles with relatively small forces of, say, a dozen units per side. It is very useful when fighting large battles, however, as it provides a means of determining when an army is defeated, short of the destruction of every one of its units. Sometimes an army is defeated before some of its units have even been fired at, due to contagious panic or general demoralization. To take that into account, each side in a battle has an army morale number. Once the total number of units and detachments destroyed (including those which have broken and fled from the battlefield) equals or exceeds the army morale number, the morale of the surviving units of the army breaks, and they will flee from the battlefield or surrender, unless the army commander succeeds in inspiring them.

An army commander may attempt to inspire his army when its morale breaks. Roll one die; if the result is equal to or less than the army commander's leadership level, the commander succeeds, and his army's morale does not break. Each time that an additional unit or detachment is destroyed, however, he must make an additional attempt to inspire his men. If he ever fails the attempt, the army disintegrates.

Elite units are immune to the effects of army morale and will go on fighting (if only to cover the retreat of the main body, or the escape of its commander) after the rest of the army has disintegrated.

To determine army morale, the referee rolls one or more dice for each army before the game. Add up the numbers thrown to determine the army morale level. The number of dice thrown is determined by the size of the army. One die is thrown for every eight units or separate detachments present with the army. Always round fractions of dice up. For example, an army with 10 units and detachments would roll one die and a fraction of a second; roll two dice instead.

A number of die roll modifiers are made. These modifiers are cumulative and apply to *each* die rolled, but can never modify a die roll to less than 1 or more than 6.

ARMY MORALE

Factor	*Modifier*
Defending Homeland	+1
Fighting Hated Enemy	+1
Defending Excellent Positions	+1
No Retreat Route Available	+1
Unpopular Cause or Leader	–1
Fighting Feared Enemy	–1
Hungry, Thirsty, or Exhausted	–1

In addition to these modifiers to the die rolls, modifications are made to the total army morale. See the Total Army Morale Modifier Table, left.

TOTAL ARMY MORALE MODIFIER

Factor	*Modifier*
Army Commander	+ Leadership
Good Troops	+1 for every three Veteran and/or Elite units or detachments
Poor Troops	–1 for every two Green units or detachments

While musketmen skirmish to cover the advance, a Martian mass of "cutters" prepare to storm the barricades. Note that the storming party is led by shield gunners. Figures from GDW.

For example, an army consists of nine companies, two separate platoons, and three gun sections, for a total of 18 units and detachments. It is defending a good position in its homeland but has been without food for several days and is very hungry. The army commander has a leadership rating of 2, there are two Veteran and two Elite units in the army, and three Green units.

The die roll modifiers are +1 (good position), +1 (defending homeland), and –1 (hungry), for a cumulative modifier on each die of +1. The army rolls three dice for morale and rolls a 2, 3, and 6. The die roll modifiers convert these to 3, 4, and 6 (since a die roll of 6 cannot be modified to 7) for a total of 13. The army has at least three Veteran/Elite units, but fewer than six, so it adds one to the total morale, bringing it to 14. Since there are more than two but less than four Green units, the army subtracts one from morale, lowering it to 13 again. Finally, the leadership of the commander is added, raising army morale to 15.

Multiple Armies: In the case of very large armies, or ones which are divided geographically, the referee should determine their morale separately. For example, a British Army of two infantry brigades and one cavalry brigade should be treated as three separate armies for morale purposes. By the same token, an army attempting to break through enemy siege lines to relieve a surrounded garrison should have its army morale determined separately from that of the garrison.

When one side has more than one army in play, the morale of all armies is lowered by two each time a friendly army has its morale broken and disintegrates. For example, suppose one side has three armies. If one army breaks, the other two react as if two of their own units have been destroyed.

One side may combine two separate armies during the play of a game. If two armies are combined, add their army morale levels together to obtain their combined morale level, but add their total destroyed units together as well.

Commander Killed: If the original commander of an army is killed, his leadership is permanently subtracted from the army morale. The next highest ranking officer then assumes command.

If he or any subsequent supreme commanders are killed, no additional subtraction is made from army morale.

Part B: Unit Organization

THE FOLLOWING section provides complete information on the organization of standard units. For regular army units, the ranks listed are those for the British Army; other armies had different titles for these ranks, and a partial list of equivalent ranks in selected armies is provided on this page and the next.

Many armies (including the British Army) differ from the standard organization given below. These differences are listed in the appropriate section of the army lists in *Book IV*.

INFANTRY

THE BASIC REGULAR infantry unit is the company. Each infantry company consists of a major, a captain, a lieutenant, a colour sergeant, and two infantry platoons. Each platoon consists of a sergeant, a corporal, and six privates. If small detachments are required, the platoon can be broken into two four-man sections, each commanded by a noncommissioned officer (sergeant or corporal). The total strength of the company is 20 men.

The infantry battalion has four companies. If, for some reason, the battalion has to be divided, the two parts are called "wings." One wing is usually commanded by the battalion commander, while the other is commanded by a major (his company in turn being commanded by a captain or lieutenant).

In addition to the men of the four infantry companies, the battalion has a small staff consisting of one lieutenant colonel (the commander), one captain (the adjutant), one lieutenant (the ensign), one sergeant major, one sapper corporal, one sapper private, one surgeon, one drum major (pipe major in highland battalions), four musicians (usually drummers, but buglers in light infantry and rifle battalions, and pipers in highland battalions), and one quartermaster. The total strength of a company is 20, a wing 40, and the battalion 93. The surgeon and the quartermaster generally remain in camp or in the rear during actions.

The battalion has two sets of colours (flags): the Queen's colours and the battalion's colours. These are rarely carried in battle, but if present, are carried and protected by the colour party. The colour party forms up with one of the battalion's companies (this duty rotates throughout the companies). The colour sergeant of that company carries the battalion's colours, the battalion's ensign carries the Queen's colours, and the two sappers form the balance of the party. The battalion's musicians usually

EQUIVALENT RANKS TABLE

Britain (& America)	*Germany*	*France (& Belgium)*
Private	Schütze	Soldat
Corporal	Gefreiter	Caporal
Sergeant	Feldwebel	Sergent
Colour Sergeant (First Sergeant)	Oberfeldwebel	Premier Sergent
Sergeant Major	Stabsfeldwebel	Sergent-Chef
Lieutenant	Leutnant	Lieutenant
Captain	Hauptmann	Capitaine
Major	Major	Major
Lt. Colonel	Oberstleutnant	Lieutenant-Colonel
Colonel	Oberst	Colonel
Brigadier	—	General de Brigade
Major General	Generalmajor	General de Division (General-Major)
Lt. General	Generaleutnant	Lieutenant-General
General	General	General d'Armee
Field Marshal	Generalfeldmarschall	Marechal

form up with the colour party.

Two battalions form a regiment. In addition to the troops of its battalions, a regiment has one colonel (the commander) and one captain (the adjutant). Total strength of the regiment is 188. All regiments have two battalions unless otherwise noted.

Irregular infantry bands consist of three chiefs, or leaders, and 16 warriors, all armed in roughly the same manner. This band is often broken down into two sub-bands (with eight warriors and one leader each) both under the overall command of the senior leader.

Canal Martian regular infantry companies are organized the same as irregulars. The company is commanded by a mounted officer while the officers commanding the two half-companies are on foot. The Canal Martian service has no equivalent to NCOs.

CAVALRY

THE BASIC CAVALRY unit is the squadron with one major, one captain, one lieutenant, one trumpeter, and two troops. Each troop consists of one sergeant, one corporal, and six privates. Thus, a troop has a strength of eight men, and a squadron has a strength of 20 men.

A cavalry regiment consists of two or more squadrons. In addition to its squadrons, the regiment has one lieutenant colonel (the commander) one captain (the adjutant), one surgeon, one sergeant major, one quartermaster, one veterinarian, one blacksmith, and one trumpet major. Cavalry regiments do not carry their colours into battle during this period. A two-squadron regiment thus has a total strength of 48 men. The surgeon,

EQUIVALENT RANKS TABLE

Russia	*Italy*	*Japan*
Armeyets	Soldato	Hei
Yefreytor	Corporale	Go-chō
Serzhant	Sergente	Gun-sō
Starshiy Serzhant	Sergente Maggiore	So-chō
Starshina	Maresciallo Maggiore	Tokumo sō-chō
Leytenant	Tenente	Chū-i
Kapitan	Capitano	Tai-i
Major	Maggiore	Shō-sa
Podpolkovnik	Tenente Colonello	Chū-sa
Polkovnik	Colonello	Tai-sa
General Major	Generale Maggiore	Shō-shō
General Leytenant	Generale Tenente	Chū-jō
General	Generale	Tai-shō
Marshal	Maresciallo	Gen-sui

Bulgaria	*Romania*	*Serbia*
Rednik	Soldat	Redov
Efreytor	Caporal	Kaplar
Kandidat Podofitser	Sergent	Podnarednik
Podofitser	Sergent major	Narednik
Feldfebel	Plutonier major	Narednik vodnik
Poruchnik	Locotenent	Porucnik
Kapitan	Capitan	Kapetan
Major	Major	Major
Podpolkovnik	Locotenent-colonel	Potpukovnik
Polkovnik	Colonel	Pukovnik
General-major	General de brigada	Brigadni djeneral
General-leytenant	General de divizia	Divizijski djeneral
General	General de armata	Armijski djeneral
—	Maresal	Vojvoda

OENOTRIA

Private: Legionnaire
Lieutenant: Bannerman
Captain: First Sword
Major: Swordmaster
Colonel: Marchmaster
General: General

quartermaster, veterinarian, and blacksmith generally remain in camp or in the rear during actions.

Irregular mounted bands consist of three chiefs or leaders and 14 mounted warriors, all armed in roughly the same manner. These are often broken into two half-bands of seven warriors and one leader each.

Canal Martian regular cavalry is organized the same as irregulars. There is no equivalent to the NCO in Martian service.

ARTILLERY

THE LARGEST permanent artillery organization is the battery. The battery consists of three gun sections, each with one sergeant, one bombardier (the artillery equivalent of corporal), and four privates. The battery, in addition to its three gun sections, has one major (the commander), one captain (the adjutant), one lieutenant, one staff sergeant (the artillery equivalent of sergeant major), one bugler, one surgeon, one veterinarian, one quartermaster, and one teamster. Battery equipment includes three guns, three limbers, and one ammunition wagon. The battery has a total strength of 27, including officers and other ranks. As with other units, the surgeon, veterinarian, and quartermaster will not generally be encountered in the front lines.

The normal allocation of men in a gun section is a four-man gun crew (consisting of three privates and the bombardier), one private with the horse team, and the section commander (sergeant). Either the sergeant or driver, or both, can fill in for casualties among the gun crew during action. Some heavy siege weapons require a larger gun crew, and in this case additional privates are added to the gun section as necessary. A 7" siege gun, for example, requires a crew of six, and so the gun section would have six privates, a bombardier, and a sergeant. Machinegun and machine cannon sections require only two gunners per weapon, and so the strength of a gun section is reduced to four, with the actual gun crew consisting of a private and a bombardier.

A British infantry company in line.

Those irregular armies which include artillery do not have a regular organization above the gun section level. Each gun section consists of one teamster, one leader, and as many gunners as are necessary to service the gun. Canal Martian regulars are organized similarly.

EQUIVALENT RANKS

ON PAGES 26 AND 27 are partial listings of equivalent ranks in some of the more important or more interesting armies of the Earth. These are presented purely for player interest and to add additional color to the role-playing game or richer background for an unusual miniatures unit raised by a player for a game.

In some cases there are no precise equivalents to the various ranks given. In most cases we have listed the closest analogous rank. Many countries do not have a precise equivalent to brigadier, in which case brigades are often commanded by major generals, divisions by lieutenant generals, etc.

Part C: Mechanical Conveyances

THE FIRST PART of the rules covers the traditional arms of service: infantry, cavalry, and artillery. This part adds mechanical conveyances to the rules. Mechanical conveyances refer to land vehicles, naval vessels, and flying machines.

A number of rules are unique to each of these categories of conveyances, but there are also a number of general rules which apply to all of them. These general rules are presented first, followed by the specific rules that apply to each type of conveyance.

SEQUENCE OF PLAY

WHEN ANY MECHANICAL conveyances are in use, the following sequence of play is used.

Both additions to the sequence are listed in bold.

- Initiative Phase
- **Ram**/Charge Declaration Phase
- Offensive Fire Phase
- Movement Phase
- Defensive Fire Phase
- **Defensive Movement Phase**
- Held Fire Phase
- Melee Phase

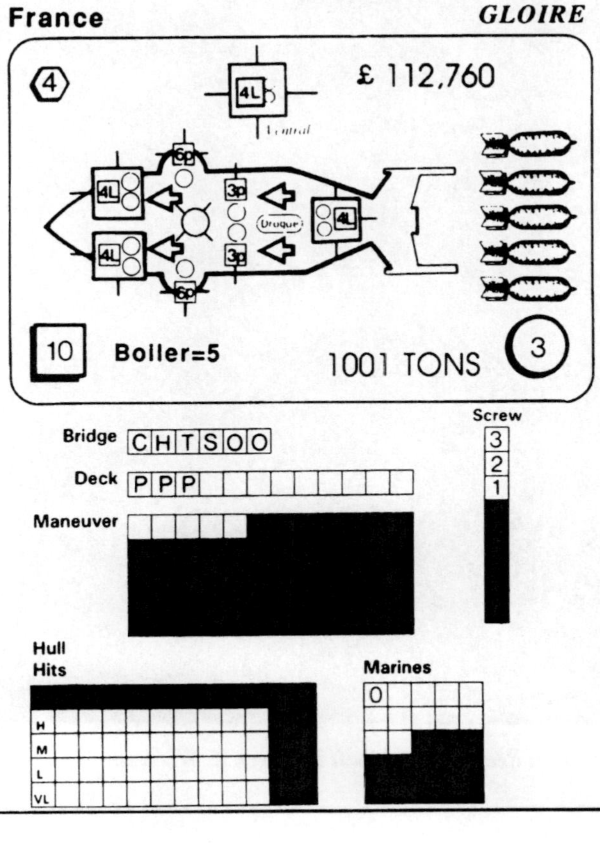

Ram Declaration: It is possible for aerial and naval vessels to ram enemy vessels.

The owning player must have the initiative and declare his intention in the ram/charge declaration phase.

Defensive Movement Phase: In the defensive movement phase the defensive player (the one who does not hold the initiative in the current phase) may move any or all of his mechanical conveyances. The nonmoving player is still not allowed to move any infantry, cavalry, or artillery, unless they are carried by a mechanical conveyance of some sort. Artillery of the nonmoving player may not limber or unlimber during the defensive movement phase, even if being drawn by a mechanical vehicle.

CONVEYANCE RECORD FORMS

EACH VEHICLE, flyer, and ship in play has a record form that details all of its important characteristics. At the back of this book there are a number of completed record forms for various vehicles, and these should be photocopied for use during a game. A sample record form for a flyer is shown to the left to illustrate its format.

THE BATTLE MAP

A BLANK HEXAGONAL grid map is included on page 31. You have permission to make additional photocopies of the map for your personal use during the game. If there are going to be a significant number of conveyances in the game, especially flyers or ships, the referee should make a battle map of the ground actually represented by the gaming table, as well as its surrounding area, with each hex on the map representing one foot on the table. Since flyers and ships move in one-foot increments, their off-table movement is easy to compute. (If you are playing with **Sky Galleons of Mars**, these hexes are also the same size as the hexes on that map.) In areas of deep ocean the referee should note the depth of the hex (in hundreds of fathoms) and should also mark each full or partial ocean or sea hex as shallow, shoal, deep coastal, or deep ocean.

TYPES OF CONVEYANCES

THE THREE TYPES of mechanical conveyances are land vehicles (called simply vehicles), nautical vessels (ships), and aerial vessels (flyers). The following is a list of the mechanical conveyances covered by these rules, grouped by conveyance type.

Nautical Vessels
- Torpedo Boat
- Gunboat
- Armored Warship
- Hydrofoil
- Submarine
- Deep-Diving Submarine
- Sailing Ship
- Galley

Motor Vehicles
- Land Juggernaut (also called a landship)
- Walking Tripod
- Tractor
- Machinegun Quadricycle
- Train

Flyers
- Glider
- Autogyro
- Aeroplane
- Helicopter
- Zeppelin
- Liftwood Flyer
- Screw Galley
- Kite
- Throckmorton Conveyor

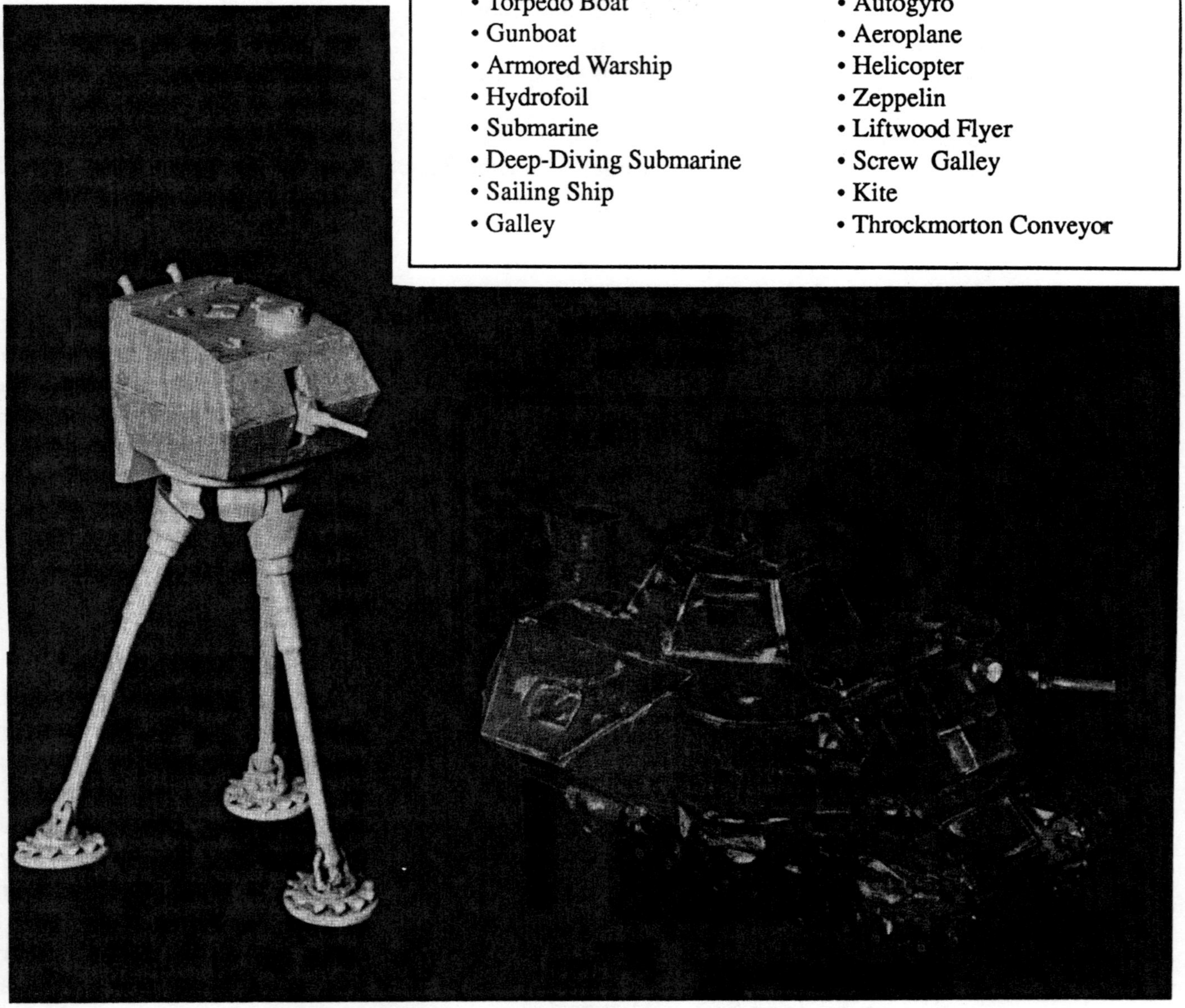

Land juggernaut built by Tom Reed. Tripod built by Loren K. Wiseman.

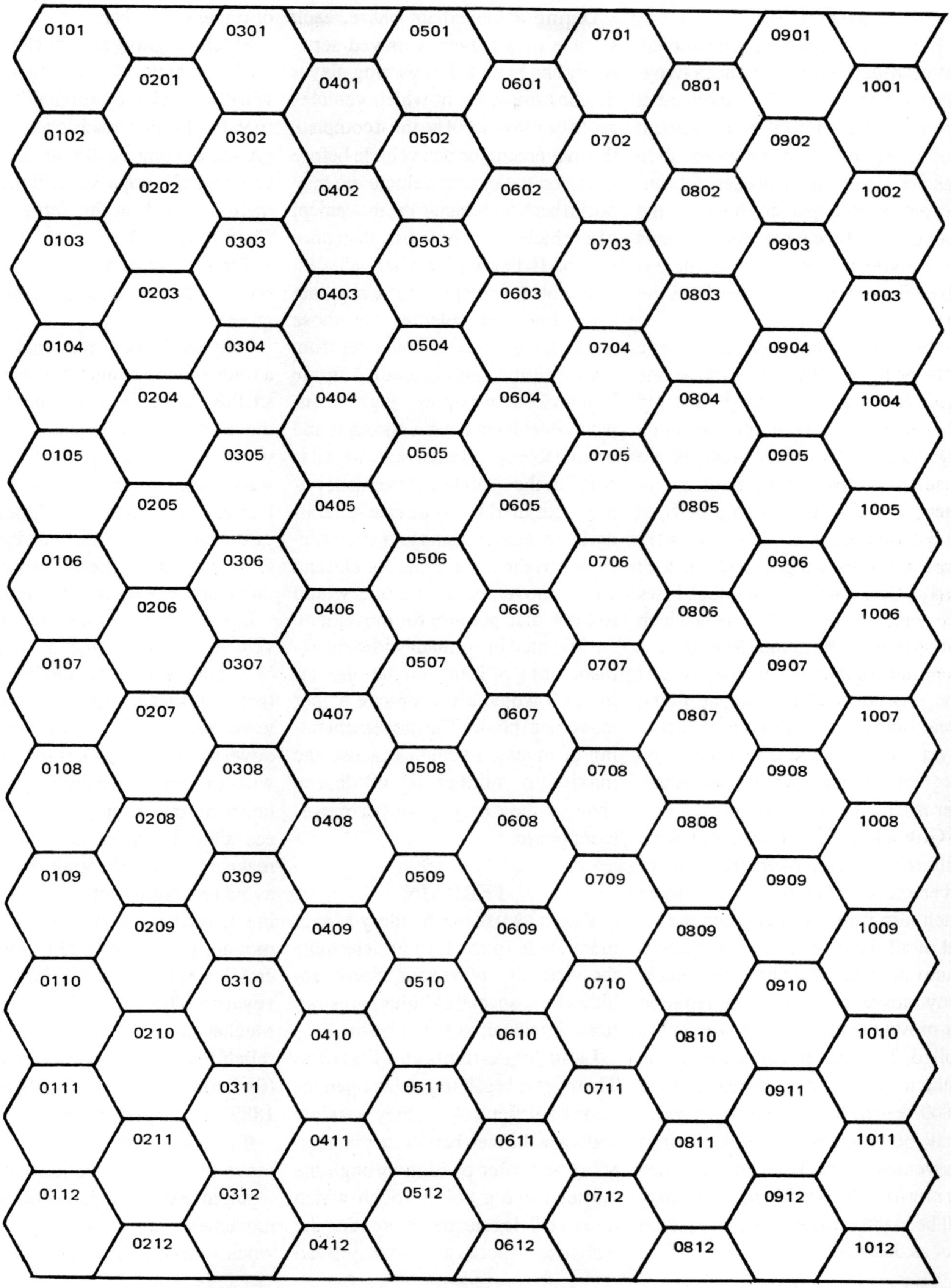
0101
0301
0501
0701
0901
0201
0401
0601
0801
1001
0102
0302
0502
0702
0902
0202
0402
0602
0802
1002
0103
0303
0503
0703
0903
0203
0403
0603
0803
1003
0104
0304
0504
0704
0904
0204
0404
0604
0804
1004
0105
0305
0505
0705
0905
0205
0405
0605
0805
1005
0106
0306
0506
0706
0906
0206
0406
0606
0806
1006
0107
0307
0507
0707
0907
0207
0407
0607
0807
1007
0108
0308
0508
0708
0908
0208
0408
0608
0808
1008
0109
0309
0509
0709
0909
0209
0409
0609
0809
1009
0110
0310
0510
0710
0910
0210
0410
0610
0810
1010
0111
0311
0511
0711
0911
0211
0411
0611
0811
1011
0112
0312
0512
0712
0912
0212
0412
0612
0812
1012

MOVEMENT

EACH CONVEYANCE has a movement rating which is noted on the conveyance's record form. The movement rating is the number of movement points the conveyance may spend in each of its movement phases. All conveyances of a player move in the movement phase when their player is the moving player, and in the defensive movement phase when he is the nonmoving player.

Each movement point spent by a ship or flyer allows it to move one scale foot (12") in a straight line and change its direction of movement by 60 degrees. Direction changes are made *at the end* of the 1' of movement, not during it. A ship or flyer may move less than 12" before making a direction change in order to dock or avoid an obstacle, but it then loses the remainder of the movement which would have been gained from the expenditure of that movement point. At the cost of one movement point, steamships and steam-powered aerial flyers may change direction by 60 degrees without moving. This maneuver is called a power turn.

Ground vehicles move somewhat differently. The movement rating of a vehicle is the number of dice thrown each turn for movement, and the total of all the dice rolled is the maximum number of inches the vehicle may move. A vehicle is not required to move the full number of inches rolled. The movement rating of the vehicle is also the maximum number of 60-degree direction changes which may be made by the vehicle in a movement phase. These may be made *at any time* during the move and may all be made at once or may be spread out as desired.

During a movement phase, each vehicle of a player is moved separately and in turn. The owning player decides the order in which vehicles are to be moved, but he must complete the movement for one vehicle before going on to the next vehicle; he may not go back and change the movement of a vehicle based on subsequent poor (or good) die rolls by other vehicles.

Invented vehicles are a separate case. Invented vehicles are those generated by a player character from the invention rules presented in the **Space: 1889** role-playing game. Invented vehicles have a constant and predictable speed each turn, which is equal to the vehicle's movement rating multiplied by its device reliability. For example, a land juggernaut designed by the rules in this booklet and with a movement rating of 2 would roll two dice per turn for movement. An invented juggernaut with a movement rating of 2 and a reliability rating of 3 would always move 6" per movement phase. The movement rating of invented vehicles is also the maximum number of 60-degree changes they may make per movement phase.

TERRAIN

VEHICLES USE the Artillery Movement Table (page 170) to determine the difficulty of terrain. Some vehicles have special abilities or restrictions, however, as noted below.

Land Juggernauts and Tractors: These treat brush terrain as open instead of difficult. Also, they treat low walls as a difficult barrier (not impassable), and after passing through the barrier leave a hole through which other vehicles can move, treating the wall in that spot as a difficult, instead of impassable, barrier.

Machinegun Quadricycles: These vehicles have narrow lightweight wheels which are designed for road travel only. For quadricycles, open ground becomes difficult, and difficult ground is impassable. Barriers remain as listed on the Terrain Types Chart (page 171).

Trains: Trains may only move on rails, and they treat rails as open ground.

Tripods: Tripods may wade across a river anywhere and may wade into shallow water off a coastline. Tripods move through rivers and shallow water as difficult ground (or may wade across a river as a difficult barrier). Tripods treat all slopes, both gentle and steep, as difficult barriers. Orchards are difficult ground for them, and woods are impassable.

Breakdowns: Whenever a land vehicle rolls all 1's for movement, it breaks down instead of moving. (Note that this means that vehicles with lower movement ratings will break down more often.) Invented vehicles will not break down during the game under normal circumstances. Referees should require an inventor to make a Difficult Piloting skill roll to avoid breakdown whenever attempting a difficult maneuver or when moving through difficult ground or crossing a difficult barrier in their conveyance. This should be done using Mechanical skill dice with the device reliability as a positive modifier. (Skill rolls are explained in the **Space: 1889** role-playing rules.)

If a vehicle breaks down, it cannot move or change direction until it is repaired. Roll for repairs during each movement phase in which the vehicle would otherwise be able to move. Roll one die per member of the engineering crew (but never less than one die); the vehicle is repaired as soon as a 6 is rolled. The vehicle may not move in the movement phase in which repairs are made, but may resume movement in the next turn.

COLLISIONS

If two hostile vessels begin a movement phase within 4" of each other at the same altitude/depth and one of them moves, there is a chance of a collision. If two friendly vessels begin a movement phase within 4" of each other at the same altitude/depth and both of them move, there is a chance of a collision.

Roll a die; a collision occurs on a roll of 1 or 2. Add one to the die roll if the two vessels are pointed in parallel directions. Add two to the die roll if the nonmoving ship or flyer declares that it intends to maneuver to avoid a collision. Subtract two from the die roll if the moving vessel attempts to turn while within 4" of the nonmoving vessel. If there is a collision, the moving vessel immediately stops and may not move further than to turn.

A friendly vessel which maneuvers to avoid a collision must expend half of its movement allowance (round fractions up) to do so. A hostile vessel which maneuvers to avoid the collision (whether successful or not) has its movement rating halved (round fractions down) for its next movement phase.

Each player involved in a collision rolls a die. If the result of the roll is equal to or less than the hull size of the other vessel, the player who rolled the die suffers a hull hit on his own vessel. If the other vessel has a hull size greater than 6, then one hit is automatically taken and a second is suffered if the die roll is less than or equal to the amount by which it exceeds six. If the other vessel has a hull size greater than 12, then two hits are automatically taken and a third is rolled for, and so on.

In addition to hull damage, roll a die. If the die roll is equal to or less than half the difference in hull size (round fractions down), then the smaller of the two vessels suffers a flooding critical (if a ship) or a critical loss of trim (if a flyer). See page 39 for an explanation of these two critical hit results.

Two British Truculent-class landships, supported by infantry, advance.

TOWING

PLAYERS MAY FIND it necessary to tow a disabled conveyance. Ships may only tow other ships, flyers may only tow other flyers, and vehicles may only tow other vehicles.

Ships: A ship may not tow another vessel if the hull size of the towed vessel is four or more times greater than that of the towing ship. To be able to tow, the two vessels must be in contact. (There is the normal risk of a collision). It then takes one complete friendly movement phase for the crews to rig a tow cable. In the next friendly movement phase the player may begin towing. All ships are towed at a speed of 1.

Vehicles: Vehicles follow the same rules for towing as do ships, except that there is no chance of a collision. When towing a vehicle at a movement rate of 1, one die is thrown for movement, even if towing with an invented vehicle which has a fixed movement allowance.

Flyers: Tow lines are rigged the same way as for ships (collision risk present). Flyers may be towed at speeds greater than 1, however, and the ability to tow is based on relative hull size.

All flyers towing other flyers have their movement allowance halved (rounding fractions up). In addition, divide the towed vessel's hull size by the hull size of the towing vessel, round all fractions down, and subtract the result from the towing vessel's speed. For example, a towing vessel with a size 2 hull, towing a ship with a size 5 hull, would have its movement rating reduced 2 (5/2=2.5, rounded down to 2) after it had already been halved.

Special Conveyances: Throckmorton conveyors, tripods, and machinegun quadricycles may not tow or be towed. Aeroplanes and autogyros may tow gliders, but may not tow anything else and may not be towed. Helicopters may tow other flyers but may not be towed. Submarines may only tow and be towed while surfaced.

ALTITUDE

THE SIX ALTITUDES are Very High (VH), High (H), Medium (M), Low (L), Very Low (VL), and Ground (G). In general, the surface of the planet is at ground level, but some mountains rise to higher altitudes. Mark the altitude of a flyer by placing a marker with the correct altitude abbreviation next to the model on the playing area.

The maximum altitude of a flyer is noted on its data form. There is a block of several rows of boxes labeled "Hull Hits." (On some unusual flyers, this block is labeled "Wing Hits" or "Rotor Hits.") The left side of each row includes the abbreviation for an altitude. The highest altitude shown is the flyer's maximum altitude.

All flyers may descend one altitude level per friendly movement phase at no cost. Each altitude the flyer descends after the first one costs 1' of movement. Each altitude level that the flyer climbs costs 2' of movement. Thus, a flyer with a movement rating of 5 could move 5' or move 3' and climb one level, or move 1' and climb two levels. A flyer whose speed is reduced to 1 may still climb 1 level instead of moving. Each level of altitude change allows a 60-degree change of direction (in addition to the 60-degree change in direction permitted for each movement point spent as explained on page 32). This does not apply to the the one free altitude drop per turn.

If a flyer is in the same hex as another vessel but is at a different altitude, there is no chance of a collision. If it changes altitude and, thus, both flyers are at the same altitude, there is the normal chance of a collision (see page 33).

If a flyer involuntarily drops to the same altitude as the surface of the planet, it crashes and is destroyed. If it voluntarily drops to the surface, it has landed. However, a flyer may only drop one altitude level and may only move 1' the turn it lands. If it moves more than 1' or drops more than one level, it crash-lands. The crew is safe, but the flyer is crippled and no longer airworthy.

If a flyer comes in contact with a landmass at an equal or higher altitude as the vessel (such as a cliff wall or mountaintop), and the vessel is moving at a speed of 1, it lands. If it is moving faster than 1, it crashes.

DEPTH

IF SHIPS ARE present in a game, the water areas of the gaming table should be divided into one or more of the following depths: Shallows, Shoals, Deep Coastal water, and Deep Ocean water. Shallows are closest to the coasts, and occur along beaches, reefs, and submerged rocks. Shoals are the boundary region between Shallow water and the deeper, navigable water off the coast. Deep Ocean waters are at least 100 fathoms deep and are often deeper. There will hardly ever be any Deep Ocean water on a gaming area, but if a hex map of the playing area and its surrounding area is used, Deep Ocean water may be present there. The referee should mark on his own map the depth of all deep ocean hexes in hundreds of fathoms.

Running Aground: Ships in Deep (either Coastal or Ocean) water have no chance of running aground. Ships in Shoals and Shallow water may run aground, depending on their draft (how deep they ride in the water).

For purposes of running aground, there are three types of vessels: deep-draft, medium-draft, and shallow-draft. To determine a ship's draft, compare its hull size to its hull length. If its hull size is greater than its length, it is a deep-draft ship. If its size is equal to or less than its length, it is a medium-draft ship. If its size is half or less of its length, it is a shallow-draft ship.

Submarines are medium-draft ships when surfaced and deep-draft ships when at Periscope depth. A hydrofoil is a shallow-draft ship, unless it has lost one complete row of hull boxes or is moving at half speed or less, in which case it is a medium-draft ship.

Shallow-draft ships never run aground. Medium-draft ships run aground in Shallow water on a die roll of 4-6, but never run aground in Shoals. Deep-draft ships always run aground in Shallows and run aground in Shoals on a roll of 4-6. Subtract one from the die roll if the ship only moved 1'. If the ship moves more that 1', roll separately for each foot of movement during which the ship was in danger of running aground.

If the ship runs aground, it stops moving until it breaks free. The owning player rolls a die at the end of every friendly movement phase. To break free, he must roll equal to or higher than twice the ship's movement rating, unless the ship was only moving at a speed of 1 when it ran aground. In that case, it breaks free on any roll of 2 or more.

A friendly ship may rig a tow line and help the grounded ship attempt to break free. Rigging the tow line is explained in the rule on towing on page 34. For a friendly ship to help, it must be at least half the hull size of the grounded ship. If it is, add one to the die roll. If the towing ship has a larger size than the grounded ship, add two to the die roll. If the towing ship is twice or more the size of the grounded ship, add three to the die roll.

Submarines: Submarines may be surfaced or submerged (Periscope depth). They may change their depth at the beginning of a movement phase. They may not fire torpedoes or any other weapons during a turn in which they change depth.

Submarines may be fired at by guns while either surfaced or at Periscope depth. Subtract two from the chances of hitting a submarine with gunfire while it is at Periscope depth.

Deep-diving submarines are inventions which may be available to player characters of the **Space: 1889** role-playing game. They may submerge to depths below Periscope depth in areas of Deep Ocean water. The device reliability of the submarine times 100 is the maximum dive depth of the submarine in fathoms. Each 100 fathoms counts as one depth level.

A deep-diving submarine may only change its depth by one level per turn, with one exception. It may "blow its tanks" at the beginning of any friendly movement phase, in which case it immediately surfaces. The submarine may not make any other movement or depth change during that movement phase or in its next movement phase.

Although the referee will not disclose the depth of any part of the Deep Ocean area of a map to the players, a deep-diving submarine can see the bottom if the bottom is one depth level below the sub through the use of searchlights and portholes. Thus, a deep-diving submarine can "chart" the depth of the Deep Ocean area by hugging the bottom, provided this does not require it diving below its maximum dive depth.

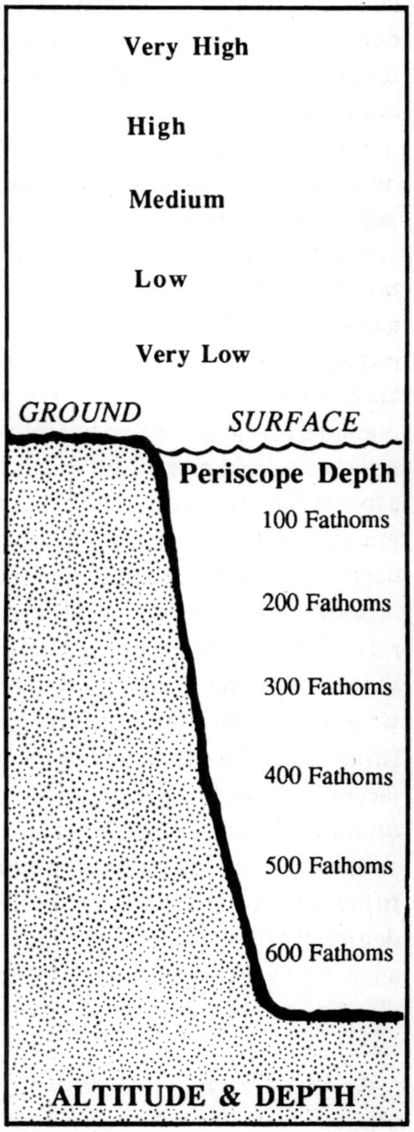

FIRE COMBAT

CONVEYANCES MAY FIRE at the same time that other units of their side fire. Conveyances of the moving player may fire in either the fire phase or the held fire phase; conveyances of the nonmoving player may fire in the defensive fire phase. Vehicles may only fire if they do not move during the turn; ships and flyers may fire and move in the same turn.

Firing Aspect: The four firing aspects of a conveyance are bow, stern, port broadside, and starboard broadside. Each aspect encompasses a 90-degree arc. And each weapon has a limited arc of fire, as shown on the conveyance's record form. Each gun mount is shown on the deck plan diagram at the top of the form and is indicated by a box.

The type of gun is noted beside the box, and its allowed field of fire is shown by the gun barrel or barrels radiating from the box. A gun with barrels pointing to the bow, stern, and one side, for example, can fire into the bow, stern, and one of the broadside aspects. The small circles next to the gun box represent the gun crew, with each circle representing one gunner.

Some guns have only a single barrel radiating from the box with a partial arc superimposed over it. These weapons can fire into one complete firing arc and half of each of the adjacent arcs and are said to have a *broad* firing arc. For example, a gun pointed to the side but with a broad firing arc can cover the entire 180-degree arc of that side of the conveyance, firing at targets directly ahead, directly astern, and at all points in between.

Artillery Firing Procedure: All artillery weapons are fired normally at and from conveyances, with several additional considerations.

High-Angle Fire: No gun may fire at a target if the difference in altitude between it and its target (in levels) is greater than the range (in scale feet). For example, a flyer cannot fire at a target 2' away but three levels lower. There are three exceptions to this rule. First, any weapon mounted in a fortress mount is capable of high-angle fire and is, thus, excused from this prohibition. Second, machine cannons on ships and field mounts (but not on flyers or vehicles) are designed to provide high-angle fire against flyers and are also exempt. Finally, all mortars, howitzers, and lob guns, regardless of their mounting, are exempt from this rule.

Altitude Difference: When firing to or from flyers, any difference in altitude affects the chance of hitting the target. All fire at targets at a different altitude than the gun firing is conducted with a die roll modification of +1 to the hit number. Thus, at close range, shots would only hit on rolls of 4, 5, or 6, and at long range they would hit only on a roll of 6.

If fire is possible at a higher target, add 1' to the range for every level higher the target is compared to the firing vessel. Thus, a target 2' away and two levels higher would be fired at as if it were at a range of 4'. Firing at targets at lower elevations does not add to the range.

Damage: When an artillery round hits a conveyance, roll a die and consult the Conveyance Hit Location Table (page 175) to determine what type of damage was inflicted on the target. In general, the damage value of the firing gun is the number of hits caused. For example, if a gun with a damage value of 2 caused a running gear hit on a vehicle, two running gear hits would be recorded on the vehicle's record form.If firing at a flyer at a higher altitude, all crew hits become hull hits instead. It is possible to inflict the following types of damage on a mechanical conveyance:

Gun: A gun hit destroys one gun. If the firing gun has a damage value greater than one, all additional hits are crew hits, with the crew of the destroyed gun suffering casualties first. The destroyed gun must be mounted in such a way that it faces the firing aspect from which it received the fire. If several such guns are present, roll a die to randomly determine which gun is hit. If no guns are present in that firing aspect, reroll the hit location and continue to reroll until a nongun hit is achieved.

Hull: A hull/running gear hit on a flyer or ship causes hull hits equal to the damage value of the gun. Each flyer and ship has a series of hull boxes on its record form. As these are marked off, the flyer or ship loses buoyancy; flyers will drop in altitude, while ships will ride lower in the water and thus become slower.

Flyers have several rows of boxes. Each row has hull boxes equal to the flyer's hull size, and each row corresponds to one of the altitudes at which the flyer can fly. For example, a flyer with a hull size of 3 and a maximum altitude of High would have four rows (one each for Very Low, Low, Medium, and High altitude), each with three boxes. Always check hull hits off from the row of the highest remaining altitude. When that row of boxes is completely filled in, the flyer's maximum altitude is reduced to the next lowest level. If the flyer is at its maximum altitude when this happens, it automatically drops one altitude level in its next movement phase. The drop in altitude does not cost the flyer movement points. When all of the hull boxes on a flyer are checked off, the ship crashes.

Ships have several rows of hull hit boxes as well, with the number of boxes in each row equal to twice the mass of the ship. Mark off all hits on the top row until it is completely full, and then begin on the next row. Each time that a complete row of hull hit boxes is marked off, the ship's movement allowance is reduced by 1. When all of the ship's hull hit boxes have been marked off, the ship capsizes and sinks.

Running Gear: A hull/running gear hit on a vehicle causes running gear hits equal to the damage value of the gun. Each vehicle has a number of rows of running gear boxes on its record form equal to its movement rating. Mark off all hits on the top row until it is completely full, and then begin on the next row. Each time that a complete row of running gear boxes is marked off, the vehicle's movement rating is reduced by 1. When all of the vehicle's running gear boxes have been marked off, the vehicle is immobilized.

Tripods constitute an exception to the above rule. Tripods treat running gear hits as misses instead (as the shot passes harmlessly between their legs).

Crew: Each crew hit causes crew casualties equal to half the damage value of the firing gun, rounding all fractions up. Crew losses are selected by the player who suffered the casualties and may be from any part of parts of the ship desired. However, the firing player also rolls an additional die, and if the result is equal to or less than the number of casualties inflicted, then one of the casualties must be an officer or petty officer (owning player's choice). This die roll is made only once at the end of the phase in which the ship suffered one or more crew casualties; it is not made separately for each casualty.

Gun crews are shown on the record form as small circles next to their respective guns. All other crew are represented by crew boxes in the main body of the record form.

Critical: If a critical hit is rolled, the firing player immediately rolls two dice, adds them together, and consults the Critical Hit Table (page 175) to determine the result.

Repairing Damage: All rolls to free jammed rudders and lifters, control flooding, put out fires, and in general repair damage are done at the end of each friendly movement phase.

Small Arms Fire: Small arms fire against a vehicle is conducted normally, assuming that the crew is the target and using all applicable modifiers to the hit roll. After hits have been achieved, but before any saving rolls are made, roll once for hit location for each small arms hit. If firing at an armored vehicle, only crew hits have any effect. Make saving throws for the crew hits that have been scored and ignore the rest.

For unarmored vehicles, structural hits against other components may produce damage. At the end of the fire phase, total the number of small arms hits in each hit location category (gun, hull, running gear, critical, etc.) and roll one die. If the die roll is less than the number of small arms hits scored, then one actual hit is scored with an assumed damage value of 1. If the roll is equal to or greater than the number of small arms hits, they have no effect. If a gun hit is scored, one gunner (selected randomly) is hit without recourse to a saving throw.

For example, eight small arms hits are scored on an unarmored wooden ship. Two of these are crew, one is a hull, three are gun, and two are critical. The ship's player first conducts two saving rolls for the two crew hits (if he is entitled to any). The firing player notes that the hull hit cannot cause any damage, as he cannot roll less than a 1. Next, the firing player rolls for the gun hits. Since he has three gun hits, he must roll a 2 or less to actually score a hit. If he does so, one gunner is shot, and no saving roll is made for him. Finally, he rolls a die for the critical hit. Since he scored two small arms hits with critical as a hit location, he must roll a 1 to actually get a critical hit. If he does, he then rolls two dice in the normal way to determine the nature of the critical hit.

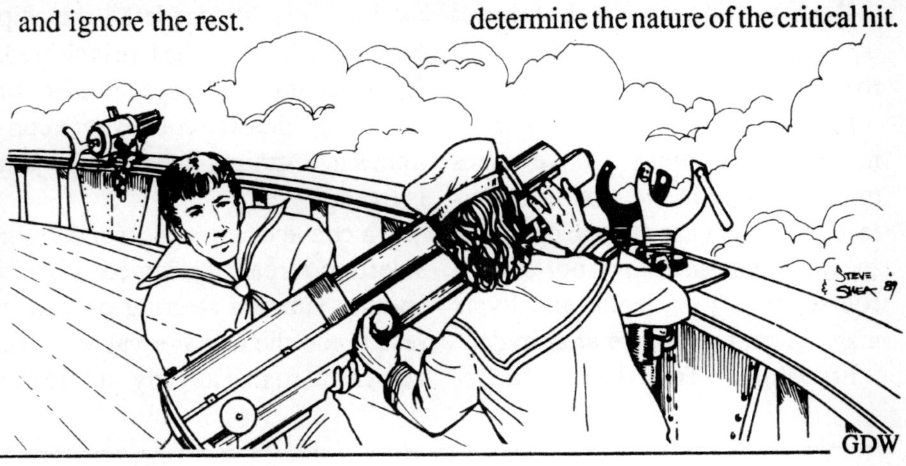

CRITICAL HITS

THE FOLLOWING CRITICAL hits are possible:

Magazine: Each large gun has its own magazine or shell locker, so detonation of a magazine will not necessarily destroy a conveyance, but it will certainly do considerable damage.

First, determine which gun's magazine has been detonated. Roll a die to randomly determine the weapon, but only guns with a damage value of 1 or more are eligible. Next, roll a single die.

If the result is less than the damage value of the gun whose magazine detonated (not the gun which fired the shot), the explosion is violent enough to completely destroy the conveyance.

If the roll is equal to or greater than the damage value of the gun whose magazine detonated, the gun serviced by the magazine is destroyed, its crew is killed, the conveyance takes hull or running gear damage equal to the damage value of the gun, and the player rolls for one additional critical hit. The additional critical hit is resolved with a damage value of the detonated magazine's gun.

If there is no gun with a damage value of 1 or more, this critical hit is treated as a fire result instead.

Bridge: Bridge crewmen are killed equal to half the damage value of the round that hit (round fractions up).

In addition to this effect, the following restrictions apply: Conveyances may not move in the next turn; surface ships may not change course or speed; submarines may not change course, speed, or depth; and flyers may not change course or altitude.

Fire/Boiler: Treat this as a fire result for conveyances which are motor-powered (such as galleys and wind-powered vessels).

Powered conveyances treat this as a boiler hit. Roll a die. If the result is less than the damage value of the firing gun, the boiler blows up. If the boiler blows up, the entire engine crew is killed, the conveyance's movement is permanently reduced to 0, the ship immediately catches fire with an initial fire level equal to the boiler size, and additional critical hits are rolled equal to the size of the boiler.

All additional critical hits are resolved with a damage value of 1.

If the boiler does not blow, the movement rating is reduced by the damage value of the firing gun. However, this movement reduction is not permanent, and the amount of the reduction is reduced by one each subsequent turn (as the engine gang patches the boiler, wraps rags around split steam lines, etc.).

Steering/Rudder: The conveyance may not change direction until the rudder is freed.

To free the rudder, roll a die for a number greater than the damage value of the firing gun.

If the hit result reads "rudder right," the ship turns 60 degrees after each move of 1' until the jam is cleared. If the hit reads "rudder left," the ship turns to the left until the jam is cleared. If the result merely says "rudder" or "steering," then the conveyance continues in a straight line until the jam is freed.

If a conveyance with its rudder or steering already jammed suffers another jammed steering or rudder result, add the damage value of the new result to that already suffered to determine the number necessary to free the jam. If the result says that the rudder jams in a different position, it remains in its original position instead.

For example, if a ship already has a rudder jammed with a damage value of 2 and suffers one with a damage value of 1, the ship's player must now roll greater than a 3 to free the rudder. However, a 6 will always free the rudder, regardless of the damage value of the firing gun. Attempts to free the rudder are made at the end of the player's movement phase, with all other repair attempts.

Running Gear: The running gear has received a direct, and potentially crippling, hit. Roll a die.

If the result is equal to or less than the damage value of the firing gun, the running gear is crippled, and the vehicle is immobilized for the rest of the game.

If the vehicle is a tripod, one leg has been shot away and the tripod topples over and is wrecked.

If the die roll is greater than the damage value of the gun, the gunning gear suffers hits equal to its damage value.

Fire: A fire is started on board the conveyance. The initial fire level is equal to the damage value of the firing gun. Once a fire has started, it will eventually spread and consume the ship unless extinguished by the crew. At the beginning of each turn, all fires presently burning are increased by one level.

Fires burning on sailing ships and Martian kites are increased by two levels. Any ship or flyer on fire receives an adverse die roll modification of one on all rolls to hit when firing weapons (including small arms fire), due to smoke interfering with the aim of the gunners. Vehicles on fire may not fire at all.

At the start of the friendly movement phase in which the fire level is greater than a conveyance's hull size, it suffers a magazine critical hit. If the conveyance has no magazines left, it instead receives one die roll worth of hull hits (on a flyer) or crew hits (on a ship or vehicle).

Fires may be fought at the end of the player's friendly movement phase. Roll one die for each deckhand on a flyer or ship and each engineer crewman on a vehicle. For each die roll of 5 or 6, the fire is reduced one level. On wooden flyers (Martian kites) and ships, the fire is reduced only on a roll of 6.

Flooding: Most ships which sink in battle do so due to uncontrolled flooding.

If a ship suffers a flooding critical, it first takes hull hits equal to the damage value of the firing gun. That number is kept track of, and the ship suffers that same number of additional hull hits at the beginning of each friendly movement phase until the flooding is controlled or the ship sinks.

If the flooding is caused by a collision or a ram, the number of hull hits caused by the collision or ram is also the number of additional flooding hits suffered each subsequent turn.

Flooding may be controlled at the end of the player's movement phase. Roll a die. If the result is greater than the amount of initial damage sustained, the flooding is halted; otherwise, it continues. However, a die roll of 6 will always control flooding, regardless of the initial damage level.

If a ship is suffering from more than one flooding critical at the same time, one separate die roll is made for each. Thus, it is possible to repair one damage result while the other continues to cause flooding.

Throttle: The vehicle's throttle is jammed. It must continue to move at the same speed in each subsequent movement phase as it did in its last movement phase before receiving the result. A jammed throttle is cleared in the same way as a jammed rudder.

Armor: The vehicle's armor has received a sharp blow which may crack it or loosen its fastening rivets. Roll a die.

If the result is less than the damage value of the firing gun, the armor value of the vehicle is reduced by one level.

Otherwise, the hit has no effect. In this case, and in this case only, the damage value of the firing gun is not affected by armor or penetration. (See the armor and penetration rule on page 40.)

Screw/Rigging: The screw (propeller) and its driving chains are hit, or the masts and rigging are damaged on a wind-powered ship or flyer. A screw-driven ship or flyer has its speed permanently reduced by 1. A wind-powered ship or flyer permanently subtracts one from its movement die roll. If a ship or flyer has its movement reduced to zero due to screw/rigging hits, it may jury-rig a mast or temporary propeller. To jury-rig a mast or propeller, a 6 must be rolled on one die at the end of the friendly movement phase. A ship or flyer may not have more than one jury-rig at a time.

Lifters: The flyer's large lifting panels are temporarily jammed in place; the flyer may not change altitude until they are freed. Freeing jammed lifters is done the same way as freeing a jammed rudder.

Loss of Trim: The flyer's trim controls are damaged, and it suffers a sudden loss of trim. The owning player immediately attempts to recover trim by rolling greater than the damage value of the firing gun. (If the loss of trim was caused by a collision, the player recovers by rolling greater than half the difference in hull sizes, rounding fractions down.)

If the trimsman is dead, the captain makes the attempt, but with a die roll modifier of –1.

If the captain is dead, any surviving officer or petty officer may make the attempt, but with a die roll modifier of –2.

If all officers and petty officers are dead, any crewman may make the attempt, but with a die roll modifier of –3.

Flyers with a hull size of 5 or larger have a +1 modification to the die roll. Ships with a hull size of 10 or larger have a +2 modification, etc.

A roll of 6 will always recover trim, regardless of the damage value of the firing gun or the die roll modifiers in use.

If the flyer recovers trim, it remains at its current altitude. If the ship does not recover trim, it immediately drops one altitude level, and the attempt to recover is repeated. This procedure continues until either the flyer recovers trim or it crashes.

In either case, the flyer may not move, fire, fight fires, or change any crew assignments for the rest of the current turn and all of the next turn. (The crew is still stunned.) If the flyer is boarded, the crew may defend itself.

ARMOR AND PENETRATION

EACH GUN HAS a penetration value which is important against heavily protected targets, such as armored aerial gunboats. The gun charts (pages 172-276) list two penetrations for guns. The first value is the penetration at close range; the second is at long range.

Each conveyance's record form lists its armor values. If the armor value of the target exceeds the penetration of the gun, halve the gun's damage value. If this results in fractional hits, roll a die to determine if the fractional hit takes effect, with a roll of 1-3 having no effect, and a roll of 4-6 causing a hit. For example, a gun with a normal damage value of 3 which hits armor of thicker than its penetration, would have a damage value of 1 1/2. If it caused a result that called for one hit per damage value, it would cause one hit automatically and a second on a die roll of 4-6.

If the armor value of a target is more than twice the penetration of the firing gun, the firing player rolls one die. If the result is equal to or less than the damage value of the gun, it causes damage as if it had an effective damage value of 1. Otherwise, it has no effect.

For example, a gun with a damage value of 3 and a penetration of 3 would have a damage value of 1 1/2 against an armor value of 6, and would have a damage value of 1 against an armor value of 7 or more if the firing player rolls a 3 or less. Guns with a penetration of 0 do full damage against unprotected targets, half damage against targets with an armor value of 1, and have no effect on targets with an armor value of 2 or more.

Armor takes different forms in different types of conveyances.

Flyers: Flyers generally have only one armor value, the hull armor. Even on armored flyers, not all parts of the vessel are protected. Armor protects the hull, magazines, bridge, trim controls, and boiler. In addition, some flyers have some or all of their guns mounted under armor to protect them. Armored guns are represented on a flyer's record form by a large box drawn around the gun symbol. Some flyers have extra armor on one or more gun mounts, and these are noted by a small number (indicating the turret's armor value) in a hexagon next to the gun mount. In all other cases, covered gun mounts are protected by the hull armor's armor value.

Ships: Ships have up to five different armor values: the belt, deck, battery, bulkheads, and turrets.

The belt is a long, wide sheet of armor that extends along the waterline of the ship. It protects the ship against boiler hits, magazine hits, and flooding hits, provided the shots were fired at close range by a naval vessel or shore battery. It also protects the ship against all hull hits, regardless of range.Some ships are equipped with a short belt covering only the midships (which is called a "midship belt"). This armor protects against the same critical hits as a full belt but only protects against hull hits suffered from a hit location die roll result of 1. Hull hits which result from a roll of 2 are not protected by the belt.

The deck is not the deck of the ship itself, but is, instead, a layer of horizontal armor placed roughly at waterline level to stop plunging fire, as from a gun firing at long range or an aerial bomb. It protects the ship against boiler hits, magazine hits, and flooding hits, provided the shots were fired by a naval vessel or shore battery at long range, or at any range by an aerial vessel.

The battery (also sometimes referred to as the citadel) is the armored covering of the sides and central superstructure of the ship. It protects the ship against bridge hits and gun hits for any gun located inside the battery, unless the hits were the result of raking fire. Raking fire is fire delivered from directly ahead or directly astern of a ship. A shot is considered to be a raking shot if the line of fire passes through the front and rear of the battery, and does not pass through either side.

Bulkheads are armored walls placed at the front and rear of the ship's battery to protect against raking fire. They protect against bridge hits and gun hits (on guns located inside the battery), provided the hits were caused by raking fire.

Turret armor protects guns which are mounted inside turrets from gun hits.

Vehicles: Vehicles have two different armor values: hull and running gear. Hull armor protects the vehicle against crew, gun, magazine, bridge, fire/boiler, and throttle hits. Running gear armor protects the vehicle against running gear hits (both regular hits and critical hits) and steering hits.

NONEXPLODING ROUNDS (OPTIONAL)

SOME ARMOR-PIERCING rounds may go completely through lightly armored or unarmored vessels without detonating. Likewise, solid shot will do less damage if it just punches through both sides of a hull than if it hits more substantial resistance.

If a conveyance is hit by a gun which has a penetration more than twice the armor value of the conveyance, roll a die. On a result of 1-3, the hit is resolved normally. On a roll of 4-6, the round passes through the target without exploding.

Hit location is still rolled, and the shot causes damage, but the round is treated as if it had a damage value of 1, regardless of its size.

Note that rounds which already have a damage value of 1 are unaffected by this rule. If this optional rule is used, this roll will always have to be made versus unarmored conveyances unless they are fired at by a gun with a damage value of 1 already.

CREWS OF CONVEYANCES

EACH CONVEYANCE is manned by officers, petty officers, and ratings (enlisted men) who carry out a variety of functions. The different types of conveyances have different types of crewmen. Each player may move his surviving crewmen to any assignment on the conveyance desired during the initiative phase of each turn.

Flyers: Flyers have a bridge crew, maneuvering crew, gun crew, and deck crew. Some flyers also have marines.

Bridge Crew: This consists of the captain and any other officers assigned to the flyer, a helmsman, a trimsman, and a signaler. The helmsman and trimsman are petty officers, while the signaler is a rating. If no officers are left on board a flyer, it will attempt to leave the battle. If it is immobilized or boarded, it will surrender. If there is no helmsman, it may not change course or speed (except as a result of combat damage or a collision). If there is no trimsman, the flyer may not voluntarily change altitude. In addition, roll a die at the end of each friendly movement phase. On a roll of 6, the vessel suffers a trim critical hit (and probably crashes). On any other result, it remains in trim.

Any petty officer from the deck crew and any officer from the bridge may take over for the helmsman or trimsman.

Maneuvering Crew: These are the ratings assigned to man the boilers, masts, or crankshaft of a flyer. On a steam vessel these engineers are referred to as the "black gang."

On a kite they are "topmen" who control the rigging, masts, and sails.

On a screw galley these are called "turncranks."

Each flyer has several rows of boxes representing the maneuvering crew. As crew casualties are taken, mark off the boxes. When a row of boxes is completely filled in, the speed of the flyer is reduced by one. When the entire maneuvering crew is eliminated, the vessel's speed is reduced to 0.

Gun Crew: Each gun mount has an assigned gun crew represented by crew circles on the flyer's record form next to the gun. As gun crew are killed, mark off crew boxes. Each gun crew casualty reduces the rate of fire of the weapon by one. For weapons with a rate of fire of 1 or less, each casualty adds one turn to the reload time.

Deck Crew: These are all crewmen not required for other duties. They are responsible for damage control, forming (or repelling) boarding parties, and replacing losses at other crew stations. Since the owning player decides which crewman is removed due to casualties, these will usually be taken against the deck crew first. This actually represents the deck crew being reduced because replacements are being sent to take the place of casualties all over the ship.

Ships: Ships have the same categories of crewmen as do flyers, and they carry out the same functions.

Vehicles: Vehicles have much smaller crews than do ships and flyers. They have only three categories of crewmen: command crew, gun crew, and engine crew.

Command Crew: The command crew on a vehicle consists of either one or two men.

On land juggernauts, two men are in the command crew: the captain and the driver.

On all other vehicles, there is only the driver. If a land juggernaut's driver is killed, the captain can take over driving.

On vehicles with no engine crew, the driver is capable of making repairs that the engineers would normally make. The vehicle cannot move while the driver is making repairs, however.

Gun Crew: This crew is identical in function to the gun crew of a ship or flyer.

Engine Crew: These men are similar to the maneuvering crew of a ship or flyer, with two differences.

First, the engine crew is responsible for making all repairs on the vehicle.

Second, engine crew casualties do not affect the speed of the vehicle unless the entire engine crew is dead. If that happens, the movement rating of the vehicle is reduced by one each turn (as the built-up head of steam is used up), until it is reduced to 0.

RAMMING

It is possible for aerial and naval vessels to ram enemy vessels. To do so, the owning player must have the initiative and must declare his intention in the ram/charge declaration phase. In the attacker's movement phase, each vessel attempting to ram is moved and makes its ramming attempt separately.

Vessels which are the targets of ramming attempts may try to avoid the ram and do so by expending half of their movement allowance for the next movement phase (rounding fractions up). Players need to remember this so that the ship moves only half of its movement allowance in its own movement phase.

To attempt to ram an enemy vessel, a ship or flyer must either move through the position of or end movement in contact with the target vessel and be at the same depth or altitude. (The only exception to this is that submarines at Periscope depth may ram any ship on the surface.) The player making the attempt then rolls a die. On a roll of 4 or less, the attempt is successful. If the enemy vessel was avoiding the attempt, subtract the number of movement points spent avoiding the attempt from the number needed to ram. If the target of the ramming attempt is immobilized due to battle damage, the ramming attempt is automatically successful.

For example, a flyer moves into contact with an enemy flyer. The enemy flyer has a movement rating of 5 and maneuvers to avoid the ram. Avoiding the ram uses half of the flyer's movement rounded up, or 3' worth. Normally the ramming vessel would roll for a 4 or less to ram, but this is reduced to a 1 because of the target's maneuver.

If the ram is successful, and the ramming vessel was a ram-equipped ship, the rammed ship immediately suffers hull damage equal to the hull size of the ramming ship. In addition, roll a die. If the result is 4, 5, or 6, the rammed ship suffers a flooding critical result. This die roll is modified as in the Flooding Roll Modifiers Table (below) based on the hull size of the two ships.

In either case, the ramming ship suffers no damage, the rammed ship is grappled (see Grappling), and the ramming ship can send a boarding party across.

If the ram is successful and the ramming vessel was a ram-equipped flyer, the rammed flyer suffers hull damage equal to half the hull size of the ramming flyer (roll for fractional hits, with a 1-3 having no effect and a 4-6 causing a hit). In addition, roll a die. If the result is less than the number of hull damage points suffered, the rammed flyer suffers a critical loss of trim. If the rammed vessel does not suffer a loss of trim, the two vessels are grappled (see Grappling), and the rammer may send a boarding party across. In either case, the ramming vessel suffers no damage.

If the ram was successful, but the ramming vessel was not equipped with a ram, the ram is resolved the same as a collision, with two exceptions. First, if the ramming vessel is the same size as or smaller than the rammed vessel, there is no chance of losing trim or suffering a flooding critical. Second, if the rammed vessel is a flyer and does not suffer a loss of trim, or is a ship under any circumstances, the two are grappled (see below) and the rammer may send a boarding party across.

FLOODING ROLL MODIFIERS

Condition	*Modifier*
Rammer three or more times the size of the rammed ship	+2
Rammer twice the size of the rammed ship	+1
Rammed ship twice the size of the rammer	–1
Rammed ship four times the size of the rammer	–2

GRAPPLING

Only ships and flyers may grapple enemy vessels. To attempt to grapple an enemy vessel, a vessel must end its move within 2" of an enemy vessel and, if it is a flyer, be at the same altitude. Steamships with a hull size of 3 or more may not be grappled unless they are immobilized due to damage.

Half the deckhands (round fractions up) may make grappling attempts. Roll a die for each attempt; it succeeds on a roll of 5 or 6. The grappling iron is attached to the point on the enemy vessel closest to the deckhand making the attempt and to the point on the friendly vessel occupied by the deckhand. The grapple is automatically tied down, and the deckhand may undertake other actions once the grapple is successful.

If grappled, a ship may be boarded immediately. It remains grappled until the grapple is cut. The grapple may be cut by any crewman of either side who is at either of the attachment points and uninvolved in melee. Grapples are cut during the initiative phase of a turn.

No vessel may move, change direction, or change altitude while grappled to another. Grappled flyers ignore any trim critical hits, and if they take battle damage which would normally force them to drop a level, they instead stay at the same height. They will drop an altitude level if the enemy ship also suffers damage requiring it to drop a level or more or at such time as the grapple is cut. If a grappled ship suffers damage that would reduce its maximum altitude to two lower than its current altitude, the grapple breaks, and the vessel drops two levels and suffers a loss of trim critical hit.

BOARDING ACTIONS

EACH PLAYER may form or disband a boarding party during the initiative phase of the turn after initiative is determined. (Nonmoving players can form boarding parties.) The player notes on his record form the composition of the boarding party and marks off crew boxes corresponding to the party members. At the same time, he should group the figures representing the boarding party at some convenient place on the vessel model. Crewmembers formed into a boarding party may not undertake any other action that turn; they may not man guns, fight fires, or fire small arms. If a boarding party is later disbanded, the survivors are distributed to various crew positions by erasing the correct number of crew casualty marks.

When two vessels are grappled, the moving player may board the other vessel. A vessel is boarded by sending an already-formed boarding party across onto the enemy ship.

Three factors restrict the number of boarders that may be sent from one vessel to another in one movement phase. First, only crew already formed into a boarding party may board. Second, the maximum number of men that can cross in a phase is five times the hull size of the smaller of the two flyers, or five times the hull length of the smaller of two ships. Thus, if a flyer with a hull size of 2 and a flyer with a hull size of 5 were grappled, the greatest number of men who could cross in a phase would be 10. If the boarding party is crossing its own bow or stern or that of the enemy, halve the number of allowed boarders (round fractions up). Third, any crew casualties suffered during the turn due to small arms fire, shrapnel, or grapeshot are taken from the boarding party and reduce the number in the above example, if 10 men were crossing and their flyer took six crew hits from small arms fire, shrapnel, or grapeshot, six boarders would be hit, and only four would be able to cross, even if there were more boarders waiting to cross. In the next friendly movement phase a total of 10 men would again be able to cross.

Attacking boarding parties fight with a defending vessel's boarding party (if one is formed), all deckhands, and marines. Melee and morale rolls are conducted normally, with two exceptions. First, both sides ignore all checked results of a morale test. Second, if the defender fails a morale test (except with a checked result), the ship surrenders. If the attacker fails a morale test (except with a checked result), the survivors of his boarding party retreat back to their own ship. Boarding actions may be fought out either on the decks of the models of the vessels or using the tactical grid superimposed over the deck plan on the vessel's record form. Each square represents 1" of deck

"Away boarders!"

SPECIAL RULES: VEHICLES

VEHICLES INCLUDE ALL mechanically-driven land conveyances.

Record Forms: Information on a vehicle record form is read as shown below.

Land Juggernaut: Also called landships, these massive armored vehicles move on endless tracks, like those of a tractor. A few, all powered by steam, are currently in service in the arsenals of the great powers. Numerous experimental prototypes also exist, the products of the fertile minds of various inventors. All vehicle rules apply to juggernauts. In addition, juggernauts may fire in the same turn in which they move, provided they expend only half or less of their allowed movement. All weapons which fire while the juggernaut is moving suffer a –1 modifier to hit.

Walking Tripod: A hit location result of hull/running gear on a tripod is, instead, treated as a miss (the shot passes between the tripod's legs). If a running gear critical hit is achieved on the tripod and is confirmed by rolling the damage value of the round or less, the tripod tips over and is wrecked. A wrecked tripod can be recovered and repaired after the battle, but it is out of play for the rest of the battle being fought.

A tripod's armament is always positioned to fire directly ahead and has a 90-degree arc of fire to the front.

At the end of each friendly movement phase, the tripod can pivot its superstructure up to 90 degrees to either side of its facing, and that position becomes its new facing for purposes of fire. Pivoting its superstructure does not count as movement, and so the tripod can fire in the same turn it pivots; it may not fire in a turn in which it moves.

Tractor: Tractors are unarmored steam-powered vehicles which move on endless tracks and are used to tow heavy loads. Tractors are often used to tow artillery pieces and can also be used to push disabled vehicles off of roads or bridges. The tractor must begin its turn next to a disabled vehicle to push it out of the way, and it requires one complete movement phase to do so. At the end of the phase, the road or bridge is clear. The tractor must spend one complete turn next to a disabled vehicle to attach tow cables and may then tow it at one-fourth of the tractor's normal speed.

Machinegun Quadricycle: This small vehicle consists of four wheels, a driver's seat, a small petrol engine, and a Maxim machinegun. A gun shield on the Maxim gives the driver/gunner the benefit of hard cover, if

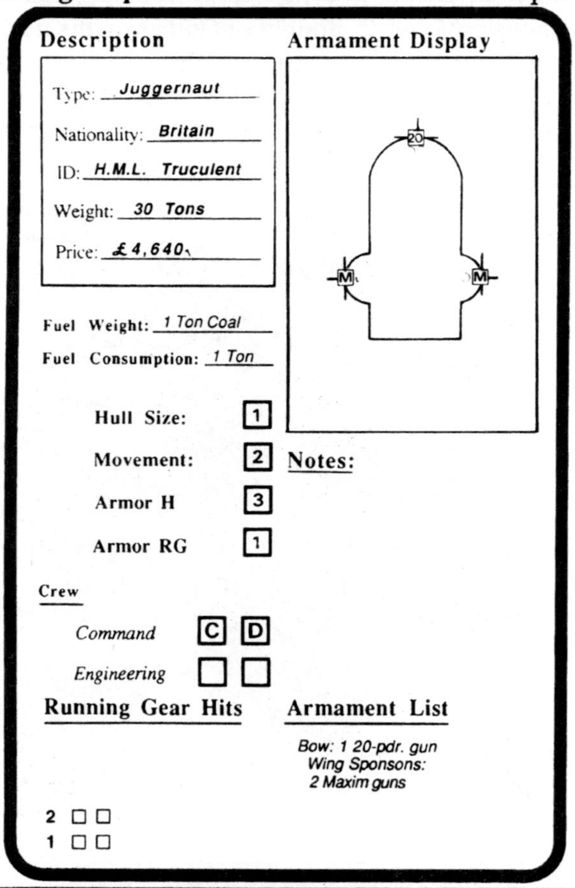
Description
Type: Juggernaut
Nationality: Britain
ID: H.M.L. Truculent
Weight: 30 Tons
Price: £4,640

Fuel Weight: 1 Ton Coal
Fuel Consumption: 1 Ton

Armament Display

Hull Size: 1
Movement: 2
Armor H: 3
Armor RG: 1

Notes:

Crew
Command: C D
Engineering: ☐ ☐

Running Gear Hits
2 ☐ ☐
1 ☐ ☐

Armament List
Bow: 1 20-pdr. gun
Wing Sponsons:
2 Maxim guns

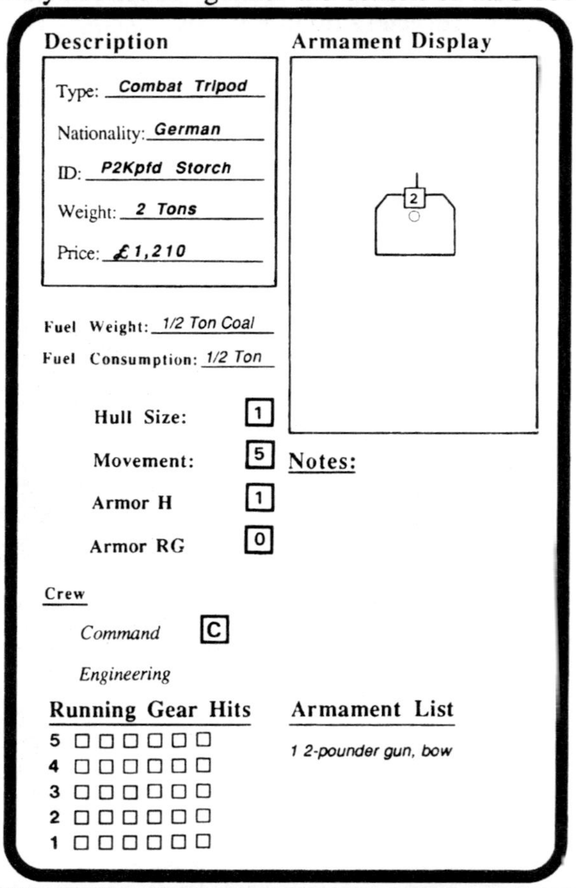
Description
Type: Combat Tripod
Nationality: German
ID: P2Kpfd Storch
Weight: 2 Tons
Price: £1,210

Fuel Weight: 1/2 Ton Coal
Fuel Consumption: 1/2 Ton

Armament Display

Hull Size: 1
Movement: 5
Armor H: 1
Armor RG: 0

Notes:

Crew
Command: C
Engineering

Running Gear Hits
5 ☐ ☐ ☐ ☐ ☐ ☐ ☐
4 ☐ ☐ ☐ ☐ ☐ ☐ ☐
3 ☐ ☐ ☐ ☐ ☐ ☐ ☐
2 ☐ ☐ ☐ ☐ ☐ ☐ ☐
1 ☐ ☐ ☐ ☐ ☐ ☐ ☐

Armament List
1 2-pounder gun, bow

fired at from the vehicle's front 90-degree arc. The machinegun has a 90-degree arc to the front, and it may be fired if the vehicle moves half or less of its movement allowance in a turn.

Train: A train has a maximum speed of 40" per turn. Its speed is always kept track of from turn to turn and the train may accelerate by up to 10" per turn, or decelerate by up to 20" per turn. Speed changes are made at the beginning of each friendly movement phase.

For example, a train moving at a speed of 30" in one turn could, in its next friendly movement phase, decrease its speed to 10" (and move 10" down the track) or increase its speed to 40" (and move 40" down the track). Trains may fire all of their weapons in any turn, regardless of how far they move, unless they decelerate by more than 10" in the turn.

A train which receives a running gear critical hit, confirmed by rolling the gun's damage value or less, is derailed. The train is wrecked, and all guns on it are out of action. All crew are stunned for one turn and may not move or fire; if the crewmembers are meleed, each attacking figure automatically kills one stunned crewman. A bridge critical kills engine crewmen. The train may not change speed for one turn and may not change speed at all if the entire engine crew is killed. A steering critical is treated as a running gear critical on trains (see above). An armor critical hit is applied to one specific car of the train, not all parts of the train. An armor critical has no effect on an unarmored train.

Weapons mounted on trains may fire while the train is moving, but they suffer an adverse modifier of 1 on their roll to hit.

SPECIAL RULES: SHIPS

SHIPS INCLUDE all nautical vessels. All ships may fire their weapons in the same turn in which they move. Ships which move 4' or more in a turn suffer a negative die roll modifier of 1 to hit when they fire any weapon, except torpedoes. Ships which move 8' or more in a turn receive a negative die roll modifier of 1 to hit when fired *at* by any other weapon.

Record Forms: Information on a ship record form is read as shown in the example below.

Torpedo Boat: A torpedo boat is a small, fast vessel designed to deliver high-speed attacks. It follows all normal ship rules.

Gunboat: A gunboat is similar to a torpedo boat, but it is generally larger and slower. Its main task is to support shore operations with gunfire. It follows all normal ship rules.

Armored Warship: Armored warships are the backbone of the fleets of the great powers. They are designed to attack ships on the high seas and have very little to do with ground combat. Nevertheless, the combat system does enable players to incorporate them into games, and so complete rules are presented which cover their occasional appearance in a game. The largest examples of these ships displace thousands of tons and are marvels of engineering. They obey all normal ship rules.

Hydrofoil: A hydrofoil is a small, fast boat, similar to a torpedo boat, which rides above the water on metal fins. This enables it to obtain very high speeds and to cruise in shallow wa-

Ship Record Form

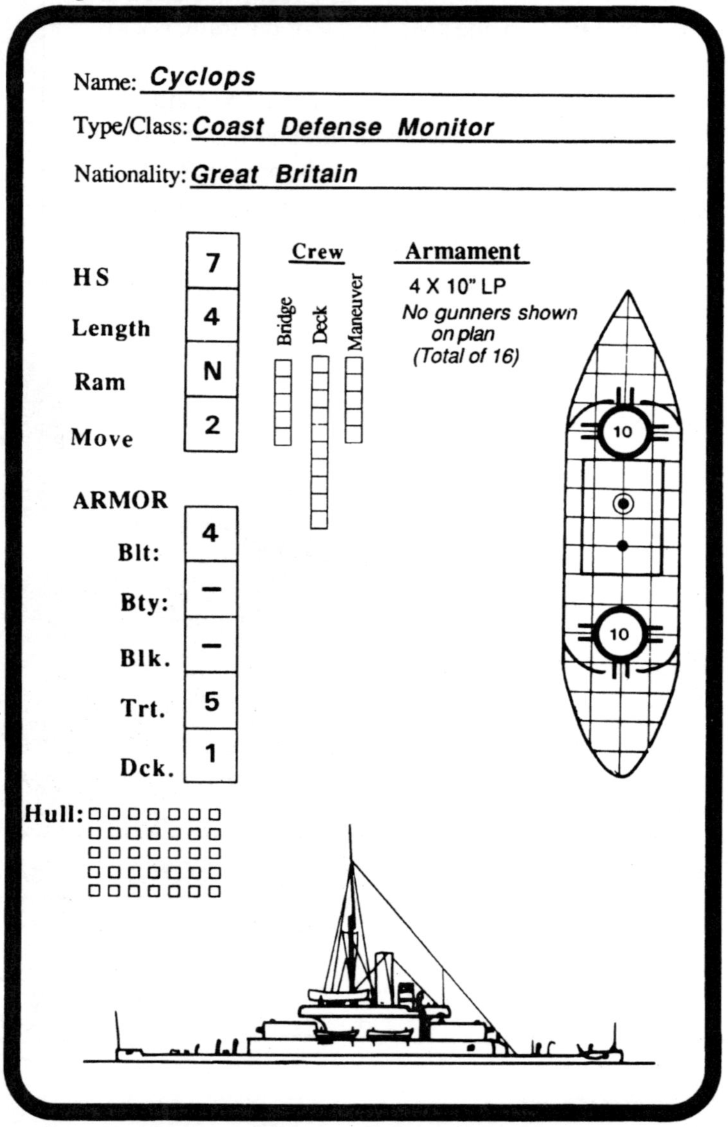

ter. (This capability severely limits its maximum weight.)

Hydrofoils ignore all hull hits caused by a die roll of 1 on the Conveyance Hit Location Table. (The shot passes under the hull of the boat). However, once one complete row of hull boxes is marked off, subtract two from a hydrofoil's movement. From then on, hull hits scored by a 1 cause actual damage, as the hydrofoil has settled into the water and is travelling as a conventional boat.

Submarine: Submarines follow all normal rules for ships and, in addition, may travel at depths lower than Surface. Submerged submarine movement should be kept track of on a hex map of the gaming table and the surrounding area, with each hex on the map equal to 1' on the table. (See the rule on depth on pages 34–35.)

Submarines which are under the surface are difficult to detect. Submarines at Periscope depth may be seen by any ship within 6' on a die roll of 3 or less and are automatically seen by any flyer within 6'. A flyer may alert ships to the presence of a submarine by spending one movement phase circling the submarine's position. Only submarines may detect other submarines which are below Periscope depth. They may only detect other submarines if the detecting submarine is submerged (Periscope depth or lower), within one level of the same depth as the other submarine, within 2' of the other submarine, and the other submarine is in their bow aspect.

Submarines may ram surface ships, but only if at Surface depth or Periscope depth. Submarines at Surface depth and Periscope depth may be attacked by bombs and gunfire; submarines at deeper depths may only be attacked by torpedoes, depth bombs, and underwater guns. A submarine which suffers a bridge hit may not change course, speed, or depth for one turn. A submarine which suffers hull hits equal to half its total possible hull hits must surface and may not submerge again.

Sailing Ship: Sailing ships are wind-powered nautical vessels. They do not have a fixed movement allowance. The movement allowance of each sailing ship, in feet, is one die roll halved (round fractions up). This die roll is made separately for each sailing ship in each friendly movement phase. Once a player rolls for a sailing ship's movement, he must complete that sailing ship's movement before moving any other conveyance. Each foot moved upwind counts as 2' of movement. Sailing ships may not sail directly into the wind. A sailing ship may change its facing by 60 degrees for each foot it moves. It may change its facing by 120 degrees if coming about (changing the angle of the wind from its port bow to its starboard bow, or vice versa). However, if a sailing ship comes about, it may not make any other turns that movement phase.

UPWIND DIAGRAM

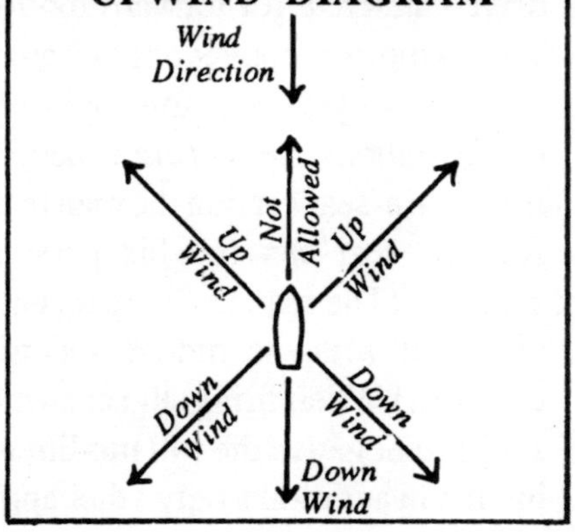

Coming About Diagram

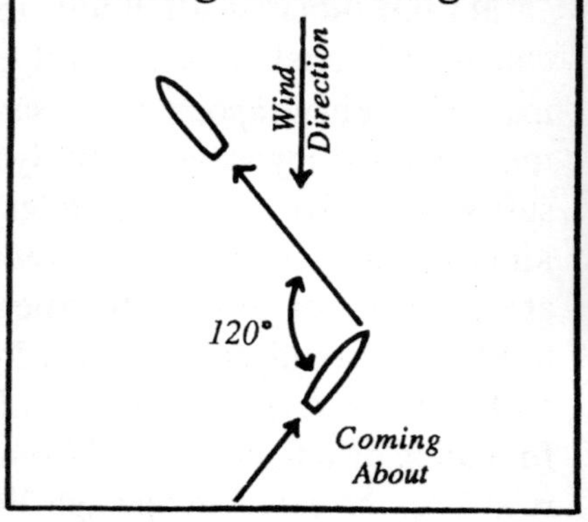

The referee will determine wind direction by rolling a die at the start of the game and consulting the wind direction diagram below.

WIND DIRECTION

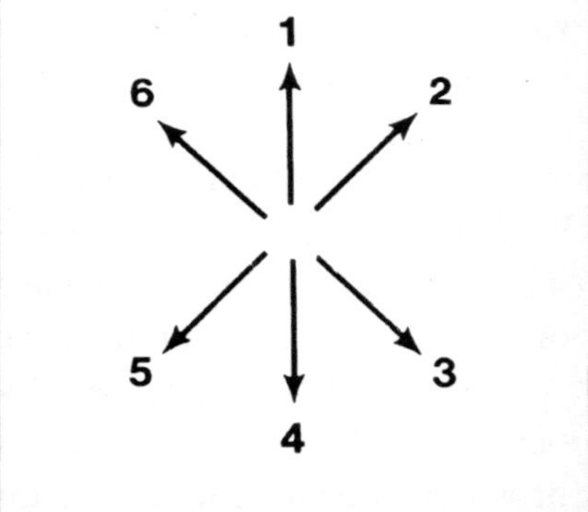

All fire/boiler results on a sailing vessel are treated as fire results. Fires on sailing vessels increase by two levels each turn. Once the level of a fire equals or exceeds the hull size of the sailing vessel, all remaining rigging boxes are marked off; the ship may not move again until it jury-rigs a mast.

Galley: Galleys are oar-powered warships which generally rely on rams for combat. Galleys follow all normal rules for ships. A fire/boiler result on a galley is treated as a fire result.

SPECIAL RULES: FLYERS

FLYERS INCLUDE all flying machines and aerial vessels. All flyers may fire their weapons in the same turn in which they move. Some flyers suffer a negative die roll modifier to hit when they fire. All flyers moving at a speed of 8 or faster suffer a negative die roll modifier of 1 to hit, as does all fire directed against the flyer. Information on a flyer's record form is read as in the example on page 29.

The listing below is divided into two sections. The first section deals with the standard flyers encountered in the service of the various nations in 1889. The second section covers special inventions which are not normally in the hands of governments but which player characters from the role-playing game may have or come in contact with.

Standard Flyers

ALL STANDARD flyers rely on a lifting agent, either hydrogen (in the case of zeppelins) or Martian liftwood.

Liftwood Flyer: Liftwood flyers obtain lift by use of thin panels of liftwood, a tree with antigravitational properties which grows in certain parts of the Martian highlands. Terrestrial liftwood flyers are generally steam-powered and driven through the air by means of a large airscrew (propeller). All normal flyer rules apply to liftwood flyers.

Screw Galley: A screw galley is a Martian liftwood flyer driven by large airscrews which are turned by the muscle power of the ship's "turncranks," or rowers. Screw galleys treat all fire/boiler hits as fire hits.

Kite: Kites are Martian wind-powered liftwood flyers. They follow all of the rules given above for sailing vessels with the following two additions: Kites have a movement allowance each turn of 1 plus the roll of one die. Kites may change altitude by one level per turn at no movement cost but may never voluntarily change by more than one level.

Zeppelin: A zeppelin relies on hydrogen as a lifting agent instead of liftwood. The hydrogen fills the large, rigid, fabric-covered hull of the zeppelin. Since the hull is only fabric supported by a few light structural members, shells pass completely through the flyer without exploding. As a result, all hull hits on a zeppelin cause only one point of damage, regardless of the damage value of the firing gun. A zeppelin never loses trim, so a trim critical hit has no effect. If a zeppelin suffers a fire/boiler critical, it explodes and is completely destroyed. If a zeppelin collides with another vessel, it suffers one die of hull hits. If rammed, a zeppelin suffers hull hits equal to the hull size of the ramming flyer unless the flyer is equipped with a ram, in which case the zeppelin suffers twice as much damage. A zeppelin may not ram another vessel.

Throckmorton Conveyors: A Throckmorton conveyor is an individual flyer which utilizes liftwood panels for flight and a small pedal-driven airscrew for forward motion. Throckmorton conveyors are available in single-seat and twin-seat configurations. Neither are armed, but in the twin-seat version the man in the forward seat can fire his personal weapon. (The man in the rear seat is occupied with the rudder and trim controls.) When firing, the crewman suffers a negative die roll modifier to hit of 1 in addition to any other applicable modifiers.

Throckmorton conveyors may face in any direction desired and may change facing as often as desired during movement. Conveyors have a movement rating of 2, pay both movement points to climb one altitude level, pay one movement point to descend a level, and may never descend more than one level per turn. If the conveyor ends its move at the same altitude and in contact with another flyer, vehicle, or ship, the conveyor's crew may board it. Conveyors are treated as troops in open order for fire purposes, with all hits being crew casualties.

Invented Flyers

THE FOLLOWING invented flyers all utilize some form of dynamic lift generated by the rapid passage of air over wings or rotors.

Glider: A glider is an aerial vessel which relies upon dynamic interaction between specially-shaped wings and the atmosphere (the same means terrestrial birds use for flight). Gliders may either be dropped from an airborne flyer (such as a zeppelin) or may be launched by catapult. All gliders have an initial movement of 10. A glider adds one to its speed for each altitude level that it descends and subtracts one from its speed for each altitude level that it climbs. A glider's speed may never be increased above 12, however, and if additional altitude levels are dropped, speed remains at 12. If a glider's speed ever falls below 3, it will immediately drop sufficient altitude levels to bring its speed back up to 3. If this brings it into contact with the ground, the glider crashes. The glider may move a total of 3' and drop one altitude level (without gaining speed) in the movement phase in which it lands. It may land on any landing field or flat grassy area 18" or more long.

A glider may make one 60-degree change in direction per movement phase. This change is made at any point after the glider has completed half of its movement. This direction change may be increased to 120 degrees by voluntarily reducing the glider's movement allowance by one.

A glider may ram, and other flyers may attempt to ram the glider. If another vessel attempts to ram it and it evades, it does so with half of its current speed, not half of its maximum movement rating. If a glider rams or is rammed, it is destroyed.

Hull hits have the normal effect on maximum altitude for a glider, but are called wing hits instead. As a glider has no airscrew, ignore all screw criticals. A lifter critical hit is treated normally, but on a glider the lifters are called flaps. A fire/boiler hit on a glider is treated as a fire. All fires increase by one level per turn on a glider. The pilot may fight the fire the same as a deckhand on a regular flyer. A bridge hit on a glider is instead treated as a trim critical hit. Any altitude lost due to a trim critical hit does not increase the speed of the glider.

Aeroplane: An aeroplane is a powered version of a glider. It follows all of the same rules as a glider, with the following exceptions. The whole crew, including the pilot, fights fires on an aeroplane.

An aeroplane may take off from any landing field or strip of flat grassland on the playing surface which is 3' or more long. Its initial speed at takeoff is 4. It may always increase or decrease its speed by half of its device reliability (round fractions up) each turn, in addition to any increases or decreases due to altitude change. Its maximum speed is 12 plus twice its device reliability.

Each screw critical hit reduces the maximum speed of the aeroplane by 5. A boiler critical hit on an aeroplane causes an additional roll. If the die roll is equal to or less than the damage value of the firing gun, the engine explodes, causing the aeroplane to crash. If the die roll is greater than the damage value of the firing gun, the engine is damaged and stops. The aeroplane then behaves like a glider for the rest of the time that it is in flight, with the exception that each turn it must reduce its speed by 1. (It may, in the same turn, regain the lost speed by reducing its altitude.)

Autogyro: An autogyro combines many of the characteristics of a helicopter and an aeroplane. Like a helicopter, it is held aloft by a rotor. However, this rotor is not powered by the engine but instead turns due to the passage of air over it and so functions much like the wing of a glider or aeroplane. The autogyro thus cannot hover and relies on its airscrew for forward motion. It is capable of flight at very low speeds, however. An autogyro follows all the same rules as an aeroplane with these exceptions:

An autogyro may take off from any landing strip or stretch of flat grassland that is 18" or more long. The autogyro has an initial take-off speed of 3. It may move a total of 2' and drop one altitude level in the movement phase in which it lands. It may land on any landing field or flat grassy area which is 18" or more long. It does not gain or lose speed for altitude changes, and it may change its own speed by only one per turn. The minimum speed for an autogyro is 2; if its speed falls below 2, it crashes. The maximum speed of the autogyro is 5 plus its device reliability. All damage on an autogyro is identical to that suffered by an aeroplane. Wing hits are called rotor hits instead, but they have exactly the same effect.

Helicopter: A helicopter is an aerial conveyance which stays aloft by means of the lift provided by its rotor blades. A helicopter does not have a separate airscrew; it achieves forward motion by tilting its rotors. A helicopter does not have hull hit boxes; instead, it has rotor hit boxes. All hull hits become rotor hits instead, and the effects of rotor damage are the same as for hull hits on a normal flyer. All screw critical hits are treated as regular hull (rotor) hits. When a complete row of boxes is marked off, the helicopter's maximum speed and maximum altitude are reduced by one.

A fire/boiler critical hit on a helicopter causes both a fire and an engine failure. The whole crew, pilot included, fights a fire. The helicopter may not move while on fire and loses one altitude level per turn until either the fire is extinguished or the helicopter crashes. Once the fire is extinguished, the helicopter may move normally. A bridge hit on a helicopter is instead treated as a trim critical hit.

A helicopter may ram, and other flyers may attempt to ram the helicopter. If another flyer attempts to ram the helicopter and the helicopter evades, it does so with half of its current speed, not half of its maximum movement rating. If a helicopter rams or is rammed, it is destroyed.

Part D: Advanced Weapons

NAVAL WEAPONS

THE FOLLOWING are naval weapons.

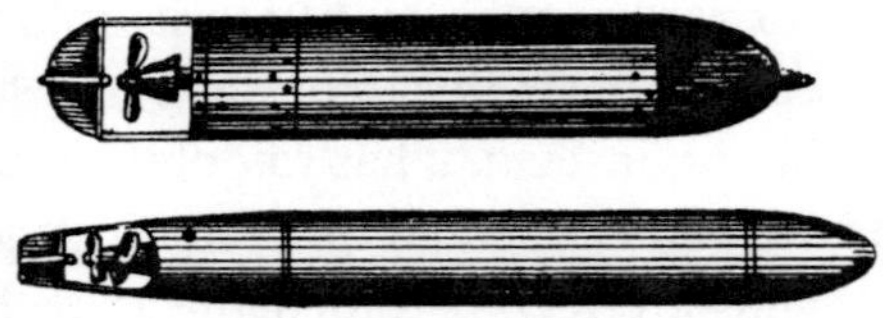

Torpedoes

MANY SHIPS have launch tubes which can fire torpedoes, and some flyers have provisions for dropping them as well.

Firing Aspect: The ship record form will indicate whether the torpedoes are fired from bow tubes (BT), stern tubes (ST), midship tubes (MT), or deck tubes (DT). Bow tubes may only fire into the bow aspect, stern tubes into the stern aspect, and broadside tubes into the broadside aspect. If a ship is listed as having broadside tubes, the number listed is the number of tubes which face *each* broadside. Deck tubes may fire into either the bow aspect or the forward half of either broadside aspect, but may *not* fire directly ahead (at any vessel within 4" of a line drawn in the direction the firing ship faces).

Aerial vessels may only fire torpedoes at ships which are directly ahead (within 4" of a line drawn in the direction the flyer faces).

Torpedo Supply: Each launch tube type has a number following it which is the number of launch tubes (and torpedoes) that are available. As many torpedoes may be fired per phase as desired (up to the total number carried), but each time a torpedo is fired, note that it is expended by marking it off on the record form.

For example, the British *Thornycroft-125* boat's listing reads "DT-4" indicating that it has four deck-mounted launch tubes and a total of four torpedoes.

Occasionally, a torpedo listing will have an additional number following it with a plus, such as "DT-2 +2." This means that two "reload" torpedoes are available. Reload torpedoes may be fired from any mount, not just the mount they are listed by. It takes one full turn to reload torpedoes, during which time the ship may not fire any other torpedoes.

Any flyer equipped with bomb racks may carry one torpedo in place of two loads of bombs.

Firing Torpedoes: Torpedoes are fired in the friendly movement phase, not the fire phase. They are fired before any other movement. In order to hit a target, the firing player rolls a die and must roll a number equal to or less than the hull length number of the target vessel. The hull length number is shown on the ship record form. However, before rolling the die, subtract the range in feet (round fractions down) and the target's movement rating in feet from the hull size number. If the attack is from directly ahead or directly behind the target ship, subtract an additional two.

If the hit number is reduced below 1, it stays at 1 but the target player is allowed a saving roll, just as with small arms fire. The saving roll number is equal to the number of excess hit modifiers.

For example, a torpedo boat is attacking a ship with a hull size of 6 and a movement rating of 2 from a range of 2'. Normally the attacking player would have to roll 6 or less to hit, but he subtracts two from this for the range and two for the target's speed, for a final modified hit number of 2. Note that if the attack took place from directly ahead or behind, the hit number would be reduced to 0. Instead, the hit number would be rolled as a 1 and, if a hit were achieved, the target player would save on a roll of 1.

Aerial vessels launch torpedoes in the same way as do ships, but can only launch them straight ahead and may only launch from Very Low altitude.

Depth: Torpedoes may only be used to attack ships at the same depth as the ship which launched the torpedo; however, Surface and Periscope depth are considered to be the same depth for purposes of launching torpedoes. Aerial-launched torpedoes may only be fired at surface ships or submarines at Periscope depth.

Torpedo Damage: All torpedo hits are hull hits. Torpedoes have a penetration of 6. Their damage value is variable and equal to the sum of the roll of four dice. All torpedo hits cause an uncontrolled flooding critical hit. To control the flooding, the player owning the damaged ship must roll a 4 or less.

Improved Torpedoes: Improved torpedoes are an invention open to inventor characters and are described in the role-playing game. Improved torpedoes are identical to regular torpedoes, except that when calculating the hit number, subtract one for every 2' of range (round fractions down) instead of every 1' of range.

Depth Bombs

ANY SHIP capable of carrying torpedoes may carry two depth bombs instead. Flyers with bomb racks may carry one depth bomb in place of each bomb load. Depth bombs are dropped at any point during movement. Flyers may only drop depth bombs from Very Low altitude. When the depth bomb is dropped, the dropping player announces the depth it is set for (Periscope, 100 fathoms, 200 fathoms, 300 fathoms, etc.) If the depth setting is correct, the referee rolls a die and halves the result (rounding fractions down); this number is the number of hull hits suffered by the submarine. If a 6 is rolled, the submarine suffers three hull hits and, in addition, an uncontrolled flooding critical result. The result of the die roll should be kept secret from the player who dropped the depth bomb.

Torpedo Nets

ONE DEFENSE against torpedo craft was torpedo netting. Torpedo nets were hung from booms alongside a ship and were intended to stop torpedoes from hitting the ship. Only warships from Earth have torpedo nets, and all are assumed to have them. Although nets are reasonably successful in protecting a ship from torpedoes, they reduce its speed considerably and cannot protect against torpedo attacks from directly ahead or behind.

Ships may begin a game with their torpedo nets deployed (in the water) or recovered (on the ship). Ships with their nets deployed have their movement rating reduced to 1. Ships with their nets deployed may only make torpedo attacks with their bow and stern tubes. (Gun attacks can be made normally.)

All torpedo attacks against ships with their nets deployed are resolved normally, with one exception. If a ship with nets out is hit by a torpedo, it makes a saving roll for 4 or less to stop the torpedo in the net. On a roll of 5 or 6, the torpedo hits anyway. Torpedo attacks made from directly ahead and directly astern are not affected by torpedo nets.

A player may attempt to deploy or recover his nets during a game if he wishes. A player declares that he is deploying or recovering his nets at the end of any friendly movement phase, when repair die rolls are made. He rolls a die, and on a roll of 5 or 6, he succeeds. Otherwise, his ship is still deploying or recovering. Once he begins to deploy or recover, he must continue to do so until he successfully rolls a 5 or 6. A ship in the process of deploying or recovering nets has its movement allowance reduced to 1 but receives no protection from the nets.

Underwater Guns

UNDERWATER GUNS are inventions available to inventor characters and described in the role-playing rules. They are treated exactly like a 4" short gun (also known as a 4" low-powered gun), except that:

• The gun may only be fired at ships.

• It may not be fired at hydrofoils unless they are stationary or riding low in the water (see the hydrofoil rule on page 46).

• The measured range to the target is doubled (thus effectively halving the range of the gun).

• All hits from the gun are hull hits.

• And the gun may be fired at submarines at any depth, provided the firing ship can see the submarine.

ARTILLERY

These weapons are generally used to fire at large targets, such as conveyances or structures, and are similar to artillery in purpose, if not in exact function.

Lightning Cannon

A lightning cannon is an invention which may be available to player characters from the role-playing game.

This weapon projects a bolt of lightning toward a target and may only be fired at large targets, such as conveyances or buildings. Its close range in feet, close range penetration, and damage value is equal to its reliability number. Its long range is twice its reliability number, while its long range penetration is half its reliability (round fractions down).

Heat Ray

A heat ray is an invention which PCs from the role-playing game may have access to. It focuses the rays of the Sun through several large lenses and produces a powerful beam of light which melts objects in the beam's path. A heat ray may only be fired at large targets, such as conveyances and buildings. It has a close range in the atmosphere in scale feet equal to five times its reliability and a close range of 1000 miles times its reliability outside the atmosphere. Its long range is twice its close range.

A heat ray has a rate of fire of 1 and a damage value of 10, although this is reduced by two in an atmosphere. In addition, the damage value is reduced by one for every orbit out from the Sun past Mercury (–1 at Venus, –2 at Earth, –3 at Mars). It has a penetration of 4 at close range and 2 at long range. If it hits a target but does not penetrate, it will instead reduce the target's armor value by 2.

Electric Rail Gun

Electric rail guns may be available to player characters from the role-playing game. They use electromagnets to accelerate steel shells down their barrels. For game purposes, an electric rail gun is equivalent to a modern 12" naval gun.

Smutts Discharger

A Smutts discharger is a steam-powered pneumatic launcher for Smutts Patent Aerial Torpedoes. These dischargers are only mounted on British steam-powered vessels and are always oriented to fire directly forward.

The Smutts Patent Aerial Torpedo is a finned projectile filled with dynamite held aloft by means of liftwood vanes and powered after launch by a propeller driven by a small flywheel. It also trails a cable with a small grapnel to snag vessels over which it passes.

On the turn it is launched, it will move directly forward from the firing ship for 6', and it does the same for the four subsequent turns. At the end of that time, it detonates (to prevent capture by the enemy).

If the Smutts torpedo passes through the model of any vessel at the same altitude or one level lower than the torpedo, it will collide with it on a roll of 2 or higher. The target vessel may attempt to avoid the collision in the same manner as avoiding a ramming attempt.

If two vessels are in the same hex, roll randomly to determine which to check first for a collision. If the Smutts torpedo misses that vessel, roll to see if it hits the other. If one or both vessels attempt to evade the torpedo, there is a chance the vessels will collide with each other (the same as if a vessel turns in a hex with another). If they collide, they do not receive the die roll modifier to avoid a ramming attempt.

If the Smutts torpedo hits, it detonates. It has a penetration of 1 and a damage value of 12. In addition, the force of the detonation will cause an automatic loss of trim critical, the same as a hit from a lob gun.

Each ship carries a limited number of Smutts aerial torpedoes. When these have all been used, the discharger may not be fired again. The Smutts aerial torpedoes are represented by small triangles on the ship's deck plan of the ship record form.

The Smutts discharger is treated as any other gun for purposes of gun hits and has a magazine. If the Smutts discharger's magazine is detonated by a critical hit, all remaining Smutts aerial torpedoes on board blow up. Roll for each torpedo separately for hit location.

Rocket Batteries

It is very difficult to fire ordnance at a steep upward or downward angle from an aerial gunboat since the angular recoil will destabilize the firing boat and cause a loss of trim. This is not a problem with rockets, however, since the thrust of the rocket can be vented in any direction required to maintain stability of the ship.

The British often employ banks of Hale rockets on their aerial gunboats to fire at higher or lower targets, and other European powers employ rockets of similar design. These rockets are also mounted on ships and some land vehicles.

Each rocket battery is a bank of rockets, all of which are fired in a single salvo at a target. As modern rockets are scarcely more accurate than their ancestor, the Congreve rocket, lack of accuracy is compensated for by volume of fire.

Each bank of rockets is directed to fire into one firing aspect, and is either level or angled up or down. Batteries angled up may only fire at targets higher than the firing conveyance, those angled down may only fire at lower ones, and level batteries may only fire at targets at the same level. Angled rocket batteries may only fire at targets if the range to the target in feet is equal to or less than the difference in altitude.

For example, a target 2' away can only be fired at if the altitude difference is at least two levels. Rockets have a maximum range of 4'. Altitude does not count against the range of the rockets.

A rocket battery is shown on the record form by a triangle with or without a tail. The triangle points in the direction the battery is faced. If the tail of the triangle is hollow, the battery is angled up; if it is filled in, the battery is angled down. If the triangle has no tail, it is level.

When a rocket battery is fired, it is not necessary to determine whether or not there was a hit. Instead, roll the die, and the number rolled is the number of rockets that hit.

If firing at a unit in open order, halve the number of hits. Rockets have a penetration of 0 and a damage value of 1.

One crewman is required to fire a battery from a conveyance (but this is normally a deckhand, not a dedicated gunner). Two gunners are required to fire a field rocket battery. Once fired, the battery is empty and may not be reloaded during the course of the game.

Rocket batteries mounted on a conveyance can be destroyed as a result of a gun hit. For purposes of determining the chance of a gun hit being on a rocket battery, count all rocket batteries on board as a single gun.

A hit destroys one rocket battery. Rocket batteries can also suffer magazine hits. If a rocket battery suffers a magazine hit, one battery detonates. Roll the die to determine how many hits are suffered, and then roll hit location on each one separately.

Fixed Batteries

FIXED BATTERIES are permanent gun mounts usually forming part of a fortress but sometimes placed by themselves to guard a harbor. Many fixed batteries have the advantage of being able to fire at high angles. Most guns still require fairly elaborate carriages to allow them to fire at high angles, and not all guns are so fitted. All machine cannon are mounted for high-angle fire. Fixed batteries of heavier guns are rigged either for high-angle or surface fire, but not for both.

Fixed batteries fire in the same manner as a field gun when mounted for surface fire. When firing at a ship, the fixed battery receives a favorable die roll modifier to hit of one . When firing at flyers, fixed batteries operate under the same limitations as ship-mounted guns (they may not fire if the altitude difference in levels is greater than the range in feet) and do not receive a +1 to hit.

Fixed batteries mounted for high-angle fire may fire at any target above them, even if the difference in altitude is greater than the range. Such a battery is still limited by the range of the gun it is firing, and still counts each altitude level higher as an additional 1' to the range.

Shore batteries mounted for high angle fire may still fire at surface targets, but do not receive the +1 modifier to hit.

Many fixed batteries are built into fortifications and so may have considerable armor. A fixed battery is fired at the same as a ship, but hull hits have no effect.

The gun crew and gun are both considered protected by armor. If a critical hit is made, only fire and magazine hits affect the battery; all other results are treated as no effect. A magazine critical hit destroys the battery.

Fire, either as a result of a critical hit or liquid fire dropped on the battery, puts a fixed battery out of action temporarily. The level of the fire will go up one level per turn. All gunners in the battery may fight the fire, and it goes down one level for each roll of a 5 or 6.

Once the fire goes out, the battery will come back into action. However, if the level of the fire ever reaches 6, the magazine blows up, destroying the battery.

Range Finder

THIS DEVICE IS an invention which may be available to PCs from the role-playing game. It allows a die roll modifier of +1 to hit targets at long range with any artillery weapon.

EXOTIC AERIAL WEAPONS

THE FOLLOWING special weapons are found only on flyers or, in the case of barrage balloons and tether mines, affect only flyers.

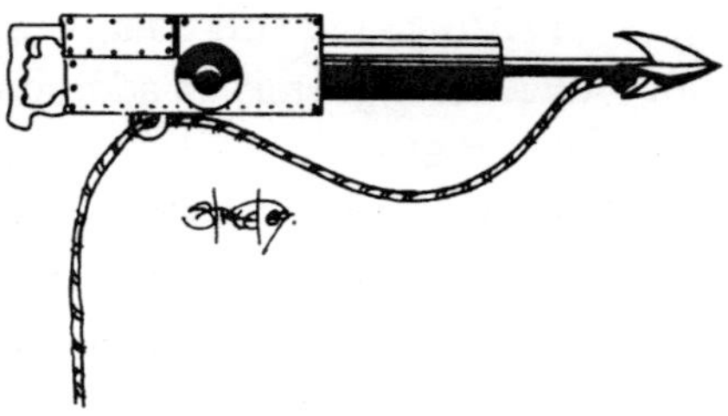

Power Grapnel

A POWER GRAPNEL is a large harpoon gun which fires a barbed, collapsing grapnel designed to forcibly pierce the side of a flyer or become entangled in its rigging or deck gear. It trails a strong steel cable which is held up by a series of small liftwood aerial buoys. The cable is attached to a power winch and, upon hitting a flyer with the grapnel, the winch is engaged and used to pull the two flyers together.

Many Martian screw galleys use a device similar in design to the above but attach the cable to the vessel's driving crankshaft and use their own turncranks to pull the vessels together.

A power grapnel is shown on the record form as a gun box with the letter "G" in it and no crew. A power grapnel is mounted like any other gun. It has a rate of fire of (2), meaning that it takes two turns of reloading between shots.

It has a crew requirement of two, but no crew requirement is provided for it, and it is instead manned by deckhands or gunners from another weapon if it fires. (It is so seldom used that there is no point in maintaining a permanent gun crew.)

Power grapnels have a short range of 6" and a long range of 12". If a power grapnel shot hits, then the two flyers are grappled and moved together. If a power grapnel hits a glider or aeroplane, it does one wing hit instead of the previous. If a power grapnel hits an autogyro or helicopter, it does one die roll's worth of rotor hits instead.

Power grapnels are treated as any other gun for purposes of taking gun hits; they have no magazine.

Tether Mines

TETHER MINES are explosive charges equipped with contact detonators, attached to liftwood buoys, and tethered in place at a selected altitude by means of a cable. Tether mines are shown on the record form by a circle with a cross superimposed on it. Tether mines may be deployed from flyers, ships, fortifications, and vehicles.

During the initiative phase of each turn, players with tether mines must state if they intend to raise or lower them that turn. If they are lowered, they have no effect. If they are raised, they are fully operational.

Conveyances with tether mines raised may not move any faster than a movement rate of 3 and may not avoid a ram. However, a player may announce at any time that he is cutting his mines loose, and then he is free to attempt to avoid a ram or move at any speed desired. Once cut free, the tether mines are lost.

Tether mines are raised one altitude level higher than the owning conveyance or fortification (called the tether point). If any flyer passes over the tether point at the same altitude as the mines, or is already above the tether point and drops to the same altitude as the mines, it automatically collides with them.

If a conveyance with tether mines raised passes under a flyer which is at the same altitude as the mines, or climbs so as to bring the tether mines to the same altitude as a flyer already in the same hex, that flyer collides with the tether mines on a roll of 6 on one die. If a flyer begins its movement above a tether point with mines raised and at the same altitude as the mines, it may move away without colliding with them.

If a tether point cuts its mines loose for any reason, they will collide with any flyer directly above them on a die roll of 6 on one die.

If a flyer collides with a tether mine, the mine detonates and is counted as a hit caused by a gun. Roll for hit location normally. All tether mines have a penetration of 0 but cause an automatic loss of trim critical hit in addition to any other damage, the same as a Martian lob gun. The damage value of the mine depends on the type being used. Martian tether mines have a damage value of 4; terrestrial tether mines have a damage value of 6.

Tether mines cannot be affected by anything except a magazine hit. If a magazine hit detonates the tether mines, each mine on board and not raised explodes. Roll a hit location for each mine separately.

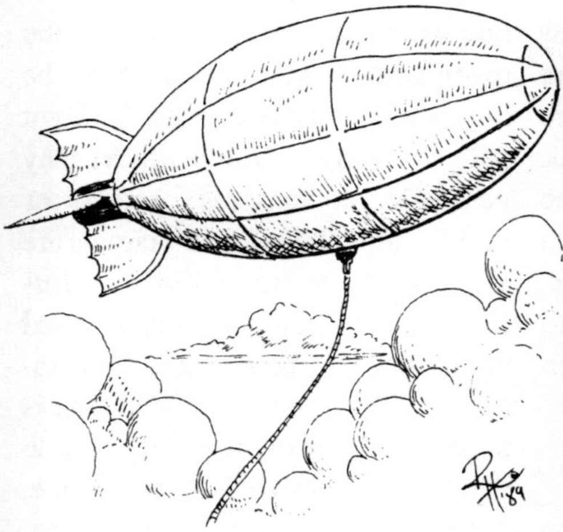

Barrage Balloons

BARRAGE BALLOONS are hydrogen-filled balloons attached to ships or fortifications by stout cables. They are sent aloft to prevent aerial gunboats from flying directly over the target below. Barrage balloons are only available on ships and fortifications; they may not be used on flyers.

Barrage balloons are suspended two altitude levels above their tether point. Any flyer which moves to either one or two altitude levels directly above a tether point with barrage balloons collides with them.

During the initiative phase of each turn, players must state if they intend to raise or lower their balloons that turn. If the balloons are lowered, they have no effect. If they are raised, they are fully operational.

Ships with barrage balloons raised may not move any faster than 2" per turn and may not avoid a ram. However, a player may announce at any time that he is cutting his barrage balloons loose, and then he is free to attempt to avoid a ram or move at any speed desired. Once cut free, the barrage balloons are lost.

When a flyer collides with a barrage balloon, the balloon explodes. The flyer suffers an automatic loss of trim critical hit. In addition, the player rolls a die. The result is the number of crew casualties taken and the level of fire started on the flyer by the explosion.

Barrage balloons may be fired at by weapons as if they were an unarmored conveyance. Any hit by a rocket battery destroys the balloon, as does any hit from liquid fire. Any gunfire hits that result in a fire or fire/boiler critical hit destroy the balloon. All other results have no effect.

A barrage balloon may be raised or lowered one altitude level per turn. A barrage balloon may be released at any time. If released, the balloon will float away and poses no further threat to any aerial vessel.

Drogue Torpedoes

A DROGUE TORPEDO is an explosive charge dangled below a flyer on a cable and equipped with a contact detonator. Drogue torpedoes are represented on the record forms by long ovals.

During the initiative phase of each turn, players commanding flyers with drogue torpedoes must state if they intend to raise or lower them that turn. If the drogue torpedoes are raised, they have no effect. If they are lowered, they are fully operational.

A flyer with its drogue torpedo lowered has its movement rating reduced by one. The drogue torpedo hangs down one level directly below the ship. Any flyer which passes directly under the ship at the same altitude as the drogue torpedo collides with the torpedo on a roll of 5 or 6. Likewise, if the flyer with the torpedo passes directly over another flyer, the torpedo collides with the target on a roll of 5 or 6.

Collision with a drogue torpedo has exactly the same effect as collision with a tether mine, except that all drogue torpedoes have a damage value of 10.

Drogue torpedoes which are lowered cannot be hit by gunfire. Drogue torpedoes on board a flyer cannot be affected by anything except a magazine hit. If a magazine hit detonates the drogue torpedoes, each torpedo on board which is not lowered explodes. Roll a hit location for each drogue torpedo separately.

EXOTIC DEVICES

THE FOLLOWING devices cover a variety of functions, from increased armor protection to unusual small arms. All of these devices are inventions which may be available to player characters from the role-playing game.

Woven Steel Body Armor

IF A CHARACTER wearing woven steel body armor is hit by small arms fire, subtract 2 from the wound determination roll (see page 13). A modified result of 0 or less means that no wound is suffered.

Gravity Focus Ray

THIS WEAPON intensifies the gravity of a planet in respect to a small (flyer-sized) object. It has a close range in feet equal to its reliability rating; its long range is twice that. Any flyer hit by the ray will plummet one altitude level, just as if it had suffered a loss of trim.

If a ship is hit by the ray, roll a die. If the result is equal to or greater than the ship's hull size, it sinks. However, a roll of 6 will always sink the ship, regardless of its hull size. Any unit or detachment hit by the ray will collapse from the additional weight and be immobilized for as long as the ray remains focused on it. A mounted unit will dismount, and its mounts will be too frightened or injured to be remounted during the game. All troops make a morale test at –4 once the ray is turned off.

Smokeless Powder

ONE OF THE reasons that a concealed unit is immediately seen when it fires is that there is an immediate cloud of black powder smoke released. This is not true of units firing smokeless powder ammunition. Units which fire smokeless powder ammunition are only spotted on a die roll of 1 or less. However, add the Fieldcraft of the closest enemy unit with a line of sight to the number needed. If, for example, the closest enemy unit had a Fieldcraft of 3, a firing unit would be spotted on a roll of 4 or less.

Electric Rifle

ELECTRIC RIFLES FIRE as bolt-action rifles on the Small Arms Firing Tables (page 170), but do so with a rate of fire of 2. Each such unit may take 20 shots per figure before the rifles have exhausted their batteries; the batteries may not be recharged within the span of a miniatures game. Electric rifles are smokeless and noiseless, and so concealed units which fire them are not revealed.

Moon Men's electric rifles are similar in design but of lower power, and so fire as if smoothbore muskets. Moon Men will only fire one shot per phase and have so many rounds in their rifles' magazines that there is no need to keep track of ammunition.

DEADFALL ORDNANCE

THE FOLLOWING weapons are unpowered weapons dropped from flyers on targets below.

Bombs

SOME FLYERS are equipped with bomb racks. These flyers have one or more bomb symbols printed on their record form. Each bomb rack carries one bomb and allows the flyer to make one bomb attack.

Unlike other attacks, bomb attacks are made at any point during movement. A ship may drop as many bombs in a movement phase as the owning player wishes. Bombs may be dropped at any point along the flight path of the flyer. Bomb attacks may be made on stationary targets or mobile targets. Stationary targets are all fixed batteries, buildings, fortifications, any ship at anchor or tied up at dock or immobilized by damage, any flyer which has landed or is immobilized by damage, any vehicle which is immobilized due to damage, and any unlimbered gun. Mobile targets are all other targets.

For each bomb dropped on a target, the attacking player rolls a die. To hit the target he must roll a number equal to or greater than the difference in altitude between him and his target. For example, if he were two altitude levels above the target, he would have to roll a 2 or higher. Add one to the number needed to hit for every 2' (or fraction thereof) the flyer moves that movement phase.

Add one to the hit number for every 60-degree turn made by the aerial vessel in its move before dropping the bombs. Add one to the hit number if the aerial vessel has already dropped a bomb on one or more targets this movement phase. Add two to the number needed to hit if the target is a mobile target.

For example, a flyer is one level above a unit of infantry (mobile target) in open order. The flyer moves 2' during its movement phase and makes one 60-degree turn before dropping its bombs. The hit number is 5 (1+1+1+2=5). Because the player must roll equal to or greater than the hit number in order to hit the target, the aerial vessel would have to roll a 5 or 6 to hit.

If the bomb hits, it does damage as

gunfire (shell) but with a penetration of 1 and a damage value of 6. Since the example target was in open order, the bomb would cause three casualties (half the damage value). Had the unit been formed, the bomb hit would have caused six casualties.

Bomb racks can be destroyed due to a gun result on the Conveyance Hit Location Chart. For purposes of determining the chance of a gun hit being on a bomb rack, count all bomb racks on board as a single gun. A hit destroys one bomb rack. Bomb racks can also suffer magazine hits. If a bomb rack suffers a magazine critical hit, all remaining bombs on board explode. Resolve each bomb explosion exactly as a single hit from a bomb.

Liquid Fire

SOME FLYERS are equipped with one or more racks of liquid fire, a chemical compound that ignites and burns fiercely once exposed to oxygen. Liquid fire is dropped on targets at lower altitudes as the flyer passes overhead. This attack is carried out during movement, not at the end of movement. No die roll is made to see whether or not liquid fire hits the target; instead, a die is rolled to see how much of it does. Roll one die and subtract one for each difference in altitude level between the flyer and its target. That is, if the flyer is two levels above its target, subtract two from the die roll. If the target is stationary, add one to the die roll. (Stationary targets are defined in the section on bomb racks above). If the target is not stationary, but the flyer is moving the same direction as the target, add one to the die roll.

The result is the level of fire started on the target. A modified die roll of 0 or less has no effect. Troop units suffer casualties equal to the modified die roll. Halve the number of casualties (round fractions down) if the troops are in open order. Liquid fire has no effect on troops in structures, but it sets the structure on fire. (See page 63.)

Each rack of liquid fire may be used only once per game. Once dropped, it is expended and may not be reloaded during the game. There is no required crew for the liquid fire racks; their release controls are on the bridge. Each liquid fire rack is represented on the record form by a checkered square.

Liquid fire may be destroyed by a gun result on the Conveyance Hit Location Chart (page 175). For purposes of determining the chance of a gun hit being on a liquid fire rack, count all racks on board as a single gun. A hit destroys one rack and starts a level 1 fire. If a magazine critical hit is made on the liquid fire, all racks are destroyed, and a fire is started equal in level to the roll of two dice.

Spike Droppers

INVENTED BY Martians but quickly copied by European powers, the spike dropper is little more than a hopper full of short metal spikes or darts with leather or wooden fins to ensure that they drop point down. Attacks with spike droppers are made in exactly the same manner as liquid fire racks, with the exception that all hits scored are casualties instead of levels of fire. If the spikes are dropped on troops in open order, halve the die roll result (round fractions down).

Each hopper of spikes may be used only once per game. Once dropped, the hopper is expended and may not be reloaded during the game. There is no required crew for the spike dropper; its release controls are on the bridge. Each spike dropper is represented on the record form by a rectangle containing several spikes.

If spike droppers are mounted on a flyer, count them as a gun for hit location rolls. For purposes of determining the chance of a gun hit being on a spike dropper, count all spike droppers on board as a single gun.

An Aphid-class gunboat supports a British attack across a canal bridge. Royal Artillery gunners by Ral Partha; naval troops by Falcon Miniatures.

Part E: The Defense of Places

IT IS OFTEN necessary in a campaign to storm or beseige an enemy fortress or defended town. The normal strategy used by the besieger was to start by digging a "parallel," a trench which roughly parallelled the enemy's positions. This was usually dug at the extremes of long range for the siege guns and was begun under the cover of night. By morning the parallel was deep enough to protect the working parties while they improved it by throwing up curtain walls and several hasty works along its length to hold the siege guns.

The next step was to begin extending the trench toward the beseiged fortress or town, although this was done in a zigzag pattern so that it never pointed directly at its target; if it did, the defender's guns could rake the length of the trench. When these approach trenches (called "saps") got to within close range, another parallel would be dug, gun positions thrown up, and the siege guns moved closer to deliver a more punishing fire. The saps would again press forward, and when very close to the walls, a final parallel would be dug. This parallel would be the jumping-off point for the infantry assault. The siege guns would pound the defender's walls to rubble or break up his earthworks, and once a breach was opened, the infantry would storm in. That, at any rate, was the theory.

What would the defender do during all of this? If he was stronger or better provided with artillery and supplies than the besieger, he could afford to fight the beseiger on fairly even terms. He would pound the attacking earthworks to dust and keep knocking them down. When a major bombardment was attempted, he might be able to silence the enemy guns long before they could soften up his defenses. In most cases, however, the defender's only hope was to conduct a more active siege.

The best example of this was the conduct of the defense of Sevastopol during the Crimean War. The Russian engineer, Todleben, kept the allies at bay for a year by turning these same techniques against them. His own work parties were constantly busy digging new fortifications and trenches. The allied saps never pointed directly toward Sevastopol, so Todleben would send out a work party at night and establish a new section of trench. Later, this would be improved into a new battery position outside the fortress trace which could enfilade a section of the allied trenches. Progress would then stop while the allies dealt with capturing this mini-fortress that had halted their progress.

Usually a defender will not have the manpower and guns to expend on extensive outworks, but a sortie is almost always a possibility. Sorties were raids out of the fortress, often at night, to disrupt or capture the enemy's work parties and destroy his works. Even the threat of sorties is a good way to keep a large part of the attacking army under arms. Every soldier under arms is one who cannot be used in a working party.

This part of the rules covers assaults against defended places, such as villages, fortresses, and walled cities. It also discusses the work of engineers, the mechanics of a siege. Small or large sieges and assaults are often a necessary part of a campaign, and these rules are designed to take what was often a fairly long, drawn out operation and make it interesting and fast-playing. The siege part of these rules can be played separately, if desired.

THE SIEGE MAP

THE SAME HEX MAP used with the vehicle rules can be photocopied for use with these rules. Unlike the map made for vehicle combat, each hex on the siege map should represent 6" on the gaming table. Since all works (such as trenches, walls, mines, etc.) are dealt with in 6" lengths, all siege activity can be plotted on the map, if desired. Bombardments can be resolved on the map, as well. Since all artillery ranges are expressed in feet, double the printed range of the gun to determine its range in hexes on the siege map.

The siege map is presented as a paper-and-pencil alternative to setting up a siege on the gaming table, but it is not required. The rules are set up in such a way that all activities associated with the siege can be represented on the gaming table without recourse to a separate map.

THE SIEGE TURN

SIEGES ARE CONDUCTED over longer periods of time than are battles, and so a modified time scale is used. Each siege turn represents a third of a day, and the turns are referred to as morning, afternoon, and night. Night turns are usually dark (but this is not so on Mercury or in the interior of the Moon). In each siege turn, both players will assign their forces to one of two general activity categories: duty or rest. Each unit may only be assigned to duty once per day; thus, an army will routinely have one-third of its force on duty at any given time. Troops on duty are further divided into troops under arms and troops on working parties. Working parties carry out the actual labor of a siege, while troops under arms defend the attacker's or defender's works, as well as his working parties.

Once both sides have assigned their men, both record on paper their activity for the current turn. Three activities are possible: work, bombard, and assault/sortie. If an army is working, the commander must record the location and activities of his various work parties and his troops under arms. If the attacker is conducting an assault (or the defender is conducting a sortie), a normal tabletop battle is conducted. The player who is making an attack or sortie will not know where there are work parties, unless and until his troops actually are able to see them. (This is why the location of the work parties is recorded on paper.) Likewise, if either army is bombarding, the owning player will conduct his bombardment without knowledge of where the enemy has work parties.

At the end of the siege turn, both sides place any new works on the table (or the map) and conduct all repairs on existing works, with one exception. Repairs conducted at night are not placed on the table or map until after both sides have recorded their activities for the turn. Thus, it is possible for an attacker to open a breach during one day's bombardment, the defender to repair it, and the attacker to unknowingly launch a morning attack against the breach only to find it repaired.

SIEGE MOVEMENT

MOVEMENT DURING a siege turn is unlimited as to distance, but is severely limited by the extent of each side's works and the position of their batteries. Units of each player may move freely within the boundaries of their own works, with the exception that no movement is allowed through a trench section which is enfiladed by an enemy gun. No movement is allowed across any open ground in the daylight which is visible to and within close range of enemy artillery. At night, movement is allowed across open ground, but a player may not move any unit into or through a position which is closer to an enemy work than to a friendly work.

If one side launches an assault or sortie, these restrictions do not apply to the normal battle movement which will follow; they do apply to the strategic siege turn movement which precedes the assault or sortie.

During an actual battle turn, movement by the defender inside the boundaries of a fortified place does not count as movement toward the enemy, even if the fortified place is completely surrounded. (See the section on normal movement and charge movement on page 8.) This means that an officer need not accompany an attachment moving to reinforce a wall, nor does a detachment moving toward the wall have to stop once it has moved half the distance toward the enemy. Troops in a fortified place still must charge in order to come into contact with an enemy unit.

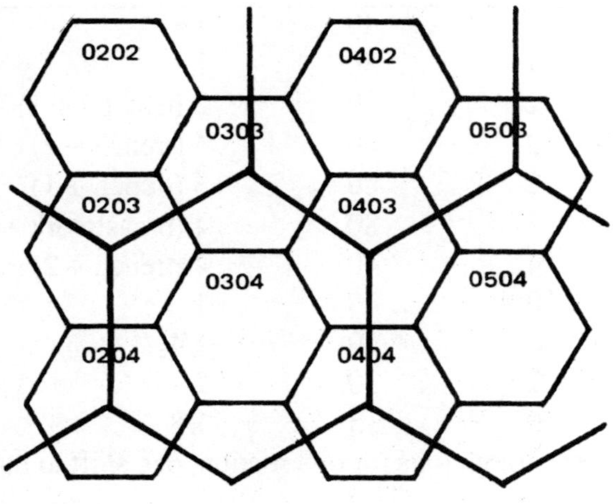

Each single hex is only half the size of a vehicle map hex. If moving a vehicle on the siege map, imagine that larger hexes are superimposed over the siege map grid.

BUILDING SIEGE WORKS

It is sometimes necessary to conduct an extended siege of a defended place, and this requires the construction of siege works. By the same token, a defender may build works during a siege to strengthen his own defenses.

Working Parties: All siege works are built by working parties. A working party generally consists of 10 men, supervised by an engineer officer or NCO, and commanded by an officer. (If supervised by an engineer officer, he also serves as commander of the work party.) Each work party undertakes one task, which is the construction of 6" of "works." Each 6" stretch of ground or works may only have one working party active on it at a time. It is possible to have two work parties working on the same trench, bridge, or causeway, provided each party is working on its own 6" segment.

All works have a cost in terms of "shifts" of labor. A shift is one working party engaged in building the work for one siege turn. At the end of the required number of shifts, the work is completed, unless there are fewer than 10 men in the working party. This is particularly true if the work party suffers casualties during the shift. If so, roll a die at the end of each shift. If the die roll is greater than the deficiency in workers, the shift counts as one shift toward completion of the work; otherwise, no significant progress was made.

For example, a 6" length of trench requires one shift to complete. If there were only eight men in the working party, the building player would roll a die. On a 1 or 2, there would be no progress on the trench; on a roll of 3 or more, the trench is completed.

Officers may not be counted as workers on a working party, nor may the engineer supervising the working party. All other engineers (or sappers) engaged in a working party count as two men each. More than 10 men may be assigned to a working party. They do not make the work go any faster, but they do make it possible to suffer several casualties without jeopardizing the completion of the work.

Improving Works: Some works may be upgraded by additional labor. A rifle pit may be upgraded to a trench, a trench to a breastwork, and a breastwork to a redoubt. Alternatively, a trench may be deepened and widened into a barrier ditch. This is done exactly as if the working party were building a new work on the site, except the working party receives the benefit of cover from existing work.

Allowed Siege Works: The types of works which can be built during a siege are listed in the Siege Works Table below, along with the shift costs to build them.

Extending Trenches: One working party may extend a trench 6" per shift while receiving the benefit of cover of the existing trench. (Note that this reduces the shift cost of the trench to one.) Several working parties may extend a trench in different directions, but each extension worked on in a single shift must be built from a different exisiting 6" segment of trench. See the examples below.

SIEGE WORKS TABLE

Siege Works	*AV*	*Damage*	*Shifts*
Log Stockade	1	40	1+1*
Rifle Pits	1	80	1
Trench	2	80	2 (rifle pit + 1)
Ditch	2	80	4 (trench + 2)
Breastwork	2	80	3 (trench + 1)
Redoubt	3	80	4 (breastwork + 1)
Gallery	4	40	4 (trench + 2)
Abatis	0	40	1
Barbed Wire	0	80	1/4
Rubble Wall	2	30	1
Barricade	0	5	1/8

* One shift to gather enough logs for one section, one shift to build the stockade section.

Examples

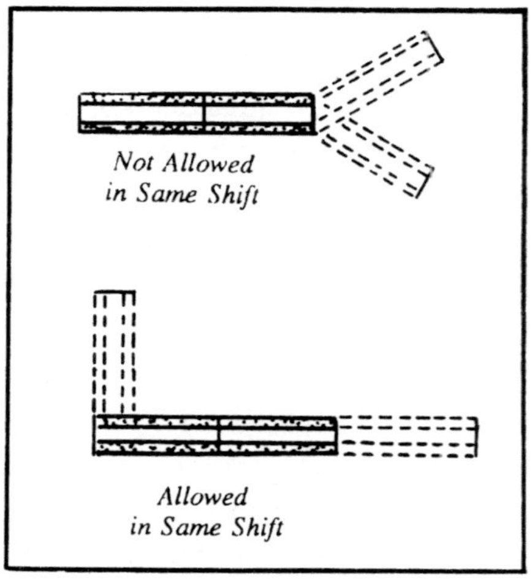

Effects of Earthworks

The different types of earthworks

have the following effects.

Log Stockade: A stockade counts as hard cover for the occupants. It has a tall wall with a firing platform behind it so infantry can fire over the top. It is an impassable barrier and may not be crossed except by an escalade.

Rifle Pits: Rifle pits count as hard cover for the occupants. Open order infantry move in rifle pits as if through difficult terrain. No other troops may occupy or move through rifle pits. Rifle pits are a difficult barrier for open order infantry to cross, an impassable barrier for formed infantry and artillery, and no barrier for cavalry. Dismounted troops in open order may fire from rifle pits.

Trench: A trench is hard cover for the occupants. Infantry in open order move through trenches as open ground; infantry in column move through as difficult ground. No other troops may occupy or move through trenches. A trench is a difficult barrier for infantry and cavalry to cross, and an impassable barrier for artillery. No troops may fire out of a trench, except at enemy troops on the parapet of the trench. No troops may fire small arms into a trench unless they occupy the parapet. Artillery may not fire into a trench unless it is an enfilading position. For a gun to enfilade the trench, it must be able to see down the length of a trench.

Ditch: A ditch is hard cover for the occupants. Infantry in open order move through ditches as open ground; infantry in column move through as difficult ground. No other troops may occupy or move through ditches. A ditch is an impassable barrier for all cavalry and artillery. Infantry may freely enter a ditch but may not leave it except by means of a ladder. Infantry leaving a ditch by means of a ladder who are unopposed roll one die per ladder, the result being the number of figures who climb up the ladder that turn and exit the ditch. Infantry leaving a ditch by means of a ladder who are opposed do so by conducting an escalade (see the assault rules on page 64). No troops may fire out of a ditch except at enemy troops on the parapet of the ditch. No troops may fire small arms into a ditch unless they occupy the parapet.

Breastwork: A breastwork is a low, packed earth wall (curtain) behind a shallow trench or ditch. It is hard cover for troops deployed behind it. Movement behind it is unrestricted. A breastwork is a difficult barrier for all infantry, and formed troops become disordered upon crossing it. Cavalry and artillery may not cross a breastwork. Troops deployed immediately behind a curtain may fire over.

Redoubt: A redoubt is a thick, elevated packed earth wall behind a deep ditch. Firing embrasures are cut in the wall to allow artillery to cover the ground in front of it. A redoubt is hard cover for troops deployed behind it. Movement behind it is restricted. Crossing a redoubt is the same as crossing a ditch.

Gallery: A gallery is an underground chamber entered from a trench. It is intended to offer protection to troops in the forward lines. Only one gallery may be attached to each trench section. Each gallery holds up to 20 troops. Galleries may only be attacked by high-angle fire.

Barricades: A barricade is a pile of random, bulky objects. It counts as medium cover for troops behind it. All troops behind a barricade can fire (provided their formation so allows). A barricade is no barrier to cavalry or open order infantry, but it is a difficult barrier for formed infantry and is impassable to artillery. The "1/8" notation under the work cost of a barricade indicates that one working party may build eight barricade sections in a shift. (If a working party has less than a full shift to work, it builds one section per hour.) Barricades may only be built if material is handy. Any village or town has ample material for barricades in the form of carts, crates, grain sacks, furniture, and so forth. Likewise, a caravan or supply train will have sufficient bundles to make at least one section of barricade, and more at the referee's option.

Abatis: Abatis is a jumble of sharp tree limbs and tangled brush. Abatis is a difficult barrier for open order infantry to cross and is an impassable barrier for all other troop types and formations.

Barbed Wire: Only terrestrial armies have access to barbed wire, usually in only limited quantities due to weight. Barbed wire has the same effects as abatis but has the advantage of being preconstructed. Allow the defender of a minor position one die roll worth of 6" barbed wire segments. Allow the defender of a major position three dice worth.

Rubble Walls: A rubble wall may only be constructed at the site of a collapsed structure or wall. One work party may build 6" of rubble wall in one shift. A rubble wall may not be built longer than the actual length of the rubble pile upon which it is built. A rubble wall is chest-high and is located on top of the rubble pile. It provides hard cover to any troops deployed behind it. For movement purposes it is treated as a breastwork.

An African war band moves through a village. Figures by Ral Partha.

DAMAGE TO STRUCTURES AND FORTIFICATIONS

ALL STRUCTURES and fortifications have an armor value and a damage capacity. The armor value is their resistance to enemy shot and shell while their damage capacity is their ability to absorb punishment and remain standing.

Hit Procedure: The normal procedure for artillery fire is followed, with each gun directed at a specific building or a specific 6" section of fortifications. The following die roll modifiers are made to the hit number, however:

- +2 to hit tall city or fortress walls
- +1 to hit a building
- –1 to hit abatis
- –2 to hit trench

Penetration and Damage: If a hit is achieved on a structure or fortification, damage is assessed in the same way as for a hit on an armored vehicle. No hit location is rolled, however, and instead all damage is structural damage. For example, a gun with a damage value of 4 and which has a penetration equal to or greater than the armor value of the target, does four points of structural damage. If its penetration is less than the target's armor value, it does two points of damage. If it is less than half the target's armor value, the firing player rolls a die and on a roll of 4 or less does one point of damage.

Damage on a structure or fortification is cumulative and should be recorded. Each structure takes damage separately, as does each 6" segment of fortification. Very large structures (such as palaces) are treated as a number of 6" by 6" structures, each of which accumulates damage separately.

When a city wall section, fortress wall section, stockade section, or structure suffers damage equal to or in excess of its damage capacity, it collapses and is replaced by a rubble pile of approximately the same size. When an earthwork suffers damage equal to or in excess of its damage value, it is breached. A breached earthwork offers cover as if it were one level lower in effectiveness; a major work becomes a hasty work, a hasty work becomes a curtain, a curtain or ditch becomes a trench, a trench becomes rifle pits, and rifle pits become open ground. A breached earthwork can continue to take hits and further reduce its cover value.

Rubble: A collapsed wall or structure produces a rubble pile. A rubble pile counts as difficult ground for open order infantry, cavalry, and unlimbered artillery. It counts as impassable for formed troops and limbered artillery. Open order infantry receive their Fieldcraft bonus when fired on in rubble; other troops receive no cover advantage.

Armor Values: An extensive list of armor values and damage capacities is provided on the Structures Chart and Siege Works Chart (page 176). Additional values can be derived from those already presented, and the following chart illustrates the armor value of various materials.

ARMOR VALUE OF 1

Inches	*Material*
2	Steel
3	Iron
12	Brick or Stone
24	Earthworks
48	Wood

Occupants of Works: Units occupying a work suffer casualties as described in the normal fire rules. In addition, occupants of works suffer casualties whenever a work's cumulative damage is sufficient to breach it or reduce it by one level. At that time half of all troops in that section of the work become casualties, and half of all guns are destroyed. Roll a die for fractional men and guns.

Repairing Damaged Works: Repair of damaged works costs only half the normal construction time. Thus, it is possible for a single working party to rebuild two shifts worth of works in a single shift. For example, a major work takes sufficient damage to breach it, and then additional damage reducing it to a breached hasty work, and then additional damage reducing it further to the level of a breached curtain. One work party can perform two shifts worth of repair; the first shift raises it to the level of an intact curtain, and the second raises it to the level of a hasty work.

FIRES

SHELLS MAY START fires if they hit wooden buildings. Roll a die; a fire starts on a 6. Such fires start at level 1 and build. Martian fire dropped from above will start fires, as will any rocket hit on an inflammable building.

Fires will burn until they exceed the damage value of the building. A building collapses then, and the fire goes down one level each turn until it goes out. Anyone in the building when it collapses is in trouble. Smoke blows downwind. The smoke trail of a fire in inches is equal to the fire level until the building collapses. Then smoke stays at the maximum level until the fire burns completely out. Then smoke decreases 1" per turn (as the embers smoulder).

Spreading Fire: Each turn there is a chance a fire will spread to an adjacent building. The chance on one die is the level of the fire minus the distance (in inches) between the buildings if downwind, or minus twice the distance if upwind. Subtract the distance from the level of fire and roll a die. If the roll is equal to or less than the modified number, the other building has a level 1 fire.

The fire level then goes up one level per turn, except in thatched roof buildings, in which case it goes up two levels. Stone and brick buildings have combustible roofs and interior walls, so they will burn. City walls and fortress walls will not burn.

Fighting Fires: Each figure that fights a fire rolls one die. (Anyone can fight fires.) Each roll of a 6 reduces the fire one level. If water is available, each roll of a 5 or 6 reduces the fire one level. Water is available to any figure within 6" of a canal, well, or other water source.

THE BOMBARDMENT

EITHER OR BOTH players may declare a bombardment during a siege. Each bombardment takes one siege turn. Players may declare several bombardments in a row, if desired. Only high-angle fire weapons (howitzer, mortars, and lob guns) may fire at night. Work parties continue to work during a bombardment, if the owning player wishes, but may suffer casualties due to the fire.

Procedure: All artillery pieces within range of an enemy target may fire during a bombardment. All fire during a bombardment is considered to be simultaneous; no casualties are removed until all guns have fired. Guns with a parenthetical ROF fire once during a bombardment; all other guns have their rate of fire doubled during a bombardment.

For example, a player has three guns. One has a rate of fire of 3, one has a rate of fire of 1, and one has a rate of fire of (2). The first gun fires six shots during the bombardment, the second fires two shots, and the third fires one shot.

A bombardment lasts for an entire siege turn, and, thus, each shot fired represents many actual salvoes. All fire is resolved normally during a bombardment with one important exception: All damage values are multiplied by 10.

Night Bombardment: During the night turn, a bombardment may only be conducted with mortars, howitzers, and lob guns. One fire phase is allowed each night. Surviving members of the working parties actually do the work; if not enough workers are left to finish the work, it is not completed. The owning player may assign extra men to a work party to ensure completion of the project it is working on.

Ammunition: The main limitation on siege bombardments is ammunition. Bombardments use up enormous quantities of powder and shell. All armies carry considerable stocks of ammunition with them, but a siege will soon use this up. All irregular armies carry one bombardment worth of ammunition; all regular armies carry two bombardments worth.

Once a siege has been declared, additional ammunition can be brought forward. If an army is on an established supply route (such as a railroad, river, or canal, or if it has access to a seaport and a friendly shipping), roll for additional ammunition once per day. If the army is at the end of a long or difficult supply line, roll once every three days. If the army is in hostile territory and does not have a regular supply line, do not roll for additional ammunition.

When rolling for additional ammunition, the besiegers receive one bombardment's worth on a roll of 2 or less, but add the leadership of the army commander to the number needed. An army commander with a leadership of 3, for example, receives additional ammunition on a roll of 5 or less. The defenders of a fortress will roll one die per leadership level of the fortress commander (but never less than one) to determine how many bombardments worth of ammunition they have at the beginning of the siege. This number must be kept secret from the attacker.

ASSAULTS AND SORTIES

AT SOME POINT during a siege, the attacker may launch an assault or the defender may launch a sortie. Both are handled similarly. The siege turn stops and time reverts to battle turns. The following additional rules cover both assaults and sorties.

Initiative: The player launching the assault or sortie will automatically have the initiative for a number of turns equal to the leadership rating of the senior officer commanding the assault or sortie. After this, the defender receives one automatic turn with the initiative, and from then on initiative is rolled for normally.

Leaving a Trench: Leaving a trench in the face of the enemy was a tricky operation that often went wrong. Roll one die for each 6" trench section that has men in it attempting to leave. The number rolled is the number of men that may leave that trench section that movement phase. No men will leave a trench in a movement phase unless an officer is one of the men to leave, or all officers have already left the trench and at least one officer remains standing on the edge of the trench. (That is, if all officers have left the trench and have all become casualties or taken a detachment forward, no more men will leave the trench.)

Leaving the trench consumes half a unit's movement. Once they have left the trench, the men of a unit may wait there or, if an officer is present to lead them, they may advance. All troops are in line formation upon leaving a trench and remain in line if they move directly away from the trench. If they move in any other direction the movement phase in which they leave the trench, they are disordered.

Escalade: Escalade is the use of a scaling ladder to climb over an otherwise impassable barrier. City walls, fortress walls, stockades, and major works may only be crossed by means of an escalade. An escalade consists of several distinct steps. A ladder party carries a scaling ladder to the wall, it erects the ladder, climbs the ladder, and then either fights the defenders at the top or moves away from the ladder into the fortification.

A ladder party may consist of as many men from a unit as desired, but must consist of at least five men. That is, it takes five men to carry a scaling ladder. Because of the bulk of the ladder, ladder parties always move at the regular movement rate. Movement to the base of an enemy occupied wall does not constitute a charge. All ladder parties are in open order.

Once at the base of the wall, a ladder party expends half of its movement to erect its ladder. If the ladder party has insufficient movement remaining, it must wait until the next friendly movement phase to erect its ladder.

Once a ladder is erected, the ladder party may climb the ladder. This consumes half of the ladder party's movement, and is treated as a charge. Roll one die per erect ladder; the result is the number of men who may climb the ladder that movement phase. If the escalade is unopposed, all of the figures are placed at the top of the wall and may move one additional die roll's worth of inches. At the end of this move they are disordered. If the escalade is opposed, the figures are lined up behind the base of the ladder in the order in which they climb the ladder, and the lead figure is placed on the parapet of the wall or work scaled.

Defensive fire is conducted normally, and all casualties from an opposed escalade are taken in order from those men actually climbing the ladder. The next remaining figure in line is then placed at the top of the ladder and fights the melee. Only one man per ladder party will fight in the melee at the top of the wall, although he may be opposed by more than one defender. The defender receives the melee benefit, both for defending higher ground and defending a work.

If the attacker wins the melee (attacker passes his morale test while the defender fails his), the rest of the men lined up behind the ladder are placed on the work and are in disorder. If the attacker fails his morale test and is checked or shaken, then all surviving attackers on the wall from his ladder party retreat to the base of the wall. If the attacker fails his morale test and is demoralized, then all surviving attackers from the ladder party will retreat to the base of the wall and then away from the wall.

If both sides pass their morale test and remain locked in melee, then one man will climb a ladder to replace any attacker who was killed or forced back down, and one man will climb the ladder and join any attacker who killed or forced back his opponent.

Destructive Mischief: The purpose of most sorties is to damage the enemy's works. A work party may accompany an assault or sortie or may be improvised from men in the assault party if an engineer is present. A work party, once it has gained the enemy works, may fill in trenches and tear down fortifications. At the end of each friendly movement phase that a work party spends tearing down a work, roll a die. On a roll of 6, the party succeeds in undoing the work of one shift. A redoubt, for instance, would be reduced to a breastwork. (It is easier to tear down works than it is to put them up.)

Ending the Battle: The assault or sortie may end in one of two ways. One side may surrender and concede defeat (which is how most battles end), or the player who launched the assault or sortie may call it off and withdraw to his original positions. The enemy may then withdraw any troops he wishes but is not required to do so.

In other words, if a player launches a sortie and his opponent counterattacks and actually captures part of the assaulting player's works, the opponent is not obligated to give up his positions just because the assaulting player has called off the sortie.

A hotly contested escalade in progress. The platoon of Australians in the foreground are Falcon Miniatures castings from their Southwest Africa line.

MINES AND COUNTERMINES

A MINE IS AN underground tunnel dug up to and under the enemy's defenses. The end of the mineshaft is filled with explosives which are then detonated to collapse part of the defender's works prior to an assault.

Digging Mines: Mines are works like any other. A mine consists of the mine opening and the shaft. The mine opening requires one shift to construct while each mine segment also requires one shift. Each mine segment is one die roll's worth of inches in length. If digging through rocky soil, subtract one from the die roll. If digging through loose soil, add one.

Once the mine is finished, it may be detonated. An assault is usually declared for that siege turn, and the mine is detonated on the first turn of the battle. First, roll a die, and consult the Mine Accuracy Table (page 176) to see if the mine was on target. Possible results are on target, right, left, short, and long. If the mine is not on target, roll two dice and move the endpoint of the mine that many inches in the direction indicated by the mine accuracy roll. It may still be under a section of the enemy's works.

Once the actual location has been determined, resolve the effects of the explosion. Roll a die and multiply the result by 100 to determine the number of damage points the explosion causes. The damage will reduce an earthwork to successively lower levels (redoubt to breastwork, breastwork to trench, trench to rifle pit). If a rifle pit is destroyed, it is replaced by a 6" crater in the ground. If there are any additional damage points remaining, they are divided between the works to either side of the destroyed work. The same procedure is followed for city and fortress walls, except that as soon as the wall takes its required amount of damage, it collapses into a pile of rubble. If it takes twice the required damage, the rubble collapses into a 6" crater. Any additional unused damage points are applied to the adjacent wall sections.

No matter how much damage is suffered, the damage never affects any fortifications except those over the mine and those adjacent to them.

Detecting Mines: Once a mine is within 18" of an enemy work, the referee will roll a die once each siege turn in which work takes place in the mine. On a roll of 6, the enemy detects the mine. This is increased to a roll of 5 or 6 at night. No roll is made during bombardment turns. Once a mine is detected, the enemy may begin a countermine.

Countermines: Countermines are dug in the same manner as regular mines and are intended to intercept enemy mines. An explosive-filled chamber is placed in front of the enemy mine and detonated. This explosion is less violent than with a normal mine, but will destroy the enemy mine, cause one die roll of casualties in the enemy work party, and make it impossible to dig further in that mine. (The ground ahead is churned up, and the mine's structural supports are badly weakened.) The countermine is detonated as soon as it reaches the head of the enemy mine.

Mole Drills: A mole drill is an invention which PCs from the role-playing game might have access to. A mole drill allows construction of a mine in one siege turn. The mole drill's mine explosion, however, only produces one die times 50 damage points, and if a 6 is rolled, the mole drill itself is trapped in the explosion and cave-in and is destroyed. (PCs in the drill are still alive, and engineers in the enemy fortress will be able to dig down and rescue them.)

OTHER TASKS

OTHER engineering tasks follow.

Bridges: Bridges are built by work parties in exactly the same manner as are siege works. Their important characteristics are summarized in the table below. Load is the heaviest vehicle which can cross the bridge without damaging it. All horse-drawn guns can cross 10-ton bridges.

When a heavy bridge suffers its full damage capacity, it is reduced to the equivalent of a stone bridge. When any other bridge suffers its full damage capacity, it is destroyed.

BRIDGES

Bridges	*Armor Value*	*Dam.*	*Shift*	*Load (tons)*
Pontoon	0	10	1	10
Foot	0	3	1	Men
Wooden	0	20	4	10
Stone	1	40	8	20
Heavy	2	80	16	40

Gate Charges: Engineers may carry gate charges to blow open city or fortress gates. The engineering party must spend one-half of a friendly movement phase adjacent to the gate, and then move away with its remaining half move. The owning player then rolls one die; the result times 10 is the number of damage points inflicted on the gate. When the gate suffers its full damage capacity, it falls open. Half of all troops within 2" of the gate and on the same side of it as the engineers are killed when the charge detonates.

MODELING SIEGE WORKS

SIEGE WORKS can be modeled quickly and easily using balsa wood, and either clay, plaster, or spackle. I prefer spackle because it is inexpensive, is usable right out of the container (no messy mixing), thins and cleans up with water, does not shrink when it hardens, and is both lighter and more durable than plaster.

Many companies also make boxes and crates, sandbag sections, earth-filled baskets, and other such materials.

While you will probably not want to make entire siege works out of these materials, you can add a lot to the appearance of your earthworks if you add a few of these accessories to them.

Balsa wood comes in a variety of sizes, but the 3" wide plank is very common, and we will use it as a base for most of our siege works. These bases will need to be sturdy, so use a nice thick piece, about 1/8". You will also need some thin sheets for planking, in addition to a quantity of 1/8" by 1/2" strips to use as reinforcing members.

Start by cutting a sheet of wood into 6" segments, each one 3" wide.

This will give you a quantity of 6" by 3" sheets that will form the bases for trenches, rifle pits, breastworks, and so forth.

Now cut several 3" segments of your 1/8" by 1/2" stripping and glue them to the base strips at right angles to the grain.

One strip per 6" segment should be sufficient for this. These reinforcing strips will prevent the bases of your siege works from splitting along the grain.

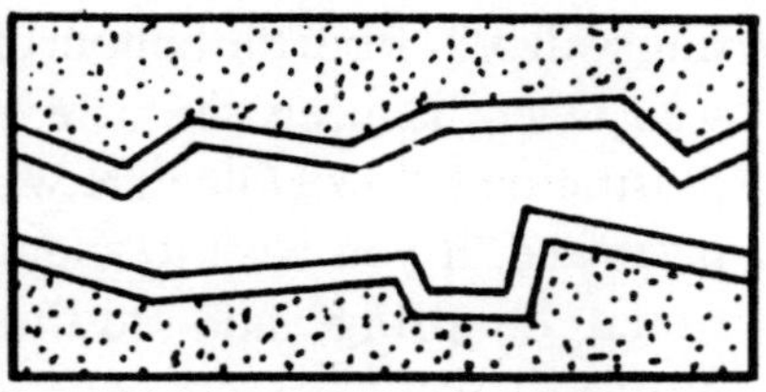

Rifle Pits: The floor of the rifle pits will be the center inch of the base, while the walls will be the 1" strip to each side. To make the walls, cut strips of planking from thin balsa and glue them in place. The wall of the rifle pit which faces the enemy should be about 3/4" high, while that facing away from the enemy can be around 1/2" high. These are rough rules of thumb, however, and rifle pits will look better if they are irregular as to the height of the walls and the width of the pit itself. Rifle pits should have a slightly meandering, haphazard look about them.

The walls of a rifle pit can be reinforced by posts cut from toothpicks or balsa wood on the inside, or right triangles of balsa glued on the outside (where they will be covered by spackle). Now fill in the section between the wall and the edge of the base with spackle (or whatever compound you are using). Smear a little bit of the compound on the floor of the rifle pit as well. When the spackle is partially dry, rough up the texture, particularly at the top near the edge of the walls, to look like upturned earth.

Once the spackle dries, paint the walls of the rifle pit gray or dark wood. Paint the floor of the pit and the outsides an earth brown. Paint the lower outside edges green and apply hobby grass. Try to come as close to matching the color of your ground cloth as possible.

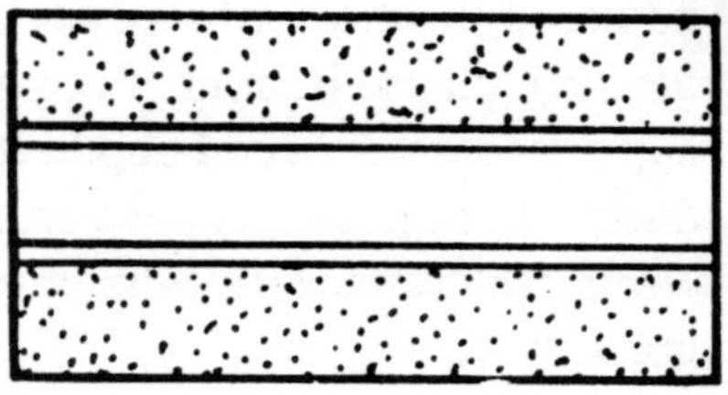

Trench: A trench section is done in exactly the same way as a rifle pit, except that it has to have a more substantial look to it. To achieve this, the walls of the trench should be straight and both walls should be the same height. The wall sections can vary from 3/4" to 1" in height, but in fairly uniform and regular segments. Paint the trench the same way as a rifle pit.

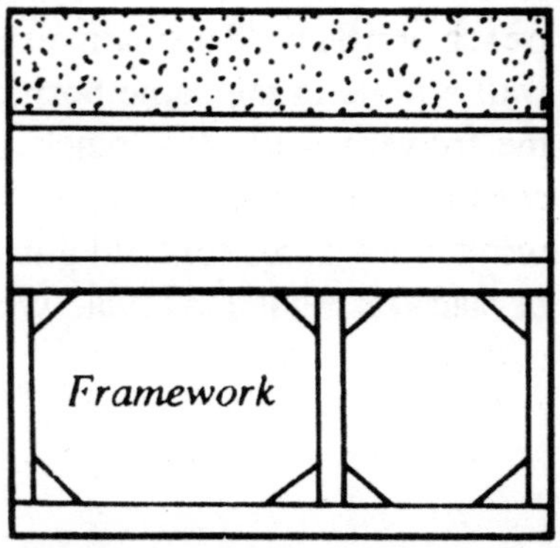

Ditch: Begin with a 3" base and make a 1" tall wall, the same as for a trench but with two differences. First, the wall should be in the middle of the base. Second, it should slope slightly toward the front of the base. Now spackle the forward half of the base and, after it dries, paint it the same as a trench. The result will look like one-half of a trench section. Now take a length of 1/2" by 1/2" square balsa wood and make a rectangular framework the size of a normal siegework base (6" by 3"). Paint the framework green on the long side (and put grass on the outside faces) and earth brown on the ends. Now any siege work can be placed on top of the framework and the ditch placed in front of it, giving a greater appearance of depth. If the ditch is to be placed in open ground, cover the framework with a plain grassy base.

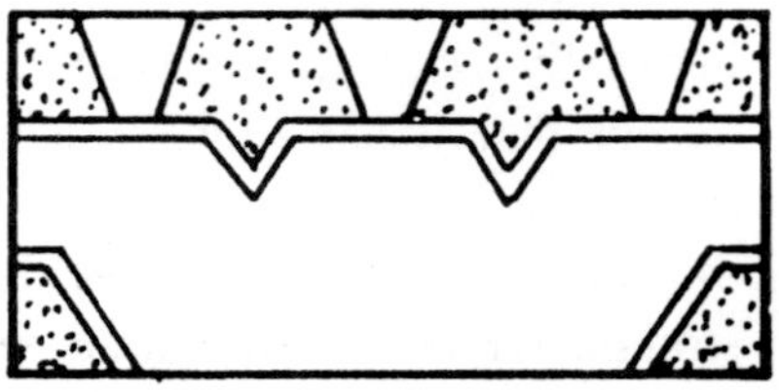

Breastwork: The breastwork section is designed to be either free-standing or to fit in with sections of trench or rifle pit. The main revetting wall will be in the same position as the forward wall of a trench but is constructed a little differently. Three firing embrasures for field guns will be placed at regular intervals, with the center of the embrasures 1", 3", and 5" from one end of the base.

Each embrasure should start as a 1/2"-wide square cut out of the revetting wall 3/8" from the bottom of the wall where it meets the base. (See illustration below.) Glue the wall in place and, if you wish to add additional detailing, add additional wedge-shaped wall sections between the firing positions.

Each such wall section should have the shape (when viewed from above) of an equilateral triangle with each side 3/4" in length. The overall height of these triangles should be 1". Finally, add a small wall section at the rear on each end of the base to match the ends of any trench or rifle pit section this earthwork will be mated with.

Now spackle the front side side of the breastwork, being careful to have the embrasures widen the farther they are from the revetting wall. Extra spackle should be piled up between the embrasures in the triangular extensions of the wall. Finally, a little spackle should be piled against the two small walls in the back, again to match any trench or rifle pit section this earthwork is mated with.

British infantry and a juggernaut overrun a German trench line. Germans by Falcon Miniatures and Wargames Foundry.

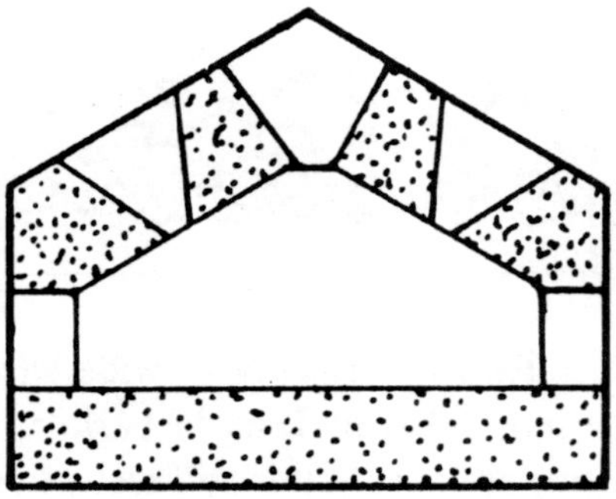

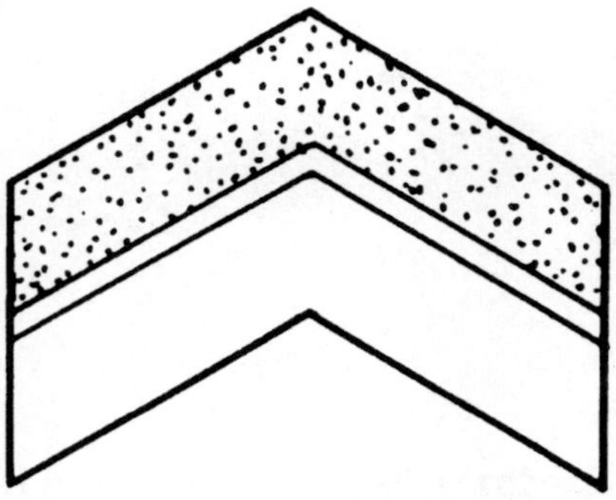

Abatis

Redoubt: This is a large work made with a larger-sized base (6" by 5"). To start, cut the base into a pentagonal shape. Mark off 3" from the back of the base on each side. Draw a line from this point on each side to the midpoint on the front edge of the base and then cut along those lines. Next, build up the firing platform of the redoubt. The firing platform is raised 1/4" above the level of the base and is in the form of a pentagon with a 5" base, 2" parallel sides, and 3" angled sides. Cut this out of sheet balsa and glue it onto a framework, which will raise it the required height. Now glue it to the base snug up against the back.

Next, construct the front revetting wall. This will start just as a trench wall would start (and should match with your other trench sections) until it meets the sides of the firing platform. It should then follow the trace of the angled sides of the firing platform. The revetting wall should be 1" high at either end, but should increase to 1 1/4" along the angle of the firing platform. Three firing embrasures are then cut in the wall: one at the point of the redoubt and one on either side. The firing embrasures are the same dimensions as on a breastwork. Now spackle the redoubt and paint it. If the firing platform is to be painted earth color, be sure to smear some spackle on it as this will give it a rough, uneven texture. It is just as acceptable to paint it as wood, however.

If the redoubt has a ditch in front of it, you will need to make a special pentagonal elevated platform and angled ditch section that fits the front of the redoubt and meets the ditch section to either side. See the illustration above for guidance.

Gallery: This is the easiest work of all to build, since it is invisible. Take a 1/2" square piece of thin balsa or plastic and glue a crumpled piece of tissue or paper to one side of it and then glue thin boards or match sticks over the paper on three sides. When dry, paint the boards brown and the crumpled paper black. This now represents the door to the gallery, complete with black curtain over the entrance. Simply place this against any interior trench wall to indicate that a gallery is present.

Abatis: Take a standard 3"-wide base and split it into three 1"-wide bases. First paint each base green and then cover it with grass. After it is dry, glue a number of crooked twigs and branches to it and paint them gray and dark brown.

Barbed Wire: Take a 1"-wide base, as used for abattis, and push the points of several 1"-long finishing nails into it at irregular intervals. Glue the nails securely to the base and then smear a light coat of spackle over it, making it a little thicker around the nails for added stability. Once it is dry, paint the base green and put grass on it. Next paint the nails steel, with some brown or rust highlights. Now find some fine electrical wire and wrap it around a pencil. Slide it off the pencil, drape it over the nail framework, and glue it to the nails on the base.

Barbed Wire

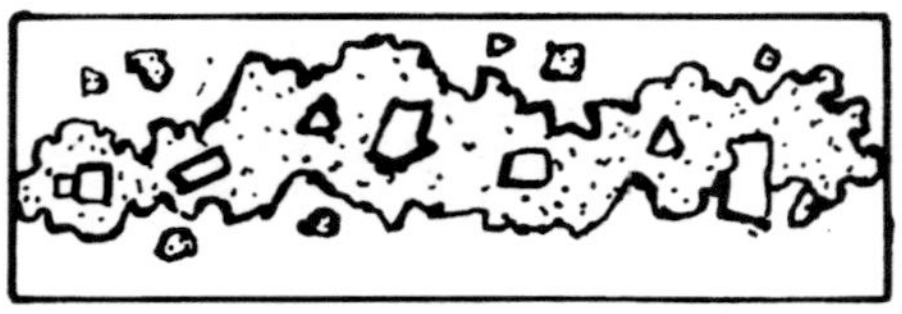

Rubble Wall: A 1"-wide base is used. Use spackle as the basic rubble pile and, while it is still wet, cover it with more angular pieces of rock, wood, and actual rubble. The best way to make rubble is to spread out a sheet of spackle or plaster and let it harden. While it is still slightly soft, carve a brick pattern into the face. Once it is hard, shatter it and use the angular pieces for rubble.

Barricade: Barricades use a 1" base as well but are represented in 3" segments, instead. Although barricades are built in 6" increments, the restricted nature of town streets makes 3" bases easier to use. For every 6" of barricades built, just place two 3" bases. Start by painting each base gray or light brown. Then, glue sandbags, barrels, and crates to it in the form of a rough barricade. The more diverse these are, the better. If you are short of these items, they can be supplemented or replaced entirely by logs carved from balsa wood, gravel from outdoors (representing boulders), and spackle for piled-up dirt.

The British besiege a Martian city. Note the use of Geo Hex™ terrain tiles.

Part A: The Role-Playing Character

THIS BOOK COVERS battles and campaigns. To start with we will examine the role of player characters from **Space: 1889** in miniatures battles.

Space: 1889 is a role-playing game, and these rules are meant to support the basic game, not supplant it. These rules are an excellent means of resolving large battles that take place in your role-playing campaigns, but you first need to know how your player characters affect the course of a battle.

PLAYER CHARACTERS AT WAR

ALL PLAYER CHARACTERS are represented by an individual casting in a miniatures battle, and the character functions the same as any other soldier on the field, with several unique exceptions.

Combat Ability: The character's basic troop quality level is determined by the character's Close Combat skill, as follows:

- 0: Green
- 1: Trained
- 2, 3: Experienced
- 4, 5: Veteran
- 6: Elite

Divide the character's Fieldcraft skill by two to find the character's Fieldcraft level for the miniatures game. If the character has a Marksmanship skill of 5 or 6, he fires as a sharpshooter. (Conversely, if he has a Marksmanship skill of 0 or 1, he fires as if Green.) Divide the character's Riding skill level by two to find his mounted melee bonus. Divide the character's Leadership skill by two to determine his leadership rating. In all cases, when dividing skill levels, round fractions up. All player characters receive the +1 leader bonus in melees if they are armed with a melee weapon, such as a sword or a rifle with attached bayonet.

For example, James Cruthingham-Caltrop has a Close Combat skill of 3, a Marksmanship skill of 5, a Fieldcraft skill of 1, a Riding skill of 5, and a Leadership skill of 2. He is an experienced sharpshooter with a Fieldcraft of 1, leadership rating of 1, and a melee bonus of +3, if mounted.

Additional Skills: The following additional skills affect specific tasks that a character can undertake during a battle or siege.

Gunnery: If the character has a skill of 1 or more, he may form part of a gun crew. If he has a skill of 5 or 6, the gun he fires has a +1 modifier to its chance to hit. If two or more characters are helping to man a gun and have high Gunnery skills, only one modifier may be used.

Engineering: A character with an Earthworks skill of 1 or more counts as an engineer when forming part of a work party (that is, he counts as two men.) A character with an Earthworks skill of 2 or more may supervise a work party.

Machinist: Machinists may attempt to repair spiked guns. Roll vs. Machinist skill once per day to repair the gun. This roll may be made in addition to the normal roll for repairs and represents the assistance the character can offer an army's ordnance men.

Stealth: Stealth allows a character to approach an enemy position noiselessly and escape detection. A character approaches at one-quarter normal movement. For each movement phase spent moving within hearing distance of the enemy, the character must make an Easy skill roll to avoid detection. For each movement phase spent moving within visibility distance of the enemy, the character must make a Moderate skill roll. If successful, the character remains undetected; if unsuccessful, he is seen or heard and the alarm is sounded.

DEEPENING YOUR CHARACTER

THE MATERIAL in this book enables you to provide considerably more depth to the background history of your character if he is a soldier or former soldier.

Age: The first step is to determine the character's age and rank based on his career selection. This can be left to the discretion of the player. However, characters with only one career should have less than 10 years service, while characters with two careers should have 10 years or more. If a character chooses one army career and then another career outside of the army, his age will be based on having served for 10 years or more, but his highest rank will be either lieutenant or corporal (or possibly private), depending on his Social Level. The following table summarizes ranks and average ages of officers and other ranks. (The ages of officers are based on the averages for the 42nd Royal Highland Black Watch in 1889.)

Although the age for a lieutenant colonel is given, it is a good idea to not allow players to start at any rank higher than major.

RANK AND AVERAGE AGES

Regimental Officers

Lieutenant: 5 years service (from 1884); 22 years old.

Captain: 10 years service (from 1879;) 27 years old.

Major: 20 years service (from 1869); 37 years old.

Lieutenant Colonel: 30 years service (from 1859); 47 years old.

Other Ranks

Private: 3 years service (from 1884); 20 years old.

Corporal: 6 years service (from 1889); 23 years old.

Sergeant: 10 years service (from 1874); 27 years old.

Colour Sergeant: 15 years service (from 1869); 32 years old.

Sergeant-Major: 20 years service (from 1864); 37 years old.

Campaign Experience

It is now possible to determine which campaigns your character has participated in. The British Army section (page 92) includes a list of major campaigns fought since 1860, as well as the campaign honors of each regiment of the army. Once you have chosen a regiment, an age, and the number of careers spent in the army, it is possible to determine which, if any, of the campigns you were present for.

For example, the 18th Royal Irish have the following campaign honors: New Zealand (68-70), the Second Afghan War (78-80), Egypt (82), the Sudan (84-5), and the Northwest Frontier (88).

Consider three characters who belong, or once belonged, to their regiment. Character A has had only one career and has spent it in the army with the regiment. Character B has had two careers, both spent in the army with the regiment. Character C has had two careers, but spent only the first one in the army with the regiment and then went on to pursue other interests.

Character A has sufficient Social Level to be an officer. Since he has only one career's service, he cannot be a captain (as that requires 10 years service), so he is a 22-year-old lieutenant with five years of service dating from 1884. (He could also be a 24-year-old lieutenant with seven years of service dating from 1882, or any other number up to nine years of service.) This means that he has probably fought through two campaigns: the Sudan in 1884-85 and the Northwest Frontier of 1888. Although only one battalion would have fought in either campaign, it was common for officers hungry for combat duty to switch places with other officers in the battalions sent overseas.

Character B is also an officer and decides to be a major. This requires that he have at least 20 years, and so he is 37 years old and has served since 1869. This means that he has served in all five campaigns of the regiment. Since he was a lieutenant for his first nine years of service (from 1869 to 1878), he served as a lieutenant in New Zealand and was promoted to captain during the Second Afghan War. He has just received his promotion to major, perhaps as a result of his performance on the Northwest Frontier last year.

Character C's record is slightly more complicated. We will assume that his Social Level makes him a non-commissioned officer. He has served two careers, and so the character decides to assume 10 years of work before the game starts, making him 27 years old. He started his first career (that is, he joined the regiment) in 1874. He had to serve 6 years to become a corporal, and so left the service in 1880. This means that he served in the Second Afghan War, but entered too late for the New Zealand campaign, and left the regiment two years prior to the Egyptian campaign.

It is possible that Character B has served, at various times, with both Characters A and C. Character C might have been a private in his company in Afghanistan when B was a newly-promoted captain. However, Character C left the army before Character A joined, and so there is no possibility that they know each other.

A SOLDIER'S LIFE

If your character is still a serving

soldier, it is fairly easy to integrate his ongoing career with a role-playing campaign, particularly if he is an officer. An officer can, and often is, placed in charge of a detachment and given a specific assignment, either of an overt or covert nature.

Overt missions would involve the character taking along his unit (a platoon or troop for a lieutenant or captain, and a full company for a major. These sorts of overt missions can be to guard caravans, hunt down bandits, quell an uprising, or anything else of that sort. The numbers of NPCs added by the unit are not overwhelming (particularly in the case of junior officers) and may provide some very welcome additional muscle, particularly for an adventuring party made up of new players.

Covert missions are secret orders issued by the player's commanding officer. These may involve a secret mission into enemy or neutral territory where an open show of force would be either unwise or impractical. In this case, the company of additional civilian travellers would be welcome as a cover to the officer's real mission. Alternatively, the player's commander may simply assign him to accompany a civilian expedition (such as that of the other players) and later report on anything he discovered which might be of interest to the Crown. This sort of added complication can greatly add to the enjoyment of the player by giving him a more sophisticated (and perhaps conflicting) set of goals and motivations.

Finally, civilian expeditions by the other players which do not fit either of these two categories need not be made without the military player, as he can simply apply for leave. Officers, in particular, were granted leave on a very generous basis. Majors, for example, could reasonably expect to be present with their unit only about half the time. Of course, any officer who is granted leave can probably arrange for an enlisted player character to be assigned to him as a batman for the duration of the expedition.

Several war bands of Pathan tribesmen storm a settlement on India's Northwest Frontier. Figures are from a variety of manufacturers.

Part B: The Military Campaign

THIS SECTION PROVIDES very simple rules for conducting a campaign. Our experience with dozens of miniatures campaigns is that most campaigns are never completed because they bog down in a morass of tediously complicated rules. These rules, therefore, are intended to be a minimalist framework to which you can attach whatever additional ruffles and flourishes you would care to.

THE CAMPAIGN MAP

ALL CAMPAIGNS require the use of a terrain map of the campaign area. The referee can use either one of the maps provided in the various **Space: 1889** products or generate his own. A blank hex grid is included in this game, and you have permission to photocopy it for your personal use in a campaign game. The campaign map should be drawn at a scale of 10 miles per hex, measured from side to side. Each hex should be evaluated as to its predominant terrain type, as this will affect movement, scouting, foraging, and the nature of any battlefield set within the confines of the hex.

MOVEMENT

CAMPAIGN MOVEMENT is expressed in terms of hexes travelled per day. Travel may be by land, water, or air.

Land Travel: The most common means by which armies travel is by marching. The Land Travel Table on page 75 lists the number of hexes which infantry and cavalry move per day based on the type of terrain covered. Pack animals (except for exceptionally large ones, such as elephants, ruumet breehr, and pacyosaurs) move as cavalry. Both infantry and cavalry may force march, if desired. This adds one hex to their movement or, if the movement rate through that type of terrain is one-half hex, increases it to one hex.

Each time that a unit conducts a forced march, roll one die. If the result is 6 or more, the unit becomes fatigued. The following additions are made to the die roll:

FORCED MARCH FATIGUE MODIFIERS

(Roll 6+ for fatigue.)

Type or Condition	*Modifier*
Veteran or Elite Troops	–1
Green Troops	+1
Difficult Terrain (normal rate of 1/2)	+1
Intense Heat (already included in Venus modifier)	+1
Humans on Mars	+1
Non-Venusian on Venus	+2
Non-Lunar on Luna	–1

Once a unit is fatigued, it remains fatigued until it spends one day resting. A fatigued unit may continue to conduct normal marches. Each time that it conducts a forced march, however, roll one die, and that many men fall out as stragglers. Once the unit stops, one die's worth of stragglers will rejoin the unit each day after the first until all have rejoined. In hostile terrain or enemy territory, however, half of all stragglers are permanently lost.

The terrain costs for vehicles are listed as multipliers because the speed of vehicles varies. All animal-drawn vehicles and artillery, with the exception of galloper guns, move at the same speed as infantry in the given terrain before the movement modifier is applied. For example, in forest the infantry speed is one-half and the vehicle modifier is ×1/2, so a horse-drawn wagon would take four days to make its way through a forest hex.

Galloper guns are any light field guns drawn by teams of horses or gashants. Galloper guns move at the same speed as cavalry before the modifiers are applied. For example, in desert the cavalry speed is two and the vehicle modifier is ×1/2, so a galloper gun would move one hex per day.

Mechanical vehicles have a speed in hexes equal to their movement rating. Tractors and land juggernauts must roll a die each day for mechanical breakdown. On a roll of 6, they experience a temporary mechanical failure and may not move that day.

LAND TRAVEL

Terrain	*Infantry*	*Cavalry*	*Vehicle*
Clear	1	2	×1
Grassland	1	2	×1
Hills	1	1	×1/2
Mountains	1/2	1/2	P
Swamp/ Marsh	1/2	1	P
Bog	1/2	1	P
Desert	1	2	×1/2
Sand Sea	1/2	1/2	P
Jungle	1/2	1/2	P
Forest	1/2	1/2	×1/2
Road	2	3	×2

Abbreviations: *P:* Prohibited.

Water Travel: Ships tend to travel at their most economical cruising speed, which is similar regardless of the vessel's maximum speed. The following table indicates the speed of various types of vessels on the open seas and on inland waterways, such as navigable rivers and Martian grand canals. Speed is given in the number of hexes travelled per day.

WATER TRAVEL
Inland Waterway

Vessel	*Hexes*
Man-Powered	2
Wind-Powered	1D6
Steamer	5

Open Seas

Vessel	*Hexes*
Wind-powered	10
Steamer	20

Aerial Travel: Aerial travel is possible by means of a variety of conveyances, as described in the rules on flyers. Liftwood flyers may not be used on Venus, as the unique magnetic field of that world greatly accelerates liftwood decay. The following table indicates the number of 10-mile hexes travelled in a day. The two different speeds for kites are for travel with or against the prevailing winds (from west to east on Mars). The speed of aeroplanes is listed in hexes per hour, and the notation "6+R" indicates that its speed in hexes is 6 plus its reliability number.

AERIAL TRAVEL

Flyer	*Hexes*
Zeppelin	30
Steam Flyer	30
Kite	20-40
Screw Galley	20
Conveyor	10
Glider	40
Helicopter	50
Autogyro	60
Aeroplane	6+R/hr

SCOUTING

SCOUTING SERVES several purposes. It can locate the enemy, determine his strength, hide your own strength, and avoid ambushes. In all cases, scouting is calculated on the basis of scouting points.

Scouting Points: Each unit of infantry and cavalry has scouting points equal to the number of men in the unit times the unit's Fieldcraft rating times the unit's movement rating in that terrain type. The unit can apply these points to scouting the hex it is in. Units on a road treat the hex as the dominant terrain type for purposes of scouting. For example, a 20-man infantry unit with a Fieldcraft of 3 would have 60 scouting points in clear terrain and hills, but only 30 points in jungle. If mounted, the unit would have 120 points in clear terrain, 60 points in hills, and 30 points in jungle.

Prebattle Scouting: Each side may committ up to 10 percent of its troops to prebattle scouting. The referee totals the scouting points of each side and compares them. If one side has 50 percent more scouting points than its opponent, that side is told how many units of infantry and cavalry and how many gun sections the enemy has. The referee tells the other side similar information, but will increase or will decrease the reported strengths by 50 percent, at the instruction of the player with the superior scouting forces.

If one side has twice the scouting points of its opponent, the same routine is followed as above, but the side with the superiority in scouting points is allowed to examine the gaming table prior to play. This side's owning player then determines whether he will set up in the middle of the table and let his opponent enter, or whether he will have his opponent set up in the center and his own forces enter.

Searching: A player may send out scouts during campaign movement to search for the enemy. The referee divides the total number of scouting points committed to a hex by 10, rounds fractions down, and adds one to the total for every four enemy units in the hex. The resulting number is the detection number for the enemy troops in the hex. The referee secretly rolls two dice, and if the total is equal to or less than the detection number of the enemy troops, he tells the scouting player of their presence.

SUPPLIES

IN MOST CASES there is little need to

worry about supplies if a campaign is properly conducted. A single large merchant kite can carry as much as 1000 tons of supplies while a canal barge or steamer can carry several hundred. In the event that a player does not have assets such as this at his disposal, however, the following simple supply rules should be used.

Rations: An army consumes one ton of rations for every 20 companies or war bands it has. Each cavalry unit or animal-drawn artillery battery counts as four units for purposes of this calculation.

If an army does not have ready access to fresh water, all units count double (cavalry and animal-drawn artillery count as eight units) due to the need to provide drinking water.

Ammunition: Troops carry enough ammunition to fight at least one battle, but they must be replenished at the end of it. One ton of ammunition will replenish 10 20-man units. Each machinegun section counts as one unit. Each gun section counts as five units times the damage value of the gun.

When conducting a siege, one ton is required per damage value per gun in order to fire one siege turn's worth of bombardment. For example, an 8" siege gun has a damage value of 8, so it requires eight tons of ammunition per bombardment.

Transport: Supplies may be transported by flyers, ships, vehicles, or animals. Flyers and ships can transport such large quantities of supply as to make the supply rules irrelevant. When conducting a small campaign in a remote area, however, a force may need to rely on animal transportation. This may take the form of wagons or pack trains. Each model wagon requires a driver and transports three tons of supplies. Each pack train requires two drivers and transports one ton of supplies. The number of animals in a pack train varies (from one ruumet breehr to 16 mules), and a train includes extra animals to carry food for the animals in the pack train. A pack train should be represented by two pack animals, except in the case of large animals (elephants or ruumet breehr), in which case one model is sufficient.

Foraging: A unit may forage for supplies, if desired. As foraging essentially involves stealing food from farmers, only cultivated hexes may be foraged. If the unit spends one full day in a hex foraging, roll a die. If the result is equal to or less than the unit's Fieldcraft, it discovers one or more tons of food, as shown on the Foraging Table below. Once food has been discovered and removed from a hex, it may not be foraged again.

Villages, towns, and cities may be foraged as well. If a village is foraged, multiply the amount on the Foraging Table by 10. If a town is foraged, multiply the amount on the table by 100. If a city is foraged, multiply the amount on the table by 1D6 times 100.

FORAGING TABLE

Season	*Tons*
Fallow Season (Winter)	2
Planting Season (Spring)	1
Growing Season (Summer)	2
Harvest Season (Fall)	1D6

Part C: Sample Scenarios

THE FOLLOWING simple scenarios are designed to get you started playing. All of the information necessary is included, as well as suggested table layouts and player briefings.

SCENARIO 1: MARTIAN MESSIAH

British Briefing: For the past several months the level of unrest has been increasing in the northern part of the Syrtis Major colony, and now that the war clouds are thickening in the south, there have been increasingly strident calls demanding open rebellion.

One Martian self-styled prophet, called Itaba Sootamaan, has been causing particular trouble, and the commander of your battalion has ordered his arrest.

As there is some chance of trouble with armed locals, it was decided to not send a mounted constabular patrol, and to instead send a platoon of British infantry under a responsible officer—you.

You will enter the southern edge of the table and search the villages until you find Sootamaan, place him under arrest, and escort him off the table.

Troops: One platoon of infantry plus one officer. *Unit Value*:V1, nine men total.

Martian Briefing: You are Itaba Sootamaan, a cleric and a holy man forced onto the path of violence by the tyranny of the hated, red off-worlders. Now that war seems likely between the British and the Oenotrian princes to the south, the time is right to strike. To convince the people to take such a bold gamble, however, you must produce a powerful victory. Fortunately, the British have presented you with such an opportunity.

Your spies have brought word that a small force has been sent to arrest you. It would be unseemly to run, and doing so would certainly undermine your ability to persuade the tribesmen here to revolt. However, you have your own small band of loyal retainers, and a carefully executed ambush can certainly wipe out the British. Not only would that provide captured arms and ammunition, it would also give the tribes a powerful sign.

Forces: One Martian war band (shooters have rifle muskets). *Unit Value:* X3, 19 men total.

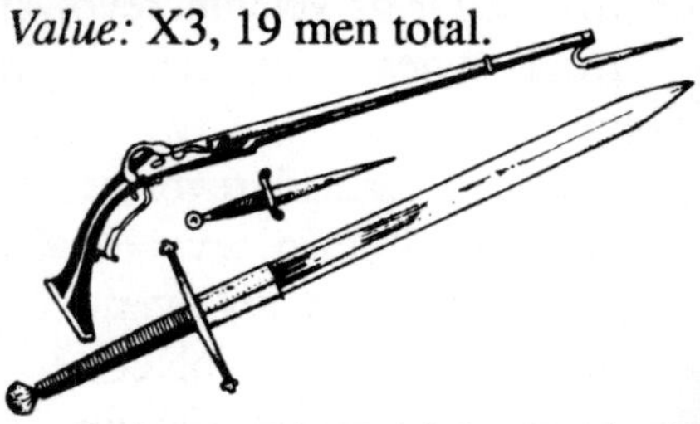

Referee: The British win a major victory if they either arrest or kill Sootamaan and escape off the south edge. They win a minor victory if they survive, but Sootamaan escapes off the board. The Martians win a minor victory if Sootamaan survives, escapes captivity, and remains in sole possession of the field at the end of the game. They win a major victory if Sootamaan survives and the British are wiped out.

SCENARIO 2: RESCUE MISSION

British Briefing: War with Oenotria has erupted and several scientific and exploratory parties have fallen under surprise attack. There is currently such a party defending a small ruined temple that was the site of an archaeological dig. Your company has been ordered to break through to them and bring them back to friendly territory.

Your first action was to round up a few horses and send an advance party on ahead to reinforce the defenders. They broke through the loose enemy siege lines and have joined the scientific party, but more enemy troops have also arrived and an assault is imminent. You have force marched to get to the temple and now need to break through as soon as possible.

Scientific Party: Three officers on leave and seven civilians, with skills and firearms as follows:

Army Officer: Veteran, revolver

Army Officer: Veteran, revolver

Navy Officer: Experienced, revolver

Scientist: Trained, revolver

Scientist: Trained, revolver

Scientist: Green, revolver

Scientist: Green, revolver

Missionary: Green, shotgun

Martian Guide: Experienced, rifle musket

Human Guide: Experienced, bolt-action rifle

Reinforcing Mounted Detachment: (Horses have been lost.) One officer with revolver, one corporal and three privates with bolt action rifles. *Unit Value:* V1.

Relief Column: One infantry company (less the mounted detachment). *Unit Value:* V1, 15 men total.

Martian Briefing: War is a good thing when directed against godless grave robbers such as these English. For months you and other officers like you on the frontier have been forced to sit by and watch while bands of temple defilers have openly crossed the border and pawed their way through the holiest of holy relics in the old temples of the north, taking as souvenirs some of the items that caught their fancy and discarding many others across the countryside as if they were so much rubbish. You and your men have held back until now for fear of provoking an incident and alerting the British to your preparations for war. Now, however, the war has begun and you are free to wipe out the latest group of vandals.

Your scouts have contained the vandals in the ruins of one of the temples and have kept them from escaping until the arrival of the rest of your force. A small party of five mounted enemy soldiers even arrived to rescue them, but your scouts have them bottled up with the others. Now you are ready to attack.

Martian Forces: One war band with smoothbore muskets. *Unit Value:* X2.

One war band with rifle muskets. *Unit Value:* T2.

One war band with smoothbore carbines. *Unit Value:* G1.

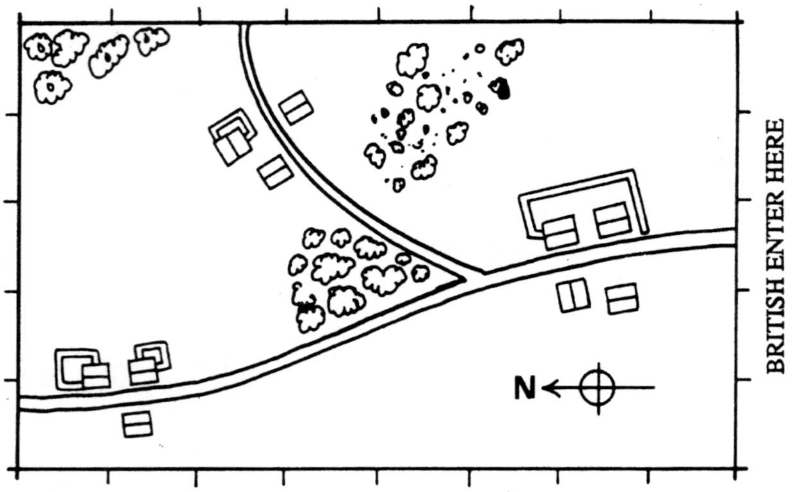

SCENARIO 1: *5' X 8' Table*

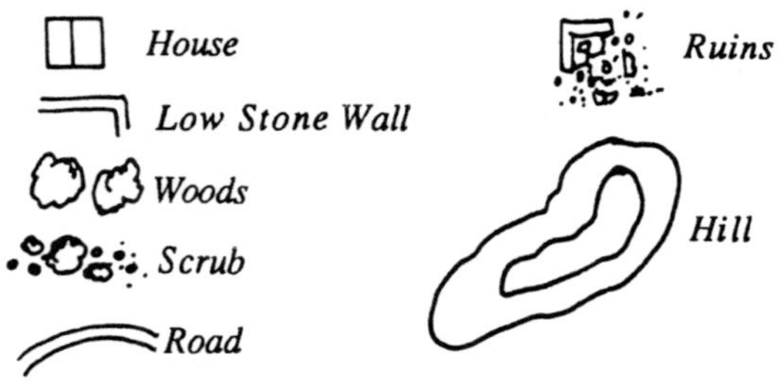

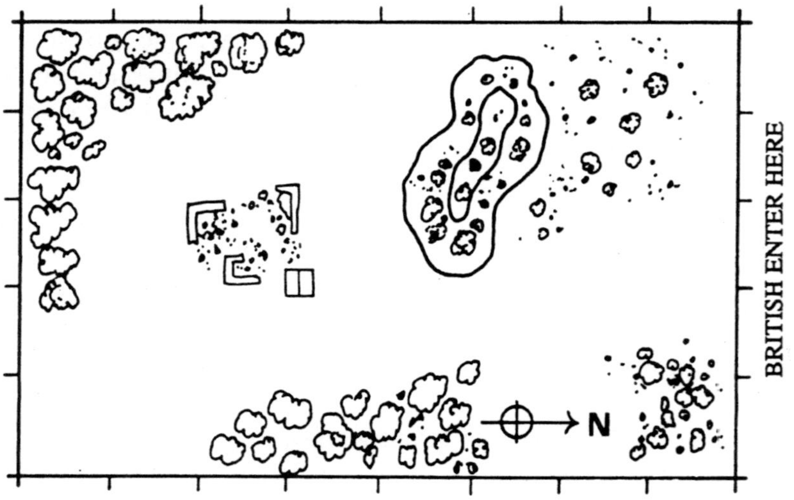

SCENARIO 2: *5' X 8' Table*

Part D: Sample Campaigns

The following are not fully developed campaigns, but rather are a collection of ideas for you to flesh out. The direction you take these suggestions will largely depend on the sort of games you enjoy and the quantity and types of troops at your disposal.

There are actually two different kinds of miniatures campaign. In the campaign that most gamers play, each player commands an army or unit on one of two opposing sides with a referee to adjudicate hidden movement and simultaneous execution of orders. This sort of campaign can be enjoyable, but it is very taxing for the referee and usually frustrating for most or all of the players since gamers do not all play at the same rate of speed. While the campaigns below can be played in that way, they are also ideally suited to be played as one-sided refereed games.

A one-sided refereed game is a somewhat more rigorous role-playing game, with a military operation as its central theme. The players all play the roles of officers on the same side, while the referee adjudicates the action of the campaign and also determines the actions of the opponents. The advantages of this sort of game are many. Play proceeds at a pace that is comfortable for everyone involved, there is generally a good deal more character identification and authentic "feel" to the game, and all players get the opportunity to work together against a common foe, thus reducing the chances for the hard feelings that seem to accompany the conclusion of many competitive campaigns.

In setting up your campaign, consult the army lists provided in this book and the background information in the other **Space: 1889** games, particularly **Conklin's Atlas of the Worlds** for maps, background, and inspiration for interesting subplots.

CAMPAIGN 1: THE RAID

This campaign takes place along and near the canal to Oenotria and is actually a small mini-campaign. The players will command various parts of a raiding forced detached from Lieutenant General Wood's column. The mission of the force is to strike behind the Martian lines and cause as much destruction as possible, then break free and rejoin the main body. It will travel fast and light, but it must carry all needed supplies with it. The most likely configuration of the force would be a company of the 2nd East Surreys, a platoon of the 4th Rifle Brigade, and perhaps a few civilian volunteers.The players will have to decide how large a pack train they will require, whether they want to take supply wagons, and whether they will need artillery. If so, they will have to try to pursuade Wood to relinquish a gun section; his initial feelings are that it will only slow the raiding force up and would be more valuable with the main body. The referee should ajudicate this exchange using the rules for persuasion from the role-playing game.

If a competitive game is desired, the Martian team should be responsible for guarding the rear area of the army facing Wood's column. A small force of regulars will be available (no more than one legion) to back up the guard detachments in the various villages and towns. (Generate these using the Martian city generation rules on pages 146-149.) The Martians must then decide where they will station their regulars. Will they be concentrated as a central reserve or spread out to stiffen the local garrisons? Do they want to appeal for more troops to the army commander? Since the main army is very hard-pressed by Wood at the moment, drawing more troops from there would probably be a bad decision.

CAMPAIGN 2: THE FRONTIER OF EMPIRE

In the highlands at Moeris Lacus, the British are faced by a foe superior in numbers and reinforced with three combat tripods of German manufacture. The canal route through Shastapsh has been cut, and overland caravans through the desert are regularly attacked by desert nomads or Shastapshan cavalry. But worst of all, the British commander at Moeris Lacus is hesitant and indecisive. No action is to be taken without his approval, and he never approves aggressive action.

The players are junior officers with various units of the highland forces and realize that they are facing imminent defeat. If the caravan route is to be reopened and the Shastapshan Army thrown off balance, some sort of imaginative, aggressive action needs to be taken. To do so, however, will mean disobeying the orders of their superior officer, and could potentially be the end of their careers.

The players must discover or invent means by which they can plausibly misinterpret or fail to receive orders so that they can undertake punitive raids on the enemy and send him reeling.

Over the course of several missions they will have to tread a fine line between simple insubordination and outright mutiny, as too blatant a disregard of orders will result in their removal from command and court martial.

CAMPAIGN 3: THE MAN WHO WOULD BE KING

FROM 1872 TO 1889, the Abyssinian Empire was ruled by a British adventurer who took the title John IV, thus achieving the goal (becoming a king) that hundreds of his countrymen strove for in vain. Who is to say, however, that his success could not be duplicated by others on Mars or Venus?

In this campaign, the characters will pool their resources to buy a quantity of modern weapons and strike off into the Martian wilderness in search of a country to rule. They will be especially interested in finding a region currently in a state of anarchy and civil war (a common enough thing on Mars), so they can step into the power vacuum, pick a side to support, and eventually take over.

The referee can generate any region on Mars using the large-scale maps in the role-playing game book and the city generation system on pages 146-149. He can doctor the results of certain rolls to create the proper levels of confused mayhem and bedlam and then inject the players.

He will need to pay special attention to the Eloquence and Leadership skills of the PCs, as these skills will be essential to attracting native followers. He should also begin computing their renown from scratch in this new region, as renown will be essential to the success of their plans. Eventually, Mars may see a new kingdom, or even empire, emerge.

CAMPAIGN 4: FREEDOM'S CALL

THE PLAYER CHARACTERS are harmless and innocent passengers on a commercial interplanetary ether flyer en route from Earth to Mars. They are in Mars orbit when an attempted hijacking by anarchists badly damages the vessel and forces it to crash on the far side of Mars, near the city of Candor.

The players are made prisoner by the locals, who are extremely hostile to humans as a result of the Belgian atrocities in the Coprates Valley to the south. They soon discover several things.

The authorities at Syrtis Major assume that all hands were lost in the crash of the liner, and all messages out of Candor are being intercepted.

The Belgians are planning a move against the city of Candor and fabricate an incident. When the players discover the falsehood, the local Belgian commander decides they must be disposed of when the city is taken. For a variety of reasons the players must throw in their lot with the Candorans and fight off the Belgian attack.

The first order of business, of course, will be to convince the Candorans that they are friends and have an interest in joining the fight against Belgian aggression. This will be difficult, and there will be some elements who will never completely trust them, and others who now hate all humans so deeply that the players' act of friendship will make no difference.

Once they have at least gained some freedom of action, it will be up to the players to chart a course of constructive action. Military men in the group may be able to train a war band or two of Veteran or Elite Candoran infantry as regulars.

Characters with a fluent knowledge of French, perhaps with a theatrical background as well, may be able to set up an effective secret service. Players can win the trust and respect of their soldiers by leading them on raids and undertaking hazardous missions.

The referee will record the effects of all this on the players' local renown, and when it is high enough, the prince will begin consulting them on military and diplomatic matters. There is a real need for the Candorans to understand the workings of terrestrial politics, and the players will be perfect "consultants."

Eventually the Belgians will make their move, and it will be up to the players to help the Candorans resist the assault.

Part A: Artillery of the Worlds

THIS BOOK of the **Soldier's Companion** deals with the large tools of war, specifically artillery, naval vessels, mechanical vehicles, and flyers.

The artillery available on the various worlds of **Space: 1889** can be divided into several broad categories, the most important of which is that of modern breech-loading guns. These guns are the most common category currently in production, although large numbers of older, less powerful, guns remain in service. The main criteria for inclusion in this category is that a gun be rifled, breech-loading, and have a muzzle velocity in excess of 1700' per second. These modern guns are characterized by excellent range and superior penetration.

Several special guns are worth noting. The 4.7" quick-firing gun is the first of a new breed of naval guns which have hydraulic recoil cylinders that allow the gun to slide back in recoil and then return easily to its original firing position. This allows for quicker delivery of aimed fire. The 4" gun listed here is usually referred to as the 4" long gun to distinguish it from its lower-velocity twin, the 4" short gun (or 20-pounder gun). That weapon is detailed in the table covering lower-powered ordnance.

Note that the 3" gun is also called a 15-pounder. This other designation is generally used when the gun is mounted in a field carriage and refers to the weight of the most common shell thrown by the gun. Since the weight of conical shells is not rigidly dictated by the diameter of the gun's bore (a longer shell of the same diameter will weigh more), it is possible to have two guns of the same bore caliber which fire different weights of shell. This is the case with the high-powered 3" gun and its shorter, low-powered version (covered later) which fires only a 12-pound shell.

Finally, some mention should be made of the diminutive Hotchkiss 2-pounder breechloader. To represent the small size of its projectile, it is allowed to fire only shell, not shrapnel. It is much prized by the United States Army for its portability, as it can be taken almosty anywhere that a horse can travel (a definite benefit in the American West).

The second important category of guns we will call "low-powered, rifled guns." These are modern, rifled guns but with a muzzle velocity less than 1700' per second. Many of these are muzzle-loading guns, but many breechloaders fall into this category as well. Virtually all of the Krupp guns, for example, are low-powered breechloaders. Most (but not all) field guns fall into this category as well, as the shorter gun tube makes for a lighter weapon, while the lower muzzle energy allows for a lighter carriage. Most guns used as field guns have an additional parenthetical identification that indicates the weight of the shell thrown by the gun. This is usually used in reference to the field

TABLE 1:
MODERN BREECH-LOADING GUNS

Weapon	*Weight*	*Pen*	*DV*	*ROF*	*Crew*	*Range*	*Cost*
18"	3400	18/9	20	(4)	8	14/28	30,000
17"	2800	17/9	18	(3)	7	13/26	27,000
16"	2250	16/8	16	(2)	6	10/20	24,000
14"	1300	14/7	14	(1)	6	9/18	12,000
12"	900	12/6	12	(1)	5	8/16	9000
10"	600	10/5	10	(1)	4	7/14	6000
8"	300	9/5	8	(1)	3	6/12	3000
6"	100	5/3	6	1	2	5/10	1000
5"	80	4/2	4	1	2	5/10	800
4.7" QF	100	4/2	3	2	2	4/8	1000
4" (long)	40	3/2	2	1	2	4/8	400
3" (15-pdr)	25	2/1	1	1	2	3/6	260
2-pdr gun	5	0/0	1*	1	2	2/4	100

*Only fires shell; cannot fire shrapnel.

Abbreviations: *QF:* Quick-Firing *Pdr:* Pounder.

TABLE 2: LOW-POWERED (LP) RIFLED GUNS

Weapon	*Weight*	*Pen*	*DV*	*ROF*	*Crew*	*Range*	*Cost*
18"	2000	14/7	18	(4)	8	9/18	24,000
16"	1600	12/6	16	(3)	6	8/16	18,000
14"	1000	10/5	14	(2)	6	7/14	12,000
13"	750	9/4	13	(1)	6	6/12	10,000
12"	500	8/4	12	(1)	5	6/12	8000
10"	400	7/3	10	(1)	4	6/12	6000
9"	250	6/3	9	(1)	3	5/10	3000
8"	200	5/2	8	(1)	3	5/10	2000
7"	140	4/2	7	(1)	3	5/10	1000
6"	80	4/2	6	(1)	2	4/8	800
4.7" (40-pdr)	50	3/1	3	1	2	4/8	600
4" (20-pdr)	30	2/1	2	1	2	3/6	300
3" (12-pdr)	20	1/1	1	1	2	3/6	240
9-pdr	10	1/0	1	1	2	3/6	220
6-pdr	10	0/0	1	1	2	2/4	100

Abbreviations: *Pdr:* Pounder.

TABLE 3: RIFLED HOWITZERS

Weapon	*Weight*	*Pen*	*DV*	*ROF*	*Crew*	*Range*	*Cost*
7" hwtzr	100	1	7	1	2	10	1000
6" hwtzr	70	1	6	1	2	8	800
5" hwtzr	60	1	4	1	2	8	600
7# MH	15	0	1	2	2	6	200

Abbreviations: *Hwtzr:* Howitzer *MH:* Mountain Howitzer *Pdr:* Pounder.

TABLE 4: SMOOTHBORE GUNS

Weapon	*Weight*	*Pen*	*DV*	*ROF*	*Crew*	*Range*	*Cost*
15"	300	4/2	7	(2)	4	4/8	6000
11"	150	3/1	5	(1)	3	3/6	3500
10"	80	2/1	4	(1)	3	2/4	2000
68-pdr	80	2/1	3	1	2	3/6	1500
9"	60	1/1	3	1	2	2/4	1000
32-pdr	60	1/1	2	1	2	3/6	1000
24-pdr	40	1/0	2	1	2	2/4	800
12-pdr	30	1/0	1	1	2	2/4	400
9-pdr	25	0/0	1	1	2	2/3	200
6-pdr	20	0/0	1	1	2	1/2	100

Abbreviations: *Pdr:* Pounder.

artillery version of the gun.

Howitzers are weapons with shorter, lighter barrels designed to throw a shell onto a position from a high angle. They are less accurate and generally have a shorter range than a comparably sized gun, but they tend to be lighter and are capable of firing over intervening obstacles. They are especially valuable for shelling fortifications. The howitzers listed to the left are all rifled.

Much older than any of the above weapons, smoothbore guns date back to the first half of the century. Although now obsolete, many of these guns are still found in the arsenals of the lesser powers and on some of the older vessels of the United States Navy. These weapons are considerably inferior to more modern guns in terms of range and effectiveness of ammunition. In game terms, these weapons can only fire shot and grapeshot. Primitive shells were fired from many of these guns as well, but they were much less effective than more modern ammunition, and so for simplicity are treated as shot. Most field guns of this type are referred to only by the weight of their shot, not their bore.

Smoothbore howitzers and mortars are similar to smoothbore guns, but have shorter barrels and are intended for high-angle, plunging fire on a target. Mortars tend to be mounted on solid carriages, rather than wheeled field carriages, as they are used almost exclusively in sieges.

The last category of terrestrial artillery is perhaps the most interesting: machine cannon. These rapid-fire, small-caliber guns were originally developed for shipboard use to provide large vessels with an effective means of defense against small, fast torpedo boats. Since most aerial vessels are small, machine cannon serve as very effective secondary armament on many vessels, and as primary armament on a few of the smaller ships. Recently there has been considerable interest in mounting these weapons on field carriages for use against various heavy vehicles and to provide ground troops with an effective means of defense against low-flying aerial vessels. As most of these guns have fairly high muzzle velocities, they have impressive penetration for their size.

Most of these guns have multiple rotating barrels which fire in succession. The Gatling 1" is nothing more than a scaled up version of the ubiquitous .50-caliber Gatling gun.

The Hotchkiss revolving cannons (often called revolvers for short) are based on a slightly more advanced mechanical principle, but externally they appear almost identical to a Gatling gun.

Of special interest, however, is the Maxim-Nordenfelt 1-pounder Pom-Pom. Only recently offered for sale, this weapon has a slightly better rate of fire than the Hotchkiss gun has, but the Pom-Pom uses the same mechanical principle as Mr. Maxim's famous machinegun.

None of these guns have an effective shrapnel shell, but they make up for it with sheer volume of shell fire.

Having dispensed with the ordnance of Earth, it is time to turn to that of other worlds. Of the other inhabited worlds of the Solar System, only Mars can be said to have developed a genuine system of ordnance.

Although metal is scarce on Mars (or perhaps because of that), Martian

TABLE 5:
SMOOTHBORE HOWITZERS AND MORTARS

	Weight	*Pen*	*DV*	*ROF*	*Crew*	*Range*	*Cost*
13" mortar	150	2	10	(2)	4	7	5000
10" mortar	90	1	8	(1)	3	6	4000
8" mortar	60	0	6	(1)	2	5	3000
5" mortar	40	0	4	1	2	4	2000
32-pdr hwtzr	40	0	3	1	2	4	1200
24-pdr hwtzr	30	0	2	1	2	3	600
12-pdr hwtzr	20	0	1	1	2	3	300

Abbreviations: *Hwtzr*: Howitzer *Pdr:* Pounder.

TABLE 6:
MACHINE CANNON

Weapon	*Weight*	*Pen*	*DV*	*ROF*	*Crew*	*Range*	*Cost*
6-pdr HRC	15	1/0	1*	3	1	3/6	220
3-pdr HRC	10	1/0	1*	3	1	2/4	180
1-pdr HRC	10	0/0	1*	3	1	2/4	160
1-pdr PP	10	0/0	1*	4	1	2/4	250
1" Gatling	5	0/0	1*	3/4	1	1/2	70

* Only fires shell; cannot fire shrapnel.

Abbreviations: *HRC:* Hotchkiss Revolving Cannon *Pdr:* Pounder *PP:* Pom-Pom.

TABLE 7:
MARTIAN ORDNANCE

Weapon	*Weight*	*Pen*	*DV*	*ROF*	*Crew*	*Range*	*Cost*
Sweeper	10	P	—	1	1	0/1	200
Light gun	20	0/0	1	1	2	1/2	400
Heavy gun	40	1/0	2	1	2	2/4	1000
Rod gun	30	2/1	1	(1)	2	3/6	800
Rogue	60	2/1	3	(1)	3	3/6	2000
Lob gun	200	2	4	(1)	3	6	2000

TABLE 8:
LUNAR CATAPULTS

Weapon	*Weight*	*Pen*	*DV*	*ROF*	*Crew*	*Range*	*Cost*
20-pdr	Hv	0/0	1	(1)	4	2/4	500
60-pdr	Sg	1/0	2	(1)	6	2/4	1000

Abbreviations: *Pdr:* Pounder.

guns tend to be well-made. Iron smoothbores are most common, although the so-called "rod gun" is becoming increasingly popular and is prized for its excellent range and penetration against armored vessels.

This weapon has four rifling grooves in the barrel and fires an oblong bar with a square cross-section and a half twist (called a rod). The rod must be matched up with the riflings before loading, and so this is a slow-firing piece for its size. Other weapons fire iron (or sometimes stone) round shot or the local equivalent of grapeshot.

The sweeper is the smallest Martian gun, closely resembling the 17th-century swivel gun in both its appearance and its function.

Only grapeshot is provided for the weapon, but it is effective against infantry at close range.

The Martian lob gun is of particular interest. It is essentially an extremely large mortar which fires a large, iron-banded boulder at a high angle. Its extreme weight and low rate of fire brings its value into some question.

Nevertheless, its ability to occasionally knock a ship out of the sky with a single lucky hit makes it a valuable, if not completely dependable, asset. (This weapon's range was seriously underrated in previous products in this series, and its performance has been upgraded here.)

Finally we come to the catapults used by the Moon Men of the Great Sea, deep within Luna. These are generally low-powered weapons, used mostly for defense against large animals and wooden-hulled vessels. If transported to Venus, Earth, or Mars, their range would be halved due to the higher gravity.

Each of these catapults operates on a torsion principle and looks like a large crossbow.

Lunar catapults throw spherical stone boulders of either 20 or 60 pounds in weight (depending on the catapult). For firing purposes they are treated as artillery but may only fire shot.

TABLE 9: RIFLED FIELD ARTILLERY

Weapon	*Weight*	*Pen*	*DV*	*ROF*	*Crew*	*Range*	*Cost*
7" gun	Sg	4/2	7	(2)	6	5/10	1000
7" hwtzr	Sg	1	7	(1)	4	10	1000
6" long gun	Sg	5/3	6	(1)	4	5/10	1000
6" short gun	Sg	4/2	6	(1)	4	4/8	800
6" hwtzr	Sg	1	6	(1)	4	8	800
5" gun	Sg	4/2	4	(1)	4	5/10	800
5" hwtzr	VH	1	4	1	4	8	600
4" gun	VH	3/2	2	1	4	4/8	400
40-pdr gun	VH	3/1	3	1	4	4/8	600
20-pdr gun	Hv	2/1	2	1	4	3/6	300
15-pdr gun	Md	2/1	1	1	4	3/6	260
12-pdr gun	Md	1/1	1	1	4	3/6	240
9-pdr gun	Lt	1/0	1	1	4	3/6	220
7-pdr hwtzr	Lt	0	1	2	4	6	200
6-pdr gun	Lt	0/0	1	1	4	2/4	100
6-pdr HRC	Md	1/0	1*	3	2	3/6	220
3-pdr HRC	Lt	1/0	1*	3	2	2/4	180
2-pdr gun	Lt	0/0	1*	1	4	2/4	100
1-pdr HRC	Lt	0/0	1*	3	2	2/4	160
1-pdr PP	Lt	0/0	1*	4	2	2/4	250
1" Gatling	Lt	0/0	1*	3/4	2	1/2	70

*Only fires shell; cannot fire shrapnel.

Abbreviations: *Hwtzr:* Howitzer *HRC:* Hotchkiss Revolving Cannon *PP:* Pom-Pom

FIELD ARTILLERY

THE PREVIOUS SECTION covers the major ordnance mounted in ships, aerial vessels, large vehicles, and fortresses in 1889. Not all of these guns were mounted on field carriages, however.

Additionally, certain characteristics of guns change when on field mounts.

All crew requirements are doubled (as there are no shell hoist, recoil gear, or other similar crew-helpers in the field).

Weight of field guns is measured in terms of the weapon's weight category, ranging from Light to Siege. Finally, the rates of fire of most siege guns are lower than their naval or fortress equivalents.

All of this information is summarized in the charts located on pages 84 and 85.

TABLE 10: SMOOTHBORE FIELD ARTILLERY

Weapon	*Weight*	*Pen*	*DV*	*ROF*	*Crew*	*Range*	*Cost*
13" mortar	Sg	2	10	(3)	8	7	5000
11" gun	Sg	3/1	5	(2)	6	3/6	3500
10" gun	Sg	2/1	4	(2)	6	2/4	2000
68-pdr gun	Sg	2/1	3	(1)	4	3/6	1500
10" mortar	Sg	1	8	(2)	6	6	4000
9" gun	Sg	1/1	3	(1)	4	2/4	1000
8" mortar	Sg	0	6	(2)	4	5	3000
5.5" mortar	Sg	0	4	(1)	4	4	2000
32-pdr gun	Sg	1/1	2	(1)	4	3/6	1000
32-pdr hwtzr	VH	0	3	1	4	4	1200
24-pdr gun	VH	1/0	2	1	4	2/4	800
24-pdr hwtzr	Hv	0	2	1	4	3	600
12-pdr gun	Hv	1/0	1	1	4	2/4	400
12-pdr hwtzr	Md	0	1	1	4	3	300
9-pdr gun	Md	0/0	1	1	4	2/3	200
6-pdr gun	Md	0/0	1	1	4	1/2	100

Abbreviations: *Hwtzr:* Howitzer.

TABLE 11: MARTIAN FIELD ARTILLERY

Weapon	*Weight*	*Pen*	*DV*	*ROF*	*Crew*	*Range*	*Cost*
Lob gun	Sg	2	4	(2)	6	6	2000
Rogue	Sg	2/1	3	(2)	6	3/6	2000
Heavy gun	VH	1/0	2	1	4	2/4	1000
Rod gun	Hv	2/1	1	(1)	4	3/6	800
Light gun	Md	0/0	1	1	4	1/2	400
Sweeper	Lt	P	1*	1	2	0/1	200

*Only fires grapeshot; does not fire shot.

TABLE 12: LUNAR CATAPULTS

Weapon	*Weight*	*Pen*	*DV*	*ROF*	*Crew*	*Range*	*Cost*
20-pdr	Hv	0/0	1	(1)	4	2/4	500
60-pdr	Sg	1/0	2	(1)	6	2/4	1000

Abbreviations: *Pdr:* Pounder.

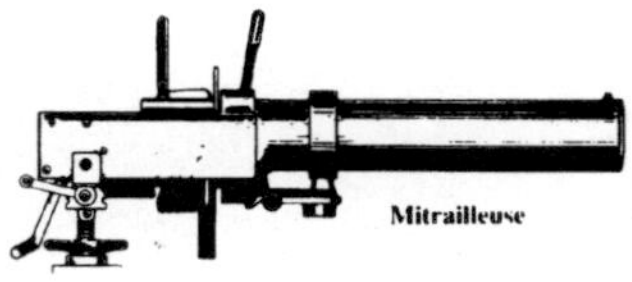
Mitrailleuse

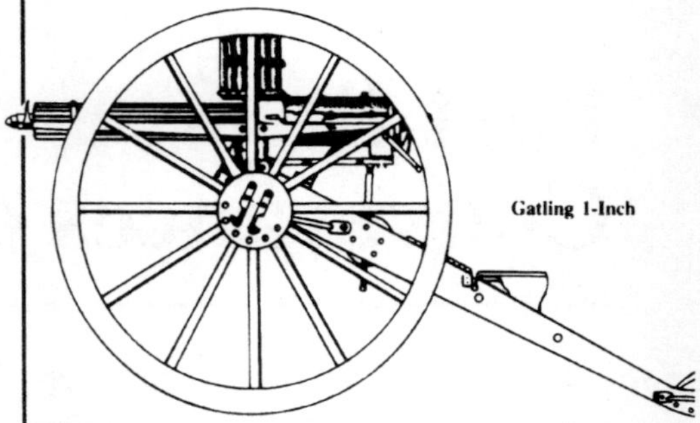
Gatling 1-Inch

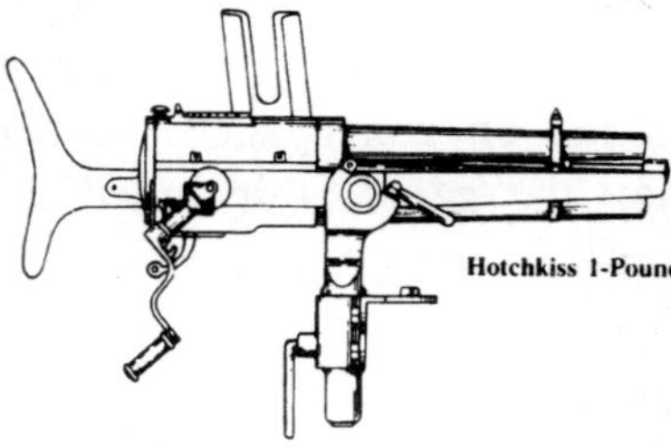
Hotchkiss 1-Pounder

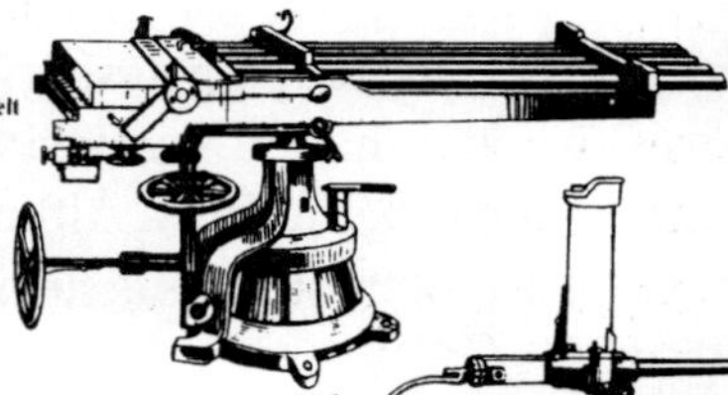
Nordenfelt

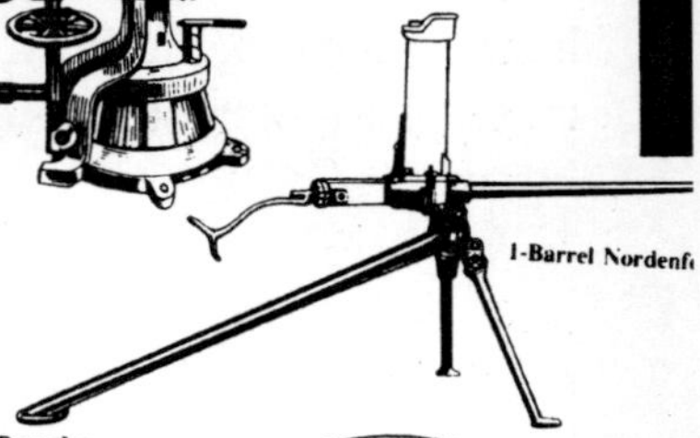
1-Barrel Nordenfelt

15-Pounder Rifled Breech-Loader

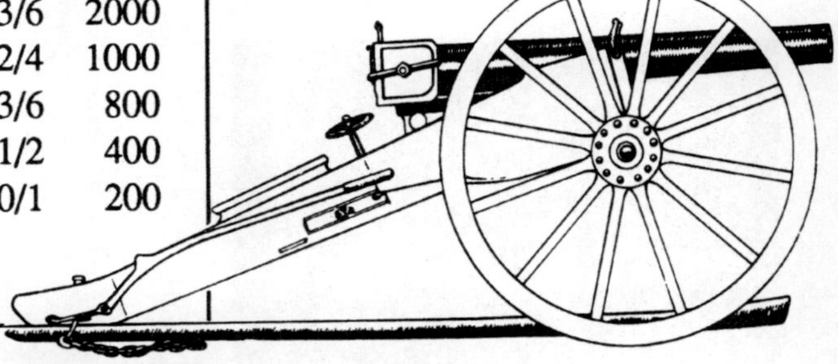

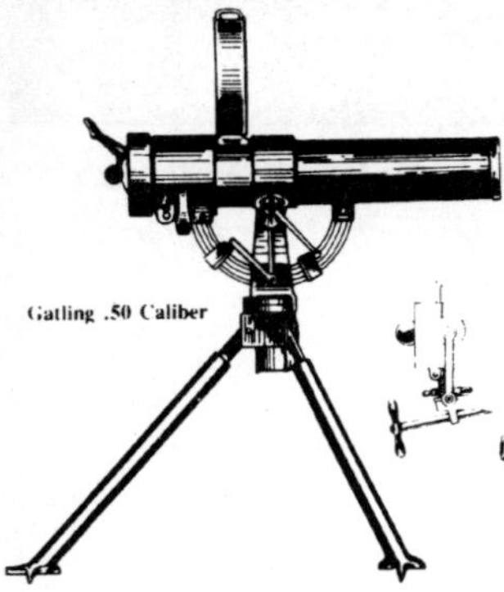
Gatling .50 Caliber

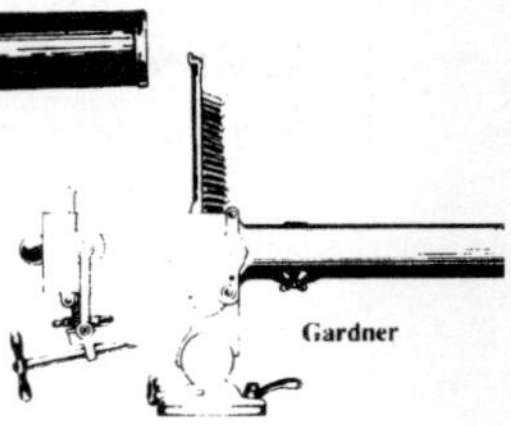
Gardner

Part B: Conveyances of the World

THIS SECTION PROVIDES a brief overview of the mechanical conveyances of the world. The bulk of the information on conveyances needed to play the game is included in the conveyance record forms.

SHIPS

THE NAVIES OF THE WORLD include fighting vessels, ranging in size from small wooden-hulled gunboats to huge armored battleships. Although the emphasis of these rules is such that most games will involve only gunboats, the naval rules can cope with any ship afloat, and to that end, a few ratings of larger vessels are also included in the ship lists that follow.

The listings in the game are only partial lists of the many types of gunboats used, but they provide enough variety that a referee should be able to find a vessel that will suit his needs in the game. The completed ship record forms provided should be photocopied for use during a game, and you have permission to do so.

Building Model Ships: This is a miniatures game, and miniatures games require models of the ship used. The models you will build of ships will not be in exact scale to model figures, or they would take up too much of the table. Instead, they will be scaled down in length and width. Their general configuration should remain the same, however. Consult the overhead schematic deck plan and the side view drawing of the ship on its record form to get a good idea of how the ship looks. The deck plan on the ship record form has a tactical grid superimposed on it, each square of the grid representing 1". For those ships which do not have an overhead view, use the general rule that the length of the model in inches is four times the listed hull length. Use this as a blueprint for the size and shape of the main hull of the model.

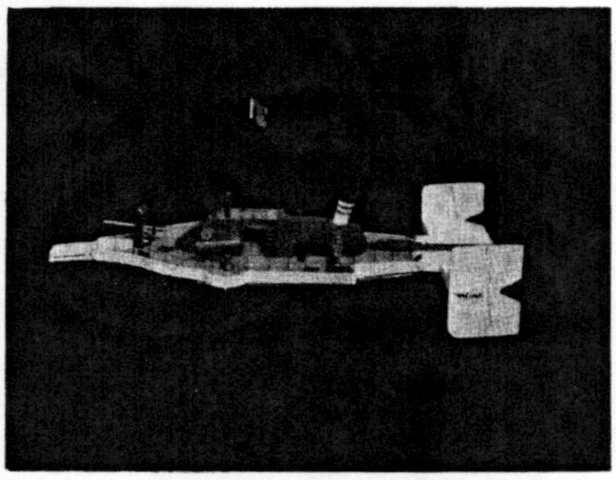

Aphid model built by Tom Harris. Ship's ordnance by Lizard's Grin.

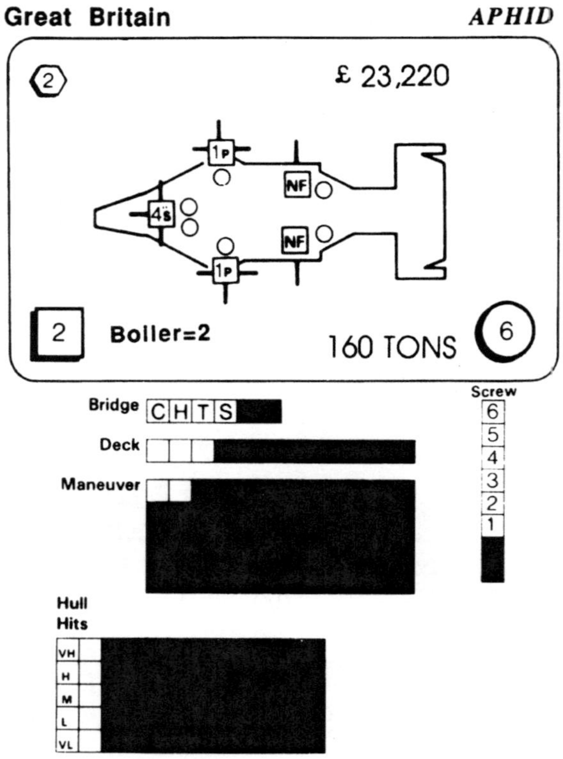

Actual construction of the ship should be as simple and durable as possible. A thick sheet of balsa wood cut and sanded to the shape of the hull with superstructure and gunwales (if any) added is a good start. Masts can be added from hardwood doweling. A variety of white metal ship fittings are available from some model specialty houses if you want to add some extra chrome, but that isn't necessary.

A number of naval gun mounts, including Nordenfelts and Hotchkiss revolvers, are available in white metal from Lizard's Grin Models. If you can't find them in a store, write them for a catalog at:

Lizard's Grin Models
P.O. Box 14522
Oklahoma City, OK 73113

We will be issuing naval ordnance in white metal ourselves at a later date, but in the mean time, these fine little models will do very nicely.

When you are adding gun mounts, superstructure, and other fittings, be sure to leave enough room for the crew figures. Although you will not want to bother with the engine room crew, deckhands and gunners in open gun mounts should be included.

Juggernauts built by Don Apperson.

FLYERS

A NUMBER OF flyer record forms are included in the game, but it is difficult to do these conveyances justice here. Much of the universe of **Space: 1889** revolves around its unusual flying machines, and these are covered in much greater depth elsewhere. Players are specifically directed to **Sky Galleons of Mars** and **Cloudships and Gunboats**, both of which provide rules for the design and construction of liftwood flyers usable with these rules. More exotic and improbable flying machines (such as gliders and aeroplanes) are covered by the invention rules in the basic role-playing game.

If players wish to build models of their flyers, the same general suggestions from the Ships section on page 86 apply here. A particularly valuable source of information as to the general look of many liftwood flyers is **Cloudships and Gunboats,** which includes detailed deck plans as well as many side views. Again, each grid square is equal to 1" on the model. A number of full-sized (1" per grid square), color deck plans are also provided, which can give you a quick feel for the final size of the model.

MECHANICAL VEHICLES

SEVERAL STOCK vehicle record forms are provided with this game. These stock vehicles can be used as is, or players can design their own juggernauts and tripods using the design sequence rules that follow.

Models should be built using the previously described guidelines, but you will want to build the models primarily out of plastic kit parts. Model tank and ship kits are particularly useful, and while much of the hull work will be made from sheet plastic, a good set of tank treads from a 1:48-scale or 1:35-scale tank are the essential basics of any juggernaut. Plastic or brass tubing, or hardwood dowel rods can form the basis for tripod legs, and a trip to the hardware store can supply the tripod's feet in the form of a variety of washers and wires to be superglued or epoxied together.

LAND JUGGERNAUT DESIGN SEQUENCE

1. Power Plant: The size of the power plant of a land juggernaut determines the overall size of the vehicle. Power plant size may be 1, 2, or 3 (referred to as the power plant number). In all cases, the maximum tonnage of the completed vehicle is its power plant number times 40. The power plant installed may be a conventional boiler or a forced draught boiler. Conventional boilers weigh six tons per power plant size number and cost £300 per power plant number. Forced draught boilers weigh three tons per power plant size number and cost £600 per power plant number.

If the vehicle is the invention of a player character from the role-playing game, the maximum power plant number is one-half of the reliability number, rounded down (but never below 1). Any power plant may be installed to which the inventor has access; the weights, costs, and fuel requirements of the various power plants are listed on page 66 of the role-playing rules book.

The power plant number of a land juggernaut is also its hull size.

2. Fuel Bunker: A boiler, whether it is of conventional or forced draught design, consumes one ton of coal per day per power plant number. A fuel bunker with a minimum of one day's fuel must be installed in the vehicle. This costs nothing, but it does increase the weight of the vehicle by the weight of the fuel.

If an inventor has installed a non-standard power plant, the minimum bunker size is determined by the fuel consumption of the engine actually installed. A gas turbine, for example, requires only one-quarter of a ton of fuel per day per power plant number, not a full ton.

3. Running Gear: Running gear for a land juggernaut includes the motors used to convert the energy generated by the steam engine into actual power, the endless track and its supporting suspension, and the complex gearboxes necessary to make the whole assembly function. Running gear weighs seven tons and costs £2000 per power plant number.

4. Armor: The armor plating on the hull of the juggernaut is fashioned from forged steel plates riveted to the girder framework of the vehicle's chassis. The larger the vehicle, the more steel is required to cover it. Armor weighs five tons and costs £500 per armor level per power plant number.

5. Armament: Any weapon listed on the gun lists (pages 172-175) may be mounted on a land juggernaut. The cost is as listed, while the weight is one-tenth of the listed design weight. Because of crew weights, no machinegun weighs less than one-half of a ton. (The listed design weight is for aerial and naval vessels and includes provisions not only for the gun and gun crew themselves, but also for very large magazines, gun hoists, crew quarters, and a large share of the general structural overhead of the vessel. Land juggernauts have smaller magazines and none of these other features.)

As each weapon is mounted, it must be allocated to a specific gun mount. The available gun mounts are bow, stern, right or left wing sponson, right or left forward sponson, right or left aft sponson, and right or left broadside. All of these gun positions are possible on each vehicle, except that a vehicle which has wing sponsons may not have forward or aft sponsons, and vice versa. Weapons mounted on the sides must be mounted in balanced pairs. That is, if the forward left sponson has a weapon weighing one ton, the forward right sponson must have a weapon weighing one ton as well.

6. Exotic Weapons: A land juggernaut may have a total of one tether mine mounted on it and as many rocket batteries as desired. Each tether mine has no weight and costs £200. Each rocket battery weighs one-half of a ton and costs £50. Each rocket battery is mounted to fire forward but may be manipulated from inside the vehicle to fire at ground targets or aerial targets.

Ratings

ONCE YOU HAVE FINISHED designing your vehicle, you need to evaluate it in terms of game statistics. Take a blank vehicle record form and fill it out as follows.

Description: Write the type (land juggernaut), total weight, and total price in the description block of the vehicle form. Write the power plant number in the hull size box. If several vehicles of the same type are involved in a battle, each should have its own form and the correct identification of the vehicle (its name or serial number) written on the I.D. line.

Movement: Divide the tonnage of the vehicle by its power plant number. If the result is 20 or less, the vehicle's movement rate is 3. If it is 30 or less, the movement rate is 2. If it is 40 or less, the movement rate is 1. If it is greater than 40, the vehicle is overweight and must be redesigned.

Fuel: Write down the total weight of fuel and its type (coal for conventional and forced draught boilers) in the correct space.

Fuel Consumption: Multiply the power plant number by the fuel consumption rate of the power plant (one for conventional and forced draught boilers). Write the result in the correct space.

Armor: All land juggernauts have an armor value of 1 for the running gear, so write a 1 in the RG box of the armor display. The armor level installed during the design sequence is the armor value for the hull; write that value in the H box of the armor display.

Running Gear Hits: All land juggernauts can suffer two running gear hits per movement rating, except for vehicles which have been invented by player characters according to the rules of the role-playing game. Invented vehicles can suffer running gear hits equal to their reliability rating for each movement rating.

Draw a line enclosing the total number of running gear hit boxes allowed, and black out the rest. For example, a vehicle with a movement rating of 2 and a reliability of 5 would have an enclosed area with two rows of five boxes each.

Command Crew: Each land juggernaut has a commander and a driver. Write C and D in the two boxes in the command crew display.

Engineering Crew: Each land juggernaut has one more engineer than its power plant number. Leave this many boxes open in the engineering crew display and black out the rest.

Armament: Draw a rough outline of the juggernaut in the space provided on the vehicle record form, and

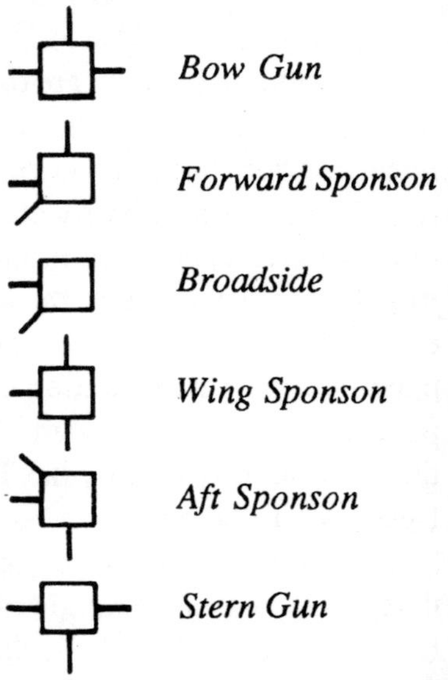

mark the location of the various weapons. Draw crew boxes next to each weapon equal to the number of gunners needed to man it. A vehicle-mounted gun requires half the number of men required to service a weapon in the field. A modern 4" long gun, for example, requires four crewmen as a field gun, and so would require only two crewmen if mounted in a vehicle.

Bow, stern, and wing sponson guns have 180-degree arcs of fire. Forward sponson guns have 135-degree arcs of fire: 90 degrees forward and 45 degrees aft. Aft sponson guns also have 135-degree arcs of fire, but in the reverse direction of the forward guns. Broadside guns have 90-degree arcs of fire: 45 degrees forward and 45 degrees aft.

Example: The example at the left is the standard land juggernaut described on page 69 of the role-playing game. It is also the British Army's *Truculent*-class land ship. The price and fuel consumption figures listed below supersede those listed in the basic game rules.

LAND JUGGERNAUT
(*TRUCULENT*-CLASS LAND SHIP)

Component	*Weight*	*Cost*
Power Plant Number: 1 (Forced Draught)	3	600
Fuel Bunker	1	0
Running Gear	7	2000
Armor: Level 3	15	1500
Armament		
Bow—1 20-pounder Gun	3	240
Wing Sponsons —2 Maxim Guns	1	300
Total	30	4640

For the ratings on this vehicle, see the vehicle record form for the HML (Her Majesty's Landship) *Truculent*.

COMBAT TRIPOD DESIGN SEQUENCE

1. Tripod Size: There are four tripod sizes available: small, medium, large, and very large. The size of the tripod determines the base weight and price of the mechanical portion of the tripod, how fast it moves, the weight of its armor (per armor level), and the maximum weight of additional components that may be added. All of these are summarized on the Tripod Design Chart below.

2. Armor: The armor column of the table indicates the weight of each level of armor for that particular size of tripod. Armor costs £100 per ton.

3. Armament: Any weapon listed on the gun lists (pages 172-175) may be mounted on a combat tripod. The cost is as listed, while the weight is one-tenth of the listed design weight. Because of crew weights, no machinegun weighs less than one-half of a ton. (The listed design weight is for aerial and naval vessels and includes provisions not only for the gun and gun crew themselves, but also for very large magazines, gun hoists, crew quarters, and a large share of the general structural overhead of the vessel. Combat tripods have smaller magazines and none of these other features.)

As each weapon is mounted, it must be allocated to a specific gun mount. The available gun mounts are bow, right sponson, or left sponson. All three of these gun positions are possible on each tripod. Weapons mounted in the sponsons must be mounted in balanced pairs. That is, if the left sponson has a weapon weighing one ton, the right sponson must have a weapon weighing one ton as well. No tripod can have more than three guns (one in each position).

4. Exotic Weapons: A combat tripod may have a total of one tether mine mounted on it and as many rocket batteries as component weight will allow. Each tether mine has no weight and costs £200. Each rocket battery weighs one-half ton and costs £50. Each rocket battery is mounted to fire forward, but may be manipulated from inside the tripod to fire at ground targets or aerial targets.

Ratings

ONCE YOU HAVE finished designing your vehicle, you need to evaluate it in terms of game statistics. Take a blank vehicle record form and fill it out as follows.

Description: Write the type (combat tripod), total weight, and total price in the description block of the vehicle form. If several vehicles of the same type are involved in a battle, each should have its own form and the correct identification of the vehicle (its name or serial number) written on the I.D. line. The base weight number of the tripod (1 for small, 2 for medium, etc.) is also the vehicle's hull size.

Movement: Consult the Tripod Design Chart below and note the correct movement number for the size of the tripod. Write the movement number in the correct space on the form.

Fuel: Write "one-half ton of coal" in the correct space.

Fuel Consumption: Write "1/2 ton per day" in the correct space.

Armor: All combat tripods have an armor value of 0 for the running gear, so write a 0 in the RG box of the armor display. The armor level installed during the design sequence is the armor value for the hull; write that in the H box of the armor display.

Running Gear Hits: All combat tripods can suffer one running gear hit per movement number, except for vehicles which have been invented by player characters according to the rules of the role-playing game. Invented vehicles can suffer running gear hits equal to half of their reliability rating (round fractions up) for each movement level.

Draw a line enclosing the total number of running gear hit boxes allowed, and black out the rest. For example, a heavy tripod (movement rating of 3) with a reliability of 4 would have an enclosed area with three rows of two boxes each.

Command Crew: Each tripod has a commander who also serves as the driver. Write C in one of the boxes in the command crew display, and black out the other one.

Engineering Crew: Tripods do not have an engineering crew; black this entire section out.

TRIPOD DESIGN CHART

Size	*Weight*	*Price*	*Move*	*Armor*	*Component*
S	1	700	5	1/2	1
M	2	1000	4	1	2
L	3	1500	3	1 1/2	4
VL	4	2500	2	2	8

Armament: Draw a rough outline of the tripod's hull in the space provided on the vehicle record form, and mark the location of the various weapons. Draw crew boxes next to each weapon equal to the number of gunners needed to man it. A vehicle-mounted gun requires half the number of men needed to service a weapon in the field. A modern 9-pounder gun, for example, requires four crewmen as a field gun, and so would require only two crewmen if mounted in a tripod.

Sponson guns have 180-degree arcs of fire. Bow guns and rockets may only fire directly to the front. However, the hull of the tripod itself has a 180-degree arc of traverse (90 degrees to the right and to the left of directly ahead), and this is the effective arc of the fixed armament.

Example: The following example is the standard tripod described on page 69 of the role-playing game. It is also the Imperial German Army's *Storch*-class light combat tripod. The price and fuel consumption figures listed below supersede those listed in the basic game rules.

Component	*Weight*	*Cost*
Frame (Light)	1	700
Armor	1 1/2	250
Armament		
2-pounder gun	1/2	260
Total	2	1210

For the ratings on this vehicle, see the vehicle record form for the PzKpfd (Panzer Kampfdreifuss, or armored battle tripod) *Storch*.

3

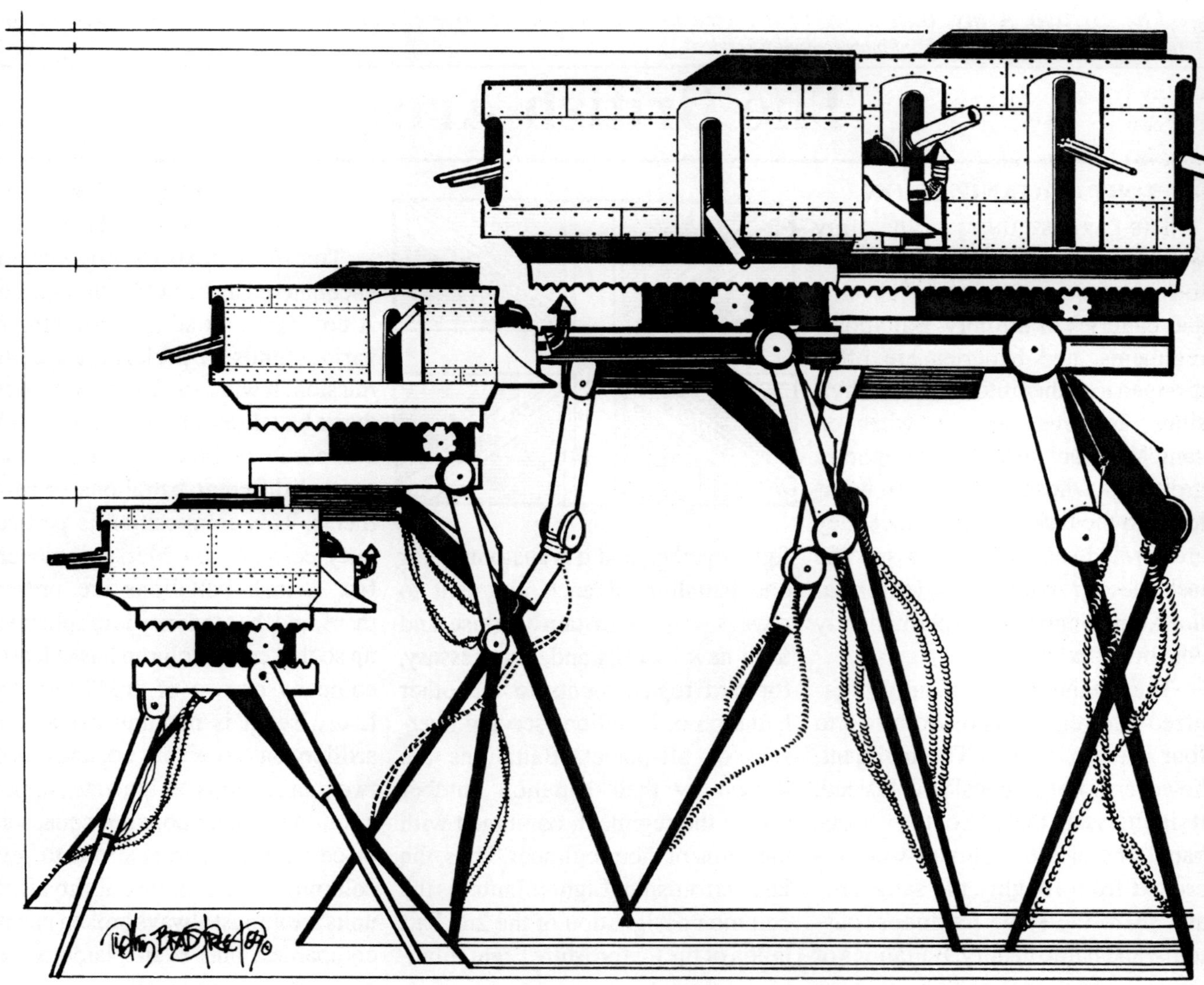

The British Army: *(Left to right.) Highland light infantry, Royal Horse Artillery, artillery, infantry (back view), infantry, naval landing party, infantry (colonial service).*

The British Army

UNIT ORGANIZATION

THE LARGEST UNITS in the army with a fixed organization are battalions of infantry, regiments of cavalry, and batteries of artillery. Battalions, regiments, and batteries are often grouped together into brigades, divisions, and even armies, when on campaign, but these are temporary groupings whose composition is tailored to the task at hand. Since they are formed especially for a specific task, these grouping are called *formations,* as opposed to permanently constituted *units*.

The infantry is nominally organized into regiments of from two to four battalions each. The regiment, however, is not a tactical unit. Instead, it signifies that the men of the various battalions of the regiment were recruited from roughly the same area and share the same traditions, customs, and battle history. Battalions of the same regiment seldom, if ever, fight together, and it is customary for one battalion of each regiment to always stay in Britain to raise and train new recruits and, if necessary, forward replacements to the other battalion or battalions serving overseas or off-planet. Battalions are known by their battalion number within the regiment, combined with the name of their regiment. Thus, the 2nd Oxfordshire Light Infantry is the common designation of the 2nd battalion of the Oxfordshire Light Infantry Regiment.

ORGANIZATION IN THE FIELD

THE MOST COMMON organization encountered in the field is the column. A column is an ad hoc grouping of various units to perform a specific mission. It will usually be no stronger than a battalion or two and is routinely composed of bits and pieces from several different battalions or regiments. This composition is particularly common on Mars, since very few British battalions are present there, and the tendency is to split them up so that every column has at least a company or two of "red" infantry. Likewise, it is not unusual to find artillery batteries split up, and one or two gun sections assigned to support a column, while troops and squadrons of cavalry are parceled out to give columns some scouting ability. Rifle units are almost always broken up into companies, and even platoons, for scouting duties as well.

BRITISH FIELD ARMY, 1887 (THE SHASTAPSH CAMPAIGN)

Commander: Major General Sir Henry Evelyn Wood, VC, GCMG, KCB[1]

Army Troops

A Troop, 10th Prince of Wales' Own Royal Hussars (cavalry)

No. 1 Company, Parhoon Sappers and Miners (Martian engineers)

No. 9 Battery, Royal Artillery (three sections, 12-pounder field guns[2])

No. 27 Battery, Royal Artillery (three sections, 12-pounder field guns)

No. 32 Battery, Royal Artillery (three sections, 12-pounder field guns)

No. 12 (Howitzer) Battery, Royal Artillery (three sections, 5" howitzers)

No. 1 Section, 19 Battery, Royal Artillery (one section .50-caliber Gatling guns)

No. 3 Battery, Parhoon Mountain Artillery (three sections, Martian 7-pounder mountain howitzers)

The Naval Brigade

Commander: Captain Oliver Stanton Randolf (Royal Navy)

Royal Marine Light Infantry (infantry battalion)

Johnson's Battery (two sections Hotchkiss 1-pounders)

Carstairs' Battery (two sections 5-barrel Nordenfelts)

Siege Battery (two 5" gun sections)

The Parhoonese (or Regency[3]) Brigade

Commander: Brigadier Robert Rollo Gillespie, CB

3rd King's Royal Rifle Corps (one wing only) (infantry)

The Parhoon Rifles (Martian infantry)

5th Parhoon Infantry (Martian infantry)

1st Gorovaangian Levies (Martian infantry)

Western (or Crown[4]) Brigade

Commander: Major General Sir George Stewart White, VC, KCB

C Company, 3rd King's Royal Rifle Corps (infantry)

1st South Wales Borderers (infantry)

2/3rd Martian Infantry {Avenel Rifles} (Martian infantry)

1/4th Martian Infantry (Martian infantry)

The Martian Guides (one squadron) (Martian cavalry)

The Eastern (or Trucial[5]) Brigade

Commander: Brigadier Charles Mansfield Clarke, CB

2nd Royal Highland Black Watch (infantry)

1st Meepsoor Fencibles (Martian infantry)

Strides in Glory {1st Moeris Lacus Foot} (Martian infantry)

Forward Shining Banners {3rd Moeris Lacus Foot} (Martian infantry)

Cavalry Brigade

Commander: Brigadier Sir Henry Peter Ewart, KCB

10th Prince of Wales' Own Royal Hussars (less A troop) (cavalry)

Governor-General's Escort (one squadron) (Martian cavalry)

1st Meepsoor Lancers (three squadrons (Martian cavalry)

Graham's Mounted Irregulars (one squadron) (Martian cavalry)

M Battery, Royal Horse Artillery (3 sections, 12-pounder field guns)

---

[1] Having broken his left leg shortly after his arrival, Major Gen. Wood led the expedition from the howdah of a ruumet breehr.

[2] In 1887 field batteries were equipped with 12-pounders, the new 15-pounders not yet available. All field batteries have since been reequipped.

[3] The Regency Brigade was so-called because the native troops forming the bulk of its strength were from Parhoon—not legally part of the crown colony but an independent state governed by a British regent in the name of its young ruler. All battalions in Parhoonese service were numbered consecutively, except the Parhoon Rifles, which formed a separate, elite battalion outside the normal sequence. Troops recruited from subjugated regions near Gorovaan were numbered separately.

[4] The Crown Brigade was so-called because its native troops were from the colonial establishment of the crown colony of Syrtis Major.

[5] The Trucial Brigade was so-called because its native trops were all drawn from the treaty dependencies on the eastern border of the colony. The parenthetical designations given for the two units from Moeris Lacus are those adopted in 1888 when the Moeris Lacus Army was reorganized along British lines.

When a mission demands a larger force than a column, a brigade is usually sent. A brigade consists of several battalions (up to five or six, but as few as two) and is commanded by either a brigadier or a major general. If no brigadier or major general is available, the brigade is commanded by the senior officer present. Normally a brigade will consist of troops of the same arm (infantry or cavalry) with only one or two other small attached units to support it. For example, an infantry brigade might consist of three battalions of infantry with one cavalry squadron and one artillery battery attached to it.

Missions which require forces in excess of a brigade are assigned to an army. An army consists of several brigades. If four or more brigades are included in the army, the brigades will generally be grouped into divisions of two brigades each. If four or more divisions are included in the army, the divisions will generally be divided into corps of two divisions each.

UNITS OF THE BRITISH ARMY

THE FOLLOWING is a complete listing of all active units in the British Army. Facing colors are given in brackets after the name of the regiment. The parenthetical notations F and VF indicate fashionable and very fashionable regiments and are of interest primarily in conjunction with the role-playing game. Unit values are shown following the notation *UV:*, with the letter indicating troop quality (*E:* Elite, *V:* Veteran, *X:* Experienced, *T:* Trained, *G:* Green) and the number indicating the unit's Fieldcraft modifier. Units with the additional notation S are sharpshooters, while those with the additional notation H are heavy cavalry.

Finally, the major campaign honors for the period from 1860 to the present (1889) are given in parentheses following the unit value. The following abbreviations are used:

AB: Abyssinian War (1867-70)
AF: Second Afghan War (1878-80)
AS: Second Ashanti War (1873-74)
BL: Bechuanaland (1884)
BR: Third Burma War (1885-7)
CH: Third China War (1860)
EG: Egypt (1882)
NWF: Northwest Frontier (1888)
NZ: Maori War in New Zealand (1868-70)
PS: Second War of the Parhoon Succession (1880)
SD: Sudan (1884-5)
SI: Sikkim Expedition (1888)
ST: Shastapsh Expedition (1887)
SU: Suakin Expedition (1888)
ZU: Zululand Uprising (1888)
ZW: Zulu War (1879)

Infantry Regiments

The Brigade of Guards

EACH REGIMENT has two battalions, except the Grenadier Guards, which has three battalions.

Grenadier Guards (VF) [blue] *UV:* E0 (EG, SD)

Coldstream Guards (VF) [blue] *UV:* E0 (EG, SD)

Scots Fusilier Guards (VF) [blue] *UV:* E0 (EG, SD)

Infantry of the Line

ALL REGIMENTS have two battalions, except for the King's Royal Rifle Corps and the Rifle Brigade, which have four battalions each. The initial number is a regiment's old number in the seniority lists. Although these are no longer officially used, all officers and men still think in terms of the old numbers as well as the new names of the regiments. Facing colors indicate the nationality of regiments, except for the royal regiments, which have blue facings. For other regiments the coding is white for English and Welsh, yellow for Scottish, and green for Irish. A few regiments (such as the Buffs and the older rifle regiments) have unique facing colors.

1 Royal Scots (F) [blue] *UV:* V1 (CH, BL, ZU)

2 Queen's Royal West Surrey (F) [blue] *UV:* V1 (CH, BR)

3 Buffs (F) [buff] *UV:* V1 (CH, ZW)

4 King's Own Royal Lancaster (F) [blue] *UV:* V1 (AB, ZW)

5 Northumberland Fusiliers (F) [white] *UV:* V1 (AF, NWF)

6 Royal Warwickshire (F) [blue] *UV:* X1

7 Royal Fusiliers (F) [blue] *UV:* V1 (AF)

8 King's Liverpool [blue] *UV:* V1 (AF, BR)

9 Norfolk [white] *UV:* V1 (AF, BR)

10 Lincolnshire [white] *UV:* X1

11 Devonshire [white] *UV:* V1 (AF)

12 Suffolk [white] *UV:* V1 (AF, NWF, NZ)

13 Somerset Light Infantry (F) [blue] *UV:* V2 (SD, BR, ZW)

14 West Yorkshire [white] *UV:* V1 (AF, NZ)

15 East Yorkshire [white] *UV:* V1 (AF, NZ)

16 Bedfordshire [white] *UV:* X1

17 Leicestershire [white] *UV:* V1 (AF, BR)

18 Royal Irish [blue] *UV:* V1 (AF, EG, SD, NWF, NZ)

19 Yorkshire [white] *UV:* V1 (SD)

20 Lancashire Fusiliers (F) [white]

UV: X1

21 Royal Scots Fusiliers (F) [blue] *UV:* V1 (SD, BR, ZW)

22 Cheshire [white] *UV:* V1 (BR)

23 Royal Welsh Fusiliers (F) [blue] *UV:* V1 (AS, BR)

24 South Wales Borderers [white] *UV:* V1 (BR, ST, ZW)

25 King's Own Scottish Borderers [blue] *UV:* V1 (AF, SU)

26 Scottish Rifles [dark green] *UV:* V3S (AB, ZW)

27 Royal Inniskilling Fusiliers (F) [blue] *UV:* V1 (ZU)

28 Gloucestershire [white] *UV:* X1

29 Worcestershire [white] *UV:* X1

30 East Lancashire [white] *UV:* V1 (AF)

31 East Surrey [white] *UV:* V1 (AF, CH, NZ, SD)

32 Duke of Cornwall's Light Infantry (F) [white] *UV:* V2 (EG, SD)

33 West Riding [white] *UV:* V1 (AB)

34 Borderers [white] *UV:* X1

35 Royal Sussex [blue] *UV:* V1 (EG, SD, NWF)

37 Hampshire [white] *UV:* V1 (AF, BR, CH)

38 South Staffordshire [white] *UV:* V1 (EG, SD, ZW)

39 Dorset [white] *UV:* X1

40 South Lancashire [white] *UV:* V1 (NZ)

41 Welsh [white] *UV:* V1 (SU)

42 Royal Highland (Black Watch) (F) [blue] *UV:* E1 (AS, EG, SD, ST)

43 Oxford Light Infantry (F) [white] *UV:* V2 (NZ)

44 Essex [white] *UV:* V1 (CH, SD)

45 Sherwood Foresters [white] *UV:* V1 (AB, EG, SK)

47 North Lancashire [white] *UV:* V1 (AF)

48 Northamptonshire [white] *UV:* V1 (NZ, ZW)

49 Royal Berkshire [blue] *UV:* V1 (AF, EG, SD)

50 Royal West Kent [blue] *UV:* V1 (EG, NZ, SD)

51 King's Own Yorkshire Light Infantry (F) [blue] *UV:* V2 (AF, BR)

53 Shropshire Light Infantry (F) [blue] *UV:* V2 (AF, EG, SD)

57 Middlesex [white] *UV:* V1 (NZ, ZW)

60 King's Royal Rifle Corps (VF) [scarlet] *UV:* E3S (AF, BR, CH, EG, SD, ST, ZW)

62 Wiltshire [white] *UV:* V1 (CH, NZ, ZW)

63 Manchester [white] *UV:* V1 (AF, EG, NZ)

64 North Staffordshire [white] *UV:* V1 (ZU)

65 York and Lancaster [white] *UV:* V1 (EG, NZ, SD)

68 Durham Light Infantry [white] *UV:* V2 (NZ, SD)

71 Highland Light Infantry (F) [yellow] *UV:* V2 (EG)

72 Seaforth Highlanders (F) [yellow] *UV:* E1 (AF, EG, NWF)

75 Gordon Highlanders (VF) [yellow] *UV:* E1 (AF, EG, SD)

79 Queen's Own Cameron Highlanders (F) [blue] *UV:* E1 (EG, SD)

83 Royal Irish Rifles [dark green] *UV:* X3S

87 Royal Irish Fusiliers [blue] *UV:* V1 (EG, SD)

88 Connaught Rangers [green] *UV:* V1 (SD, ZW)

91 Argyll and Sutherland Highlanders [yellow] *UV:* E1 (ZW)

100 Leinster [blue] *UV:* X1

101 Royal Munster Fusiliers [blue] *UV:* V1 (BR)

102 Royal Dublin Fusiliers [blue] *UV:* X1

The Rifle Brigade (F) [black] *UV:* E3S (AF, AS, SD, BR)

Cavalry Regiments

ALL FASHIONABLE unless marked.

The Household Cavalry

1st Life Guards (VF) [dark blue] *UV:* V0H

2nd Life Guards (VF) [dark blue] *UV:* V0H

Royal Horse Guards {The Blues} (VF) [red] *UV:* V0H

The regiments of the household cavalry never take the field as a whole. However, it is customary in time of war to make up a composite regiment of three squadrons (one per regiment) and send it instead. This composite force is always referred to as The Household Cavalry Regiment.

The Household Cavalry Regiment *UV:* V0H (EG, SD)

The Dragoon Guards

1 (King's) Dragoon Guards [blue] *UV:* V0H (CH, ZW)

2 (Queen's) Dragoon Guards [buff] *UV:* V0H (SD)

3 (Prince of Wales') Dragoon Guards [yellow] *UV:* V0H (AB)

4 (Royal Irish) Dragoon Guards [blue] *UV:* V0H (EG, SD)

5 (Princess Charlotte of Wales') Dragoon Guards [green] *UV:* V0H (SD)

6 Dragoon Guards (Carabiniers) [white] *UV:* V0H (AF)

7 (Princess Royal's) Dragoon Guards [black] *UV:* V0H (EG)

The Cavalry of the Line

1 (Royal) Dragoons [blue] *UV:* V0H (SD)

2 Dragoons (Royal Scots Greys) [blue] *UV:* V0H (SD)

3 (The King's Own) Hussars [blue] *UV:* V1 (SD)

4 (The Queen's Own) Hussars

[yellow] *UV:* V1 (SD)

5 (Royal Irish) Lancers [red] *UV:* V1 (SD)

6 (Inniskilling) Dragoons [yellow] *UV:* V0H (BL, ZU)

7 (The Queen's Own) Hussars [red] *UV:* V1 (SD)

8 (The King's Royal Irish) Hussars [red] *UV:* V1 (AF)

9 (The Queen's Royal) Lancers [red] *UV:* V1 (AF)

10 (The Prince of Wales' Own Royal) Hussars [red] *UV:* V1 (AF, SD, ST)

11 (Prince Albert's Own) Hussars (VF) [crimson] *UV:* V1 (SD)

12 (The Prince of Wales' Royal) Lancers [red] *UV:* V1

13 Hussars [buff] *UV:* V1

14 (The King's) Hussars [yellow] *UV:* V1

15 (The King's) Hussars (VF) [red] *UV:* V1 (AF, SD)

16 (The Queen's) Lancers [blue] *UV:* V1 (SD)

17 (Duke of Cambridge's Own) Lancers (VF) [white] *UV:* V1 (ZW)

18 Hussars [blue] *UV:* V1 (SD)

19 (The Princess of Wales' Own) Hussars [white] *UV:* V1 (EG, SD)

20 Hussars [crimson] *UV:* V1 (SD)

21 Lancers [gray] *UV:* V1 (SD)

Other Regiments

Royal Marine Light Infantry [dark blue] *UV:* V1

Royal Marine Artillery [red] *UV:* V0

Royal Artillery [red] *UV:* V0

Royal Horse Artillery [red] *UV:* V0

Royal Engineers [dark blue] *UV:* V2

Royal Navy

Naval parties serving guns *UV:* V0

Naval parties fighting as infantry *UV:* X0

UNIFORMS

Line Infantry: *Headgear:* Plain white or khaki Sun helmet, sometimes replaced by a dark blue glengarry. *Jacket:* Red with collar and cuffs in the facing color (see pages 94-95 for facing colors of the regiments). Often (but not always) plain khaki on campaign (no facing distinctions). *Pants:* With a red jacket, dark blue with red stripe down the outside seam. With a khaki jacket, plain khaki pants. Pants worn tucked into brown leather leggings over black boots. *Equipment:* White leather. Officers wear a brown leather Sam Brown belt.

Rifles: *Headgear:* As line infantry, but helmet was rifle green. For colonial service, khaki was usually worn. *Jacket:* Rifle green with collar and cuffs in the facing color. For colonial service a plain khaki jacket instead. *Pants:* Rifle green with a black stripe down the outside seam. For colonial service, plain khaki pants. Pants worn tucked into black leather leggings over black boots. *Equipment:* Black leather. Officers wear a black leather Sam Brown belt.

Highlanders: *Headgear:* Same as line infantry. *Jacket:* Same as infantry. *Kilt:* Kilt with sporran worn both at home and on campaign, and with both the red jacket and the khaki. Instead of boots, black shoes with white leggings over long, red and white, checked stockings were worn with the red jacket. Khaki leggings were worn with the khaki jacket. *Equipment:* Same as line infantry.

Marine Light Infantry: *Headgear:* White tropical helmet with brass plate and chin scales. *Jacket:* Dark blue with dark blue collar and cuffs. *Pants:* As line infantry. *Equipment:* As line infantry.

Cavalry: The full dress uniforms of the various regiments of cavalry were spectacular, but no longer worn in the field. Instead, cavalry wore essentially the same uniform as line infantry (white helmet, red jacket with collar and cuffs in facing colors, blue trousers with red stripe, or sometimes helmet, jacket and pants all in khaki). In the light cavalry (hussars and lancers) the jacket was blue instead of red. Three exceptions to this pattern of red for the heavies and blue for the lights were: The Royal Horse Guards and 6th Dragoon Guards, blue jackets; and 16th Lancers, red. Other major differences between infantry and cavalry uniforms were that cavalry wore taller boots with spurs, and generally wore a brown leather cartridge bandolier over their other equipment.

Royal Artillery: *Headgear:* As line infantry. *Jacket:* Dark blue with red collar. Cuffs and shoulder straps were dark blue with red piping. Khaki was sometimes worn on campaign. *Pants:* Dark blue with a red stripe down the outside seam. Sometimes wore khaki on campaign. Pants were tucked into black boots. *Equipment:* White leather. Officers wore a brown leather Sam Brown belt.

Royal Horse Artillery: The Royal Horse Artillery wore an elaborate variation of the Hussar uniform for full dress and home service, but on campaign, exclusively wore khaki at this time. Uniform was the same as for Royal Artillery.

Royal Marine Artillery: *Headgear:* White Sun helmet with brass plate and chin scales. *Jacket:* Dark blue with collar and cuffs in red. *Pants:* As Royal Artillery. *Equipment:* Black leather. Officers wore a black leather Sam Brown belt.

Engineers: As line infantry.

Naval Officer: *Headgear:* Dark blue cap with black brim. *Jacket:* Dark blue double-breasted coat. *Pants:* Dark blue. *Equipment:* Black leather.

Naval Rating: *Headgear:* Dark blue sailor's hat with black band. In summer and tropical climates, a broad straw hat. *Jacket:* Dark blue jumper (white in the summer or tropics) with a wide, light blue collar. *Pants:* Dark blue. White in summer and the tropics. *Equipment:* Black leather.

Other Uniform Items: *Patrol Jacket:* Officers in all services often wore the patrol jacket in place of either the standard uniform jacket or the khaki jacket when in the field. The patrol jacket was dark blue (almost black) with black lace. *Glengarry:* The casual cap worn by other ranks (and sometimes by officers as well) was a dark blue glengarry, and it was sometimes worn in the field in place of the helmet. *Puttees:* Shoes with khaki, gray, or blue-gray puttees were often worn in place of boots with the khaki campaign uniform. *Neck Cloth:* A khaki neck cloth was often worn with the khaki helmet in tropical climates. *Shirt:* The standard shirt was a gray flannel pullover with a narrow, white, stand-up collar. When on fatigue duty, the jacket was removed, and the soldier worked in his shirtsleeves. White braces (suspenders) were worn over the shirt.

Rank Distinctions: NCO chevrons were "V" shaped and displayed with the points down. They were in white on red jackets, khaki outlined in black on khaki jackets, and in black for rifle regiments (whether wearing green or khaki). Chevrons were worn on both sleeves midway between the shoulder and elbow. The various non-commissioned officer ranks were distinguished as follows:

Corporal/Bombardier: Two chevrons

Sergeant: Three chevrons

Colour Sergeant: Three chevrons with crossed colours and a crown

Sergeant Major: Four chevrons

When wearing the red jacket, officers' collars and cuffs were outlined in gold, and shoulder straps were replaced with twisted gold cord. Collar and cuff outlining and twisted shoulder cords were in black on the green jackets of the rifle regiments and on patrol jackets. Khaki officers' jackets were essentially identical to those for other ranks.

Officer ranks were distinguished by silver rank insignia on the shoulder straps or twisted shoulder cords:

Lieutenant: One star

Captain: Two stars

Major: One crown

Lieutenant Colonel: One star, one crown

Colonel: Two stars, one crown

Brigadier: Crossed sword, baton

Major General: Crossed sword, baton, one star

Lieutenant General: Crossed sword, baton, one crown

General: Crossed sword, baton, one star, one crown

Field Marshal: Crossed sword, baton, two stars, one crown

WEAPONS

Infantry: All officers carry sabers and revolvers. Other ranks carry a breech-loading rifle and a bayonet. The Brigade of Guards, the Rifle Brigade, the King's Royal Rifle Corps, and all battalions deployed on Mars have been equipped with the Lee-Metford bolt-action rifle instead.

Cavalry: All ranks carry a saber and revolver. Enlisted men also carry a breech-loading carbine and, in lancer regiments, a lance.

Engineers: Officers carry sabers and revolvers. Other ranks carry a breech-loading rifle and a bayonet.

Artillery: Officers carry sabers and revolvers. Other ranks carry a breech-loading carbine and a bayonet instead, although these are usually left with the gun limber. Field batteries are equipped with the 15-pounder field gun. Royal Horse Artillery batteries are equipped with the 12-pounder field gun. Position batteries use either the 40-pounder gun or the 5" howitzer, while mountain batteries use the 7-pounder mountain howitzer or the 6-pounder gun. Machinegun sections manned by Royal Artillery gunners are equipped with .50-caliber Gatling guns.

Royal Navy: Many land expeditions include a Naval Brigade, which is often little more than a battery or two protected by a force of marines, ranging in strength from a company to a battalion. Marines and sailors are armed as infantry or artillery, depending on their role. Naval gunners are generally used to man machineguns, or machine cannon on field carriages, or big naval guns used in sieges. Naval machineguns include Gardners, three-barrel Nordenfelts, and five-barrel Nordenfelts. Machine cannons include Hotchkiss 1-pounder revolvers. The most common naval gun used in siege work is the 5" gun. (This is actually a modern 4.7" gun, but we have labeled it a 5" gun to avoid confusion with the low-power 4.7" or the high-power 4.7" quick-firing gun.)

Martian Colonial Troops: *(Left to right.) Infantry, cavalry, engineer.*

The Martian Colonial Establishment

UNIT ORGANIZATION

Units in the Martian Colonial Establishment include three nominally distinct types of units: colonial, regency, and trucial. Colonial units are those raised in the British colony itself and which are legally a part of the Imperial armed forces. Regency units are those raised from Parhoonese territory and which are nominally independent. Trucial units are those raised in Meepsoor and Moeris Lacus, which are treaty dependencies of the British Crown, and which thus come under British control by treaty arrangement. In fact, all three types of units are organized and equipped identically.

Battalions of Martian infantry are organized similarly, except that there is never more than one British officer in a company. Two companies in the battalion are commanded by lieutenants, one by a captain, and one by a major. All officers (including the surgeon and quartermaster) are British; each company also has one British sergeant. The battalion does not have an ensign, but instead has a British sergeant major in addition to the native sergeant major. All other ranks are native. There is usually, in addition, a native surgeon with the battalion.

Martian infantry battalions are generally designated in the same manner as British battalions. For example, the 3rd Queen's Own Martian Rifles is the designation of the 3rd Battalion of the Queen's Own Regiment of Martian Rifles. Regular Martian native line infantry regiments, however, are generally numbered instead of named, and thus battalions are designated by two numbers separated by a slash. For example, the 1/5th (spoken "first fifth") Martian Infantry designates the first battalion of the 5th Regiment of Martian Infantry.

Martian cavalry is organized similar to British cavalry, but the number of squadrons in a regiment may vary from only one (The Governor-General's Escort) to as many as four (1st Meepsoor Lancers). All officers are British, and other ranks are native.

Martian field and mountain batteries are organized the same as British batteries, except that instead of three officers there are only two (a captain and a lieutenant), both of whom are British, along with a British staff sergeant in addition to the Martian staff sergeant. The battery quartermaster is British as well, and all other ranks are Martian.

UNITS IN THE MARTIAN ESTABLISHMENT

Infantry

Martian Colonial Infantry

Two battalions each:

1 Infantry (Syrtis Major) [white]

UV: T1

2 Infantry (Haat and Syrtis Major) [buff] *UV:* T1

3 Infantry (Avenel) {The Avenel Rifles} [dark green] *UV:* T2S

4 Infantry (Syrtis Major and Avenel) [dark blue] *UV:* T1

5 Infantry (Syrtis Major) [light blue] *UV:* T1

6 Infantry (Haat and Syrtis Major) [red] *UV:* T1

Parhoonese Infantry

Queen's Own Martian Rifles {The Parhoon Rifles} [dark blue]

1 Battalion *UV:* E3S

2, 3 Battalions *UV:* V3S

1 Parhoon Infantry (two battalions) [white] *UV:* X2

2 Parhoon Infantry (two battalions) [red] *UV:* X2

3 Parhoon Infantry (two battalions) [green] *UV:* X2

Gorovaangian Levies (four battalions) [none] *UV:* T1

Meepsoori Infantry

The Meepsoor Fencibles (three battalions) [none] *UV:* X2

The Anwaakaan Guard (one battalion) [red] *UV:* V2

Moeris Lacus Infantry

(All of these are one-battalion regiments.)

1 Foot [red] *UV:* T2

2 Foot [blue] *UV:* T2

3 Foot [white] *UV:* T2

4 Foot [violet] *UV:* T2

5 Foot [yellow] *UV:* T2

Cavalry

Martian Colonial Cavalry

Martian Guides (two squadrons) [yellow] *UV:* E3S

Governor General's Escort (one squadron) [blue] *UV:* X1

Graham's Irregulars (one squadron) [none] *UV:* T3

Mounted Constabulary (four squadrons) [red] *UV:* T1

Parhoonese Cavalry

Parhoon Light Dragoons (two squadrons) [red] *UV:* T1

Parhoon Guides (one squadron) [yellow] *UV:* X2

Meepsoori Cavalry

1 Meepsoor Lancers (four squadrons) [red] *UV:* E2

2 Meepsoor Lancers (two squadrons) [black] *UV:* X2

Moeris Lacus Cavalry

Moeris Lacus Dragoons (three squadrons) *UV:* T1

1 squadron [green]

2 squadron [orange]

3 squadron [black]

Other Branches

Colonial Troops

Martian Garrison Artillery [black] *UV:* T0

Martian Field Artillery [red] *UV:* T0

Martian Sappers and Miners [blue] *UV:* T1

Parhoonese Troops

Parhoon Garrison Artillery [khaki] *UV:* T0

Parhoon Mountain Artillery [black] *UV:* X1

Parhoon Engineers [red] *UV:* X3

Meepsoori Troops

Meepsoor Artillery [black] *UV:* T0

Moeris Lacus Troops

Moeris Lacus Artillery [red] *UV:* T0

UNIFORMS

Martian Native Infantry: *Headgear:* A loose Martian turban in white with black or red stripes for Meepsoor (black for the Fencibles, red for the Guard), green for Moeris Lacus, rifle green for the Parhoon Rifles and Avenel Rifles, red for other Parhoon infantry, and khaki for all others. *Jacket:* Khaki jacket (rifle green for the Parhoon Rifles) with collar and cuffs in facing color. Cuff design in black lace. Battalions of the Meepsoor Fencibles and Gorovaangian Levies are differentiated by the battalion number in black worn on the shoulder strap. *Pants:* Khaki (rifle green for the Parhoon Rifles) with a facing color stripe down the outside seam, tucked into leggings worn above sandals. *Equipment:* White leather (black leather in rifles). *Officers and NCOs:* All British officers and NCOs wear standard infantry or rifle uniforms, usually khaki.

Martian Native Cavalry: *Headgear:* A brass, spiked helmet (steel for the Meepsoor Lancers). The loose Martian turban wrapped around it is yellow with black stripes for the Martian Guides, blue for the Governor-General's Escort, white with black stripes for the Meepsoor Lancers, green for Moeris Lacus, red for Parhoon (and Parhoon Guides), and khaki for others. *Jacket:* Khaki with cuffs and collar in the facing color. *Pants:* Khaki with a facing color stripe down the outer seam. *Equipment:* White leather, with a brown leather cartridge bandolier over it. *Officers and NCOs:* All British officers and NCOs wear standard cavalry uniforms, usually khaki.

Martian Native Artillery: *Head-*

gear: A brass spiked helmet with a loose khaki Martian turban wrapped around the outside. *Jacket:* Khaki with red collars and cuffs. Cuff design in black lace. *Pants:* As Martian infantry, but with a red stripe on the outside seam. *Equipment:* White leather. *Officers and NCOs:* British officers and NCOs wear standard artillery uniforms, usually khaki.

Martian Native Engineers: *Headgear:* Black leather cap with peak and neck flap. *Jacket:* Khaki, with cuff design in black lace. *Pants:* As for infantry. *Equipment:* Black leather. *Officers and NCOs:* All British officers and NCOs wear standard engineer uniforms, usually khaki.

WEAPONS

Infantry: All officers carry sabers and revolvers. Other ranks carry a rifle musket and bayonet. The Queen's Own Martian Rifles and Avenel Rifles have breech-loading rifles.

Cavalry: Officers carry a saber and revolver. Other ranks carry sabers and rifle musket carbines. Lancer regiments also carry a lance. The Martian and Parhoon Guides carry breech-loading carbines.

Engineers: Officers carry sabers and revolvers. Other ranks carry rifle muskets and bayonets.

Artillery: Officers carry sabers and revolvers. Other ranks carry rifle musket carbines and bayonets, although usually they are left with the gun limber. Parhoon Mountain Artillery has 6-pounder guns or 7-pounder mountain howitzers. Other colonial artillery has traditional Martian ordnance.

Other Colonial Troops: *(Left to right.) Canadian militia (Amazonian), West Indies Regiment, African levy, Victoria Mounted Rifle, New South Wales Lancer.*

Other Colonial Units

WEST INDIES REGIMENT

Organization: Along British lines, with British officers and all other ranks native. One battalion was usually stationed in the West Indies (the Carribean), the other on the west coast of Africa, usually in Nigeria. Served in the Ashanti War. *UV:* X2.

Weapons: European officers carry revolvers and sabers. Native other ranks carry breech-loading rifles and bayonets.

Uniform: *Headgear:* White turban *Jacket:* Red zouave-style vest with yellow braid worn over a white, long-sleeved waistcoat. *Pants:* Baggy, blue, zouave pants with red stripes tucked into French-style, white gaiters over black shoes. *Equipment:* White leather.

GOLD COAST HAUSAS

Organization: Organized along British lines, with British officers and native other ranks. One battalion strong, with companies in the Gold Coast and Nigeria. *UV:* X2.

Weapons: European officers carry revolvers and sabers. Native other ranks carry breech-loading rifles and bayonets.

Uniform: *Headgear:* Low, dark blue fez. *Jacket:* Light blue zouave-style vest with red lace worn over a light blue, long-sleeved waistecoat with dark blue collar. *Pants:* Baggy, dark blue zouave pants tucked into French-style, white gaiters over black shoes. *Equipment:* White leather.

AFRICAN IRREGULARS

Organization: Individual companies, usually with only one or two European officers and all other ranks native. *UV:* T2.

Weapons: Officers carry revolvers and sabers. Other ranks carry muskets or rifle-muskets and bayonets.

Uniform: Civilian clothes with some common uniform element. This element would usually be a colored armband or headband but could also be a colored cloth hat or even an old uniform jacket or fatigue cap.

HONG KONG VOLUNTEERS

Organization: An enlarged artillery battery with five gun sections. All ranks were European volunteers from the Hong Kong colony. *UV:* T0.

Weapons: Officers carry revolvers and sabers. Other ranks carry breech-loading carbines and bayonets. Three gun sections have 6-pounder guns and two with Maxims.

Uniform: *Headgear:* Khaki Sun helmet. *Jacket:* Khaki with large bullet loops stitched above the breast pockets. *Pants:* Khaki tucked into blue leggings worn over black shoes. *Equipment:* Brown leather.

AUSTRALIA

AUSTRALIA DID NOT, at this time, consist of a single government, but rather comprised five separate and independent states: Queensland, Victoria, New South Wales, South Australia, Western Australia, and Tasmania.

Organization: All of these states maintained small standing forces, mostly garrison infantry and fortress gunners in the major seaport towns. All of these have *UV:* X0.

Each state also maintains one company of regular light horse or one squadron of lancers. These are the Upper Clarence Light Horse (Queensland), New South Wales Lancers, Victoria Mounted Rifles (light horse), South Australia Lancers, Western Australian Mounted Infantry (light horse), and Tasmanian First Light Cavalry (light horse). All of these have *UV:* V2S. In times of crisis, additional companies were raised and named after the state in which they were raised along with the description "mounted rifles," "mounted infantry," "light horse," or "bushmen," all of which amount to about the same thing. All of these units have *UV:* X2.

Uniform: Uniforms were invariably a brownish khaki. Headgear was a distinctive khaki bush hat with one side pinned up. Lancers wear a khaki jacket with red collar, shoulder straps, cuffs, and plastron, and khaki trousers tucked into brown cavalry boots. The New South Wales Lancers wear a bush hat with green feathers on the side; the South Australia Lancers wear a khaki Sun helmet with a silver spike and badge.

Weapons: All officers carry revolvers and sabers. All other ranks carry breech-loading rifles and bayonets. Lancers (except officers) also carry a lance when mounted.

NEW ZEALAND

NEW ZEALAND maintains a small permanent garrison force, just as the Australian states. In the event of hostilities, companies of mounted rifles were raised. Uniforms, equipment, and unit values were the same as for Australia.

ADOPTION OF THE LEE-METFORD RIFLE

ENGLAND HAS LATELY adopted a small-bore—0.303-inch calibre—modified Lee magazine rifle...after making a long series of most amusing steps of development in order to reach the conclusion that this arm was suited to her needs. For some years she has been more than content with her famous 0.45-inch calibre single-loading Martini-Henry rifles and Boxer cartridges—guns almost as bad in principle of breech mechanism as our own Springfields, and cartridges even worse than the United States' regulation ones—and in her late "wars with people who wear not the trousers," her soldiers have gallantly fired on the enemy when they knew full well what a horrible punishment they were to receive from the brutal recoil of their weapons, and have borne their torture with true English grit. An English officer informed the writer that the practice was a great aid to gallantry in battle in South Africa, for "when a fellow has been so brutally pounded by his own rifle half a hundred times, he doesn't so much mind having an assegai as big as a shovel stuck through him; it's rather a relief, don't you know."

(Reprinted from "The Small Arms of European Armies," W. W. Kimball, *Scribner's Magazine*, September 1889.)

The Indian Army: *(Left to right.) Gurkha rifleman, line cavalry, line infantry.*

The Indian Army

THE INDIAN ARMY was strictly under British control, and could properly be covered as part of the British Army. Its sheer size and organizational quirks make it worthwhile to consider it as a separate entity. The Indian Army was divided into four separate and independent armies, as well as a number of auxiliary units. Officially there were the three Presidency Armies and the Punjab Frontier Force, but, for the sake of convenience, all four will be referred to as armies. The names of the armies and their areas of principal responsibility were as follows:

Madras: Southern India and Burma

Bengal: Eastern India

Bombay: Western India, including Sind, Aden, and Quetta

Punjab Frontier Force: Punjab and the Northwest Frontier

All four armies reported to the commander-in-chief in India, and while by 1889 supply and administrative services were pooled on a subcontinent-wide basis, each army tended to operate as a separate organization whenever possible. Promotion lists were kept on an army basis, for example, with the result that an officer's chance of promotion depended on which army he was serving in.

In the event of a major conflict, troops could and would be sent from any command to the scene of action, with the result that one could find elements of all four armies serving in the same area. The best example of this happened in the 2nd Afghan War (1878-1880) when units of all four Armies ended up in action together on the Northwest Frontier.

UNIT ORGANIZATION

ALL INDIAN INFANTRY regiments (with the except of several Gurkha regiments dealt with below) consisted of a single battalion, which was organized as a standard battalion with the following changes:

Each company had 20 men. One of these (the commander) was a British officer. The four company commanders for the battalion included one British major, one British captain, and two British lieutenants. The other two officers in the company were an Indian first lieutenant and an Indian second lieutenant.

The battalion staff was similar to that of a British battalion, except that it included two surgeons, instead of one. The regimental commander and adjutant were British (a lieutenant colonel and a captain), as was the quartermaster and one of the surgeons. Instead of a sergeant major, the battalion had a subedar major, who ranked as the senior Indian officer in the battalion, but was still outranked by the British lieutenants. The ensign was an Indian second lieutenant.

Cavalry regiments were larger than their British counterparts, and were organized with three squadrons instead of two. The squadron was organized normally, except that there was one British officer in each squadron, along with an Indian first lieutenant and an Indian second lieutenant. All other ranks in the squadron were Indians. The regiment had one British major, one British captain, and one British lieutenant acting as squadron commanders. The regimental staff was identical to that of a normal cavalry regiment, except that instead of a sergeant major, the regiment had an Indian rissaldar major, who was the senior Indian officer of the regiment (but, again, was outranked by British lieutenants). The regiment's commander, adjutant, quartermaster, veterinarian, and surgeon were British. The rissaldar major, trumpet major, and blacksmith were Indian.

Indian mountain artillery was organized as a normal battery, but all officers were British.

Below is a list of Indian Army ranks and their British equivalents.

UNITS OF THE INDIAN ARMY

Madras Army

ONCE CONSIDERED to produce the best troops in India, by 1889 the Madras forces had gained a reputation for being the poorest of the combat troops.

Infantry Regiments: The infantry consists of 32 regiments of one battalion each, numbered from 1 to 17 and from 19 to 33. *UV:* T1 (except as noted below).

Three battalions were trained as light infantry: 3rd (Palamcottah) Madras Light Infantry, 23rd (Wallajahbad) Madras Light Infantry, and 31st (Trichinopoly) Madras Light Infantry. *UV:* T2.

Cavalry Regiments: The cavalry totaled four regiments: 1st and 2nd Madras Lancers, 3rd Madras Light Cavalry, and 4th (Prince of Wales' Own) Madras Light Cavalry. *UV:* X1.

Engineers: The army had six companies of Madras Sappers and Miners, numbered from 1 to 6. *UV:* T2.

Bengal Army

THE BENGAL ARMY had been responsible for the Great Mutiny, and while those regiments that had mutinied were disbanded, there remained a blot on the honor of this army.

Infantry Regiments: The army had 44 single-battalion regiments, numbered from 1 to 40 and from 42 to 45. *UV:* X1, except as noted below.

Six battalions were trained as light infantry: 2nd (Queen's Own) Bengal Light Infantry, 5th Bengal Light Infantry, 6th Bengal Light Infantry, 42nd (Gurkha) Bengal Light Infantry, 43rd (Gurkha) Bengal Light Infantry, and 44th (Gurkha) Bengal Light Infantry. The first three are rated *UV:* X2S, the last three (Gurkhas) as *UV:* V3S.

In addition to the Bengal regiments, there are five separate regiments of Gurkha light infantry administratively part of the Bengal Army. These are unique regiments in that each has two battalions instead of one. The regiments are the 1st, 2nd (The Prince of Wales' Own) The Sirmoor Rifles, 3rd, 4th, and 5th Gurkha Regiments. *UV:* V3S.

Cavalry: The army possessed 19 regiments of cavalry, numbered from 1 to 19. *UV:* X1, except as noted below.

The 18th Regiment was the famous Bengal Lancers, and their rating should be *UV:* V2.

Other than the 18th regiment, a total of six regiments were equipped with the lance. These were the 9th, 10th (Duke of Cambridge's Own), 11th (The Prince of Wales' Own), 13th (Duke of Connaught's), 14th, and 19th.

Engineers: Eight companies of Bengal Sappers and Miners were in this army, numbered from 1 to 8. *UV:* X2.

Artillery: The army had two batteries of Bengal Mountain Artillery, numbered 1 and 2. *UV:* V1.

Bombay Army

THE BOMBAY ARMY had, for the most part, remained loyal during the Great Mutiny, and had guarded the southern reaches of the Northwest

INDIAN RANKS TABLE

British Army	*Indian Infantry*	*Indian Cavalry*
Private	Sepoy	Sowar
Corporal	Naik	Lance Daffadar
Sergeant	Havildar	Daffadar
Color Sergeant	Havildar Major	Kot Daffadar
2nd Lieutenant	Jemedar	Jemedar
1st Lieutenant	Subedar	Rissaldar
Senior Officer	Subedar Major	Rissaldar Major

Frontier. It was regarded as the best of the Presidency Armies.

Infantry: The infantry possessed a total of 26 one-battalion regiments, numbered from 1 through 30, but skipping the numbers 6, 11, 15, and 18. *UV:* X2, except as noted below.

There were two regiments of grenadiers: 1st Bombay Grenadiers and 2nd (The Prince of Wales' Own) Bombay Grenadiers. Note that these are included in the above total of 26 regiments. *UV:* V2.

There were six regiments trained as light infantry: 3rd, 5th, 10th, 23rd, 25th, and 27th (Beluch Light Infantry). *UV:* X3S.

Engineers: The army had four companies of Bombay Sappers and Miners, numbered from 1 to 4. *UV:* X3.

Artillery: The army included two batteries of Bombay Mountain Artillery, numbered 1 and 2. *UV:* V1.

Punjab Frontier Force

KNOWN AS the PIFFers, the force was formed in 1851 as the Punjab Irregular Force and soon became famous for its service along the Northwest Frontier. The PIFFers were the first units in British service to wear the khaki uniform. Their independence and their promise of hard action allowed them to skim the cream of those British officers who wished to serve in India.

Infantry: The army included a total of 17 one-battalion infantry regiments. These were the 1st through 4th Sikhs, 1st through 6th (but skipping 3rd) Punjabs, 1st through 6th Hyderabad, the Mhairwaira Battalion, and the Bhopaul Battalion. Sihks and Punjabs were *UV:* V2; others were *UV:* X2.

In addition to the above complete battalions, the following smaller detachments of infantry existed: Malwah Bheel Corps (one wing), Meywor Bheel Corps (one wing), The Resident Escoort at Katmandu (one company). *UV:* X2.

Cavalry: Eight regiments of cavalry fleshed out the force: the 1st, 2nd, 3rd, and 5th Punjab and the 1st, 2nd, 3rd, and 4th Hyderabad. *UV:* V1.

Mixed Corps: Three mixed corps each consisted of one battalion of infantry and one squadron of cavalry (except for the guides, which had two squadrons). The battalion commander was also the overall commander of the corps. The corps were the Queen's Own Corps of Guides, The Deolee Irregular Force, and the Erinpoorah Irregular Force. *UV:* V3, except the Guides had *UV:* E3.

Artillery: There were four mountain batteries (No. 1 Kohat, No. 2 Derajat, No. 3 Peshawur, and No. 4 Hazara) and four field batteries (Nos. 1, 2, 3, and 4 Hyderabad). *UV:* V1.

UNIFORMS

THE UNIFORMS VARIED considerable between armies, and sometimes between regiments. The following general notes should help. Headgear was always a turban, although the color and pattern varied from unit to unit. Virtually all troops wore a long-skirted, khaki tunic in service. Trousers were dark blue or khaki and tucked into white leggings, or khaki puttees over black shoes. Equipment was white.

The Gurkha regiments wore a uniform of dark green, almost black. Headgear was a dark green pillbox hat. Equipment was black leather.

WEAPONS

Infantry: All officers carry sabers and revolvers. Other ranks carry breech-loading rifles and bayonets.

Cavalry: Officers carry sabers and revolvers. Other ranks carry sabers and breech-loading rifles. In some regiments the other ranks also carry lances.

Engineers: Officers carry sabers and revolvers. Other ranks carry breech-loading carbines and bayonets.

Artillery: Officers carry sabers and revolvers. Other ranks carry breech-loading carbines and bayonets instead, although they are usually left with the gun limber. Field batteries are equipped with the 9-pounder field gun. Mountain batteries are equipped with either the 7-pounder mountain howitzer or the 6-pounder gun.

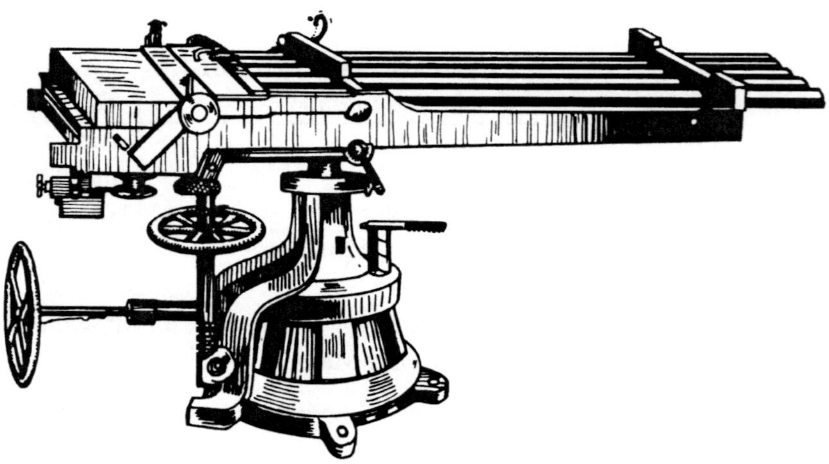

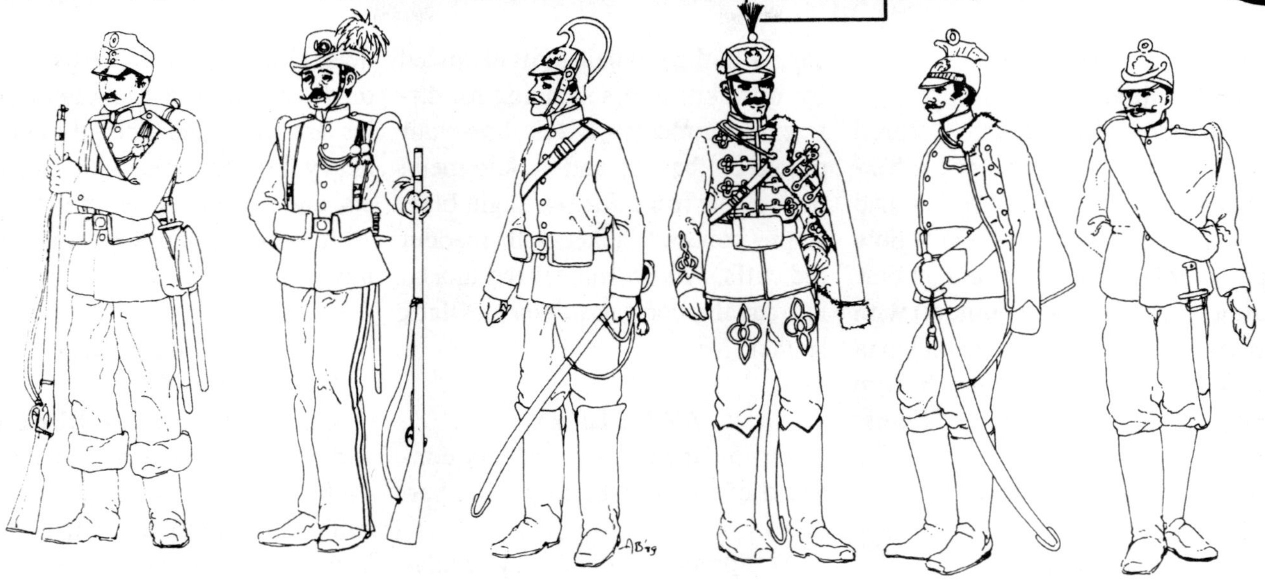

Austria-Hungary: *(Left to right.) German infantry, jäger, dragoon, hussar, lancer, artillery.*

Austria-Hungary

INFANTRY

Organization: Infantry was organized into regiments of four fusilier battalions and one grenadier battalion.

Only three fusilier battalions and the grenadiers took the field; the fourth fusilier battalion was a reserve battalion used to train and forward replacements to the field battalions. There was no regimental command structure; on campaign, all the field battalions of a single regiment, along with one separate jäeger battalion, comprise a brigade commanded by a major general.

Weapons: Officers carry revolvers and sabers. Other ranks carry box magazine bolt-action rifles and bayonets.

German and Hungarian Line Infantry

Unit Value: Fusiliers X1, grenadiers V1

Uniform: *Headgear:* Black shako with Austrian double eagle plate and cockade. *Jacket:* Dark blue, with each regiment having a different combination of colored patches and buttons (which were either white or yellow). *Pants:* Light blue loose trousers for "German" regiments, tight-fitting, light blue trousers for Hungarian regiments. *Equipment:* Black leather.

Jäegers

Unit Value: X3S

Uniform: *Headgear:* Black jäeger hat with dark green cock's feathers worn on the left side. *Jacket:* Bluish-gray with grass green collar, cuffs, and piping, and yellow metal buttons. *Pants:* Bluish-gray, worn loose. *Equipment:* Black leather.

CAVALRY

Organization: The cavalry was organized in standard regiments.

Weapons: All ranks carry sabers. Officers carry revolvers; other ranks carry breech-loading carbines. Lancers also carry a lance.

Dragoons

Unit Value: X0H

Uniform: *Headgear:* Black dragoon helmet. *Jacket:* Light blue with collar, cuffs, and piping in distinctive regimental colors, and buttons, either white or yellow (depending on the regiment). *Pants:* Red, tucked into cavalry boots. *Equipment:* White leather.

Hussars

Unit Value: X2

Uniform: *Headgear:* Colored shako, with regiments having different distinctive colors. All shakos had a black plume, and black and yellow cords. *Jacket:* Dark blue or light blue Attila (depending on regiment) with a pelise of the same color, trimmed in black fur. (The pelise was seldom worn on campaign, however.) *Pants:* Madder red tucked into cavalry boots. *Equipment:* White leather.

Lancer

Unit Value: X1

Uniform: *Headgear:* Black lancer cap, with the top half individualized by different colors standing for different regiments. Black horsehair plume on the left, and yellow metal plate in the front. *Jacket:* Light blue, single-breasted jacket with madder red cuffs. *Pants:* Madder red tucked into cavalry boots. *Equipment:* Black leather.

ARTILLERY

Organization: The artillery consisted of standard three-section batteries.

Weapons: Officers carry revolvers and sabers. Other ranks carry breech-loading carbines and bayonets, although these are usually left on the gun limber. Light field batteries are equipped with 9-pounders, heavy field batteries with 15-pounders, and siege batteries with 5" guns, 7" howitzers, and 5.5" smoothbore mortars.

Field Artillery

Unit Value: X0

Uniform: *Headgear:* Black shako with yellow metal plate and red cord. *Jacket:* Dark brown with red collar, cuffs, and shoulder straps. *Pants:* Light blue; fortress artillery has red stripes as well. *Equipment:* Black leather.

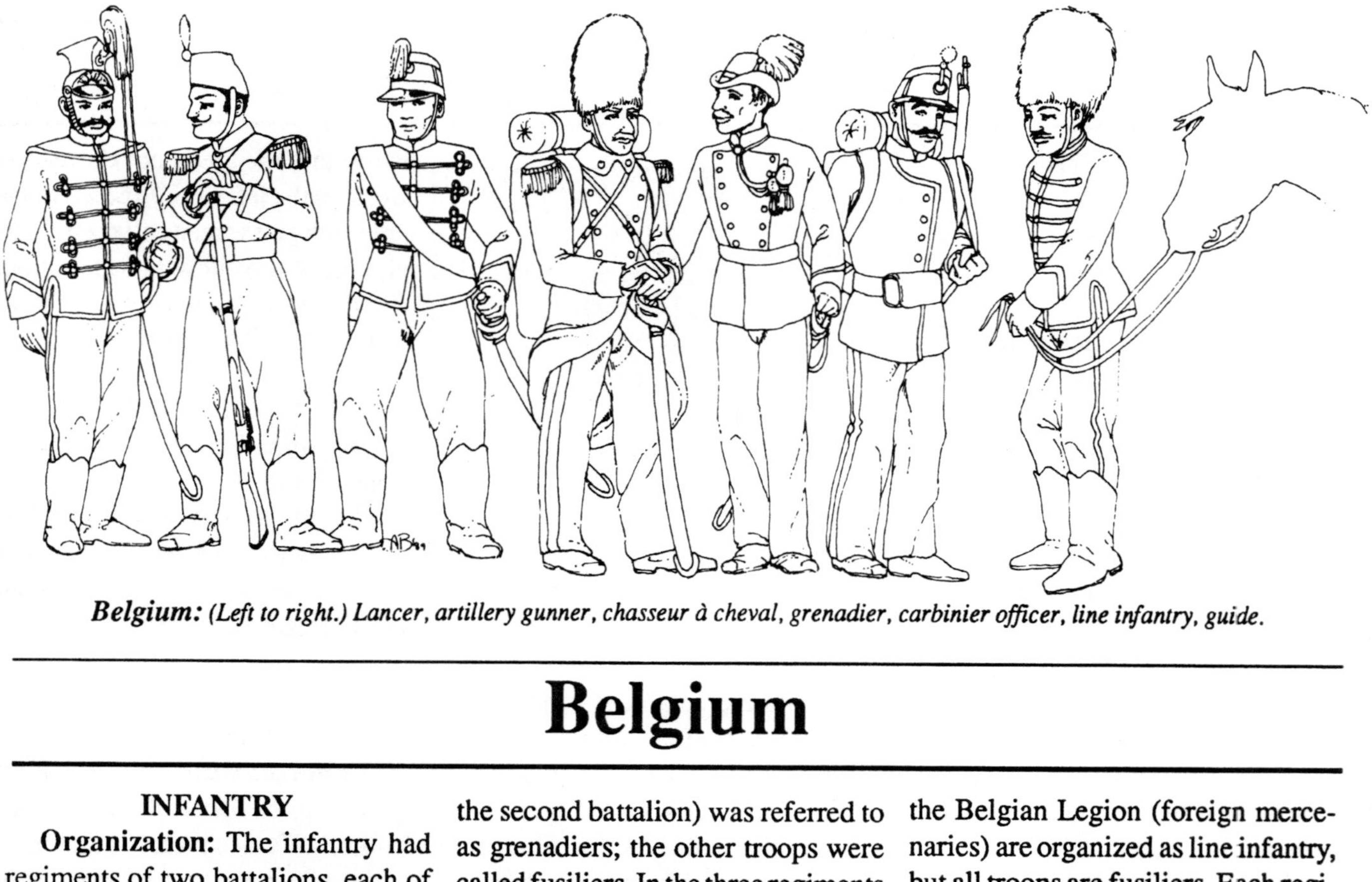

Belgium: *(Left to right.) Lancer, artillery gunner, chasseur à cheval, grenadier, carbinier officer, line infantry, guide.*

Belgium

INFANTRY

Organization: The infantry had regiments of two battalions, each of four companies. However, the 1st platoon of the lowest numbered company in each battalion (1st company in the 1st battalion, 5th company in the second battalion) was referred to as grenadiers; the other troops were called fusiliers. In the three regiments of *chasseurs a pied* (light infantry), the 1st platoon of each battalion is referred to as carbiniers, and the others as chasseurs. The three regiments of the Belgian Legion (foreign mercenaries) are organized as line infantry, but all troops are fusiliers. Each regiment of the legion also includes one battery of three gun sections (12-pounders) and one squadron of cavalry *(chasseurs a cheval).*

Weapons: Officers carry sabers and revolvers. Other ranks carry bolt-action rifles and bayonets.

Line Infantry

Unit Value: Fusiliers T1, grenadiers X1

Uniform: *Headgear:* Black shako with yellow metal plate, red plume, pompon, and trim (except grenadiers, who wore a tall black bearskin hat). *Jacket:* Royal blue, double-breasted coat with two rows of yellow buttons, red collar, cuffs, and shoulder wings (except grenadiers, who had red epaulettes). In the legion, the coat was green, trimmed in orange. *Pants:* Gray with narrow red stripe (except grenadiers, who wore black trousers with a broad red stripe). Trousers were worn over the boots. Trouser stripe was black in the legion. *Equipment:* White leather.

Light Infantry

Unit Value: Chasseurs T2, carbiniers X2

Uniform: *Headgear:* Black shako with yellow metal plate, yellow plume, and pompon (except for carbiniers, who wore a black jäeger hat with dark green cock's feathers on the left side). *Jacket:* Green with yellow piping. *Pants:* Gray with yellow piping worn over the boot. *Equipment:* Black leather.

Belgian Legion

Unit Value: X1

Uniform: *Headgear:* Black shako with yellow metal plate and trimmed in orange. This was often replaced in the field by a white or khaki Sun helmet. *Jacket:* Green, double-breasted coat with two rows of yellow buttons, orange collar, cuffs, and shoulder wings. This was often replaced in the field by a khaki jacket with an orange collar. *Pants:* Gray with a narrow, black stripe. These were often replaced in the field by white or khaki trousers without stripes. *Equipment:* White leather.

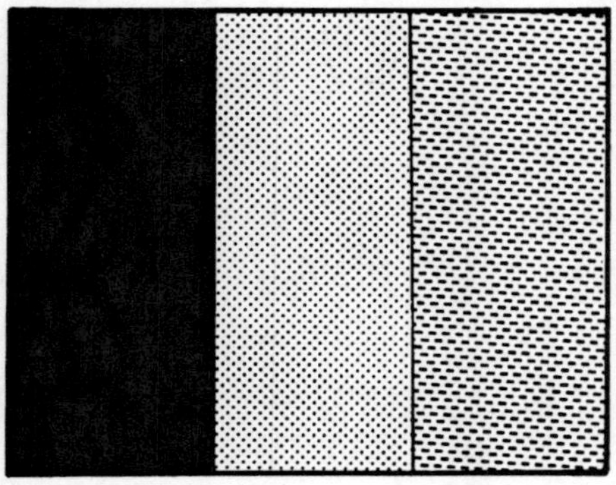

CAVALRY

Organization: The cavalry had a standard regimental organization.

Weapons: All ranks carry sabers. Officers carry revolvers. Other ranks carry breech-loading carbines. Lancers also carry lances.

Guides

(Total of two regiments.)

Unit Value: X1

Uniform: *Headgear:* Black bearskin caps *Jacket:* Green dolman with red pointed cuffs and collar and orange-yellow loopings. *Pants:* Red with double yellow stripes worn over the boots. *Equipment:* Black leather.

Chasseurs a Cheval

(Total of two regiments, plus one squadron per regiment of the legion.)

Unit Value: T2

Uniform: *Headgear:* Yellow shako in 1st Regiment, scarlet shako in 2nd, black shako in the legion. Shakos were trimmed in white lace and had a small white plume, but were usually worn with black oilskin covers. *Jacket:* Royal blue (green in the legion) dolman with white loopings (orange in the legion). Collar and cuffs are yellow in 1st Regiment and the legion, scarlet in 2nd Regiment, and orange in the legion. *Pants:* Gray-blue (light gray in the legion) with white stripes, worn over the boots. *Equipment:* White leather.

Lancers

(Total of four regiments.)

Unit Value: T1

Uniform: *Headgear:* Lancer cap in red (1st Regiment), yellow (2nd), white (3rd), or ultramarine (4th). *Jacket:* Royal blue dolman with white loopings for the 1st and 2nd regiments, and yellow loopings for the 3rd and 4th regiments. The collar and cuffs were the same color as the cap. *Pants:* Gray-blue with white stripes, over the boot. *Equipment:* Black leather.

ARTILLERY

Organization: The artillery had batteries of three gun sections.

Weapons: Officers carry revolvers and sabers. Other ranks carry breech-loading carbines and bayonets, although these are usually left on the gun limber. Field artillery uses 12-pounder guns. Heavy artillery uses 5" guns and 6" howitzers.

Field Artillery And Heavy Artillery

Unit Value: T0

Uniform: *Headgear:* Low-crowned fur cap with red cloth bag (except for heavy batteries, which wore a black shako). *Jacket:* Blue (green in the legion) with red collar and piping. *Pants:* Blue with red stripes, worn over the boot. *Equipment:* Black leather.

Bulgaria: *(Left to right.) Infantry, infantry in summer uniform, cavalry.*

Bulgaria

INFANTRY

Organization: Standard organization.

Weapons: Officers carry sabers and revolvers. Other ranks carry breech-loading rifles and bayonets.

Foot Guards

(Total of three regiments.)

Unit Value: V2

Uniform: *Headgear:* Low, black, fur cap with the Bulgarian Cross in white metal on the front. In summer, this was replaced by a white linen peaked cap. *Jacket:* Dark green with collars, shoulder straps, and cuff patches in the distinctive color of the regiment (red for the Alexander Regiment, white for the Ferdinand Regiment, light blue for the Clementine Regiment). In the summer, this was replaced by a white linen tunic. *Pants:* Dark green tucked into tall boots. In the summer this was replaced by white linen. *Equipment:* Black leather.

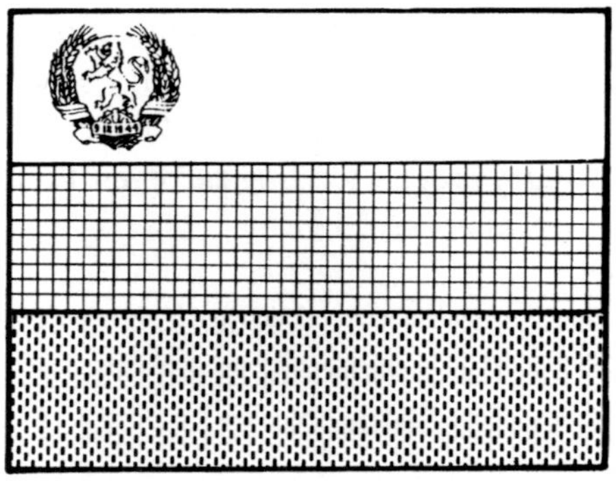

Line Infantry

Unit Value: X2

Uniform: *Headgear:* Low, black, fur cap with the Bulgarian Cross in white metal on the front. In summer, a white linen peaked cap. *Jacket:* Dark green with collar, cuffs, and shoulder straps in the same color. In summer this was replaced by a white linen tunic. *Pants:* Dark green tucked into tall boots. In the summer this was replaced by white linen. *Equipment:* Black leather.

CAVALRY

Organization: Standard regiments.

Weapons: All ranks carried sabers. Officers carry revolvers; other ranks carry muzzle-loading carbines.

Line Cavalry

(Total of four regiments.)

Unit Value: X2

Uniform: *Headgear:* Low, black, fur cap with a white, upright plume. *Jacket:* Dark blue with red, silver embroidered, collar and cuffs. Edges and seams were piped in the regimental color (white for 1st; red, 2nd; yellow, 3rd; blue, 4th). *Pants:* Dark blue with red stripes, tucked into cavalry boots. *Equipment:* Black leather.

Prince's Lifeguard

(One squadron only.)

Unit Value: V2

Uniform: *Headgear:* White, low, fur cap with red top. *Jacket:* Red Attila with white loops. *Pants:* Dark blue with red stripes, tucked into black cavalry boots. *Equipment:* Black leather.

ARTILLERY

Organization: Standard battery organization

Weapons: Officers carry revolvers and sabers. Other ranks carry breech-loading carbines and bayonets (usually left on the gun limber). Field batteries have 9-pounder guns. Siege batteries have 5" guns.

Field Artillery

Unit Value: X0

Uniform: *Headgear:* Low, black, fur cap with a red cloth top. *Jacket:* Dark blue with black collar and cuffs. *Pants:* Dark blue with red stripes, tucked into boots. *Equipment:* Black leather.

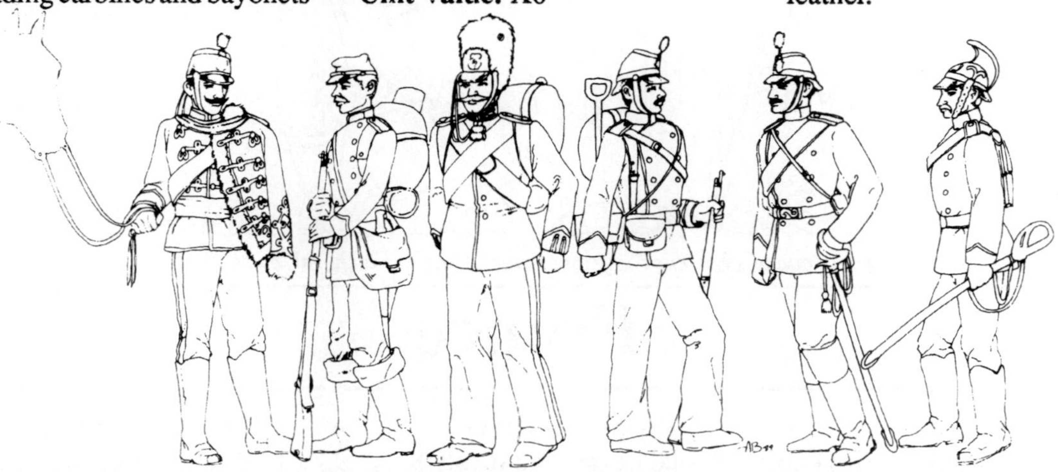

Denmark: *(Left to right.) Hussar officer, infantry, guard grenadier, engineer, artillery officer, dragoon.*

Denmark

INFANTRY

Organization: Standard regiments.

Weapons: Officers carry sabers and revolvers. Other ranks carry breech-loading rifles and bayonets.

Line

Unit Value: T1

Uniform: *Headgear:* Shako with white metal fittings. For field service, this was replaced with a light blue kepi. *Jacket:* Dark blue with red collar patches and red-piped, pointed cuffs. *Pants:* Light blue worn over the boots, in the field often rolled up to mid-shin. *Equipment:* Black leather.

Lifeguard

(Total of one regiment.)

Unit Value: X1

Uniform: *Headgear:* Black, fur grenadier cap. *Jacket:* Red with light blue collar, shoulder straps, and pointed cuffs, all piped white. *Pants:* Light blue with wide, white stripes. *Equipment:* White leather.

CAVALRY

Organization: Standard regiments.

Weapons: All ranks are armed with sabers. Officers carry revolvers; other ranks carry breech-loading carbines.

Dragoons

Unit Value: T1H

Uniform: *Headgear:* Black, crested cavalry helmet with white metal fittings. *Jacket:* Light blue tunic with dark red collar, cuff patches, and piping. *Pants:* Light blue, tucked into cavalry boots. *Equipment:* Black leather.

Hussars

(Total of one regiment.)

Unit Value: T2

Uniform: *Headgear:* Light blue kepi. *Jacket:* Light blue Attila with five rows of white loopings, and a carmine collar and cuffs. *Pants:* Light blue, tucked into hussar boots. *Equipment:* Black leather.

ARTILLERY

Organization: Standard batteries.

Weapons: Officers carry revolvers and sabers. Other ranks carry breech-loading carbines and bayonets, although these are usually left on the gun limber. Field batteries are equipped with 9-pounder guns (light batteries) or 15-pounder guns.

Field Artillery

Unit Value: T0

Uniform: *Headgear:* Black shako, white metal fittings. *Jacket:* Dark blue tunic with carmine collar patches and piping. *Pants:* Dark blue tucked into boots. *Equipment:* Black leather.

France: (Left to right.) Zouave, chasseur d' Afrique, spahi, chasseur à cheval, cuirassier, Turco, line infantry.

France

INFANTRY

Organization: Standard regiments. A third battalion exists for each regiment, but was generally left behind to train new recruits and forward replacements to the field.

Weapons: Officers carry sabers and revolvers. Other ranks carry bolt-action rifles and bayonets.

Line Infantry

Unit Value: X1

Uniform: *Headgear:* Red kepi, blue band. *Jacket:* Officers wear a black dolman. Other ranks wear a blue jacket with red collar and blue collar patches. *Pants:* Madder red tucked into short, white gaiters over black shoes. *Equipment:* Black leather.

Chasseurs a Pied

(Light infantry.)

Unit Value: V2S

Uniform: *Headgear:* Blue kepi, yellow piping. *Jacket:* Blue with blue collar and cuffs, yellow piping. *Pants:* Iron gray with yellow stripes, tucked into low, white gaiters over black shoes. *Equipment:* Black leather.

Zouaves

(Total of four regiments.)

Unit Value: V2

Uniform: *Headgear:* Red fez. *Jacket:* Dark blue waistcoat and jacket with red lace and light blue sash. *Pants:* Baggy red, tucked into white gaiters over black shoes. *Equipment:* Black leather.

Tirailleurs Algerien

ALGERIAN COLONIAL infantry, also called Turcos. All officers are European, all other ranks native. (Total of three regiments.)

Unit Value: X3

Uniform: *Headgear:* Red fez. *Jacket:* Sky blue waistcoat and jacket with yellow lace and red sash. *Pants:* Baggy sky blue, tucked into low, white gaiters over black shoes. *Equipment:* Black leather.

Tirailleurs Senegalais

(Senegalese infantry.) All officers are European; all other ranks are native. (Total of one regiment.)

Unit Value: V3

Uniform: Same as for Turcos.

French Foreign Legion

(Total of three regiments.)

Unit Value: E2

Uniform: *Headgear:* Stiff, white kepi with Sun curtain at back. Sometimes replaced by a white Sun helmet in the tropics. *Jacket:* Blue with red collar and green epaulettes. Replaced by a khaki jacket in the tropics. *Pants:* White, worn tucked into or over black boots. *Equipment:* Black leather.

Colonial Infantry

ALL RANKS WERE Europeans recruited from colonists.

Unit Value: X2

Uniform: *Headgear:* Dark blue kepi with red piping, replaced by a white or khaki Sun helmet in the tropics. *Jacket:* Dark blue, replaced by khaki in the tropics. *Pants:* Gray-blue with red piping tucked into low, white leggings over black shoes. In the tropics, replaced by khaki or white pants tucked into khaki leggings. *Equipment:* Black leather.

CAVALRY

Organization: Standard regiments.

Weapons: All ranks carry sabers. Officers carry revolvers. Other ranks carry breech-loading carbines. Half of all dragoon other ranks (two men per section) carry lances.

Cuirassiers

Unit Value: V0H

Uniform: *Headgear:* Steel helmet with brass band, black criniere. *Jacket:* Blue with red collar and cuff patches and scarlet epaulettes. Steel cuirass with yellow metal straps. *Pants:* Red with leather strapping to the knees. *Equipment:* Black leather.

Dragoons

Unit Value: X1H

Uniform: *Headgear:* White metal helmet with yellow metal band, mounts, and comb, and black criniere. *Jacket:* Blue dolman with black loopings. *Pants:* Red with leather strapping to the knees. *Equipment:* White leather.

Hussars

Unit Value: X2

Uniform: *Headgear:* Light blue kepi with red band. *Jacket:* Light blue Attila with white loopings. *Pants:* Red with leather strapping to the knees. *Equipment:* Black leather.

Chasseurs d'Afrique

(African light cavalry.) All ranks were Europeans recruited from colonists in Africa. (Total of three regiments.)

Unit Value: V3

Uniform: *Headgear:* Stiff, white kepi with Sun curtain in back. *Jacket:* Light blue with yellow collar and cuff patches and red sash. *Pants:* Red with leather strapping to the knees. *Equipment:* Black leather.

Spahis

(Light cavalry.) Officers were French; other ranks were native North Africans. (Total of three regiments.)

Unit Value: X3

Uniform: *Headgear:* Officers wear a light blue kepi. Other ranks wear a large, long, red Arabian cloak. *Jacket:* Officers wear a red jacket with blue cuffs. Other ranks wear a red jacket and waistcoat with black lace and red sash. *Pants:* Officers wear light blue tucked into cavalry boots; other ranks wear medium blue over shoes. *Equipment:* Black leather.

Foreign Legion Cavalry

(One regiment.)

Unit Value: E2

Uniform: Same as legion infantry, but pants were tucked into cavalry boots.

ARTILLERY

Organization: Standard batteries.

Weapons: Officers carry revolvers and sabers. Other ranks carry breech-loading carbines and bayonets, although these are usually left on the gun limber. Light and horse batteries are equipped with 9-pounder guns, mountain batteries with 6-pounder mountain guns, field batteries with 15-pounder guns, and heavy and siege batteries with either 5" guns, 6" howitzers, or 6" guns.

Artillery

Unit Value: V0

Uniform: *Headgear:* Blue kepi with red piping. *Jacket:* Blue with black hussar loopings, red collar, and pointed cuffs. *Pants:* Blue with red stripes worn over the shoes. *Equipment:* Black leather.

Germany

INFANTRY

Organization: Standard regiments. Each has a third battalion, but this was normally left at home to train recruits and forward replacements to the regiments in the field.

Weapons: Officers carry revolvers and sabers. Other ranks carry bolt-action rifles and bayonets.

Line Infantry

Unit Value: V1

Uniform: *Headgear:* Black, spiked helmet with yellow metal fittings. *Jacket:* Dark blue with red collar, cuffs, and piping down the front seam. Cuff patches were either red or white (depending on the regiment), and shoulder straps were any of a variety of colors (varying with the regiment). *Pants:* Black with red piping down the seam, tucked into black boots. *Equipment:* Black leather.

Saxon Line Infantry

Unit Value: X1

Uniform: *Headgear:* Black, spiked helmet with yellow metal fittings. *Jacket:* Sky blue with red collar, cuffs, cuff patches, shoulder straps, and piping down the front seam. *Pants:* Sky blue with red piping down the seam, tucked into black boots. *Equipment:* Black leather.

Bavarian Line Infantry

Unit Value: X1

Uniform: *Headgear:* Black, spiked helmet with yellow metal fittings. *Jacket:* Light blue with red collar, cuffs, cuff patches, shoulder straps, and piping down the front seam. *Pants:* Light blue with red piping down the seam, tucked into black boots. *Equipment:* Black leather.

Jäegers

Unit Value: V3S

Uniform: *Headgear:* Black shako with yellow metal eagle on front. *Jacket:* Green with red collar, cuffs, shoulder straps, and piping down the front seam. *Pants:* Black with red piping down the seam, tucked into black boots. *Equipment:* Black leather.

Guard Infantry

(Total of eight regiments.)

Unit Value: E1

Uniform: Same as line infantry on campaign.

Note on Colonial Uniforms

Whenever any of the above German regular troops were stationed in the colonies overseas or off-planet, they wore the following uniform.

Uniform: *Headgear:* Black, spiked helmet with yellow metal fittings, or black shako for jäegers. This was sometimes replaced by a white or gray-green Sun helmet, particularly by officers. *Jacket:* Gray-green with red collar and cuffs. *Pants:* White, gray-green, or light gray (depending on the preference of the unit) tucked into black boots. *Equipment:* Black leather.

German East African Schutztruppen

(Colonial infantry.)

Unit Value: T2

Uniform: *Headgear:* European officers and NCOs wear a white Sun helmet with a black, white, and red cockade on the front. Native other ranks wear a red fez with a blue tassel. *Jacket:* White or khaki for European officers and NCOs, khaki for native other ranks. *Pants:* White, tucked into black boots for European officers and NCOs; khaki, tucked into blue puttees over black shoes for native other ranks. *Equipment:* Brown leather.

Southwest African Schutztruppen

(Colonial infantry.)

Unit Value: X2

Uniform: *Headgear:* Light gray slouch hat with the right side pinned up. *Jacket:* Light gray. *Pants:* Light gray. *Equipment:* Brown leather.

Cameroon Schutztruppen

(Colonial infantry.)

Unit Value: T2

Uniform: *Headgear:* Light gray slouch hat with the right side pinned up. *Jacket:* Light gray with red collar and cuffs. *Pants:* Light gray. *Equipment:* Brown leather.

Togo Police

Unit Value: T2

Uniform: Same as Cameroon *Schutztruppen.*

Venusian Schutztruppen

(Troops raised from human colonists.)

Unit Value: T1

Uniform: *Headgear:* Black leather, spiked helmet with yellow metal fittings. *Jacket:* Gray-green with blue collar, cuffs, and shoulder straps. *Pants:* Gray-green tucked into black boots. *Equipment:* Brown rubberized canvas.

Venusian Feld Kompanie

(Separate companies of Lizard-man infantry with human officers and NCOs.)

Unit Value: G2

Uniform: *Headgear:* European officers and NCOs wore a white Sun helmet with a black, white, and red cockade on the front. Native other ranks wore a leather helmet reinforced with bone and *Oma Jolima* ribs, with a crest. *Jacket:* White or khaki for European officers and NCOs. Other ranks do not wear a jacket. *Pants:* White tucked into black boots for European officers and NCOs; nothing for native other ranks. *Equipment:* Brown, rubberized canvas. Native other ranks wear cross belts and a web harness.

CAVALRY

Organization: Standard regiments.

Weapons: Officers carry revolvers and sabers. Other ranks all carry sabers, lances, and bolt-action carbines.

Cuirassier

(Total of eight regiments.)

Unit Value: X0H

Uniform: *Headgear:* Steel spiked

helmet. (This was yellow metal in the 6th regiment). *Jacket:* White with collar patches, cuffs, and piping in the distinctive regimental color (1st, black; 2nd, crimson; 3rd, light blue; 4th, orange; 5th, light red; 6th, blue; 7th, yellow; 8th, green). The metal cuirass was not worn in the field. *Pants:* White, tucked into black cavalry boots. *Equipment:* White leather.

Guard Cuirassier

(Total of two regiments.)

Unit Value: V0H

Uniform: *Headgear:* Yellow metal spiked helmet. *Jacket:* White with collar patches, cuffs, and piping in distinctive regimental color (*Garde du Corps*, red; *Guard Cuirassiers*, blue). Metal cuirass was not worn in the field. *Pants:* White, tucked into black cavalry boots. *Equipment:* White leather.

Guard Dragoons

(Total of two regiments.)

Unit Value: V1

Uniform: *Headgear:* Black, spiked helmet with yellow metal fittings. *Jacket:* Light blue with red collar and cuffs and with buttons in the distinctive regimental color (1st, yellow; 2nd, white). *Pants:* Gray-blue, tucked into black knee boots. *Equipment:* White leather.

Leibgarde-Husaren

(Lifeguard hussars—one regiment.)

Unit Value: V2

Uniform: *Headgear:* Low, black fur cap with red cloth bag. *Jacket:* Red Attilla with five rows of yellow loopings. *Pants:* Dark blue, with stripes the same color as jacket loopings, tucked into black hussar boots. *Equipment:* White leather.

Dragoons

(Total of four regiments.)

Unit Value: X1

Uniform: *Headgear:* Black, spiked helmet with yellow metal fittings. *Jacket*: Light blue with collar and cuffs in the distinctive regimental color (1st, red; 2nd, black; 3rd, light red; 4th, sulfur yellow). *Pants:* Gray-blue, tucked into black knee boots. *Equipment*: White leather.

Hussars

(Total of 16 regiments.)

Unit Value: X2

Uniform: *Headgear:* Low, black fur cap with colored cloth bag (red in 1st, 3rd, 6th, 7th, 11th, 13th, and 14th regiments; white in 2nd and 12th; yellow in 4th, 15th, and 16th; dark red in 5th; pompadour red in 10th; cornflower blue in 8th and 9th.) *Jacket*: Attila in distinctive color with

Germany: *(Left to right.) Line infantry, jäger, cuirassier, hussar, dragoon, lancer, artillery.*

five rows of lace (black with white loops in 1st and 2nd; red with white loops in 3rd; brown with yellow loops in 4th; dark red with white loops in 5th; dark green with white loops in 6th and 11th; Russian blue with yellow loops in 7th; dark blue with white loops in 8th, 14th, and 15th; cornflower blue with yellow loops in 9th; dark green with yellow loops in 10th; cornflower blue with white loops in 12th, 13th, and 16th). *Pants:* Dark blue, with stripes the same color as jacket loops, tucked into black hussar boots. *Equipment:* White leather.

Uhlans (Lancers)

Unit Value: X1

Uniform: *Headgear:* Black lancer helmet with yellow metal fittings. *Jacket:* A distinctive, dark blue, high-collared jacket was worn, with the whole of the chest covered by the broad lapel. Collars, cuffs, and the lapels were in the regimental distinctive color (red in the 1st through 8th, white in the 9th and 13th, crimson in the 10th and 14th, yellow in the 11th and 15th, light blue in the 12th and 16th.) *Pants:* Dark blue, tucked into black cavalry boots. *Equipment:* White leather.

Guard Uhlans

(Three regiments.)

Unit Value: V1

Uniform: *Headgear:* Black lancer helmet with yellow metal fittings. *Jacket:* The same as the line regiments (Uhlans), but with different distinctions. The collar, cuffs, and lapels were red in the 2nd regiment and yellow in the 3rd. The 1st regiment has red collar and cuffs with white lapels. *Pants:* Dark blue, tucked into black cavalry boots. *Equipment*: White leather.

ARTILLERY

Organization: Standard batteries.

Weapons: Officers carry revolvers and sabers. Other ranks carry breech-loading carbines and bayonets, although these are usually left on the gun limber. Light batteries and horse artillery batteries have 9-pounder guns, field batteries have 15-pounder field guns, heavy batteries have 6" howitzers, and mountain batteries have 6-pounder guns.

Artillery

Unit Value: V0

Uniform: *Headgear:* Helmet similar to that worn by the infantry, but with a yellow metal ball in place of the spike. *Jacket:* Dark blue, with black collar and cuffs, and white shoulder straps. *Pants:* Dark gray, tucked into black boots. *Equipment:* Black leather, except for the guard artillery, which wore white leather.

Italy

INFANTRY

Organization: Standard regiments. Regiments were permanently grouped into brigades, named after the geographic region from which they were recruited.

Weapons: Officers carry revolvers and sabers. Other ranks carry bolt-action rifles and bayonets.

Grenadiers

(Total of two regiments.)

Unit Value: V1

Uniform: *Headgear:* Dark blue shako with red pompon, but in the field, a white cloth shako cover was worn. *Jacket:* Dark blue with red piping around the collar, cuffs, and edges of the jacket, and red collar patches, black wings and shoulder straps. Officers had red collars and cuffs. *Pants:* Blue-gray with red piping worn over black shoes. White trousers were usually worn in the field. *Equipment:* White leather with black cartridge box.

Line Infantry

Unit Value: X1

Uniform: *Headgear:* Dark blue shako with red pompon, but in the field a white cloth shako cover was worn. *Jacket:* Dark blue with red piping around the collar, cuffs, and edges of the jacket, and black collar patches, wings, and shoulder straps. Officers had black collars and cuffs. *Pants:* Blue-gray with red piping worn over black shoes. White trousers usually worn in the field. *Equipment:* White leather with black cartridge box.

Bersaglieri

Unit Value: V3S

Uniform: *Headgear:* Black, wide-brimmed hat with dark green cock's feathers on the right side. *Jacket:* Dark blue with carmine piping around the collar, cuffs, and edges of the jacket, and carmine collar patches, black wings and shoulder straps. Officers had carmine collars and cuffs. *Pants:* Dark blue, worn over black shoes. White trousers were usually worn in the field. *Equipment:* Black leather.

Alpini

Unit Value: V3

Uniform: *Headgear:* Tall, round, black leather hat with a brown eagle feather worn upright on the left side. In the field, a white cloth cover was worn and the feather was attached to this. *Jacket:* Dark blue with red piping around the collar, cuffs, and edges of the jacket, and green collar patches, black wings and shoulder straps. Officers had black collars and green cuffs. *Pants:* Blue-gray with red piping worn over black shoes. White trousers were usually worn in the field. *Equipment:* White leather with black cartridge box.

CAVALRY

Organization: Standard regiments.

Weapons: Officers carry revolvers and sabers. Other ranks carry breech-loading carbines and sabers. Other ranks in line cavalry and lancer regiments also carry a lance.

Cavalleria di Linea

(Line cavalry—total of four regiments.)

Unit Value: X0H

Uniform: *Headgear:* White metal helmet, with yellow metal comb and chin scales and black turban. *Jacket:* Dark blue with regiments differentiated by combinations of collar, cuff, and piping color. *Pants:* Gray-blue with black stripes, worn over black boots. Officers have stripes matching the piping on their jacket. *Equipment:* White leather.

Lancieri

(Lancers.)

Unit Value: X1

Uniform: *Headgear:* Dark fur caps with brown feather. *Jacket:* Dark blue with regiments differentiated by combinations of collar, cuff, and piping color. *Pants:* Gray-blue with black stripes, worn over black boots. Officers have stripes matching the piping on their jacket. *Equipment:* White leather.

Cavalleggeri

(Light cavalry.)

Unit Value: X2

Uniform: *Headgear:* Dark fur caps with brown feather. *Jacket:* Dark blue with regiments differentiated by combinations of collar, cuff, and piping color. *Pants:* Gray-blue with black stripes, worn over black boots. Officers have stripes matching the piping on their jacket. *Equipment:* White leather.

ARTILLERY

Organization: Standard batteries.

Weapons: Officers carry revolvers and sabers. Other ranks carry breech-loading carbines and bayonets, although these are usually left on the gun limber. Field batteries are equipped with 12-pounder guns. Garrison and siege batteries are equipped with heavier pieces.

Artillery

Unit Value: X0

Uniform: *Headgear:* Dark blue shako with red pompon and black horsehair plume. *Jacket:* Dark blue with orange piping around the collar, cuffs, and edges of the jacket, and black collar patches, wings, and shoulder straps. Officers have orange collars and cuffs. *Pants:* Dark blue with red piping worn over black shoes. White trousers were usually worn in the field. *Equipment:* White leather with black cartridge box.

Italy: *(Left to right.) Bersaglieri, Alpini, infantry, line cavalry, lancer, light cavalry, cuirassier officer.*

Montenegro

INFANTRY

Organzation: There was no standing army in the principality, only locally drilled peasant militias. These are organized as irregular bands.

Weapons: Officers carry sabers and revolvers. Other ranks carry rifle muskets and bayonets.

Militia Infantry

Unit Value: T1

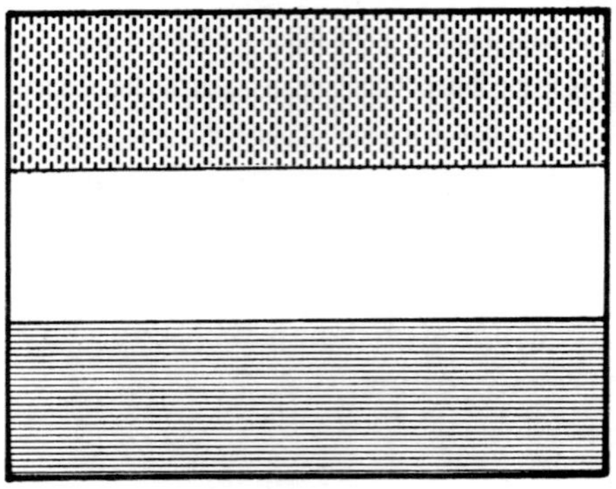

Uniform: There were no infantry uniforms as such, but the militia fought while they were wearing the distinctive national peasant costume. *Headgear:* Low, rounded cap was worn with a badge on the front. *Jacket:* Braided jacket with loose, hanging sleeves. *Pants:* Broad knee breeches were worn by the infantry, along with white stockings and ankle boots. *Equipment:* Black or brown leather.

Graustark

INFANTRY

Organization: There were no regiments. Infantry was organized in separate battalions, with standard battalion organization, and named for the region they were recruited from.

Weapons: Officers carry sabers and revolvers. Other ranks carry breech-loading rifles and bayonets in the regulars, and rifle muskets in the militia.

Line Infantry

Unit Value: X1

Uniform : *Headgear:* Blue-gray shako with black trim, but on campaign a blue-gray kepi was worn. *Jacket:* Blue gray with black collar, cuffs, and shoulder straps. *Pants:* Black, tucked into black boots. On campaign, unbleached linen trousers were worn instead. *Equipment:* White leather.

Light Infantry

(Total of three battalions.)

Unit Value: X2S

Uniform: *Headgear:* Blue-gray shako with yellow trim and a green plume. The plume was not worn on campaign, and the shako was covered with black oilskin. *Jacket:* Blue-gray with yellow collar, cuffs, and shoulder straps. *Pants:* Black, tucked into black boots. On campaign, unbleached linen trousers were worn instead. *Equipment:* Black leather.

Militia Infantry

Unit Value: T1 (irregulars)

Uniform: *Headgear:* Blue-gray kepi. *Jacket:* Brown peasant smock. *Pants:* Unbleached linen, tucked into black boots. *Equipment:* Brown leather.

CAVALRY

Organization: Standard regiments.

Weapons: Officers carry sabers and revolvers. Other ranks carry sabers, lances, and breech-loading carbines.

Line Cavalry

(Two regiments.)

Unit Value: X1

Uniform: *Headgear:* Light blue kepi with red piping. *Jacket:* Light blue Attila with red loopings. *Pants:* Light blue with red stripes, tucked into black cavalry boots. *Equipment:* White leather.

ARTILLERY

Organization: Standard batteries, but usually deployed as single gun sections.

Weapons: Officers carry revolvers and sabers. Other ranks carry breech-loading carbines and bayonets, although these are usually left on the gun limber.

Each battery has two sections of 9-pounder smoothbore guns and one section of 12-pounder smoothbore howitzers.

Artillery

Unit Value: X0

Uniform: *Headgear:* Blue-gray shako with red piping. *Jacket:* Black Attila with red loopings. *Pants:* Black with red stripes, tucked into black boots. *Equipment:* White leather.

Ruritania

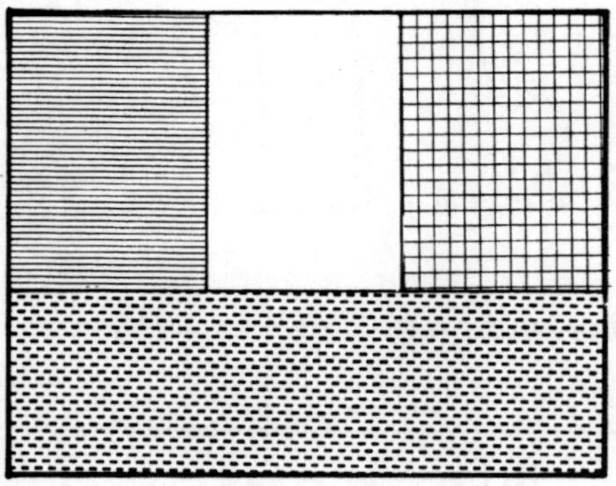

INFANTRY

Organization: Standard regiments. The first company of each regiment was a grenadier company, and the eighth was a light infantry company.

On campaign, these were routinely stripped off to form one or two *ad hoc* grenadier and one or two light infantry battalions of two or three companies each. (There were a total of six regiments in the army). Militia battalions were separately raised and were named after the region from which they were recruited.

Weapons: Officers carry sabers and revolvers. Other ranks carry breech-loading rifles and bayonets in the regulars, rifle muskets in the militia.

Line Infantry

Unit Value: X1

Uniform: *Headgear:* Black shako with green trim. *Jacket:* Gray with green collar, cuffs, and shoulder straps. *Pants:* Gray with green stripes tucked into black boots. On campaign, white trousers were usually worn instead. *Equipment:* White leather.

Grenadiers

Unit Value: V1

Uniform: *Headgear:* Black shako with red trim. *Jacket:* Gray with red collar, cuffs, and shoulder straps. *Pants:* Gray with red stripes tucked into black boots. On campaign, white trousers were usually worn. *Equipment:* White leather.

Light Infantry

Unit Value: X3S

Uniform: *Headgear:* Black shako with yellow trim. *Jacket:* Gray with yellow collar, cuffs, and shoulder straps. *Pants:* Gray with yellow stripes tucked into black boots. On campaign, white trousers were usually worn instead. *Equipment:* Black leather.

Militia Infantry

Unit Value: T1 (irregulars)

Uniform: *Headgear:* Gray forage cap. *Jacket:* Brown peasant smock. *Pants:* White, tucked into black boots. *Equipment:* Brown or black leather.

CAVALRY

Organization: Standard regiments.

Weapons: Officers carry sabers and revolvers. Other ranks carry breech-loading rifles and bayonets.

Mounted Rifles

(Mounted infantry—total of two regiments.)

Unit Value: X2S

Uniform: *Headgear:* Black, round-brimmed hat with right side pinned up and a fall of green cock's feathers. *Jacket:* Gray with black collar, cuffs, and shoulder straps. *Pants:* Gray with black stripes, tucked into black boots. *Equipment:* Black leather.

ARTILLERY

Organization: Batteries have only two gun sections each.

Weapons: Officers carry revolvers and sabers. Other ranks carry breech-loading carbines and bayonets, although these are usually left on the gun limber. Batteries are equipped with 9-pounder guns.

Field Artillery

Unit Value: X0

Uniform: *Headgear:* Black shako with black plume. *Jacket:* Gray Attila with black loopings. *Pants:* Black tucked into black boots. *Equipment:* White leather.

The Netherlands: *(Left to right.) Line infantry, line cavalry.*

Netherlands

INFANTRY

Organization: Standard regiments. The regiment "Grenadiers and Jägers" consists of one battalion of each type.

Weapons: Officers carry a revolver and saber. Other ranks carry breech-loading rifles and bayonets.

Line Infantry

Unit Value: T1

Uniform: *Headgear:* Dark blue shako with red plume. *Jacket:* Dark blue with white collar, cuff patches, and piping. *Pants:* Light blue with red stripes over black shoes. *Equipment:* Black leather.

Grenadiers

(Total of one battalion.)

Unit Value: V1

Uniform: *Headgear:* Dark blue shako with red plume and white cords. *Jacket:* Dark blue with red collar, cuff patches, piping, and shoulder wings. *Pants:* Light blue with red stripes over black shoes. *Equipment:* Black leather.

Jägers

(Total of one battalion.)

Unit Value: X3S

Uniform: *Headgear:* Green shako with yellow plume and piping. *Jacket:* Green with yellow piping. *Pants:* Green with yellow stripes, worn over black shoes. *Equipment:* Black leather.

Colonial Infantry

(Dutch Indies garrison.)

Unit Value: X2

Uniform: *Headgear:* Dark blue tropical helmet with white metal fittings. *Jacket:* Dark blue Attila with orange piping in the shape of a plastron on the front, as well as around collar and cuffs. Officers wore black silk loopings on their jackets. *Pants:* Dark blue with orange stripes, worn over black shoes. *Equipment:* Black leather.

CAVALRY

Organization: Standard regiments.

Weapons: Officers carry a revolver and saber. Other ranks carry breech-loading carbines and sabers.

Line Cavalry

(Total of four regiments.)

Unit Value: T2

Uniform: *Headgear:* Dark fur cap with white metal chin scales and a light blue pompon (red in the 3rd Regiment). *Jacket:* Blue-black Attila with light blue loopings (red in the 3rd Regiment). *Pants:* Dark blue overalls worn over cavalry boots. *Equipment:* Black leather.

Colonial Cavalry

(Dutch Indies Garrison—total of one regiment.)

Unit Value: X2

Uniform: *Headgear:* Dark blue tropical helmet with white metal fittings. *Jacket:* Dark blue Attila with red piping in the shape of a plastron on the front, as well as around collar and cuffs. Officers wore black silk loopings on their jackets. *Pants:* Dark blue with red stripes over black shoes. *Equipment:* Black leather.

ARTILLERY

Organization: Standard batteries.

Weapons: Officers carry revolvers and sabers. Other ranks carry breech-loading carbines and bayonets, although these are usually left on the gun limber. Field batteries are equipped with 12-pounders. Garrison artillery is equipped with a variety of heavier weapons.

Field Artillery

Unit Value: T0

Uniform: *Headgear:* Dark blue shako with yellow metal plate, red pompon, and black plume. *Jacket:* Dark blue with black collar and red piping on the collar and cuffs. *Pants:* Dark blue with red stripes, worn over black shoes. *Equipment:* Black leather.

Colonial Artillery

(Dutch Indies garrison.)

Unit Value: T1

Uniform: *Headgear:* Dark blue tropical helmet with white metal fittings. *Jacket:* Dark blue Attila with red piping in the shape of a plastron on the front, as well as around the collar and cuffs. Officers wore black silk loopings on their jackets. *Pants:* Dark blue with red stripes, over black shoes. *Equipment:* Black leather.

Portugal: *(Left to right.) Artillery, engineer officer, infantry, lancer.*

Portugal

INFANTRY

Organization: Standard infantry regiments and separately numbered rifle battalions.

Weapons: Officers carry a revolver and saber. Other ranks carry breech-loading rifles and bayonets.

Line Infantry

Unit Value: T1

Uniform: *Headgear:* Black spiked helmet with yellow metal fittings. *Jacket:* Brown with red collar, shoulder straps, and cuff piping. *Pants:* Blue-black with red piping, worn tucked into black boots. White trousers were usually worn in the field. *Equipment:* White leather.

Rifles

Unit Value: X3S

Uniform: *Headgear:* Black spiked helmet with yellow metal fittings. *Jacket:* Brown with black collar, shoulder straps, and cuff piping. *Pants:* Blue-black with black piping, worn tucked into black boots. White trousers were usually worn in the field. *Equipment:* Black leather.

CAVALRY

Organization: Standard regiments.

Weapons: Officers carry a revolver and saber. Other ranks carry breech-loading carbines, sabers, and (in the lancer regiments) lances.

Lancers

(Total of two regiments.)

Unit Value: X1

Uniform: *Headgear:* Black spiked helmet with yellow metal fittings. *Jacket:* Dark blue with red collar, cuffs, and piping around the lower edge of the jacket, and yellow collar patches. Yellow metal shoulder scales. *Pants:* Blue-black with red stripes, tucked into black cavalry boots. *Equipment:* White leather.

Light Cavalry

Unit Value: X2

Uniform: *Headgear:* Black spiked helmet with yellow metal fittings. *Jacket:* Dark blue with red collar, cuffs, and piping around the lower edge of the jacket, and black collar patches. Yellow metal shoulder scales. *Pants:* Blue-black with red stripes, worn tucked into black cavalry boots. *Equipment:* White leather.

ARTILLERY

Organization: Standard batteries.

Weapons: Officers carry revolvers and sabers.

Other ranks carry breech-loading carbines and bayonets, although these weapons are usually left on the gun limber.

Field batteries have 12-pounder guns. Garrison artillery has a variety of heavier pieces.

Field Artillery

Unit Value: X0

Uniform: *Headgear:* Black spiked helmet with yellow metal fittings. *Jacket:* Dark blue with red collar, shoulder straps, and piping on the cuffs. *Pants:* Blue-black with broad, red stripes, worn over black shoes. *Equipment:* White leather.

Rumania: *(Left to right.) Infantry, Rosiori, rifles, Dorobanze, Calarasi, artillery, engineer.*

Rumania

INFANTRY

Organization: Standard regimental organization.

Weapons: Officers carry sabers and revolvers. Other ranks carry breech-loading rifles and bayonets.

Line Infantry

Unit Value: X1

Uniform: *Headgear:* Dark blue kepi with red capband. *Jacket:* Dark blue with red piping, collar patches, shoulder straps, and cuffs. *Pants:* Dark blue with red piping, tucked into black boots. *Equipment*: Black leather.

Rifles

Unit Value: X2S

Uniform: *Headgear:* Round,

black, leather hat with sides pinned up and a fall of green cock's feathers on the right side. *Jacket:* Brown with green piping and cuffs. *Pants:* Dark gray with green piping, tucked into black boots. *Equipment:* Black leather.

Dorobanze

(Auxiliary infantry.)

Unit Value: T1

Uniform: *Headgear:* Black fur cap. Moslem *Dorobanze* wear a red fez with a light blue tassel instead. *Jacket:* Dark blue with light blue piping, collar patches, shoulder straps, and cuffs. *Pants:* White, tucked into black boots. *Equipment:*Black leather.

Frontier Guards

Unit Value: V2

Uniform: *Headgear:* Dark blue kepi with light green capband. *Jacket:* Dark blue with light green piping, collar patches, shoulder straps, and cuffs. *Pants:* Dark blue with light green piping, tucked into black boots. *Equipment:* Black leather.

CAVALRY

Organization: Standard regiments.

Weapons: Officers carry sabers and revolvers. Other ranks carry sabers, breech-loading carbines, and (in the three *Rosiori* regiments) lances.

Rosiori

(Regular cavalry.)

Unit Value: V1

Uniform: *Headgear:* Black fur cap with white feather plume in front, yellow cords, and cloth bag on the left side in the regimental color (1st, yellow; 2nd, white; 3rd, green). Officers instead wore a black kepi with a band of the regiment's distinctive color. *Jacket:* Red dolman with black loopings. *Pants:* White hussar breeches with black loopings, tucked into black hussar boots. *Equipment:* White leather.

Calarasi

(Auxiliary cavalry.)

Unit Value: X1

Uniform: *Headgear:* Black fur cap with white feather plume in front, yellow cords, and a red cloth bag. Officers instead wore a black kepi with a red band. *Jacket:* Dark blue dolman with red loopings. *Pants:* White hussar breeches with red loopings, tucked into black hussar boots. *Equipment*: White leather.

ARTILLERY

Organization: Standard batteries.

Weapons: Officers carry revolvers and sabres. Other ranks carry breech-loading carbines and bayonets, although these are usually left on the gun limber. Field batteries are equipped with 9-pounder guns. Siege batteries are equipped with 6" howitzers.

Artillery

Unit Value: X0

Uniform: *Headgear:* Dark blue kepi with black band and red piping. *Jacket:* Brown with black collar and pointed cuffs piped with red. *Pants:* Gray, tucked into black boots. *Equipment:* Black leather.

Serbia

INFANTRY

Organization: Standard organization.

Weapons: Officers carry sabers and revolvers. Other ranks carry breech-loading rifles and bayonets.

Line Infantry

Unit Value: X2

Uniform: *Headgear:* Dark blue kepi with green piping. This was sometimes replaced in the field by a gray-blue, peakless field cap. *Jacket:* Dark blue with green collar, cuffs, and shoulder straps. *Pants:* Gray-blue, tucked into black boots. *Equipment:* Black leather.

Levy (Militia) Infantry

Unit Value: T2

Uniform: *Headgear:* Gray-blue, peakless field cap. *Jacket:* Brown peasant smock. *Pants:* Brown, tucked into black boots. *Equipment:* Black leather.

CAVALRY

Organization: Standard regiments.

Weapons: Officers carry sabers and revolvers. Other ranks carry sabers and breech-loading carbines.

Line Cavalry

Unit Value: X2

Uniform: *Headgear:* Light blue kepi with dark blue band. In the field this was often replaced by a plain, light blue kepi. *Jacket:* Light blue with dark blue collar, cuffs, and shoulder straps. In the field this was often replaced by a plain, light blue jacket. *Pants:* Madder red, tucked into black boots. *Equipment:* White leather.

Levy (Militia) Cavalry

Unit Value: T1

Uniform: *Headgear:* Red, peak-

Serbia: *(Left to right.) Infantry, artillery officer, cavalry, engineer officer.*

less field cap. *Jacket:* Brown peasant smock. *Pants:* Madder red tucked into black boots. *Equipment:* White leather.

ARTILLERY

Organization: Standard battaries.

Weapons: Officers carry revolvers and sabers. Other ranks carry breech-loading carbines and bayonets, usually left on the gun limber. Light batteries have 9-pounder guns,

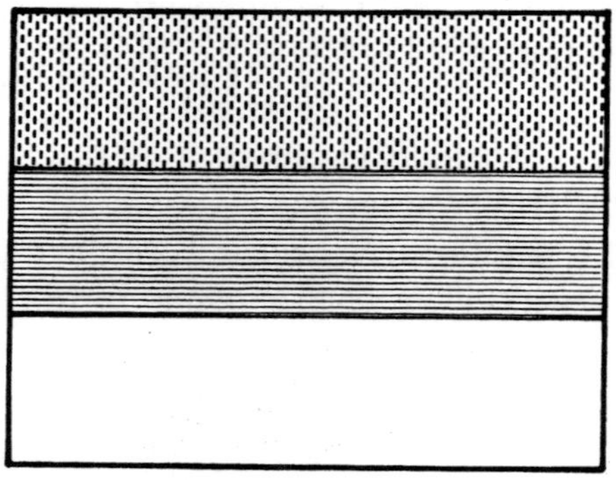

field batteries have 12-pounder guns, and siege batteries have 5" guns.

Artillery

Unit Value: X0

Uniform: *Headgear:* Dark blue kepi with green piping. Sometimes replaced in the field by a black, peakless field cap. *Jacket:* Dark blue with black collar, cuffs, and shoulder straps. *Pants:* Gray-blue, tucked into black boots. *Equipment:* Black leather.

Russia

INFANTRY

Organization: Standard organization except that each regiment has four battalions. In the event of war one battalion stayed behind to train recruits and forward replacements to the other battalions of the regiment.

Weapons: Officers carry a revolver and saber. Other ranks carry breech-loading rifles and bayonets.

Guard Infantry

(Total of 12 regiments.)

Unit Value: V1

Uniform: *Headgear:* Dark green shako with red plume and piping. *Jacket:* Dark green with red piping. The different regiments were identified by the combinations of different colored collars, cuffs, and cuff patches. *Pants:* Dark green, tucked into black boots. *Equipment:* White leather.

Grenadiers

Unit Value: V1

Uniform: *Headgear:* Dark green forage cap with red band and piping. *Jacket:* Dark green with red piping. The shoulder straps were yellow and the color of the piping on the strap indicated to which division the regiment belonged (1st Grenadier Division, red; 2nd, blue; 3rd, white; 4th, yellow), while the color of the collar patch indicated the regiment's position in the division (1st Regiment, red; 2nd Regiment, blue; 3rd Regiment, white; 4th Regiment, dark green). *Pants:* Dark green, tucked into black boots. *Equipment:* White leather.

Line Infantry

Unit Value: X1

Uniform: *Headgear:* Dark green forage cap with red band and piping. *Jacket:* Dark green with red piping. The shoulder strap color indicated to which brigade of the division the regiment belonged (1st Brigade, red; 2nd Brigade, blue), while the color of the collar patch indicated the regiment's position in the division (1st Regiment, red; 2nd Regiment, blue; 3rd Regiment, white; 4th Regiment, dark green). *Pants:* Dark green, tucked into black boots. *Equipment:* White leather.

Rifles

(Total of 10 line battalions and four lifeguard battalions.)

Unit Value: X2S

Uniform: *Headgear:* Dark green forage cap with raspberry red band and piping. Lifeguards wore a low, black, lambskin cap with a yellow metal star on the front. *Jacket:* Dark green with raspberry red (light blue in Finnish units) shoulder straps and a carmine collar and piping. The guard units had lace on their collars as well (white for the 1st Lifeguard Rifles and 3rd Finnish Lifeguard Rifles, yellow for the 2nd and 4th Lifeguard Rifles). *Trousers*: Dark green, tucked into black boots. *Equipment*: Black leather.

CAVALRY

Organization: Standard regiments.

Weapons: Officers carry a revolver and saber. Other ranks carry breech-loading carbines and sabers. Half of all the other ranks in each squadron also carry the lance and form the front rank of the unit when it charges. All cossacks and guard uhlans carry lances.

Guard Heavy Cavalry

(Total of four regiments.)

Unit Value: V0H

Uniform: *Headgear:* Yellow metal helmet with white metal fittings and a spike. In the field this was usually replaced by a white forage cap with red piping in the Chevalier Guard and Lifeguard of Horse, yellow piping in the Czar's Lifeguard, and light blue piping in the Czarina's Lifeguard. *Jacket:* Green with piping around the collar, cuffs, and shoulder straps in the same color as on the forage cap. *Pants:* Gray with stripes the same color as the piping, tucked into cavalry boots. *Equipment:* White leather.

Guard Dragoons

(Total of two regiments.)

Russia: *(Left to right.) Cossack officer, guard cuirassier (field dress on dismounted picket), line infantry, artillery officer, guard uhlan, guard hussar, line dragoon.*

Unit Value: V1

Uniform: *Headgear:* Green forage cap with red piping and band. *Jacket:* Green with red collar, pointed cuffs, shoulder straps, and lapels, yellow lace on the collar, cuffs, and lapels, and metal shoulder scales with red fringe. In the Lifeguard Dragoon Regiment, the shoulder scales were white metal; in the Lifeguard Grenadier Regiment of Horse, they were yellow. *Pants:* Gray with red piping, tucked into cavalry boots. *Equipment:* White leather.

Guard Hussars

(Total of two regiments.)

Unit Value: X2

Uniform: *Headgear:* Black fur cap. *Jacket:* Red dolman and white pelisse with yellow loopings in the Guard Hussar Regiment; green Attila and pelisse with white loopings in the Grodno Hussar Regiment. *Pants:* Gray tucked into hussar boots. *Equipment:* Black leather. The Guard Hussar Regiment rode white horses while the Grodno Hussar Regiment rode browns.

Guard Uhlans

(Lancers—total of two regiments.)

Unit Value: X1

Uniform: *Headgear:* Lance cap with red capband and sides in the Czarina's Lifeguard Uhlans and red capband with yellow sides in the Czar's Lifeguard Uhlans. *Jacket:* Blue lancer jacket with red collar, shoulder straps, piping, pointed cuffs, and sash. Lace loopings were yellow in the Czarina's Lifeguard Uhlans, and white in the Czar's Lifeguard Uhlans. *Pants:* Gray, tucked into cavalry boots. *Equipment:* White leather.

Line Dragoons

Unit Value: T1

Uniform: *Headgear:* Green forage cap with red piping and band. *Jacket:* Green with collar patch and cuff piping in the distinctive color of the regiment. *Pants:* Gray with red piping, tucked into cavalry boots. *Equipment:* White leather.

ARTILLERY

Organization: Standard batteries, except that each of the batteries has four gun sections.

Weapons: Officers carry revolvers and sabers. Other ranks carry breech-loading carbines and bayonets, although these are usually left on the gun limber. Light batteries are equipped with 12-pounder guns, heavy batteries with 20-pounder guns, and garrison and siege batteries with 6" guns and howitzers.

Field Artillery

Unit Value: XO

Uniform: *Headgear:* Black lambskin cap with yellow metal plate. *Jacket:* Dark green with red piping and shoulder straps. Officers had black collars and cuffs with gold lace. *Pants:* Dark green (blue in the horse artillery), tucked into black boots. *Equipment:* Black leather.

Spain

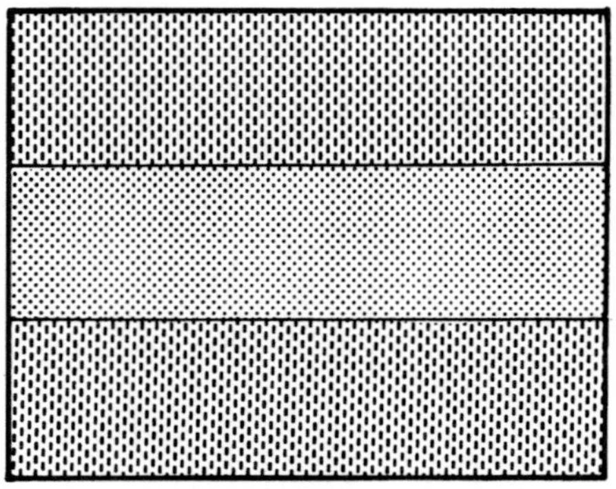

INFANTRY

Organization: Standard regiments with separately numbered rifle battalions.

Weapons: Officers carry a revolver and a saber. Other ranks carry breech-loading rifles and bayonets.

Line Infantry

Unit Value: T1

Uniform: *Headgear:* Dark blue Ros with black or white cover. *Jacket:* Dark blue with red collar, cuffs, piping, and shoulder wings. *Pants:* Madder red. *Equipment:* White leather.

Rifles

Unit Value: T3S

Uniform: *Headgear:* Dark blue Ros with black or white cover. *Jacket:* Dark blue with green collar, shoulder wings, and piping on the shoulder straps. *Pants:* Madder red. *Equipment:* Black leather.

CAVALRY

Organization: Standard regiments.

Weapons: Officers carry a revolver and a saber. Other ranks carry breech-loading carbines, sabers, and (in lancer regiments) lances. Other ranks in

***Spain:** (Left to right.) Line infantry, light cavalry, lancer, hussar officer.*

the mounted rifles have breech-loading rifles and bayonets.

Cuirassiers

(Total of one regiment.)

Unit Value: X0H

Uniform: *Headgear:* Yellow metal helmet with black plume. *Jacket:* Blue with yellow collar and epaulettes. Steel cuirass with yellow metal fittings. *Pants:* Light blue, tucked into cavalry boots. *Equipment:* White leather.

Lancers

Unit Value: T1

Uniform: *Headgear:* Steel helmet. *Jacket:* Light blue dolman with red collar and cuffs, and black loopings. *Pants:* Red with light blue stripes, tucked into cavalry boots. *Equipment:* White leather.

Hussars

(Total of two regiments.)

Unit Value: X2

Uniform: *Headgear:* White kepi in the Princess' Hussars, and blue kepi in the Pavia Hussars. *Jacket:* Light blue dolman with yellow loopings and white pelisse in the Princess' Hussars, red dolman with yellow loopings and light blue pelisse in the Pavia Hussars. The pelisse was not usually worn in the field. *Pants:* Light blue tucked into hussar boots. *Equipment:* White leather.

Mounted Rifles

(Count as light horse.)

Unit Value: T1

Uniform: *Headgear:* Light blue kepis with red lace around the top. Steel helmet. *Jacket:* Light blue dolman with red collar and cuffs and black loopings. *Pants:* Red with light blue stripes, tucked into cavalry boots. *Equipment:* White leather.

ARTILLERY

Organization: Standard batteries.

Weapons: Officers carry revolvers and sabers.

Other ranks carry breech-loading carbines and bayonets, although these are usually left on the gun limber. Field batteries are equipped with 12-pounder guns.

Artillery

Unit Value: T0

Uniform: *Headgear:* White Ros with red lace and plume. *Jacket:* Dark blue with red collar, cuffs, piping, and shoulder wings. *Pants:* Dark blue with red stripes worn over black shoes. *Equipment:* White leather.

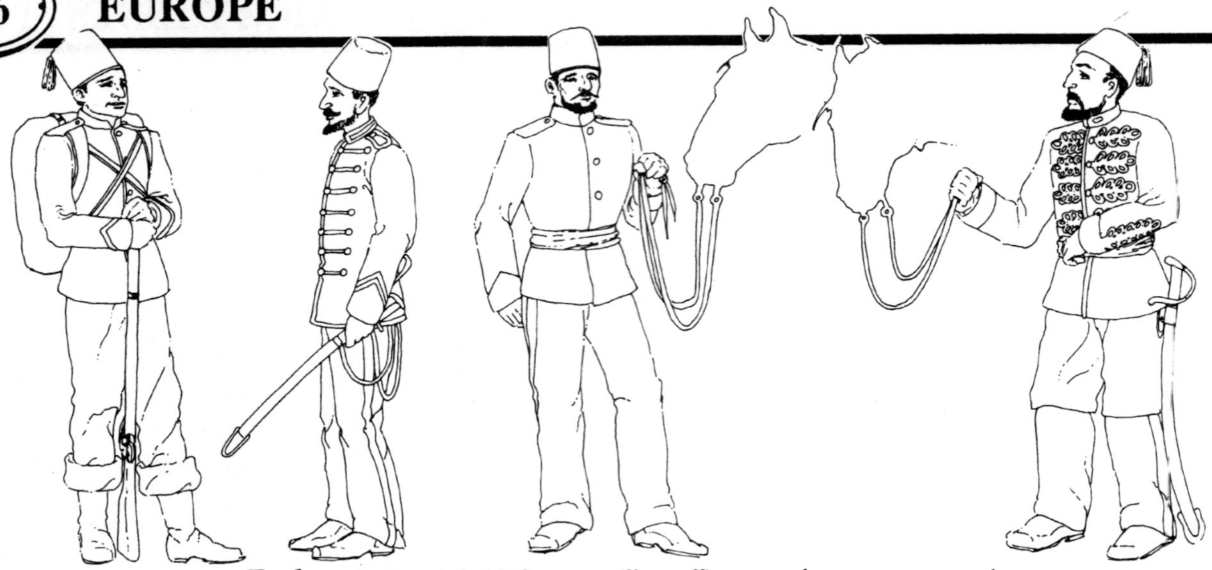

Turkey: *(Left to right.) Infantry, artillery officer, cavalry trooper, general.*

Turkey

INFANTRY

Organization: Standard infantry regiments with separate rifle battalions.

Weapons: Officers carry sabers and revolvers. Other ranks carry breech-loading rifles and bayonets.

Regular Infantry

Unit Value: X1

Uniform: *Headgear:* Red fez with dark blue tassel. *Jacket:* Dark blue with red collar patches, shoulder straps, and piping. *Pants:* Dark blue with red piping, tucked into black boots. *Equipment:* White leather.

Reserve Infantry

Unit Value: T1

Uniform: *Headgear:* Red fez with dark blue tassel. *Jacket:* Dark blue with red collar patches, shoulder straps, and piping. *Pants:* Dark blue with red piping, tucked into black boots. *Equipment:* White leather.

Rifles

Unit Value: X2S

Uniform: *Headgear:* Red fez with dark blue tassel. *Jacket:* Dark blue with dark green collar patches, shoulder straps, and piping. *Pants:* Dark blue with dark green piping tucked into black boots. *Equipment:* Black leather.

CAVALRY

Organization: Standard regiments.

Weapons: Officers carry sabers and revolvers. Half of the other ranks in each regiment carry lances and sabers, while the other half of the other ranks carry sabers and lever-action rifles. The lancers form the front rank when charging.

Line Cavalry

Unit Value: X1

Uniform: *Headgear:* Black kolpak. *Jacket:* Dark blue with collar and pointed cuffs in regimental distinctive color (usually red or green), yellow metal shoulder scales. *Pants:* Light gray with piping the same color as the collar and cuffs. *Equipment:* Black leather.

ARTILLERY

Organization: Standard batteries.

Weapons: Officers carry revolvers and sabers. Other ranks carry breech-loading carbines and bayonets, although these are usually left on the gun limber. Light batteries have 9-pounder guns, field batteries have 15-pounder guns, and garrison and siege batteries are equipped with heavier pieces.

Artillery

Unit Value: X0

Uniform: *Headgear:* Black fur cap. *Jacket:* Dark blue Attila with black loopings. *Pants:* Gray with broad, red stripes, tucked into black boots. *Equipment:* Black leather.

Trans-Balkania

INFANTRY

Organization: A small regular army of separately named infantry battalions exists. The bulk of the infantry is made up of militia levies.

Weapons: Officers carry sabers and revolvers. Other ranks carry breech-loading rifles and bayonets in the regulars, rifle muskets in the militia.

Lifeguard Foot

(Total of one battalion.)

Unit Value: V1

Uniform: *Headgear:* Black fur cap with yellow metal plate. *Jacket:* Light blue with red collar, cuffs, and shoulder straps. *Pants:* Blue-gray tucked into black boots. *Equipment:* Black leather.

Line Infantry

(Total of three battalions.)

Unit Value: X1

Uniform: *Headgear:* A light blue shako with green trim in the Nevrekop Battalion, dark blue trim in the Dschumaja Battalion, and a red fez with a white tassel in the Bunjsko Battalion. *Jacket:* Light blue with collar, cuffs,

and shoulder straps in the same color as the shako trim or fez tassel. *Pants:* Blue-gray, tucked into black boots. *Equipment:* White leather.

Militia Infantry

Unit Value: T3S (irregulars)

Uniform: Officers wore the infantry uniform with red-brown distinctions. Other ranks wore peasant garb with brown leather equipment.

CAVALRY

Organization: Only one squadron exists—the Prince's Escort.

Weapons: Officers carry sabers and revolvers. Other ranks carry sabers, lances, and breech-loading carbines.

The Prince's Escort

Unit Value: V1

Uniform: *Headgear:* Black fur cap with yellow metal plate. *Jacket:* Light blue Attila with red loopings. *Pants:* White hussar breeches with red loopings, tucked into black hussar boots. *Equipment:* White leather.

ARTILLERY

Organization: Standard battery organization.

Weapons: Officers carry revolvers and sabers. Other ranks carry breech-loading carbines and bayonets, although these are usually left on the gun limber. The one field battery in the army has two 9-pounder guns and one 7-pounder mountain howitzer.

Artillery

Unit Value: X0

Uniform: *Headgear:* Light blue shako with black trim. *Jacket:* Light blue with black collar, cuffs, and shoulder straps. *Pants:* Blue-gray, tucked into black boots. *Equipment:* Black leather.

Abyssinia

INFANTRY

Organization: Regiments, each with three bands of irregulars and one senior leader

Weapons: Royal regiments have rifle-muskets, levies have muskets.

Royal Regiment

(About half of any army.)

Unit Value: X3

Uniform: Loincloth, feathered headdress.

Tribal Levies

Unit Value: T2

Uniform: Loincloth, feathered headdress.

ARTILLERY

Organization: Individual gun sections.

Weapons: Smoothbore guns, equivalent to 9-pounders for field artillery, and 24-pounders for fortress guns.

Artillery

Unit Value: T0

Uniform: Loincloth.

Boers

THE BOERS of the Transvaal and Orange Free State have no formal standing army. Instead, mounted "commandos" are formed when needed from local farmers.

COMMANDO

Organization: Each commando is treated as a band of irregular mounted infantry.

Weapons: Breech-loading rifles.

Boer Commando

Unit Value: V3

Uniform: Civilian clothing.

ARTILLERY

Organization: Individual gun sections.

Weapons: Officers carry revolvers. Other ranks carry breech-loading rifles, although these are usually left on the gun limber. Guns range from primitive smoothbores to a few modern breech-loading pieces.

Boer Artillery

Unit Value: V1

Uniform: Civilian clothing.

Egypt

THE EGYPTIAN ARMY revolted several years ago, was defeated and mostly disbanded by the British, and is now struggling to reform under British sponsorship. The hard-fighting core of the army remains the Sudanese battalions, but the Egyptian battalions are beginning to respond to training and discipline as well.

INFANTRY

Organization: Standard battalions, consecutively numbered. There are no regiments.

Weapons: Officers carry revolvers and sabers. Other ranks carry breech-loading rifles and bayonets.

Egyptian Infantry

Unit Value: T1

Uniform: *Headgear:* Red fez. *Jacket:* White. *Pants:* White. *Equipment:* Black leather.

Sudanese Infantry

Unit Value: V2

Uniform: *Headgear:* Red fez. *Jacket:* Dark blue. *Pants:* White. *Equipment:* Black leather.

CAVALRY

Organization: Standard regiments.

Weapons: Officers carry sabers and revolvers. Other ranks carry sabers and muzzle-loading rifled carbines. Some regiments carry lances.

Egyptian Cavalry

Unit Value: T1

Uniform: *Headgear:* Red fez. *Jacket:* White. *Pants:* White. *Equipment:* Black leather.

ARTILLERY

Organization: Standard batteries.

Weapons: Officers carry revolvers and sabers. Other ranks carry breech-loading carbines and bayonets, although these are usually left on the gun limber.

Field batteries are equipped with 9-pounder guns.

Field Artillery

Unit Value: T0

Uniform: *Headgear:* Red fez. *Jacket:* Dark blue. *Pants:* Dark blue. *Equipment:* Black leather.

Other Arabs

OTHER ARAB ARMIES are treated as irregulars, mostly cavalry (except for troops defending cities), with some bands on camels. All are armed with sabers and rifle-muskets. The average band is trained, but the occasional Green, Experienced, or even Veteran band may be encountered. The referee may alter this for his campaign.

Dahome: *(Left to right.) Regular infantry (2 views).*

Dahome

DAHOME IS AN EXAMPLE of how extensively organized some of the native armies of the African kingdoms can be, although it should in no way be considered a typical army. The Dahomean Army is most famous for its regiments of "Amazons," and the female regiments of the army are the best of the lot, known both for their bravery and determination in pressing home a charge and for their skill in infiltration and Fieldcraft. The Royal Bodyguard and the regulars are considered regular troops; the hunters and tribal levies are irregulars.

INFANTRY

Organization: "Regiments," each of two war bands, plus one leader, one flagman, and one drummer.

Royal Bodyguard

(Total of one regiment of men and one of women.)

Unit Value: V2 (women E3)

Weapons: Breech-loading rifles and bayonets.

Uniform: *Headgear:* Red fez. *Jacket:* Red tunic. *Pants:* White knee-length trousers (blue skirts for women). *Equipment:* White cross-straps.

Regular Infantry

(Total of four regiments of men and four regiments of women.)

Unit Value: T1 (women X3)

Weapons: Rifle-muskets and bayonets.

Uniform: *Headgear:* White fez. Officers wore white turbans. *Jacket:* White, long tunic with blue stripes, although this was usually discarded for battle. *Pants:* White knee-length trousers for men, blue skirts for women. *Equipment:* Various types.

Hunters

(Total of four regiments of men.)

Unit Value: G3S

Weapons: Rifle-muskets.

Uniform: Loincloths, animal skins, and feathered headdresses.

Tribal Levies

(Total of 15 regiments.)

Unit Value: G1

Weapons: One band with smoothbore carbines, one with spears.

Uniform: Loincloth and feathered headdress.

ARTILLERY

Organization: Total of four gun sections, each with two to four gunners (as required by the piece), plus a total of two German officers (in civilian safari dress) as battery commanders.

Weapons: Two 6-pounders and two Mitrailleuse.

Artillery

Unit Value: G0

Uniform: As regular infantry.

Equatoria

THE ENTIRE ARMY of Equatoria consists of two battalions of Sudanese infantry stationed there before the Mahdi's uprising and stranded there ever since. The battalions have undertaken some local recruiting to keep up to strength but have maintained a high state of readiness and training.

INFANTRY

Organization: Standard infantry battalions.

Weapons: Officers carry sabers and revolvers. Other ranks carry breech-loading rifles and bayonets.

Sudanese Infantry

Unit Value: V3

Uniform: *Headgear:* Red fez. *Jacket:* Dark blue. *Pants:* White. *Equipment:* Black leather.

Herreros

THE HERREROS are the most important inhabitants of German Southwest Africa. They are relatively few in number (as the land is not fertile enough to support a dense population) but are extremely westernized. They tend to be freeholding farmers and are temporarily content with German rule. There are growing signs of friction, however, between the German colonial authorities and the Herreros. Although German military leaders are confident that they could easily deal with any trouble, the recent defeat of the British by the Boers in the Transvaal casts some doubt upon this. It is perhaps significant that German colonial troops stationed in the region sometimes call the Herreros "Black Boers."

INFANTRY

Organization: Separate irregular bands of mounted infantry. Never more than two or three bands are at one place in the event of a revolt.

Weapons: Half the bands would be equipped with rifle muskets, half with breech-loading rifles.

Unit Value: V3

Uniform: Civilian clothes.

Mahdist Empire (The Dervish Empire)

ORIGINALLY FANATICALLY brave, the *ansars* (soldiers) of the Mahdist empire are now showing signs of corruption and decline.

The "Fuzzy Wuzzies" (warriors of the eastern Sudan) under their leader Osman Dinga remain fierce foes, however.

Most dervish armies are liable to contain a small nucleus (about 10 percent of the total) of Sudanese riflemen (called *jehadia*) who fight under black flags and who are mostly deserters from the Sudanese regulars of the Egyptian army.

INFANTRY

Organization: Separate war bands, several of which will be gathered together under an emir (general) for a battle.

Weapons: Fuzzy Wuzzies are armed with swords and shields, with four men in each war band having rifle muskets. Dervish *ansar* bands are armed, half with melee weapons and half with firearms. Half of the *ansar* bands will have smoothbore muskets, and half will have rifle-muskets. Sudanese *jehadia* riflemen have breech-loading rifles and bayonets and are treated as regulars.

Ansars

Unit Value: T1

Uniform: *Headgear:* White turban.

Jacket: White robe with square colored patches on the sleeves, front, and back. *Pants:* White baggy pants. *Equipment:* Various.

Jehadia

Unit Value: V2S

Uniform: Mixtures of the old Sudanese uniforms and Dervish costumes.

Fuzzy Wuzzies

Unit Value: V3

Uniform: Loincloth.

ARTILLERY

Organization: Individual gun sections.

Weapons: Leaders carry sabers. Other ranks carry smoothbore muskets, although these are usually left on the gun limber. Gun sections are equipped with a mixture of old smoothbore guns and a few modern 9-pounders captured from the Egyptian army.

Artillery

Unit Value: T0

Uniform: As dervish infantry (*ansars*).

Other Sub-Saharan Nations

OTHER SUB-SAHARAN natives are treated as irregular infantry. On the average, half are armed with smoothbore muskets, half with spears and shields. The tribes very close to European or Arab enclaves are armed with muskets almost exclusively, while those deep in the interior have virtually no firearms. In the organized states, half the bands are Trained and half are Experienced, with a few Green and a few Veteran. In the unorganized tribal areas, about half are Trained and half are Green, with only an occasional Experienced band.

Malagasy (Island of Madagascar)

INFANTRY

Organization: A very large regular army existed, equipped and trained along European lines, supplemented by a larger provincial, or reserve, army. The regulars were organized in separate battalions. Provincials were treated as irregular war bands.

Weapons: Regular officers carry sabers. Other ranks carry breech-loading rifles and bayonets. About one-quarter of the provincial war bands are equipped with smoothbore muskets; the rest have spears and shields.

Regular Infantry

Unit Value: X1

Uniform: *Headgear:* Broad, blue cylindrical hat with the sides taller than the front or back. *Jacket:* Blue or white with either red or blue pointed cuffs, depending on the battalion. *Pants:* White. *Equipment:* Black leather.

Provincials

Unit Value: T2

Uniform: *Headgear:* Sweatband, broad-brimmed hat, or turban. *Jacket:* Loose, flowing tunic or robe, gathered by a belt at the waist. Musket-equipped bands often wore a white cloak wrapped around the upper body over the shoulders. *Equipment:* Black leather.

ARTILLERY

Organization: Standard batteries.

Weapons: Officers carried sabers. Gunners do not appear to have been armed.

Three batteries are equipped with 6-pounder guns, one battery is equipped with 12-pounder guns, and three batteries are equipped with Gardner machineguns.

Artillery

Unit Value: X1

Uniform: *Headgear:* Broad, blue cylindrical hat with the sides taller than the front or back. *Jacket:* Blue. *Pants:* White. *Equipment:* Black leather.

Malagasy: *(Left to right.) Artillery gunner, provincial rifleman, regular officer, provincial rifleman, regular infantry, provincial spearman.*

Matabeles: *(Left to right.) Elite unmarried regiment, married regiment.*

Matabeles

THE MATABELES had broken away from the Zulu kingdom in the 1820s and moved north. They quickly carved a new kingdom of their own from the land of the Mashona north of the Limpopo River. Their military system was based loosely on that of the Zulus, with age-based regiments. Unlike the Zulus, they had very few married regiments. The army consisted exclusively of infantry.

Organization: All troops were irregulars. Two or three war bands make up a regiment, of which there were approximately 30. These were about evenly divided between *zansi* regiments (made up of descendants of the original immigrants from Zululand), *enhla* (descendants of those who joined the tribe while it travelled through the Transvaal), and *holi* (made up of the Matabeles' Mashona subjects).

Weapons: Two men in each war band have smoothbore muskets. All others have spears and shields.

Married Regiment

(Probably no more than five total.)

Unit Value: V2

Uniform: *Headgear:* Stuffed headband of otter skin with a single crane feather on each side sticking straight up. *Pants:* Loin covering made from hanging strips of jackal skin. *Shields:* Zulu-style with regiments differentiated by the shield pattern.

Young Elite Regiment

(Probably no more than five total.)

Unit Value: V3

Uniform: *Headgear:* Circlet of black ostrich feathers around the head with a large, clipped pompon of the same material worn over the forehead. Some regiments were differentiated by the color of an additional plume or feather worn in the pompon. *Pants:* Loin covering made from hanging strips of jackal skin. A kilt made from strips of monkey fur was worn over this. *Shields:* Zulu-style with regiments differentiated by the shield pattern.

Average Young Regiment

(Perhaps 10 total.)

Unit Value: X2

Uniform: Same as elite regiments, but no kilt.

Young Holi Regiment

(Perhaps 10 total.)

Unit Value: T2

Uniform: Same as the other young regiments, but of inferior material. A loincloth was usually worn instead of the more elaborate covering, and the ostrich feather circlet and pompon tended to have a thin and ratty look to them.

Western Soodan: *(Left to right.) Bola infantry, bola infantry (alternate), sofa infantry, cavalry.*

Western Soodan (Samorian Empire)

THE WESTERN SOODAN was, at this time, an empire carved out by a remarkable leader, Samori Toure. The empire was not a nation in any real sense of the word and was held together solely by the personality and will of the *Alamamy* Samori. Samori is under increasing pressure from the French to the west, and both sides know that war is inevitable. Samori has managed to organize a remarkable army, the best parts of which were trained, equipped, and uniformed in reasonably good style.

The Samorian Army is divided into a Royal Army commanded by Samori himself and five field armies, one in each of the provinces of the empire, each commanded by a *keletigi*. Each field army contains up to 25 war bands, while the Royal Army contains about 40. Naturally, not all of these will be available to take the field at the same time, as many are tied up with occupation duty.

INFANTRY

Organization: The majority of troops are irregulars. Each irregular band (called a *bola)* was commanded by a mounted officer *(bolokuntigi)* and two junior officers on foot. The hard core of the army, however, were the *sofas* (sharpshooters). These units were equipped with modern rifles, uniformed, and were drilled and disciplined as regulars. Each *sofa* is smaller than a normal company, with 15 men each and including only two officers on foot. *Sofas* were grouped into regiments of four *sofas* each, and were commanded by a mounted officer. A typical army might be made up of half *bolas* and half *sofas,* with the *sofas* being about half Elite and half Experienced.

Weapons: *Bolas* carry smoothbore muskets. *Sofas* carry breech-loading rifles.

Bola

Unit Value: T2 (irregulars)

Uniform: *Headgear:* A mixture of flat conical hats (very much like Chinese "coolie" hats) and cotton bags which hung down on one side or to the rear. Chiefs wear turbans, usually red. *Jacket:* Thigh-length, loose smock with large sleeves. Colors varied within a unit, but most were dark yellow to light brown. *Pants:* Large, baggy pants which narrow toward the ankles, sometimes cut off at the knee. Colors varied as with the smock. *Equipment:* A red cord holding a knife sheath or powder horn.

Sofas

Unit Value: X2 (regulars)

Uniform: *Headgear:* A mixture of native hats (see above) and European slouch hats, top hats, etc. Officers wear turbans or red fezes. *Jacket:* A mixture of European clothing, including uniform coats, frock coats, and various pieces of formal wear. *Pants:* Large, baggy pants which narrow toward the ankles, sometimes cut off at the knee. Color was usually a shade of blue. *Equipment:* A mixture of black, brown, and white leather.

Elite Sofas

(Includes the Royal Guard.)

Unit Value: V2 (regulars)

Uniform: *Headgear:* Red or red-brown fez. *Jacket:* Dark blue with red sash. *Pants:* White or blue European trousers. *Equipment:* A mixture of black, brown, and white leather.

CAVALRY

Organization: There was very little cavalry in Samori's army. What cavalry existed was all irregular and organized in small companies, each of which had one chief and eight warriors.

Weapons: All ranks carried sabers, and the warriors carried lances as well.

Irregular Cavalry

Unit Value: T1 (irregulars)

Uniform: Very similar to the uniform of the *bolas,* but with a wide-brimmed leather hat. Chiefs wore turbans.

ARTILLERY

Organization: There was very little artillery in this army. There should be no artillery present at most battles, and only rarely would there be more than a single gun section.

Weapons: Old, smoothbore 6-pounders or 9-pounders.

Artillery

Unit Value: T0 (irregular)

Uniform: Unknown.

Rabeh's Empire

Rabeh Fadal Allah, also known as Rabah Zubeir, in the early 1880s was a lieutenant of Sulayman, the son of Zubeir Pasha, the powerful slaver of the southwestern Sudan. When Gordon broke the power of Zubeir, scattered his army, and executed his son Sulayman, Rabeh fled to the west with a small band of followers. As his men were disciplined Sudanese riflemen armed with breech-loading rifles, they soon defeated the poorly trained and equipped forces of the petty sultans in the Lake Chad region. Known as "The Napoleon of Africa," Rabeh now has a substantial empire held together by an army small by African standards, but exceptionally effective.

INFANTRY

Organization: The basis of Rabeh's army was his Sudanese riflemen, now expanded to a force of 15 companies. All of these were considered regulars. They were supplemented by tribal levies, although Rabeh puts little faith in them for anything more than police work. All tribal levies were treated as irregular war bands.

Weapons: All of the regular companies are armed with breech-loading rifles. All tribal levies are equipped with swords, or spears and shields.

Regular Infantry

Unit Value: V2

Uniform: *Headgear:* White turban. *Jacket:* Baggy, white jacket. *Pants:* Baggy, white pants. *Equipment:* Black leather.

Tribal Levies

Unit Value: T2

Uniform: Loincloth and feathered headdress in the south; white turban, baggy jacket and pants in the north.

Zulus

The Zulu nation commanded one of the most powerful armies of southern Africa until defeated 10 years ago by Great Britain. It was disbanded and broken up into smaller tribal holdings, but some sentiment for rebellion remains, and violence occurs. (Ten years ago the regiments would probably have been rated one level higher.)

INFANTRY

Organization: Regiments, each with one *induna* (commander) and five *iviyos* (war bands)

Weapons: One or two bands per regiment have half their men equipped with smoothbore muskets. All others are equipped with spears and shields.

Married Regiment

Unit Value: X3 each

Uniform: Headring, loincloth, distinctively patterned shield.

Unmarried Regiment

Unit Value: T2

Uniform: Loincloth, distinctly patterned shield.

Latin American Armies: *(Left to right.) Mexican infantry, Chilean infantry, Argentinian horse grenadier, Brazilian infantry, Brazilian presidential guard.*

Argentina

INFANTRY

Organization: Independent battalions (standard organization).

Weapons: Officers carry sabers and revolvers; other ranks carry breech-loading rifles and bayonets.

Line Infantry

Unit Value: T1

Uniform: *Headgear:* Black leather shako with green plume. *Jacket:* Turquoise-blue with green collar, cuffs, and epaulettes. (Sometimes a tan, linen jacket without markings was worn in the field.) *Pants:* Baggy, red trousers tucked into white gaiters. (Tan trousers if worn with the linen jacket.) *Equipment:* White leather.

CAVALRY

Organization: Regiments (stan-

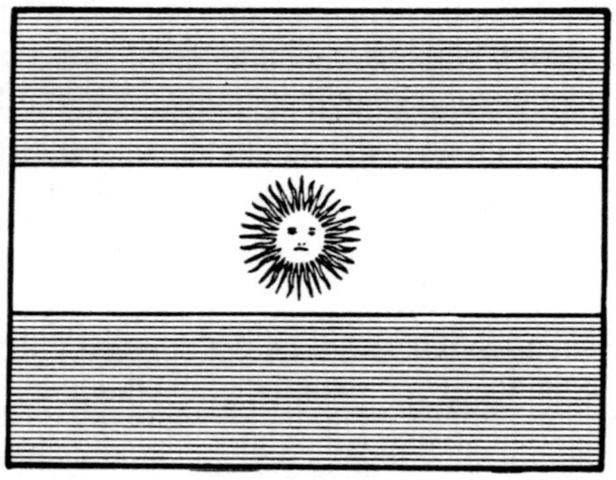

dard organization).

Weapons: All ranks carry sabers. Officers carry revolvers; other ranks carry breech-loading carbines.

Line Cavalry

Unit Value: T1

Uniform: *Headgear:* Red kepi and plume. *Jacket:* Dark blue dolman with red collar, pointed cuffs, and epaulettes. *Trousers:* Red, tucked into black cavalry boots *Equipment:* White leather.

Horse Grenadiers

(One regiment only.)

Unit Value: X0H

Uniform: *Headgear:* Black bell-top shako with red band around the top, red plume, and cords. In the field, a khaki, peaked service cap. *Jacket:* Blue coat and lapels with red collar, piping, and epaulettes. In the field, a khaki service jacket. *Pants:* Turquoise with red stripes, tucked into black cavalry boots, or khaki service trousers when the khaki jacket was worn. *Equipment:* White leather.

ARTILLERY

Organization: Batteries of two gun sections each, but usually deployed in individual sections.

Weapons: Officers carry sabers and revolvers. Other ranks carry breech-loading carbines and bayonets, but these are generally left on the ammunition limber in action. Batteries are equipped with 6-pounder and 12-pounder guns and 7-pounder howitzers.

Line Artillery

Unit Value: T0

Uniform: *Headgear:* Dark blue kepi with red piping and plume. *Jacket:* Dark blue dolman with red collar, cuffs, and epaulettes. *Pants:* Dark blue trousers with double red stripes. *Equipment:* White leather.

Brazil

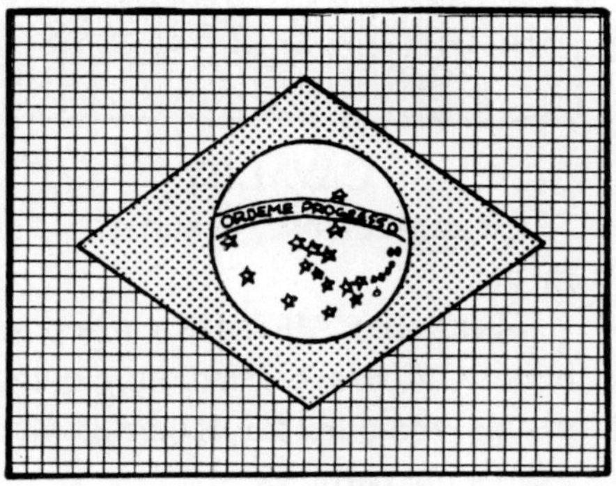

INFANTRY

Organization: Battalions were organized normally and numbered sequentially. There were no infantry regiments.

Weapons: Officers carry sabers and revolvers. Other ranks carry breech-loading rifles and bayonets.

Fusilier

Unit Value: T1

Uniform: *Headgear:* Dark blue spiked helmet with black front and back peaks and a yellow metal plate. In the field, this was usually replaced by a dark blue kepi with red band and piping. *Jacket:* Dark blue with red collar and cuff patches. *Pants:* Dark blue with red stripes, tucked into black gaiters. *Equipment:* White leather.

Rifle

Unit Value: T2S

Uniform: Same as fusiliers.

CAVALRY

Organization: Standard regiments.

Weapons: All ranks carry sabers. Other ranks carry muzzle-loading carbines.

Line Cavalry

(Total of four regiments.)

Unit Value: T1

Uniform: *Headgear:* Red cavalry helmet with yellow metal comb, white horsehair criniere, and small white plume at the front. *Jacket:* Dark blue with red collar and cuff patches and white piping, and yellow metal shoulder scales. *Pants:* Royal blue with broad red stripes, tucked into black cavalry boots. *Equipment:* White leather.

Presidential Guard

(One regiment only.)

Unit Value: X0

Uniform: *Headgear:* Black cavalry helmet with yellow metal comb and front plate, and a red plume and horsehair criniere. *Jacket:* White coat with red collar, cuffs, and piping, and yellow metal shoulder scales. White gauntlets were usually worn which covered the cuffs. *Pants:* White breeches tucked into black cavalry boots. *Equipment:* Black leather.

ARTILLERY

Organization: Standard battery organizations. Batteries were administratively grouped into two battalions of foot artillery and one of horse artillery, but individual batteries or single gun sections were the standard tactical unit used in the field.

Weapons: Officers carry sabers and revolvers. Other ranks carry breech-loading carbines, but these are generally left on the ammunition limber in action. Horse batteries are equipped with 6-pounder guns. Foot batteries are equipped with 12-pounder guns.

Foot Artillery, Horse Artillery

Unit Value: G0

Uniform: *Headgear:* Spiked infantry helmet for foot artillery, except that the main body of the helmet was red instead of blue. Horse artillery wore a red cavalry helmet, similar to that worn by the line cavalry, but with a red criniere and a red and black plume. *Jacket:* Dark blue jacket. First battalion had red collar patches and black cuffs; the second, black collar patches and red cuffs; the horse artillery, red collar patches and cuffs. *Pants:* Royal blue with broad, red stripes, tucked into black gaiters or, in the horse artillery, black cavalry boots. *Equipment:* Black leather.

Chile

INFANTRY

Organization: Battalions were organized normally and numbered sequentially. There were no infantry regiments.

Weapons: Officers carry sabers and revolvers.

Other ranks carry breech-loading rifles and bayonets.

Line Infantry

Unit Value: X2

Uniform: *Headgear:* Black shako. Usually replaced by a blue kepi in the field. *Jacket:* Dark blue with red collar and cuffs. Usually replaced by a tan or khaki jacket in the field. *Pants:* Red, tucked into boots. Usually replaced by tan or khaki in the field. *Equipment:* Black leather.

CAVALRY

Organization: Standard regiments.

Weapons: All ranks carried sabers. Officers carried single-shot pistols, and other ranks carried muzzleloading carbines.

Line Cavalry

Unit Value: X2

Uniform: Considerable latitude was allowed, and most regiments had a distinctive uniform. Hussar styles may have predominated. In the field, a simple tan or khaki uniform was worn with a blue kepi or black shako.

ARTILLERY

Organization: Standard batteries.

Weapons: Officers carry sabers and revolvers. Other ranks carry breech-loading carbines, but these are generally left on the ammunition limber in action. Batteries are equipped with 12-pounder guns.

Field Artillery

Unit Value: T0

Uniform: Details are not known, but it was believed to be a simple khaki or tan uniform in the field with a blue kepi trimmed in red.

Mexico

INFANTRY

Organization: Battalions were organized normally and numbered sequentially. There were no regiments.

Weapons: Officers carry sabers and revolvers. Other ranks carry breech-loading rifles and bayonets.

Line Infantry

Unit Value: T1

Uniform: *Headgear:* Black leather shako with a red band around the edge, sometimes replaced by a leather kepi in the field. *Jacket:* Linen jacket with red collar patches. *Pants:* Linen or white canvas, worn over the shoes, and often worn with the cuffs rolled up to mid-shin. *Equipment:* Black leather.

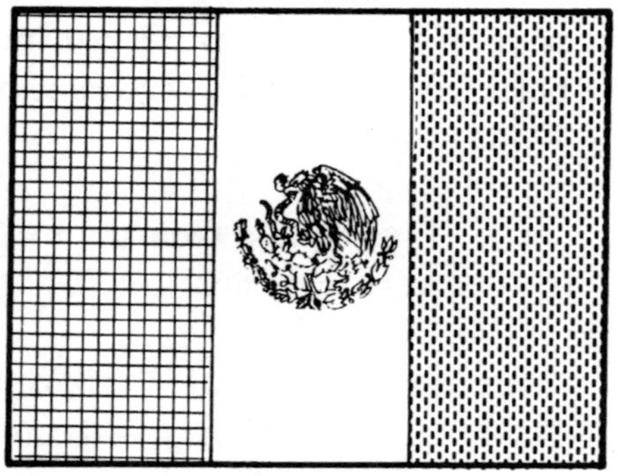

Rifles

(Total of two battalions.)

Unit Value: T2S

Uniform: Same as line infantry.

CAVALRY

Organization: Standard regiments.

Weapons: Officers carry sabers and revolvers. Other ranks have sabers, lances, and breech-loading carbines.

Line Cavalry

Unit Value: T2

Uniform: *Headgear:* Black leather shako with a red band around the edge, a red pompon, and a yellow metal plate with the number of the regiment. *Jacket:* Gray with light green collar, cuffs, and turnbacks (turned-back corners of the coattails).

Pants: Gray with light green stripes, worn pover the boots, and with leather covering the bottom. *Equipment:* Black leather.

ARTILLERY

Organization: Standard batteries, but usually deployed in single gun sections.

Weapons: Officers carry revolvers and sabers. Other ranks carry breech-loading carbines and bayonets, although these are usually left on the gun limbers during action. Batteries are equipped with 6-pounder and 9-pounder guns and 7-pounder howitzers.

Field Artillery

Unit Value: T0

Uniform: Same as line infantry.

***USA:** (Left to right.) Marine sergeant, infantry, infantry officer, artillery officer.*

United States of America

INFANTRY

Organization: Regiments, each of battalion size. The regiment had eight companies, each consisting of a normal platoon plus one officer. In half of the companies, the officer was a lieutenant; in the other half, a captain. The regimental staff was a battalion staff except that there was a major on the staff in place of the battalion ensign. Colors were not carried in the field.

Weapons: Officers carry sabers and revolvers. Other ranks officially carry breech-loading rifles and bayonets, but detachments in the West routinely exchanged these for Winchester lever-action rifles.

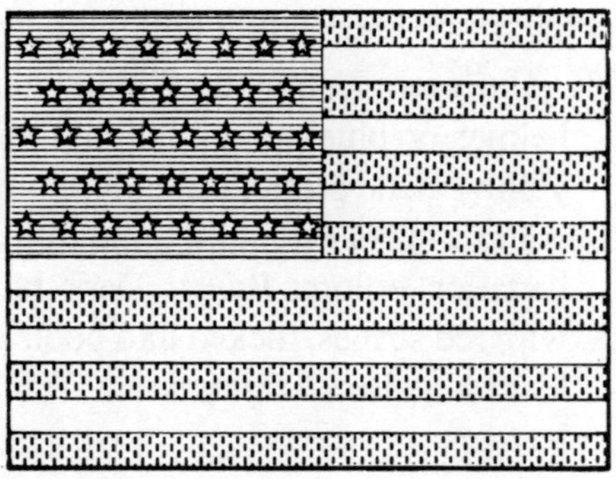

Infantry

(Total of 25 numbered regiments.)

Unit Value: T1

Uniform: *Headgear:* Light gray slouch hat, although this was often replaced by a white or light tan hat instead. *Jacket:* Dark blue. *Pants:* Light blue tucked into canvas gaiters. Officers and NCOs had a white stripe down the outside seams. *Equipment:* Black leather. A rolled gray or brown blanket was often worn over the shoulder in the field in place of a knapsack.

CAVALRY

Organization: Normal regiments, except that regiments consist of three squadrons, instead of two.

Weapons: Officers carried sabers and revolvers. Other ranks carried revolvers and breech-loading carbines. Sabers were not carried by other ranks, although the revolver was effectively used as a mounted melee weapon.

Cavalry

(Total of 10 numbered regiments.)

Unit Value: X1 (9th and 10th Cavalry "Buffalo Soldiers" V2)

Uniform: *Headgear:* Light gray slouch hat, but this was often replaced by a variety of civilian headgear. *Jacket:* Dark blue. *Pants:* Light blue tucked into cavalry boots. Officers and NCOs had yellow stripes down the outside seams. *Equipment:* Black leather.

ARTILLERY

Organization: Artillery was administratively grouped into regiments, each of five standard batteries. One battery in each regiment was trained as "light artillery," which is to say a field battery. The others were trained as heavy artillery and manned coastal fortifications, but they were often pressed into service as infantry companies. Battery organization is standard.

Weapons: Officers carry revolvers and sabers. Other ranks carry breech-loading rifles and bayonets. Light batteries are equipped with 2-pounder mountain guns, 12-pounder guns, and 7-pounder mountain howitzers. Heavy artillery mans a variety of fixed fortification guns, and 40-pounder guns for siege work. Gatling guns are manned by scratch gun crews drawn from infantry and cavalry regiments, not by the artillery.

Light Artillery

Unit Value: X0 (as artillery, T0 as infantry)

Uniform: Same as infantry, except that officers and NCOs had red stripes on the seams of their trousers.

MARINES

Organization: Separate companies numbered consecutively. If a larger force was required, composite battalions were made up of two or more companies under a lieutenant colonel or major. Companies use standard organization except that there are two lieutenants, one captain, and no major, and the captain is not mounted.

Weapons: Officers carry sabers and revolvers. Other ranks carry bolt-action rifles and bayonets. NCOs sometimes carried lever-action shotguns.

Marines

Unit Value: V1

Uniform: *Headgear:* Dark blue, peaked forage cap, although this was sometimes replaced on shore duty by a light gray slouch hat. *Jacket:* Dark blue. *Pants:* Blue with red stripe down outside seam, tucked into canvas gaiters. *Equipment:* Black leather. A rolled gray or brown blanket was often worn over the shoulder in the field in place of a knapsack.

Canada

INFANTRY

Organization: One regular battalion supplemented by regionally-raised militia. Standard battalions. No regimental organization existed.

Weapons: Officers carry sabers and revolvers. Other ranks carry breech-loading rifles and bayonets.

Royal Canadian Regiment

(Total of one battalion.)

Unit Value: V2

Uniform: Same as British line infantry.

Militia Infantry

Unit Value: X1

Uniform: *Headgear:* Either white helmet or blue spiked helmet with yellow metal plate. *Jacket:* Red with collar and pointed cuffs in individual battalion colors. *Pants:* Dark blue with red stripes, tucked into boots or leather gaiters. *Equipment:* White leather.

Militia Rifles

Unit Value: X2S

Uniform: *Headgear:* Dark green glengarry. *Jacket:* Dark green with red piping. *Pants:* Dark green tucked into boots or leather gaiters. *Equipment:* Black leather.

"Amazonians"

Company A, 62nd St. John Fusiliers, New Brunswick. (See designer's notes.)

Unit Value: T0

Uniform: *Headgear:* Khaki slouch hat pinned up on left side. *Jacket:* Khaki with red collar. *Skirt:* Khaki. *Equipment:* Black leather.

CAVALRY

Organization: One regular regiment supplemented by separate militia troops, and grouped into squadrons and regiments.

Weapons: All ranks carry sabers.

Officers carry revolvers; other ranks carry breech-loading carbines.

Royal Canadian Dragoons

(Total of one regiment.)

Unit Value: V2

Uniform: As British dragoons.

Governor-General's Bodyguard

(Total of one squadron.)

Unit Value: X2

Uniform: *Headgear:* Light blue forage cap. *Jacket:* Light blue dolman. *Pants:* Light blue pants. *Equipment:* White leather.

Militia Cavalry

Unit Value: T1

Uniform: A variety of uniforms were worn, mostly reminiscent of British regulars.

ARTILLERY

TWO FIELD BATTERIES and two garrison batteries of the Royal Canadian Artillery were permanently active. These units were uniformed and equipped the same as the British Royal Artillery.

In the field, these artillery units wore dark blue pants tucked into their boots, a khaki jacket, and a white glengarry.

American Mountain Indians

THE INDIANS of the American mountains, such as the Apaches and the Nez Pierce, were a completely different sort of adversary than the plains Indians. While the plains warriors waged war haphazardly and as a means of gaining personal glory, the mountain Indians fought with a much more purposeful and ruthless style. Instead of emphasizing individual feats of courage, the mountain Indians approached warfare as they did a hunt, with the members of a band working together to achieve their purpose with the fewest possible casualties.

Although the mountain Indians were mostly subdued by 1889, an uprising or escape by reservation Indians is still possible. There will never be more than one band of mountain Indians involved in such a raid or escape, but they will be treated as Veterans with a Fieldcraft of 3. Nez Pierce are, in addition, treated as sharpshooters. Weapons are the same as for the plains Indians.

American Plains Indians

THE INDIANS of the plains were brave warriors on an individual basis, but largely ineffective as military forces, due to their complete lack of organization and strategic direction. By 1889 the Plains Indian Wars were all but over, and the great war chiefs were all on reservations. Treat any plains Indian war party as irregular cavalry, with half of the bands Trained and half Experienced. Weapons consist of a mixture of breech-loading carbines, rifle-musket carbines, and lever-action carbines. (Roll a die for each band: 1-2, rifle muskets; 3-4, breechloaders; 5-6, lever-action carbines.) All plains Indians are treated as Green troops when they fire, are given a +1 on all melee rolls, and have a Fieldcraft of 2 (with Experienced bands having a Fieldcraft of 3).

Other American Armies

TREAT ALL OTHER armies of South America, Central America, and the Caribbean as regulars, with half of the troops Trained and half Green. Uniforms were almost universally linen or white canvas tunics and trousers worn loose over shoes. Hats were mixtures of slouch hats, kepis, and sombreros. Weapons consisted of a mixture of breech-loading rifles and rifle muskets. All units have a Fieldcraft of 1.

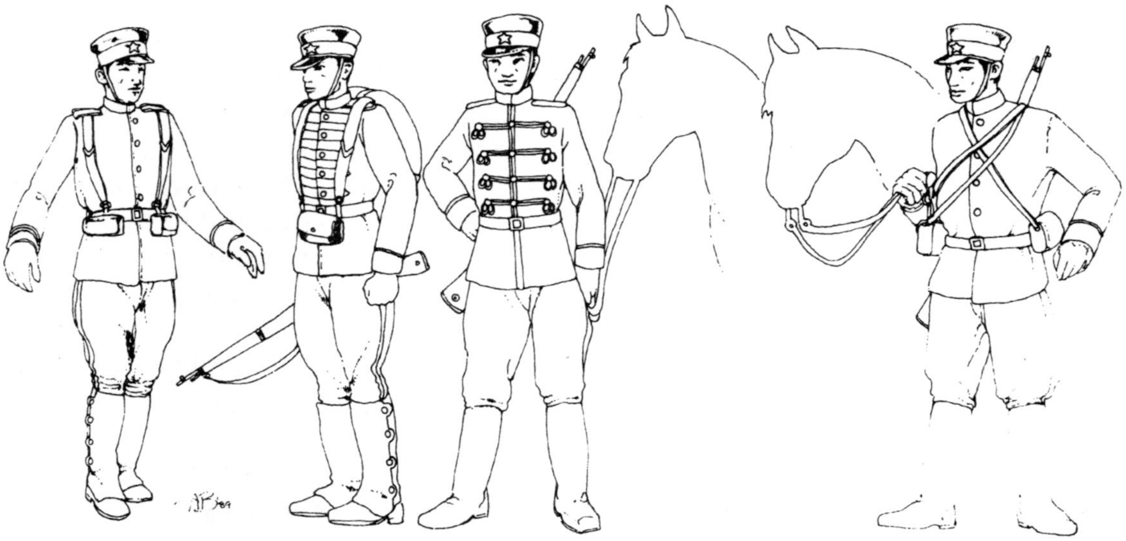

Japan: *(Left to right.) Line infantry, guard infantry, line cavalry, line cavalry in summer field uniform.*

Japan

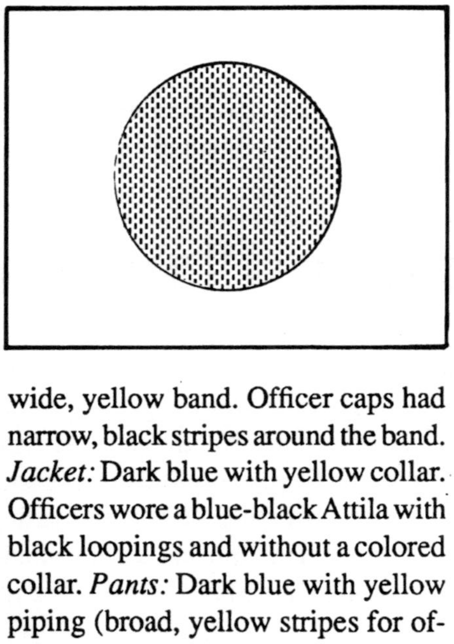

INFANTRY

Organization: Standard regiments.

Weapons: Officers carry revolvers and sabers. Other ranks carry breech-loading rifles and bayonets.

Guard Infantry

Unit Value: E1

Uniform: *Headgear:* Dark blue peaked caps with a narrow top and a wide, red band. Officer caps had narrow, black stripes around the band. *Jacket:* Dark blue with a red collar and white lace loopings. Officers wore a blue-black Attila with black loopings and without a colored collar. *Pants:* Dark blue with red piping (broad, red stripes for officers), tucked into black boots. *Equipment:* Black leather.

Line Infantry

Unit Value: V2

Uniform: *Headgear:* Dark blue peaked caps with a narrow top and a wide, yellow band. Officer caps had narrow, black stripes around the band. *Jacket:* Dark blue with yellow collar. Officers wore a blue-black Attila with black loopings and without a colored collar. *Pants:* Dark blue with yellow piping (broad, yellow stripes for officers), tucked into black boots. *Equipment:* Black leather.

CAVALRY

Organization: Standard regiments.

Weapons: Officers carry sabers and revolvers. Other ranks carry sabers and breech-loading carbines.

Guard Cavalry

(Total of two regiments.)

Unit Value: E1

Uniform: *Headgear:* Dark blue peaked caps with a narrow top and a wide, red band. Officer caps had narrow, black stripes around the band. *Jacket:* Dark blue Attila with red loopings (black loopings for officers). *Pants:* Red, tucked into black boots. *Equipment:* Black leather.

Line Cavalry

Unit Value: V2

Uniform: *Headgear:* Dark blue peaked caps with a narrow top and a wide, green band. Officer caps had narrow, black stripes around the band. Plain white caps were worn in the summer. *Jacket:* Dark blue Attila with white loopings (black loopings for officers). Plain, white jackets were worn in the summer. *Pants:* Red with green stripes tucked into black boots. Plain, white trousers were worn in the summer. *Equipment:* Black leather.

ARTILLERY

Organization: Standard batteries.

Weapons: Officers carry sabers and revolvers. Other ranks carry breech-loading carbines, but these are usually left on the gun limber in action. Field batteries are equipped with 15-pounder guns. Siege batteries are equipped with a variety of heavier pieces.

Artillery

Unit Value: V0

Uniform: *Headgear:* Dark blue peaked caps with a narrow top and a wide, white band. Officer caps had narrow, black stripes around the band. *Jacket:* Dark blue with white collar. Officers wore a blue-black Attila with black loopings and without a colored collar. *Pants:* Dark blue with white piping (broad, white stripes for officers), tucked into black boots. *Equipment:* Black leather.

Khmer Empire

THE KHMER EMPIRE has a standing army, but it is poorly trained and equipped and is treated as irregulars.

The empire has the following characteristics.

"REGULAR" INFANTRY

(Treated as irregulars.)

Weapons: Rifle muskets.

Unit Value: T1

Militia Infantry

Weapons: Half the bands have smoothbore muskets, half have melee weapons.

Unit Value: G1

CAVALRY

Weapons: Melee weapons.

Unit Value: T1

ARTILLERY

Weapons: A wide variety of ordnance is used, most of it smoothbore.

Unit Value: T0

Afghanistan

AFGHANISTAN is famous for its fierce Pathan tribesmen, expert mountaineers and crack shots with their *jezails* (long rifled muskets). Treat all Pathans as irregulars as follows.

INFANTRY

Weapons: Half of each band has rifle muskets, half has melee weapons.

Unit Value: X3S

CAVALRY

Weapons: All have melee weapons, and half also have muzzle loading carbines.

Unit Value: X1

Burma

ALTHOUGH THE MAIN Burmese armies were defeated by 1889, the British continued to fight a bitter guerrilla war in the jungle-covered hills of the north.

Treat all Burmese as irregulars and as in the following manner.

INFANTRY

Weapons: Half of each Burmese infantry band is provided with rifle muskets.

The other half is provided with melee weapons.

Unit Value: T2

Tonkin

ALL TONKINESE are treated as irregulars with these characteristics.

INFANTRY

Weapons: Half of each band has rifle muskets, and half, melee weapons.

Unit Value: X1

China

Several minor actions were fought during this period in China.

Although China had a standing army, it was poorly trained and equipped and wore civilian clothing at this time. Treat all Chinese units as irregulars with the following characteristics.

INFANTRY

Weapons: Some bands are equipped exclusively with melee weapons.

Other bands of Chinese infantry are equipped exclusively with rifle muskets.

Unit Value: T1

CAVALRY

Weapons: Melee weapons.

Unit Value: T1

ARTILLERY

Weapons: A wide variety of ordnance is used, most of it smoothbore.

Unit Value: T0

Hawaii

INFANTRY

The kingdom of Hawaii had one battalion of regular infantry. All other Hawaiians are treated as irregular bands.

Regular Infantry

Weapons: Breech-loading rifles and bayonets.

Unit Value: T1

Uniforms: Blue.

Irregular Bands

Weapons: Half the bands have only melee weapons, the other half only smoothbore muskets.

Unit Value: G2

Siam

The Siamese Army is a regular force which is organized and equipped along European lines. This army has the following characteristics.

INFANTRY

Weapons: Officers have sabers and revolvers; other ranks have breech-loading rifles and bayonets.

Unit Value: X1

CAVALRY

Weapons: Officers have sabers and revolvers. Other ranks have sabers and lances.

Unit Value: X1

ARTILLERY

Weapons: Officers carry sabers and revolvers. Other ranks carry breech-loading carbines, but these are usually left on the gun limber in action.

Field batteries are equipped with 9-pounder guns.

Fortress and siege batteries are equipped with a variety of heavier pieces, including some smoothbore weapons.

Mars

This section covers the armed forces currently deployed on Mars, both of the colonial powers of Earth and of native Martian armies. The colonial powers are armed and equipped as detailed in the appropriate section of these Army Lists. The Martian native forces, however, require some elaboration.

ORGANIZATION

The basic building blocks of Martian forces are the company or band of infantry and the squadron or band of cavalry. There is no significant difference between the organization of regular companies/squadrons and irregular bands; all have three officers (chiefs or leaders) and 17 enlisted men (warriors). Although Martian regular units contain a few equivalents to the

Mars: *(Left to right.) Canal infantry, Oenotrian shield gunner, canal infantry with coddling chopper, senior officer, canal infantry with spear and shield.*

noncommissioned officer, they have nowhere near the same authority or responsibility as in units from the Earth.

The Martian city-states of the canals build their armies around a core of regular troops raised from their own citizenry, uniformed (after a fashion), drilled, and equipped at public expense. However, very few of the Martian city-states boast an army sufficiently well drilled and disciplined to count as regulars under these rules. The notable exceptions to this are the armies of the Tossian Empire and the Oenotrian Empire. (Other than this, only a city-state with an army quality result of "excellent" is considered to have genuine trained regulars.)

The citizen soldiers are almost always supplemented, however, by hired mercenary bands. These mercenary irregulars usually have better Fieldcraft skills than the regulars and are used for scouting and outpost duties, while the citizens are expected to bear the brunt of the fighting. Cities outside the old seabeds make extensive use of the magnificent Hill Martian nomads for cavalry, and these nomads are also often used as shock troops.

WEAPONS

Most Martian regular infantry is armed with smoothbore muskets, as well as some sort of melee weapon. Swords are common, as are elaborately bladed halberds. Officers usually carry a saber and a single-shot pistol, although some high-ranking officers have obtained revolvers. Between a quarter and a half of all regular units are armed with rifle muskets. Increasing numbers of American, breech-loading, Remington rifles are finding their way into the hands of Martian troops as well, as are a very few Winchester lever action rifles and carbines. These rifles are most common in the Chryse area, as far east as the Meridiani Sinus and as far west as the Coprates, but a few examples can be found almost anywhere on Mars, particularly in the hands of a canal prince's personal bodyguard.

Cavalry is armed with sabers, and some units carry the lance as well. Most officers carry a single-shot pistol, and other ranks carry a smoothbore carbine.

Again, a smattering of more modern weapons, particularly of American manufacture, is finding its way into Martian hands.

Irregulars who have firearms are almost exclusively equipped with smoothbore weapons, and in very remote areas (such as the deserts of Eden, Moab, Arabia, and Amazonia) bows and even slings are still used. The various High Martian hosts are all considered irregulars for the purposes of these rules. Their warriors are armed almost exclusively with bows and melee weapons.

GENERATING MARTIAN CITIES

MARTIAN CITIES are marked on the various maps provided, but their exact size and makeup are not specified, for several reasons. Predetermining their complete makeup would limit the ability of the referee to provide imaginative input. Listing all the important statistics of the cities would take a small book of its own. Finally, once all the basic facts are written down, players will get ahold of them, and this will ruin some of the suspense in the game.

As an alternative, the following system is designed to provide you with a simple means of generating the important information concerning a city with a series of die rolls. As with all such systems in **Space: 1889**, however, the referee should not feel bound by its results; he is perfectly free, and is actively encouraged, to make up cities with radically different characteristics than those presented here. Continuous novelty is one of the keys to an intriguing and enjoyable world.

The basic procedure for generating a city is explained below. All the actual tables needed, along with a brief recapitulation of the procedure, are found on page 148-149.

Population

ROLL TWO DICE and add one to the result for every canal that flows into the city. (Astrapsk, for example, which lies south of Syrtis Major, has seven canals flowing into it, so you would add seven to the dice roll.) The modified die roll is referred to as the population number. Make a note of it, as it will be used in some of the later calculations. Now multiply the population number by 10,000 to determine the population of the city.

Form of Government

VIRTUALLY ALL the city-states of Mars are ruled by hereditary princes. However, the exact means by which a prince rules, the extent to which other political factions control the government, and his exact "style" of leadership may differ. These are determined by making two die rolls. The first die roll determines whether the city is ruled by a strong prince or a weak one (a result of 1-3 is a strong prince; 4-6 is a weak prince).

If a strong prince rules, the second die roll determines his style of government. If a weak prince rules, the second die roll determines what faction exerts the real power over the city. Consult the Form of Government Table on page 148.

Strong prince styles of government include the following.

Despotic princes are absolutists who suffer no dissent and who arrange the affairs of the city solely for their own benefit. *Ambitious* princes are interested in increasing their power and prestige, either through intrigue or military conquest. *Popular* princes rule with the welfare of their subjects in mind. *Decadent* princes largely ignore affairs of state and have given themselves over to the pursuit of sensual pleasure.

In the case of a weak prince, the second roll indicates which social force has taken real control of the city. The entry *subject city* means that the city is actually ruled by the prince of a neighboring city.

Corruption

CORRUPTION REFERS to the willingness of local officials to take bribes. The three levels of corruption are *honest*, *corrupt*, and *very corrupt*. Officials in an *honest* city will not take bribes and will be inclined to arrest anyone offering a bribe. Officials in a *corrupt* city will often take bribes to hurry action on a request or will look the other way in the face of a transgression, provided it is not too serious. Officials in a *very corrupt* city will do virtually nothing without a bribe and will do anything if the bribe is large enough.

Consult the Corruption Table on page 148 to determine the corruption level of the city, roll a die, and make the modifications listed. If the modified die roll is 2 or less, the city is honest. If it is 3 or 4, it is corrupt. If it is 5 or more, it is very corrupt.

Economic Type

ECONOMIC TYPE is an indication of the principal means by which the city produces excess wealth. All cities have some mercantile activity, some manufacturing, and extensive farmlands up and down the canals radiating from the city. This die roll merely tells which type predominates. Consult the Economic Type Table on page 148. A result of *mixed* indicates that no one type predominates. A *special resources* result indicates that the city has access to some special commodity. Examples of this would be *bhutan* spice from the city of Umbra, *gumme* from the plantations outside Melas, or petroleum from the wells near Galen. Metal is scarce on Mars as well, and a city which has a special resource result might have large (by Martian standards) deposits of iron ore or tin.

Economic Vitality

IS THE CITY POOR, prosperous, or wealthy? This is determined, to a certain extent, by its location and form of government. Roll a die, make the listed modifications, and consult the Economic Vitality Table on page 148.

Quality of the Army

FOR EASE OF record keeping, the size of all Martian armies is calculated in terms of 60-man bands, with each man in the band being of the same NPC experience level (Green, Trained, Experienced, Veteran, Elite). The overall quality of the army determines the percentage of the army made up of each individual troop type, as shown on the Army Quality Table on page 148. The highest quality troops are often formed into a special royal bodyguard unit.

To determine the army quality level, roll a die, make the modifications listed on page 148, and consult the table.

Mercenary Troops

IN THE UPLANDS, all mercenary cavalry will be Hill Martian nomad free lances, (with troop quality proportioned as for Excellent troops, regardless of the army quality of the city-state itself). All other mercenaries, in both the uplands and old seabeds, are Canal Martian mercenaries. Troop quality will either be the same, one better, or one worse than that of the city-state. Roll a die and consult the Mercenary Quality Table on page 148.

Example: A city rolls a 3 for army quality (Fair) and then rolls a 5 for mercenary quality, indicating that it is one higher than the city's, thus making the mercenary troops Good.

Size of the Army

THE MODIFIED population die roll is also the army size number, after the listed modifications on page 149 have been made.

The army size number determines the number of bands in the army. There are two bands of infantry, one band of cavalry, and two guns for every army size number rolled. Prosperous cities have one additional band of mercenary foot or horse, and one additional gun for each army size number. Wealthy cities have one additional band of mercenary infantry and one additional band of mercenary cavalry, as well as two additional guns, for each army size number.

Fleet Quality

A CITY'S MIGHT is measured more by its cloud fleet than its army. Crew quality for cloud fleets is determined by rolling a die, making the listed modifications on page 149 to the die roll, and consulting the Fleet Quality Table on the same page.

Fleet Size

THE FLEET SIZE is measured in terms of the construction cost of its ships, and it depends on the wealth and population of the city. However, the population number is modified as shown on page 149. Once the modified population number has been determined, the level of economic vitality of the city determines the value of the fleet per population number.

Attitude

THIS IS THE GENERAL attitude prevalent in the city and of its government toward humans from Earth. Roll a die, make the listed modifications on page 149, and consult the Prevalent Attitude Table on that page.

Settlements

CANAL MARTIAN settlements are found throughout the fertile seabeds and along the remaining active grand canals. These rules are designed to give the referee an easy means of generating these settlements.

Number Appearing: Without considering such things as nomadic encampments and High Martian kraags, there are two types of settlements: villages and towns. Villages are usually small, inland farming communities, while towns tend to be trade and transportation centers along the grand canals. Both towns and villages are often surrounded by stone walls, particularly in the uplands. These are generally low walls for villages, but can sometimes be quite elaborate for towns, with occasional towers and strong gates.

Canal Hexes: Each 100-mile hex of the medium-scale maps used in **Space: 1889** and **Conklin's Atlas** have the following numbers of villages and towns.

Grand Canal Hex in the Old Seabeds: 3D6 villages scattered throughout the hex and 1D6 towns along the canal.

Grand Canal Hex in the Uplands: 1D6 villages scattered throughout the hex and 1D6 towns along the canal.

Noncanal Hex in the Old Seabeds: 1D6 villages scattered throughout the hex.

Population: Each village has a population of 1D6×200. Each town has a population of 1D6×1000.

Garrison: Each village has a garrison of 2D6 soldiers. Each town has a garrison of one band of infantry, one band of cavalry, and 1D6 guns. The largest town in the hex is the provincial capital and has a garrison three times this size. Roll one die and consult the following table to determine the troop quality of the garrison of each village and town. Add one to the die roll in the uplands.

GARRISON TROOP QUALITY

Die	*Quality*
1	Green
2-4	Trained
5-6	Experienced
7	Veteran

To determine which types of guns are present on the walls of a town, roll once on the following table for each gun present.

TOWN GUNS

Die	*Gun*
1	Light
2-3	Heavy
4	Rod
5	Rogue
6	Lob

CITY GENERATION SEQUENCE

1. Population equals (2D6+number of canals)×10,000.

2. Form of Government: Roll one die. 1-3, Strong Prince; 4-6, Weak Prince. Roll again for specific type.

FORM OF GOVERNMENT

Die	*Strong Prince*	*Weak Prince*
1	Despotic	Strong Counselor
2	Despotic	Strong Nobles
3	Ambitious	Strong Warriors
4	Ambitious	Strong Merchants
5	Popular	Strong Priests
6	Decadent	Subject City

3. Corruption: Roll one die: 2 or less, honest; 3-4, corrupt; 5 or more, very corrupt.

Corruption modifiers follow.

Despotic Prince, Decadent Prince, Strong Priests, or Subject City: +1

Popular Priest or Strong Merchants: –1

CORRUPTION TABLE

Die	*Type*
1-2	Honest
3-4	Corrupt
5-6	Very Corrupt

4. Economic Type: Roll one die.

ECONOMIC TYPE TABLE

Die	*Type*
1	Agricultural
2	Mercantile
3	Manufacturing
4	Special Resource
5-6	Mixed

5. Economic Vitality: Roll one die.

The following are economic vitality modifiers.

City in Old Seabed: +1

City Honest: +1

City Very Corrupt: 1

City in Upland: 1

City in Upland Not on Grand Canal: –2

Government Decadent, Strong Priests, Subject City, Strong Warriors: –1

Government Popular, Strong Merchants, Strong Counselor: +1

ECONOMIC VITALITY TABLE

Die	*Vitality*
1-2	Poor
3-4	Prosperous
5-6	Wealthy

6. Army Quality: Roll one die.

The following are army quality modifiers.

Government Decadent, Strong Warriors: –1

Government Popular: +1

ARMY QUALITY TABLE

Die	*Army*	*El*	*Vt*	*Ex*	*Tr*	*Gr*
1-2	Poor	—	10	20	60	10
3-4	Fair	—	20	50	20	10
5	Good	10	40	40	10	—
6	Excellent	10	60	30	—	

7. Mercenary Quality: Roll 1 die.

MERCENARY QUALITY TABLE

Die	*Quality*
1-2	One level worse
3-4	Same
5-6	One level better

8. Army Size: Size number equals population number, as modified.

The following are modifiers.

Government Despotic, Ambitious: +1

Government Strong Warriors: +3

Government Decadent, Strong Merchants: –1

Poor Army: +1

Excellent Army: –1

9. Fleet Quality. Roll one die.

The following are modifiers.

Government Decadent, Strong Warriors: –1

Government Ambitious: +1

FLEET QUALITY TABLE

Die	*Quality*
1	Green
2-5	Trained
6	Crack

10. Fleet Size: Size number equals modified population number.

The following are modifiers.

Government Decadent, Subject City: –1

Government Ambitious: +2

Government Strong Warriors: +3

Fleet Value: Calculate as detailed below.

Poor Cities: £20,000 value per population number.

Prosperous Cities: £30,000 value per population number.

Wealthy Cities: £40,000 per population number.

11. Attitude: Roll one die.

The following are modifiers.

Despotic, Strong Counselor, Strong Nobles: –1

Strong Priests: –2

Popular, Strong Merchants, Subject City: +1

PREVALENT ATTITUDE TABLE

Die	*Attitude*
1	Very Hostile
2	Hostile
3-4	Indifferent
5	Friendly
6	Very Friendly

MAJOR POLITICAL ENTITIES OF MARS

THE PREDOMINANT form of government on Mars is the city-state, routinely consisting of a major city on a grand canal which controls the towns and villages for perhaps 100 or 200 miles in all directions. Isolated stretches of canal farther away than this are often controlled by the closest large town, which often flatters itself with the title of city-state, but which is, in fact, far less important than that. In very remote areas, particularly in the uplands, it is not uncommon to find regions where every town along the canal is independent, with varying degrees of control over the surrounding villages.

Large political entities above the city-state level are rare, but several are worth noting. Two of these are European colonial holdings, while the others are native governments.

The Belgian Coprates

THIS REGION is held by a mixture of Belgian regulars, the Belgian Legion, and locally recruited native levies. Legally it is actually two distinct entities. The Upper Coprates is the personal domain of Leopold II, the Belgian king. It comprises the former city-states of Melas and Po-Poo-Hanna-Kitai (renamed New Amsterdam in 1888), as well as all the villages and towns along the canals between them, many of which were previously independent of either of these states. The Lower Coprates is a protectorate of the Belgian state and includes the former city-state of Melas Lacus (renamed Copratia in 1888) and vast tracts of surrounding territory.

The formal boundary of the Upper Coprates extends along the escarpment of the old seabeds in the north. Thus, Belgian power did not extend north beyond the canal locks at Uri-Babaat until the last 12 months. Hot pursuit of rebel raiding forces, however, has gradually been followed by permanent garrisons as far north as Oo-Tareen, a town which was autonomous, but which the city-state of Ophir always considered part of its legitimate sphere of interest. Ophir has protested any further Belgian advances, but has no real authority in the region and is not in a position to guarantee a cessation of rebel raids into Belgian territory. Thus, tensions continue to mount between the two neighbors.

Syrtis Major

THE BRITISH crown colony, along with its treaty dependencies and the jointly administered regency territory of Parhoon, covers the entire Syrtis Major basin, as well as parts of the adjoining uplands. Relations with the Parhoonese, Meepsoori, and Moerus Lacus highlanders are good, but relations are somewhat more strained with the subjects of the lowland cities. Britain is currently at war with the Oenotrian Empire.

Oenotrian Empire

THE FORMAL NAME of this political entity is the Six Cities League. It is nominally a federation of the six city-states of Oenotria, Astrapsk, Crocea, Deltoton, Iapygia, and Skorosia. In practice, the leadership councils and high administrative posts are completely dominated by Oenotrian nobles, and the league is almost universally referred to as the Oenotrian Empire.

One major advantage of this multicity league is that all the towns and villages within the area defined by the member cities have been brought under central rule, and incidents of brigandage and piracy are now virtually unknown. However, Oenotrian ambitions in the north (exemplified by a long-standing claim against the city of Avenel) have brought the empire into conflict with Britain. Despite the vast industrial might of Britain, the limited cargo capacity of existing interplanetary ether flyers and long transit times from Earth to Mars rule out quick, massive reinforcement of the colony, and the war which has recently broken out shows signs of potentially turning into a long, bloody affair.

The Boreosyrtis League

THE LEAGUE IS A loose, mercantile confederation comprised of the cities of Umbra, Meroe, Coloe, and Saardaar. Merchant interests predominate in the governments of all the cities, and the principal source of revenues is *bhutan* spice, the production of which is a monopoly jealously guarded by the league members. The league has signed trade agreements which give the British exclusive rights to purchase the spice in return for certain defensive guarantees. Relations between the two have been cordial, although the current war with Oenotria is considered bad for business and is a troubling complication.

The Tossian Empire

THIS IS A IS A genuine empire, ruled by Emperor Krahaanik IV from the emerald throne in Tossia. The sprawling empire includes the cities of Hyoraotes, Thymiamata, Aram, Duecalionis, Pandora, Noachis, Pyrrhae, Tobansoor, Erythria, and Protei, and dominates most of its neighboring cities. Increasingly concerned with Belgian expansionism, the empire has recently (and temporarily) put aside its differences with the stubbornly independent Prince Sitaani of Nectar and entered into certain defensive agreements with him. The exact details of these arrangements remain secret. However, Tossian heavy cavalry units have recently arrived in Nectar and are apparently being used to augment Nectaran patrols along the western frontier where Belgian raiding columns have made periodic penetrations in pursuit of rebels. Should Tossian patrols clash with Belgian raiding columns, the results could have far-reaching repercussions.

Oenotrian Army

LEGIONS

ALL REGULAR INFANTRY is organized in legions, with from two to six companies of infantry in each legion, as well as artillery and mercenary auxiliaries (covered later). Legions are numbered sequentially and most have an honorific designation. Each legion is recruited from the citizens of a single city-state. The number, name (if any), city of origin, number of companies, and unit values of the 38 imperial Oenotrian legions are listed on page 151.

Each legionary company is divided into two half-companies, called the "shooters" and the "cutters." The shooters are equipped with missile weapons, almost universally muskets, although the better units often have rifle muskets. Very few modern breechloaders have found their way to Oenotria yet, although at least one company of the 1st "Victorious" has them, and there may be others scattered throughout the army. The cutters are exclusively equipped with melee weapons, either spears or the massive two-handed sword the Martians call a "coddling-chopper."

CAVALRY

ALL CAVALRY is organized into units whose title roughly translates as *flight*. There are a total of 35 flights of cavalry. Each flight has two squadrons of cavalry with the exception of Skorosia's, which have three squadrons each.

Cavalry flights are known in Oenotrian service by the names of their current commanders. This information is not available on a reliable basis, and so the table on page 152 merely lists the flights in numeric order by city and their unit values.

MERCENARIES

CONSIDERABLE NUMBERS of mercenary irregulars are attached to the Oenotrian legions. These units are used for light scouting and skirmishing in advance of the main force of a legion.

Each of the eight Oenotrian legions has one band of mercenary infantry and one band of mercenary cavalry attached. These are *UV:* E3 in the 1st Legion, and *UV:* V2 in the others. The mercenary infantrymen are equipped with muskets or, in some cases, bows in their shooter half-company.

Each of the six Crocean legions has one band of mercenary infantry and one band of mercenary cavalry attached. All are *UV:* T2 and are equipped the same as those attached to the Oenotrian legions.

Each of the six Deltoton legions has two bands of mercenary cavalry and two bands of mercenary infantry attached. In each legion, one of each type is *UV:* V2, and the other is *UV:* X2. All are equipped the same as those attached to the Oenotrian legions.

The legions from Astrapsk, Iapygia, and Skorosia do not have mercenary auxiliaries.

ARTILLERY

EACH LEGION has one light and two heavy guns permanently assigned to it. All other guns are city defense guns, although large expeditions often will take several of the big guns along from a city to form a siege train. The heavy artillery strength of the various cities is listed below.

Oenotria: Six rod guns, 10 rogues, eight lob guns.

Astrapsk: Three rogues, four lob guns.

Crocea: Six rod guns, six rogues,

LEGIONS OF THE OENOTRIAN EMPIRE

	Legion	*City*	*Companies*	*Quality*
1	"Victorious"	Oenotria	4	*UV:* E1
2	"Ferocious"	Oenotria	2	*UV:* V1
3	"Faithful"	Oenotria	4	*UV:* X1
4	"Triumphant"	Crocea	5	*UV:* T2
5	"Vigilant"	Skorosia	5	*UV:* T1
6	"Aggressor"	Crocea	5	*UV:* X2
7	"Bellicose"	Oenotria	4	*UV:* X1
8		Skorosia	4	*UV:* T1
9	"Steppe Tigers"	Astrapsk	2	*UV:* V1
10	"Ravenous"	Iapygia	2	*UV:* E1
11		Astrapsk	2	*UV:* G0
12		Iapygia	5	*UV:* X1
13	"Glorious"	Iapygia	3	*UV:* X1
14	"Vindicators"	Skorosia	6	*UV:* T1
15	"Lightning"	Oenotria	6	*UV:* V1
16	"Cleansers"	Crocea	5	*UV:* T2
17	"Bedrock"	Deltoton	6	*UV:* X1
18	"Blood Spillers"	Deltoton	2	*UV:* V1
19		Astrapsk	3	*UV:* T0
20	"Dauntless"	Skorosia	3	*UV:* V1
21	"Fortunate"	Iapygia	5	*UV:* V1
22	"Marchers"	Crocea	3	*UV:* T2
23	"Horrendous"	Astrapsk	3	*UV:* T0
24	"Avenger"	Iapygia	3	*UV:* V1
25		Iapygia	2	*UV:* T1
26	"Quiet Killers"	Astrapsk	6	*UV:* T0
27	"Punishers"	Crocea	3	*UV:* V3
28	"Guardians"	Skorosia	3	*UV:* T1
29		Crocea	3	*UV:* G2
30	"Vengeance"	Astrapsk	4	*UV:* X0
31	"Alert"	Deltoton	6	*UV:* X1
32	"Reckless"	Oenotria	4	*UV:* T1
33	"Fruitful"	Deltoton	3	*UV:* V1
34		Deltoton	2	*UV:* G0
35		Skorosia	3	*UV:* G1
36	"Slashers"	Oenotria	4	*UV:* V1
37	"Frenzied"	Oenotria	4	*UV:* X1
38		Deltoton	5	*UV:* T0

CAVALRY FLIGHTS OF THE OENOTRIAN EMPIRE

	Oenotria	*Astrapsk*	*Deltoton*	*Iapygia*	*Crocea*	*Skorosia*
1	*UV:* E0H	*UV:* X1	*UV:* V0H	*UV:* V0H	*UV:* V1H	*UV:* X1
2	*UV:* V0H	*UV:* T1	*UV:* X0H	*UV:* :V1	*UV:* X2	*UV:* T1
3	*UV:* V0H	*UV:* T1	*UV:* X0H	*UV:* V1	*UV:* T2	*UV:* T1
4	*UV:* V1	*UV:* T1	*UV:* X1	*UV:* X1	*UV:* T2	*UV:* T1
5	*UV:* X1	*UV:* G0	*UV:* T1	*UV:* X1	*UV:* T2	*UV:* T1
6	*UV:* X1	—	*UV:* G1	—	*UV:* T2	—
7	*UV:* T1	—	—	—	—	—

six lob guns.

Deltoton: Eight rod guns, six rogues, 10 lob guns.

Iapygia: Two rogues, one lob gun.

Skorosia: Three rod guns, five rogues, four lob guns.

GARRISONS

City garrisons are provided by the regular forces of legions and flights.

Village and town garrisons are locally raised.

Generate village and town garrisons using the normal settlement generation rules.

DISTRIBUTION OF FORCES

The exact distribution of Oenotrian forces is unknown, but the following is a rough indication of their troop allocations. Exact unit identifications and strengths are in a state of flux and cannot be determined precisely at this time.

Garrisons

Oenotria: Two legions and two flights.

Astrapsk: One legion.

Deltoton: Two legions and three flights.

Iapygia: One legion and two flights.

Crocea: Two legions.

Field Armies

Avenel Canal: Eight legions and eight flights.

Oenotria Canal: Six legions and six flights.

Astrapsk Canal: Four legions and five flights.

Crocea Canal: Twelve legions and nine flights.

Shastapsh

The Army of Shastapsh is a hastily-raised citizen's army built around the cadre of the old city-state's municipal guard. It is not very proficient, but is quite numerous. Furthermore, it is stiffened by a volunteer battalion made up mostly of Irish revolutionaries and supported by three German combat tripods, flown in and assembled in the city recently and manned by German "volunteers" on leave from the Imperial German Army.

The locally raised forces are organized in "flags" of two infantry war bands, one cavalry war band, and one gun section each. The first five listed flags have heavy gun sections, the second five have light gun sections. About half the men in each infantry war band have muskets or bows; the rest have only swords or spears. The Black Flag, however, appears to be entirely equipped with rifle muskets.

Black Flag: *UV:* V2
Red Flag: *UV:* X2
Star Flag: *UV:* X2
Blue Flag: *UV:* T1
Stripped Flag: *UV:* T1
Green Flag: *UV:* T1
Yellow Flag: *UV:* T1
Orange Flag: *UV:* T1
Sun Flag: *UV:* T1
Quartered Flag: *UV:* G1

Very little cavalry is stationed in Shastapsh, and the flags assigned to defend the city usually have their cavalry stripped off and assigned to the field forces. Bands of cavalry and infantry are also sometimes swapped between flags in the field to reinforce a flag for some particular mission, and then often stay with the flag later. Gun sections are usually collected under central control of the commander of a field army and assigned where needed, regardless of their flag affiliation.

ARTILLERY

The army has two batteries of heavy field artillery, each with one rod gun and two heavy guns. In addition, the following heavy ordnance is mounted on the walls of Shastapsh, some of which may be taken into the field for use as siege artillery: one heavy gun, one rod gun, seven rogues, and six lob guns.

MERCENARIES

TEN BANDS of mercenary steppe nomad cavalry are in Shastapshian service. One is *UV:* E3, six are *UV:* V3, and three are *UV:* X3. All are irregulars.

The Fenian Battalion: A weak battalion of Fenians (Irish revolutionaries) is now present at Shastapsh and is willing to undertake mischief against Britain.

It is organized as a standard battalion, but each company has only six privates, two NCOs, and one officer. The company officers include two lieutenants, one captain, and one major. The battalion has a single gun section equipped with a 9-pounder smoothbore gun.

Staff and 1st Company: *UV:* V1
2nd Company: *UV:* X1
3rd Company: *UV:* X1
4th Company: *UV:* T0
Gun Section: *UV:* T0

The Tripod Squadron: There is a squadron of three light PzKpfd *Storch* combat tripods present at Shastapsh. They were flown to the city by chartered merchant ships and are manned by veteran "volunteers" from the German service. Germany has listed these men as deserters, and so is not legally liable for their actions. The German authorities do not seem to be making any effort to recover the deserters, however.

The British Army on Mars

THE FOLLOWING TROOPS are currently deployed on Mars. Most of these are locally raised, stiffened by a few British units and a small number of colonial troops from Earth. Administratively, they are divided into three broad categories: Imperial, Parhooni, and trucial. The Imperial troops are all those of Britain, the Dominions (such as Canada, New South Wales, Southern Australia, etc.) and the Martian colony of Syrtis Major. Parhooni troops are those from the city state of Parhoon and its dependency Gorovaan. The trucial troops are those from the treaty dependencies of Meepsoor and Moeris Lacus, and are commonly referred to as Highland brigades (not to be confused with Scottish highlanders, of which there are several battalions on Mars), due to their location on or above the boundary of the old seabed.

The troops are organized in brigades of from two to five battalions or regiments plus supporting arms. A series of territorial brigades are given the task of defending a city and its surrounding territory, and are generally named for the city they garrison, as well as a series of field brigades that comprise the three columns currently mobile and in the field. The three columns operate along the axes of the three easternmost canals that lead from Syrtis Major into Oenotrian territory.

Number 1 Column's task is to act aggressively along the axis of the canal to Oenotria proper and draw forces off the main Oenotrian drive toward Avenel. Reinforced by HML *Truculent,* the column has succeeded admirably, winning several pitched battles against numerically superior enemy forces and forcing a major redistribution of forces (particularly heavy artillery) to this canal.

Number 2 Column's task is to screen the axis of the Astrapsk canal, guard against any overland raid toward the capital, and maintain overland contact between the other two columns. Although weak in infantry, this column is particularly strong in light cavalry to enable it to dominate the surrounding grasslands.

Number 3 Column is the strongest, and comprises the bulk of the actual field army. It operates on the canal to Crocea and has been actively engaged in driving south against stiff resistance in an effort to take Crocea and the main Oenotrian shipyards located there. While the column has pushed 50 miles into enemy territory, the Oenotrian forces on this axis have been reinforced, and the column is temporarily halted, neither side willing to risk a decisive battle.

GARRISONS

Parhoon (1st Parhoon Brigade)

B Co. 3rd King's Royal Rifle Corps *UV:* E3S

2nd Queen's Own Martian Rifles (The Parhoon Rifles) *UV:* V3S

1/1 Parhoon Infantry *UV:* X2

2nd Gorovaangian Levies *UV:* T1

A Troop, Parhoon Guides *UV:* X2

No. 1 Battery, Parhoon Mountain Artillery (6-pounder guns) *UV:* X1

1st Battalion, Parhoon Garrison Artillery *UV:* T0

Gorovaan (3rd Parhoon Brigade)

A Co. 3rd King's Royal Rifle Corps

UV: E3S

3rd Queen's Own Martian Rifles (The Parhoon Rifles) *UV:* V3S

1/2 Parhoon Infantry *UV:* X2

3rd Gorovaangian Levies *UV:* T1

B Troop, Parhoon Guides *UV:* X2

No. 3 Battery, Parhoon Mountain Artillery (7-pounder howitzers) *UV:* X1

2nd Battalion, Parhoon Garrison Artillery *UV:* T0

Haat (Haat Brigade)

Right Wing, 1st Highland Light Infantry *UV:* V2

1/1 Martian Infantry *UV:* T1

2/4 Martian Infantry *UV:* T1

C Squadron, Mounted Constabulary *UV:* T1

Haat Battalion, Martian Garrison Artillery *UV:* T0

Syrtis Major (Capital Brigade)

Major General Frederick W. E. F. Walker, CB, CMG (Ldr: 0)

Left Wing, 1st Highland Light Infantry *UV:* V2

Co. A, 62nd St. John Fusiliers (Amazonians) *UV:* T0[1]

1/2 Martian Infantry *UV:* T1

1/5 Martian Infantry *UV:* T1

A Squadron, Mounted Constabulary *UV:* T1

No. 23 Company, Royal Engineers *UV:* V2

One section, No. 19 Battery, Royal Artillery (.50-caliber Gatlings) *UV:* V0

1st Capital Battalion, Martian Garrison Artillery *UV:* T0

2nd Capital Battalion, Martian Garrison Artillery *UV:* T0

Avenel (Avenel Brigade)

2nd Argyll and Sutherland Highlanders *UV:* E1

1st South Wales Borderers *UV:* V1

1/3 Martian Infantry (Avenel Rifles) *UV:* T2S

2/2 Martian Infantry *UV:* T1

2/6 Martian Infantry *UV:* T1

D Squadron, Mounted Constabulary *UV:* T1

No. 19 Company, Royal Engineers *UV:* V2

Avenel Battalion, Martian Garrison Artillery *UV:* T0

No. 2 Field Battery, Martian Artillery (heavy guns) *UV:* T0

Meepsoor (Meepsoor Brigade)

D Co. 3rd King's Royal Rifle Corps *UV:* E3S

Meepsoori Anwaakaan Guard *UV:* V2

3rd Meepsoor Fencibles *UV:* X2

Meepsoor Garrison Artillery *UV:* X0

Meepsoori Anwaakaan Guard Battery *UV:* V0

Moeris Lacus

Highland Frontier Force

Lieutenant General Edward Newdegate, CB (Ldr: 0)

Moeris Lacus Garrison Artillery *UV:* T0

No. 1 Field Battery, Moeris Lacus Artillery (heavy guns) *UV:* T0

1st Highland Infantry Brigade:

C Co. 3rd King's Royal Rifle Corps *UV:* E3S

2nd Moeris Lacus Foot *UV:* T2

4th Moeris Lacus Foot *UV:* T2

2nd Meepsoor Fencibles *UV:* X2

Field Battery, Meepsoori Artillery (two sections light guns, two sections heavy guns) *UV:* X1

1st Highland Cavalry Brigade:

Graham's Irregulars *UV:* T3

Moeris Lacus Dragoons *UV:* T1

D Squadron, 1st Meepsoor Lancers *UV:* E2

2nd Meepsoor Lancers *UV:* X2

No. 1 Light Battery, Moeris Lacus Artillery (light guns) *UV:* T0

Number 1 Column
(Oenotrian Canal)

Lt. General Sir Henry Evelyn Wood, VC, GCMG, KCB (Ldr: 3)

Column Troops:

HML *Truculent*

No. 27 Battery, Royal Artillery (15-pounders) *UV:* V0

One section, No. 19 Battery, Royal Artillery (.50-caliber Gatlings) *UV:* V0

2nd Brigade:

C Co. 4th Rifle Brigade *UV:* E3S

2nd East Surreys *UV:* V1

1/4 Martian Infantry *UV:* T1

Mounted Infantry Brigade:

British Mounted Infantry Regiment UV:V1[2]

Australian Mounted Infantry Regiment UV:V3[3]

Number 2 Column
(Astrapsk Canal)

Major General Charles Mansfield Clarke, CB (Ldr: 2)

Column Troops:

No. 9 Battery, Royal Artillery (15-pounders) *UV:* V0

One section, No. 19 Battery, Royal Artillery (.50-caliber Gatlings) *UV:* V0

3rd Brigade:

Right Wing, 4th Rifle Brigade *UV:* E3S

Right Wing, 2/3 Martian Infantry (Avenel Rifles) *UV:* T2S

2/5 Martian Infantry *UV:* T1

2nd Highland Cavalry Brigade:

21st Lancers *UV:* V1

1st Meepsoor Lancers (less D Squadron) *UV:* E2

Parhoon Light Dragoons *UV:* T1

No. 2 Light Battery, Moeris Lacus Artillery *UV:* T0

Colonial Light Horse Brigade:

New South Wales Lancers *UV:* E2

Royal Canadian Dragoons *UV:* V2

The Martian Guides *UV:* E3S

B Squadron, Mounted Constabulary *UV:* T1

Number 3 Column

General Sir George Willis, KCB (Ldr: 1)

Column Troops:

No. 22 Company, Royal Engineers *UV:* V2

No. 12 Battery, Royal Artillery (5" howitzers) *UV:* V0

No. 3 Field Battery, Martian Artillery (rod guns) *UV:* T0

The Naval Brigade: Captain Fitzhugh Green, RN

1 wing, Royal Marine Light Infantry *UV:* V0

Angstrom's Battery (three sections, 5" siege guns) *UV:* V0

Fairweather's Battery (four sections, five-barrel Nordenfelts) *UV:* V0

1st Division: Lt. General Sir John McLeod, KCB (Ldr: 2)

Division Artillery:

No. 32 Battery, Royal Artillery (15-pounders) *UV:* V0

1st Brigade:

1st Royal Highland Black Watch *UV:* E1

2nd Royal Welsh Fusiliers *UV:* V1

Left Wing, 2/3 Martian Infantry (Avenel Rifles) *UV:* T2S

2/1 Martian Infantry *UV:* T1

1/6 Martian Infantry *UV:* T1

No. 1 Field Battery, Martian Artillery (heavy guns) *UV:* T0

2nd Highland Infantry Brigade:

D Co. 4th Rifle Brigade *UV:* E3S

1st Meepsoor Fencibles *UV:* X2

1st Moeris Lacus Foot *UV:* T2

3rd Moeris Lacus Foot *UV:* T2

5th Moeris Lacus Foot *UV:* T2

No. 1 Field Battery, Moeris Lacus Artillery (Heavy guns) *UV:* T0

2nd (Parhoon) Division: Major General Arthur Lyon-Fremantle, CB (Ldr: 0)

Division Artillery:

Ridgeway's Battery, Royal Navy (three sections, Hotchkiss 1-pounder revolvers) *UV:* V0

2nd Parhoon Brigade:

Right Wing, 1st Queen's Own Martian Rifles *UV:* E3S

1/3 Parhoon Infantry *UV:* X2

2/3 Parhoon Infantry *UV:* X2

No. 2 Battery, Parhoon Mountain Artillery (6-pounders) *UV:* X1

4th Parhoon Brigade:

Left Wing, 1st Queen's Own Martian Rifles *UV:* E3S

2/4 Parhoon Infantry *UV:* X2

2/5 Parhoon Infantry *UV:* X2

No. 4 Battery, Parhoon Mountain Artillery (7-pounder howitzers) *UV:* X1

Cavalry Division: Major General Sir Redvers Buller, VC, KCB, KCMG (Ldr: 3)

Division Artillery:

M Battery, Royal Horse Artillery (12-pounders) *UV:* V0

Heavy Brigade:

Household Cavalry Regiment *UV:* V0H

4th Royal Irish Dragoon Guards *UV:* V0H

Hussar Brigade:

10th Prince of Wales's Own Royal Hussars *UV:* V1

14th King's Hussars *UV:* V1

BRITISH COLONIAL ARTILLERY ON MARS

THE GARRISON ARTILLERY of the various cities is made up of old Martian guns brought back into service with local crews. Each garrison artillery battalion is commanded by a British colonel of Royal Artillery, with a staff of one major, one captain,

[1] Co. A (Amazonians), 62nd St. John Fusiliers is actually only represented by a composite volunteer platoon, with one officer. This unusual Canadian militia unit from the province of New Brunswick consists entirely of women (except for the captain commanding the detachment). Its equipment and passage out to Mars were financed by private subscription. As it is an official component of the Canadian militia, the colonial authorities have been obligated to accept its services, despite the protests of General Willis. The company has been assigned garrison duties in the capital.

[2] The British Mounted Infantry Regiment includes one platoon of mounted infantry from each British infantry regiment on Mars, grouped into the Rifle Company (platoons from the King's Royal Rifle Corps and the Rifle Brigade), the Welsh Company (platoons from the South Wales Borderers and the Royal Welsh Fusiliers), the Highland Company (platoons from the Black Watch and the Argyll and Sutherland Highlanders), and the Mixed Company (platoons from the East Surreys and the Highland Light Infantry). Normally each battalion in the field has enough men trained as mounted infantry to form a platoon and strips one soldier out of each platoon to do so. In this case, however, the mounted infantry contingents were formed from volunteers from the home service battalions of the regiments, and thus the infantry battalions on Mars are at full strength.

[3] The Australian Mounted Infantry Regiment includes the Queensland Mounted Infantry, the Victorian Bushmen, the South Australian Bushmen, and the Western Australian Mounted Infantry (one company each).

and two lieutenants. Batteries are formed on an ad hoc basis from the existing weapons and crews and placed at strategic points along the city walls and outworks. There are also a few modern mountain guns and howitzers in service with the Parhoon Mountain Artillery. The field artillery sections of the colony and the trucial cities are equipped with older Martian guns.

Parhoon Garrison Artillery

1st Battalion: Two heavy guns, two rod guns, four rogues, two lob guns.

2nd Battalion: Four heavy guns, four rogues, two lob guns.

Parhoon Mountain Artillery

No. 1 Battery: Three 6-pounder guns.

No. 2 Battery: Three 6-pounder guns.

No. 3 Battery: Three 7-pounder howitzers.

No. 4 Battery: Three 7-pounder howitzers.

Martian Garrison Artillery

1st Capital Battalion: Two light guns, six heavy guns.

2nd Capital Battalion: Three rod guns, four rogues, six lob guns.

Haat Battalion: Two light guns, two heavy guns, four rogues, two lob guns.

Avenel Battalion: Two light guns, four heavy guns, one rod gun, three rogues, four lob guns.

Martian Field Artillery

No. 1 Field Battery: Three heavy guns.

No. 2 Field Battery: Three heavy guns.

No. 3 Field Battery: Three rod guns.

Meepsoor Artillery

Field Battery: Two light guns, 1 heavy gun.

Garrison Battery: Two heavy guns, one rod gun, two rogues, one lob gun.

Anwaakaan Guard Battery: One light gun, two heavy guns, one rogue.

Moeris Lacus Artillery

No. 1 Light Battery: Two light guns.

No. 2 Light Battery: Two light guns.

No. 1 Field Battery: Two heavy guns.

No. 2 Field Battery: Two heavy guns.

Garrison Artillery: One rod gun, four rogues, two lob guns.

SENIOR BRITISH OFFICERS ON MARS

THE FOLLOWING BRIEF sketches provide the complete wartime service of the senior British officers on Mars—all officers with the rank of major general or higher. They are listed in order of seniority, so if two officers of the same rank should be present with a body of troops, the officer higher on this list takes command of the force.

General Sir George Harry Smith Willis, KCB (commissioned April 23, 1841, promoted to general on May 11, 1887) served without interruption throughout the Crimean War from April 1854 to July 1856; with 77th Regiment until May 1855, after which as D.A.Q.M. General at Headquarters, and as A.Q.M. General of the 4th Division; was present at the affairs on the Bulganac and at Balaklava, battles of Alma and Inkerman, assault of the Quarries, attack of the Redan on June 18, battle of Tchernaya, final assault of the Redan on September 8, and served for upwards of seven months in the trenches, including the repulse of several sorties, and was frequently in command of the advance trenches (medal with three clasps, brevets of major and lieutenant colonel, Grand Officer of the Legion of Honor, Sardinian and Turkish medals, and 5th Class of the Order of Medjidie). Served in the Egyptian War of 1882 in command of the 1st Division and was present at the engagements of El Magfar, Tel-el-Mahuta, and Kassasin (September 9), and in the battle of Tel-el-Kebir—slightly wounded (five times mentioned in dispatches, received the thanks of both Houses of Parliament, KCB, medal with clasp, 2nd Class of the Order of Osmanieh, and Order of the Khedive's Star). Currently commander-in-chief, Mars, and in direct command of Number 3 Column.

Referee: For all his personal bravery, General Willis is a fearful commander—cautious at the best of times and prone to panic when faced with unexpected developments or incomplete intelligence. Wolseley described him as, "a very plucky fellow personally, but an alarmist." He was an acceptable commander-in-chief in peacetime, but an unfortunate one in time of war. His tentative approach to campaigning has resulted in the main field army taking weeks to advance 50 miles down-canal toward Crocea and allowed the Oenotrians to shift reserves to that axis. The concept of the Crocean drive was excellent: capture of the Oenotrian's principal shipyard with the probable result of an immediate cessation of hostilities. The lack of energy in its pursuit has resulted in a disastrous stalemate.

Lieutenant General Edward Newdegate, CB (commissioned May 29, 1842, promoted lieutenant general May 11, 1887) served with the 2nd Battalion Rifle Brigade during the Crimean War of 1854 and up to July 1855, including the battles of Alma and Inkerman (wounded), and siege of Sebastopol (medal with three clasps, brevet of major, Knight of the Legion of Honor, 5th Class of the Order of Medjidie, and Turkish Medal). Served in the Zulu War of 1879 in command of the 2nd Division, and was present in the engagement at Ulundi (medal with clasp, and CB). Lieutenant General Newdegate is currently commanding the Highland Frontier Force, given the task of defending Moeris Lacus from any attacks along the Shastapsh Canal, protecting the overland caravan routes to the north, and launching an expedition to retake Shastapsh.

Referee: Newdegate was a competent serving officer a decade ago, but is well past his prime and now unfit for a separate command, as he lacks both initiative and energy. As a result, there has been little organized forward movement by his command, and hostile cavalry from Shastapsh raid the caravan routes almost at will.

Lieutenant General Sir Henry Evelyn Wood, VC, GCMG, KCB (commissioned September 7, 1855, promoted lieutenant general October 6, 1887) entered the navy in April 1852, and served in the Naval Brigade during the Crimean War as aide de camp to Captain Peel from October 1, 1854 to June 18, 1855, when he was severely wounded carrying up scaling ladders to the Redan; mentioned in Lord Raglan's dispatches (medal with two clasps, Knight of the Legion of Honor, 5th Class of the Order of Medjidie, and Turkish Medal).

Transferred to the army in September, 1885. Served in the Indian Mutiny in 1858 as brigade major in Somerset's Brigade and was present at Rajghur, Sindwaho (mentioned in General Michel's dispatch), Kharee, and Barode—mentioned in dispatches (medal). Employed is 1859-60, while commanding 1st Regiment Beatson's Horse, in hunting down rebels in the Seronge Jungles; thanked by the Government of India for an attack made on a band in December 1859, and gazetted to the Victoria Cross "for having on 19th October, 1858, during action at Sindwaho, when in command of a troop of the 3rd Light Cavalry, attacked with much gallantry, almost single-handed, a body of rebels who had made a stand, whom he routed. Also for having subsequently, near Sindhora, gallantly advanced with a daffadar and one sowar of Beatson's Horse, and rescued from a band of robbers a potail, Chemmum Singh, whom they had captured and carried off to the jungles, where they intended to hang him." Raised the 2nd Regiment, Central India Horse. Accompanied Sir Garnet Wolseley to the Gold Coast in September 1873 on special service and served throughout the Ashanti War of 1873-74.

Organized the natives forming "Wood's Regiment." Commanded the attacking force at the actions of Essaman (received the expression of Her Majesty's approbation). Commanded the troops at the head of the road, following the enemy from Mansu to the River Prah prior to the arrival of the European troops, including the reconnaissance in force of the November 27. Commanded the Right Column at the battle of Amoaful (slightly wounded); and commanded the headquarters of his regiment at the battle of Ordahsu and capture of Coomassie (several times mentioned in dispatches, brevet of colonel, CB, medal with clasp). Served throughout the Gaika War of 1878 in command of a column (several times mentioned in dispatches). Served throughout the Zulu War of 1879 in command of No. 4 Column. As political agent raised aa contingent of 1000 friendly Zulus known as "Wood's Irregulars." Two days after the British reverse at Isandhlwana he surprised and defeated a force of several thousands of the enemy and then maintained an advance position in the enemy's country for which he was specially commended by the high commissioner. (Nominated KCB.) Defeated the Zulus in the battle of Kambula on the 29th of March.

Appointed brigadier general in April. Led the advance on Ulundi with a flying column and was present in the engagement there on the 4th of July (mentioned in dispatches, medal with clasp). Served in the Boer War of 1881 with the rank of major general, and on the death of Sir George Colley, as the governor of Natal and commander-in-chief of the British forces (GCMG). Served in the Egyptian war of 1882 in command of the 4th Brigade in the operations near Alexandria, including the surrender of Kafr Dowar and Damietta (mentioned in dispatches, received the thanks of both Houses of Parliament, medal, 2nd Class of the Order of Medjidie, and the Khedive's Star).

Served during the Nile Expedition of 1884-85 in command of the Line of Communications (mentioned in dispatches, 1st Class of the Order of Medjidie, clasp). Served in the campaign against Shastapsh in 1887 as commander of the field army, and was present at the actions of Coonaraam (lightly wounded) and the storming of Shastapsh. (Received the thanks of both Houses of Parliament, promoted lieutenant general, medal with clasp.) Commands Number 1 Column.

Referee: Talented, but injury-prone—he has never served in a campaign without suffering some sort of injury—Wood leads his current command with his left arm in a sling, it having been scalded by an accidental discharge of live steam from the boiler of HML *Truculent*. Despite this injury, and the fact that he is almost completely deaf, Wood is the best of the British commanders on Mars, although outranked by both Willis and Newdegate. Willis has had the good sense to give him an independent command, the important Number 1 Column covering Avenel's left flank and threatening the capital of the Oenotrian Empire. Wood has driven down the Oenotrian Canal with dash and determination, forcing the Oenotrians to call off the siege of Avenel and reinforce the approaches to the capital. Wood still harries the enemy with swift columns of infantry and cavalry and is gradually forcing the front back into enemy territory.

Wood is charming, bright, and a good conversationalist. He is a favorite of the Queen and popular in government circles. A former protege of Wolseley and close friend of Redvers Buller, he has become estranged from both men, as both resent his popularity. (The fact that there is jealousy and bad feelings between the two most talented British officers on Mars is a potential source of serious trouble.)

Lieutenant General Sir John Cheatham McLeod, KCB (commissioned April 21, 1846, promoted lieutenant general August 12, 1888) served with the 42nd Highlanders (Royal Black Watch) throughout the Crimean War of 1854-55, including the battles of Alma and Balaklava, expedition to Kertch and Yenikale, siege and fall of Sevastopol (medal with three clasps, Knight of the Legion of Honor, and Turkish Medal). Served also in the Indian Mutiny, including the actions at Cawnpore (December 6, 1857), Seraight (mentioned in dispatches), Khodagunj, and Shumsabad, siege and fall of Lucknow and assault of the Martiniere, Banks' Bungalow, and Begum's Kottee (mentioned in dispatch), attack on the Fort of Rooyah, action at Allgunge, and capture of Bareilly (medal with clasp, brevet of lieutenant colonel, and CB). Embarked for the Gold Coast in command of the 1st Black Watch; served through the second phase of the Ashanti War, in 1874.

Commanded the battalion until ordered up to the front from Mansu to the north side of the Adansi Hills to take command of the advance guard of the army, now composed of Lord Gifford's Scouts, Russell's Regiment, headquarters of Wood's Regiment, headquarters of 2nd West India Regiment, and Rait's Artillery. Commanded the force at the capture and destruction of Adubiassie, and capture of Borborassie; commanded the Left Attack at the battle of Amoaful; commanded the Advance Guard at the capture and destruction of Becquah, the Advance Guard engagement of Jarinbah, and the skirmishes and ambuscade affairs between Adwabin and the Ordah River. Commenced the attack at the battle of Ordahsu with portions of Wood's and Russell's Regiments, three companies of the Rifle Brigade, and one field gun (light, contused wound of the hand). Afterward with the Black Watch, a gun, and a rocket detachment, forced the position and, pressing the fugitives with the Highlanders, entered Coomassie the same evening and was appointed commandant of the place (several times mentioned in dispatches, KCB, medal with clasp). Currently serving as commander, 1st Division.

Referee: Unquestionably brave and a talented commander in his day, McLeod is now over 60 and suffers from shortness of breath in the thinner atmosphere of Mars. His mind, however, remains sharp, and he has the instincts of a natural soldier. He is a solid, dependable division commander, a "fighter," and could easily take over command of the field army, if necessary, until Lt. General Wood could arrive and take over. There is some tension between Wood and McLeod, as Wood served under McLeod in the Ashanti War but is now senior to him. McLeod gives a +3 morale bonus to the 1st Black Watch instead of +2, as it is his old regiment, and the men are attached to him.

Major General Arthur James Lyon-Fremantle, CB (commissioned December 10, 1852, promoted major general April 1, 1882) commanded at the defense of Suakin from July 1884 until February 1885, and in the Sudan campaign of 1885, he commanded the Brigade of Guards, including the engagement at Hasheen and the destruction of Temai (mentioned in dispatches, CB, 2nd Class of the Order of Medjidie, medal with clasp). Commands the 2nd (Parhoon) Division.

Referee: Lyon-Fremantle has risen to the rank of major general by virtue of family connections, seniority, and an ability to stay out of trouble. He is almost completely ignorant of the technical aspects of soldiering, lacks extensive experience at either command or combat, and is too much of a snob to accept advice from his "inferiors." He has very little regard for the Parhoonese troops under his command, calling them, and all Martians for that matter, "spooks" due to their pale ghost-like complexions. His lack of faith in his division is returned in kind by his troops.

Major General Sir Redvers Buller, VC, KCB, KCMG (Commissioned May 23, 1858, promoted major general May 21, 1884) served with the 2nd Battalion of the Rifle Brigade throughout the campaign of 1860 in China (medal with two clasps). Served with the 1st Battalion on the Red River Expedition of 1870. Accompanied Sir Garnet Wolseley to the Gold Coast in September, 1873, and served as D.A. adjutant, quartermaster general, and head of the Intelligence Department throughout the Ashanti War of 1873-74, including the action of Essaman, battle of Amoaful, advance guard engagement at Jarbinbah, battle of Ordahsu (slightly wounded) and capture of Coomassie (several times mentioned in dispatches, brevet of major, CB, medal with clasp). Served in the Kaffir War of 1878-79, and commanded the Frontier Light Horse in the engagement at Taba ka Udoda and in the operations at Molyneux Path and against Manyanyoba's stronghold (several times mentioned in dispatches). Served throughout the Zulu War of 1879, and commanded the cavalry in the engagement at Hlobane Mountain and Kambula; conducted the reconnaissance before Ulundi, and was present in the engagement at Ulundi (several times mentioned in dispatches, thanked in the general orders, brevet of lieutenant colonel, aide de camp to the Queen, Victoria Cross, CMG, medal with clasp); received the VC "for his gallant conduct at the retreat at Inhlobana, on the March 28, 1879, in having assisted, whilst hotly pursued by Zulus, in rescuing Captain D'Arcy, of the Frontier Light Horse, whose horse had been killed under him, to a place of safety. Later on, Colonel Buller, in the same manner, saved a trooper of the Frontier Light Horse, whose horse was completely exhausted, and who otherwise would have been killed by the Zulus, who were within eighty yards of him."

Served in the Boer War of 1881 as chief-of-the-staff to Sir Evelyn Wood with the local rank of major general. Served in the Egyptian War of 1882 in the battle of Tel-el-Kebir (mentioned in dispatches, KCMG, medal with clasp, 3rd Class of the Order of Osmanieh, and Khedive's Star). Served in the Sudan Expedition under Sir Gerald Graham in 1884 in command of the 1st Infantry Brigade and as second in command of the expedition, and was present in the engagements at El Teb and Temai (twice mentioned in dispatches, promoted major general for distinguished service in the field, two clasps). Served in the Sudan campaign in 1884-85 as chief of staff to Lord Wolseley (mentioned in dispatches, KCB, and clasp). Currently commanding the Cavalry Division of Number 3 Column.

Referee: Buller is a great, hulking officer of immense personal strength, courage, and endurance. He is an energetic, relentless commander, known to spend two or three days at a time in the saddle without sleep while on campaign, and is feared by the Oenotrians who recognize in him a ruthless, implacable foe. In some of the early skirmishes in the war, Buller overran and destroyed several incautious Oenotrian war bands. He always leads from the front, and General Willis has been careful to keep him on a tight leash. Buller's faults as a commander are that, while not exactly stupid, he is not an intellectually gifted commander; he lacks imagination and is often too direct in his approach to a problem. While in charge of intelligence for Wolseley in the Egyptian campaign, for example, his main means of gathering information was to lead an attack on the enemy position. A second problem is jealousy. Buller resents the success of others, and this has alienated him from his former friend Lt. General Wood.

Major General Charles Mansfield Clarke, CB (Commissioned March 1, 1856, promoted major general August 12, 1888) served in the 57th Regiment with the column under Colonel Warre on the Taptee River in cooperation with the Central India Field Force in 1858. Served also in the New Zealand War of 1861, and was present at the operations before Te Arei. During the war in 1863-66, present as adjutant of the 57th at the actions of Katikara (mentioned in dispatches), and as D.A.Q.M. general from June 1863 to March 1866 in the Province of Taranaki, including the action near Poutoko; capture of the Maori positions at Ahuahu, Kaitake, Mataitawa, and Te Arei; operations at Warea and Te Puru; and various minor affairs (repeatedly mentioned in dispatches, medal). Served in the Zulu campaign of 1879; commanded the 57th Regiment in the engagement at Gingindhlovu (mentioned in dispatches) and the relief of Eshowe; afterwards commanded the 2nd Brigade, 1st Division, and subsequently was appointed to the command of "Clarke's Column"—a force of all arms—formed by Sir Garnet Wolseley for the following objects: the second advance to Ulundi, the capture of King Cetewayo, the subjugation of the Zulu tribes near the Middle Drift of the River Tugela. All were accomplished. Thanked in general orders (mentioned in dispatches as having "performed the duties of his responsible command in the most highly efficient manner," brevet of colonel, CB, medallion with clasp). At the conclusion of the war was appointed commandant general of the Colonial Forces in South Africa. Served in the Shastapsh Campaign of 1887; commanded the Eastern Brigade of Infantry in the overland advance, and commanded at the engagements at Coonaraam and Quabaat. Lead his brigade in the storming of the Palace District in Shastapsh (lightly wounded, mentioned in dispatches, thanked in general orders, medal with three clasps, promoted major general). Commands Number 2 Column.

Referee: Clarke is an outstanding fighting officer and is ideally suited to command of an independent column. He is physically fit, intelligent, and displays great personal initiative. He also has experience commanding large bodies of troops on Mars, and has developed a good working relationship with Lt. General Wood, who commands the column to the north.

Major General Frederick W. E. F. Walker, CB, CMG (commissioned September 1862, promoted major general December 31, 1887) served as assistant military secretary to Lieutenant General Sir Arthur Cunynghame during the Kafir War of 1878 (mentioned in dispatches, CB). Was employed on special service throughout the Zulu War of 1879, first as principal staff officer to Number 1 Column, being present at the action of Inyezane, and during the occupation of Ekowe, and subsequently on the line of communications, and in command of Fort Pearson and the Lower Tugela District (mentioned in dispatches, medal with clasp). Served with the Bechuanaland Expedition under Sir Charles Warren in 1884-85 as assistant adjutant and quartermaster general (CMG). Serving as adjutant and quartermaster general to the Army of Syrtis Major; commands the Capital Brigade.

Referee: Walker is an extremely competent staff officer but has never commanded many troops in combat and lacks the basic talent to do so. He has worked miracles in supplying the army, and the troops lack nothing in the way of food, ammunition, or equipment. He is the right man at the right place, provided the enemy does not penetrate as far as the city of Syrtis Major itself (highly unlikely).

Belgian Troops on Mars

BELGIAN LEGION (MOSTLY MERCENARIES)

1st Regiment, Belgian Legion: The permanent garrison of New Amsterdam; troops are permanently stationed there. One or more companies, plus a troop of cavalry, are usually in the field on sweeps for rebel bands.

2nd Regiment, Belgian Legion: Broken up into platoon and company garrisons in the towns along the New Amsterdam-Melas Lacus (Copratia) canal. First Battalion (with one gun section from the regimental battery) is responsible for the canal from New Amsterdam to Po-Narang. One company is in Po-Narang, but the bulk of the battalion is in the troublesome Eta-Pan and Gam-Chut area. The bulk of the regiment holds the canal from Nya-Narang to Melas Lacus (Copratia), with the regimental headquarters and many troops at Oo-Taroo. Flying columns and cavalry sweeps are frequently launched to the north.

3rd Regiment, Belgian Legion: This is the permanent garrison of Melas. One or more companies of infantry, plus a troop of cavalry, are often in the field searching for rebels.

4th Regiment, Belgian Legion: This regiment is broken up into platoon and company garrisons in the towns along the New Amsterdam-Melas canal. The regiment is deployed in the same manner as the 2nd

Regiment, with the first battalion holding the western half of the canal and the regimental main body holding the more dangerous eastern half. Cavalry patrols are constantly active around the fringes of the vast forests and broken hills southwest of Melas, a haven for guerrilla bands.

5th Regiment, Belgian Legion: The first battalion is broken up into platoon and company garrisons along the canal between Melas and Melas Lacus (Copratia). The main body of the regiment is at Oo-Tareen, with garrison companies left behind at Van-Tareen and Eeta-Babaat.

BELGIAN ARMY

4th Regiment *Ligne:* Permanent garrison of Melas Lacus (Copratia). One or more companies usually engaged in sweeps.

6th Regiment *Ligne:* Broken up into platoon and company garrisons along the Melas Lacus (Copratia) Nectar canal.

1st Regiment *Chasseurs a Pied:* Garrisons the frontier with Nectar and organizes hot pursuit columns into Nectar territory.

Foreign Troops on Mars

U.S. TROOPS ON MARS

THE UNITED STATES maintains a small force on Mars. At the main trading center in Thymiamata are three companies (A, B, and D) of the 14th Infantry Regiment, Battery G of the 2nd Artillery, and C Troop, 5th Cavalry. One company of marines is at the U.S. legation in Syrtis Major.

JAPANESE TROOPS ON MARS

THE JAPANESE 23rd Infantry Regiment, reinforced by a battery of field guns and a squadron of the 1st Cavalry Regiment, is stationed at Unebi Station. One company of the regiment is detached and stationed at the Japanese Residency at Euxinus Lacus.

RUSSIAN TROOPS ON MARS

ONE BATTALION of the Kamchatka Infantry Regiment and two artillery batteries (both equipped with .50-caliber Gatlings) are on Mars.

FRENCH TROOPS ON MARS

FRANCE MAINTAINS a considerable force of troops in the Ideas Fons area, which currently include the following units: 2nd Foreign Legion Infantry, 3rd Marine Infantry, 79th Infantry, 81st Infantry, 114th Infantry, 1st Foreign Legion Cavalry, 6th Hussar Regiment, Composite Regiment of Spahis (squadrons drawn from the 1st and 2nd regiments), and five batteries of field artillery.

THE HESPERIAN BASIN TRADING COMPANY

THIS COMMERCIAL concern, which holds trading rights throughout the Hesperian Basin and several fortified trading centers, has two battalions of privately recruited troops, all human. These are generally dispersed as individual companies throughout the region. Uniform is a simple version of the British Army khaki field uniform without any colored distinctions. The battalion number is embroidered on the shoulder straps. *Unit Value:* T1.

The Armies of Venus

THIS SECTION covers both the human troops of the colonial powers on Venus as well as various native bands.

GERMANY

ONE REGIMENT of regular infantry is deployed on Venus (the 17th Infantry Regiment). It routinely has one battalion at Venusstadt and one in the countryside. On Venus the troops wear a white tropical uniform with a white Sun helmet, although troops on guard duty at Government House in Venusstadt wear the standard uniform, complete with spiked helmet. There is one section of field guns in each major town in the colony and a complete field battery in Venusstadt.

There are also several regiments of *Schutztruppen* which are purely administrative groupings of separate *Schutztruppen* companies. No battalions exist, and the post of regimental commander is purely ceremonial. The individual companies are treated as irregular bands. The three officers are German while all troops are Lizard-men. Officers wear a white tropical uniform. The Lizard-men wear no clothing, but have a rubberized can-

Venusians: *(Left to right.) Ishtar tribal rifleman, typical tribal spearman, warrior chieftain from the Eastern Aphrodite Mountains, German Schutztruppen officer in dress uniform.*

vas harness to hold their bayonet, cartridge pouch, and so on. The officers carry revolvers, while the other ranks carry breech-loading carbines. The Unit Value for these companies is T2.

BRITAIN

BRITAIN CURRENTLY has two battalions of regular infantry on Venus, the 2nd Somerset Light Infantry and the 2nd Royal Munster Fusiliers. In addition, there are several company-size units of colonial volunteers. These are almost entirely human colonists, but most units include a half-dozen or so Lizard-men as scouts, laborers, or even occasionally armed fighters. No specific uniform is authorized, and most fight in civilian clothing. Some local communities have outfitted their militia volunteers along uniform lines, however. The Miroton Fusiliers, for example, are dressed in gray cord pants and jackets with red collars and shoulder straps. Their gray slouch hats are pinned up on the side, and they have brown rubberized canvas equipment.

Each small settlement has a company of colonial militia, and there are seven companies raised from the inhabitants of the capital. Unit Values for all of these are T2.

One of the companies in Fort Collinswood is mounted on pacyosaurs, is designated the Venusian Mounted Rifles, and wears a khaki uniform with white collar and shoulder straps with white Sun helmets. Two mountain batteries are deployed on Venus, one equipped with 6-pounder guns and one with 7-pounder howitzers. The gun sections are dispersed among the settlements.

All British and colonial troops on Venus have breech-loading rifles. The Venusian Mounted Rifles also have purchased a Maxim gun and have outfitted a pacyosaurus with a pintle mount where the saddle pommel would normally be placed. Most of the outlying settlements have either a Gatling gun or Nordenfelt manned by soldiers assigned from their militia company.

UNITED STATES OF AMERICA

ONE COMPANY of marines is at the U.S. Legation at Venusstadt, and one platoon each at the consulates in the British Russian and Italian capitals.

ITALY

ONE REGIMENT of infantry on Venus, the 7th "Cuneo" Infantry Regiment. One platoon is detached as consulate guards in each of the three other colonial capitals, and one battalion is usually dispersed in the field as plantation guards.

RUSSIA

THE RUSSIAN COLONY is guarded by two battalions of specially raised colonial troops (the only ones in Russian service), designated the 1st and 2nd Venus Rifle Battalions. Their uniforms consist of the standard green trousers tucked into black boots with a white smock and forage cap. Equipment is white canvas and all men are armed with breech-loading rifles. Unit Value is X1. First Battalion guards the capital, while the other battalion is broken up into company and platoon detachments which are used to stiffen Western Aphrodite mountain tribesman war parties in their struggles with the eastern plains Lizard-men. One platoon is also in Venusstadt, and one section each in the British and Italian capitals at legations.

THE LIZARD-MEN

LIZARD-MAN TRIBES often have unique totems and standards, but there are no specific uniforms worn by the soldiers. Many warriors carry shields, but the shield pattern is invariably the wearer's belly pattern, and thus unique. In general, the more warlike tribes tend to have a higher proportion of helmets and shields, but there is little other visible means of distinguishing them.

Lizard-men are all irregulars. Half of the men in each war band will be equipped with bows, the others with melee weapons, although there are a few exceptions to this. The war bands of the Eastern Aphrodites have received a number of metal edged weapons from the Russians, and about half of their war bands are so equipped (as are all of their chiefs). Lizard-men with metal edged weapons treat all other lizard men as weak opponents in melee. About half the war bands from the Kaiser Wilhelm and Ishtar ranges have substituted breech-loading carbines for bows. (Any weapon which does not use a sealed, metallic cartridge is virtually worthless on Venus.)

About half of the war bands from a tribe will be warriors with a Unit Value of T2. The other half will be hunters armed exclusively with bows and have a Unit Value of G2S. Warrior and hunter bands from the Gula Mountains have a Fieldcraft of 3 instead. War bands from Eastern Ishtar, the western coasts, and Western Aphrodite have Unit Values of X2, while hunting bands are T3S.

Armies of Luna

ARMIES OF THE MOON MEN

THE MOON MEN inhabit a large (several hundred miles across) cavern deep beneath the surface of the moon. While the City of Light and Science has troops armed with relics of an ancient technology, the other cities are iron-age civilizations using edged weapons, bows, and catapults.

Since Moon Man weaponry will only be encountered on Luna, its firing statistics were not included on the main firing charts on pages 170-176. If fighting a battle in the Land of the Moon Men, you may photocopy the chart on the next page and use it as a supplemental reference sheet.

SMALL ARMS TABLE

Weapon	*Dice*	*Range*
Electric Rifle	2	6"/12"
Spear	1/2	2"/4"
Bow	1	4"/8"

Note: A unit may only throw spears twice.

BRANTU

BRANTU IS AN ISLAND city-state which relies on its fleet to control commerce through the Brantu Straits. It generally levies a tariff on commerce and a tax on fishermen, and enforces this with its navy. (Some of the other city-states consider this to be little more than extortion bordering on piracy.) All of the city's catapults are mounted either on its wall or on ships. Brantu relies mostly on its navy for defense, and has a fairly small army, all of which is trained to fight on shipboard as marines, as well as manning the city defenses.

Organization: All infantry are irregulars and are organized in companies (each the size of a war band).

Weapons: About two-thirds of the companies are spearmen, each of which has a stout thrusting spear and two throwing spears. The remainder are bowmen who also carry short swords for close in fighting.

Unit Value: Spearmen X0, bowmen T0

Uniforms: Brantu soldiers wear a dark green-black tunic reminiscent of the color of the Great Sea. Their helmets are generally nautical in appearance, with the skull of a large fish being a common and popular image. The soldier's face appears to look out through the open jaws, with the mock skull's lower jaw forming the helmet's chin guard.

CITY OF THE FISHERMEN

THE CITY OF THE FISHERMEN makes its living primarily, as its name suggests, by fishing. Its citizens are not a warlike people and take pains not to antagonize their neighbors the Science Priests (of the City of Light and Science).

Organization: All infantry are irregulars and are organized in companies (each the size of a war band).

Weapons: All are spearmen and carry two throwing spears. A long fisherman's knife is also carried for melee, if necessary.

Unit Value: Half the bands are T0, the other half G0.

Uniforms: Generally brown or gray tunics are worn, with little attempt at uniformity even within the same band.

CITY OF THE HILLS

SANTAM, the Warlord of the Hills, has taken the tough, hearty hillmen of the central part of the peninsula and turned them into a military force worthy of concern. Santam managed to unite the scattered bands of hill bandits and organize their activities so that he has developed a virtual stranglehold on overland trade and appears ready to attempt the conquest of First Town.

Although the bulk of Santam's army are the city forces, about one-fourth are made up of hillmen, and these hillmen form the most potent striking force at his disposal.

Organization: All infantry are irregulars and are organized in companies (each the size of a war band). Artillery consists of individual catapult sections when it is taken into the field.

Weapons: The hillmen are equipped with bows and short swords. About a third of the city forces are bowmen with short swords while the rest are spearmen.

Unit Value: Hillmen V3S, city forces X1

Uniforms: The Hillmen wear mottled, gray-brown tunics, and usually have a distinctive colored scarf that marks the band the soldiers belong to. The city forces wear red tunics trimmed in a distinctive color. All artillerymen are from the city forces.

CATAPULTS

Weapon	*Weight*	*Pen*	*DV*	*ROF*	*Crew*	*Range*
20-pounder	Sg	0/0	1	(1)	6	2/4
60-pounder	Hv	1/0	2	(1)	4	2/4
Bolt Thrower	Md	0/0	P	1	2	2/4

Note: The bolt thrower has a damage value of "P," indicating that it may only be fired at personnel, not at conveyances or structures. If fired at troops, it is resolved the as artillery firing shot with a damage value of 1.

CITY OF IRON

THE IRONMEN are excellent miners and smelters, and alone among the

Moon Men: *(Left to right.) Brantu bowman, fisherman spearman, City of Light and Science guardsman, Ironman Civic Guard officer.*

cities of Luna have luxurious quantities of meat, tools, and armor. Paparatoomu, the chairman of the Civic Council, has spent the last two years training and drilling the city's army, alarmed at the growth of Santam's power to the south.

Organization: Most infantry are irregulars and are organized in companies (each the size of a war band). There are two regiments of Civic Guards, however (the Gate Guard and the Water Guard), each with two companies of regulars.

Weapons: All troops have steel swords in addition to their other melee weapons. The Civic Guard has plain iron helmets and breastplates. Half the men of each company have bows and the other half have spears and iron shields. (The spearmen form the front rank in battle).

Half of the nonguardsmen companies are equipped with bows and the other half with swords and iron shields.

Unit Value: Guard V1S, nonguard T1

Uniforms: Guardsmen wear white tunics while all other troops wear yellow. Officers have tall spikes on their helmets with long, red (white in the guard) ribbons attached to the top.

Special Rules: Ironmen equipped with iron shields treat all other Moon Men as weak opponents in melee (see the Melee Modifiers Table, page 170).

CITY OF LIGHT AND SCIENCE

The City of Light and Science, ruled by a council of Science Priests, has little need for an army beyond internal security functions. Its soldiers are policemen or gunners on the lightning cannons that guard the walls.

Organization: All infantry are irregulars and are organized in companies (each the size of a war band).

Weapons: Electric rifles.

Unit Value: T0

Uniforms: White tunics.

CRESCENT CITY

Relying on its relative isolation from the other cities as its best defense, the inhabitants of Crescent City carry on a peaceful and friendly trade with the fishermen of Nicolan and the smiths of the City of Iron.

Organization: All infantry are irregulars and are organized in companies (each the size of a war band). Artillery consists of individual catapult sections when it is taken into the field.

Weapons: One-third of the war bands have bows and long knives, the rest have spears.

Unit Value: One-half of the bands are T1, the others G0.

Uniforms: Civilian clothes.

FARTHERTON

This coastal city is a major trading center and is particularly concerned both with Brantu's increasing interference in naval commerce and the growing incidence of bandit raids on caravans bound for the City of Iron.

Organization: All infantry are irregulars and are organized in companies (each the size of a war band). Artillery consists of individual catapult sections when it is taken into the field.

Weapons: Half the men in each company have bows, the remainder of them have spears and carapace shields. (The spearmen form the front rank in battle).

Unit Value: Half the companies are T1, the others, G0. There is one company of Municipal Guard which is X1S.

Uniforms: Municipal Guard wears red tunics and flowing red streamers on their helmets.

Other troops wear red-brown tunics and have no helmet streamers.

FIRST TOWN

This inland town relies heavily on caravan trade, which has been virtually choked off by the hillmen. The defensive troops are now bracing themselves for an attack from the Warlord of the Hills.

Organization: All infantry are irregulars and are organized in companies (each the size of a war band). Artillery consists of individual catapult sections when it is taken into the field.

Weapons: One-third of the war bands have bows and long knives, the rest have spears.

Unit Value: Half of the spearmen are X1, the others T1. Bowmen are X2S.

Uniforms: Blue tunics.

JUNCTION CITY

This trading city has profited from First Town's troubles and now virtually controls the overland trade to the City of Light and Science. Its new-found commercial strength has encouraged the oligarchs to take a stronger stand in territorial disputes with Seaside.

Organization: All infantry are irregulars organized in companies (each the size of a war band). Artillery consists of individual catapult sections when it is taken into the field.

Weapons: Half the men in each company have bows; the rest, spears and carapace shields. (The spearmen form the front rank in battle).

Unit Value: One-third of the bands are X2, the remainder T1.

Uniforms: Yellow-brown tunics.

NICOLAN

THIS ISOLATED CITY-STATE on the far coast has little contact with other cities. Fishermen ply the waters east of the archipelago, free from Brantu war galley harassment, and carry on commerce with merchants of Crescent. It has virtually no navy; its catapults are mounted on its city and town walls.

Organization: All infantry are irregulars and are organized in companies (each the size of a war band).

Weapons: One-third of the war bands have bows and long knives, the rest have spears.

Unit Value: T1

Uniforms: Usually gray tunics.

SEASIDE

FISHING AND FARMING are both important to Seaside, but its fishermen are harassed endlessly by war galleys and motorboats from Brantu while Junction City is pressing claims to strips of farmland between the two.

Organization: All infantry are irregulars organized in companies (each the size of a war band). Artillery consists of individual catapult sections when it is taken into the field.

Weapons: Half the men in each company have bows; the rest, spears and carapace shields. (The spearmen form the front rank in battle).

Unit Value: About one-fourth of the bands are X2, one-half T1, and the final one-fourth, G0.

Uniforms: Brown tunics trimmed in blue or green.

Glossary of Uniform Terms

THIS GLOSSARY is exerpted from *Uniforms Of The World* by Knötel, Knötel, and Sieg, and readers are directed to that authoritative work for a more detailed coverage.

HEADGEAR

Chenille: Close-fitting caterpillar-like crest on the comb of the helmet.

Cockade: Circular bow or ribbon bearing national colors or emblem worn on the headgear.

Criniere: Long, flowing horsehair crest attached to the comb of a helmet.

Forage Cap: Low, cloth cap with a broad crown all around and a peak.

Glengarry: British side cap with black tapes hanging from the back.

Kepi: A close-fitting, small-crowned round cap, usually of cloth, with a leather peak.

Kolpak: Tall, round, peakless fur cap, with a crown usually done in colored cloth.

Lancer Hat: Round helmet, usually of leather, with a square top. The four sides of the top were often painted the distinctive color of the regiment.

Martian Sapper Cap: A round-topped, leather cap with a peak and a long flap in the rear covering the neck.

Martian Turban: A very loose turban covering most of the back of the head. It is often worn wrapped around a spiked steel or brass helmet.

Ros: A hat unique to the Spanish army. It is a wide, low shako with the crown higher at the front than at the back.

Shako: Stiff, tapering, peaked hat, usually made of felt or leather.

Turban: Headdress made of cloth wrapped around the head in a distinctive pattern.

JACKET

Attila: Short-skirted tunic or jacket with cord or braid loopings across the front. Worn mostly by light cavalry from about the middle of the century.

Dolman: Short, single-breasted jacket with loopings across the front. Worn mostly by light cavalry. Similar to an Attila, but does not extend below the waist.

Jumper: The loose upper garment worn by virtually all sailors at this time. It had a vee neck and a large square hanging collar in back.

Loopings: Cord or braid extending across the front of certain uniform jackets, particularly as worn by cavalry or officers.

Patrol Jacket: A dark blue jacket very similar to an Attila, but with broad, black tapes replacing the customary cord loopings. Very popular with British officers.

Pelisse: Hussar overgarment covered with loopings or braid and usually edged with fur or imitation fur. Normally slung by a cord over the left shoulder.

Plastron: The broad lapel, usually of a distinctive color, that covers the front of a lancer's jacket.

Waistcoat: A tight-fitting coat, sometimes sleeveless, worn under the jacket. The jacket is usually then worn open to expose the waistcoat's color.

Zouave Vest: A collarless vest with lace or braid trim and decorative loopings.

PANTS

Gaiters: A cloth or leather one-piece covering for the lower leg. It usually buttoned or laced up the outside seam.

Leggings: Similar to gaiters.

Puttees: Strips of cloth wound around the lower leg, serving the same purpose as gaiters.

Sporran: The white and black fur ornamental pouch worn at the front of a kilt by highlanders.

Strapping: Leather sown to the outside of the trouser, usually in imitation of a boot.

Zouave Pants: Very large, baggy pants, usually of a bright color and worn tucked into gaiters.

EQUIPMENT

Sam Brown Belt: An arrangement of leather officer's equipment invented by General Brown featuring several attachment rings on the waist belt and detachable, narrow shoulder belts to support the weight of a pistol or saber evenly.

Bibliography

Adjutant General's Office of the United States Army. *Actions &c With Indians From January 15, 1837 to January 1891*. The Old Army Press, 1979.

Barthorp, Michael. *The British Army on Campaign 1816-1902 (4): 1882-1902*. London: Osprey. ISBN 0-85045-849-8.

Lord Brassey, K.C.B. and F. K. Barnes, M.I.N.A. *The Naval Annual: 1888-9*. London: J. Griffin & Co., 1889.

Brom, Larry V. *The Sword and the Flame*. Royal Oak, MI: Greenfield, 1984.

Chappell, Mike. *The Canadian Army at War*. London: Osprey, 1985. ISBN 0-85045-600-2.

Clammer, David. *The Zulu War.* Newton Abbot, Devon: David & Charles Publishers, 1973. ISBN 0-7153-9246-8.

Conway's All the World's Fighting Ships, 1860-1905. London: Conway Maritime Press, 1979. ISBN 0-85177-133-5.

deRoos, Dirk, "Un Personage Nefaste," *Savage & Soldier* (three parts).

Elting, Col. John R. and Michael J. McAfee. *Military Uniforms in America Vol. IV—The Modern Era From 1868*. Novato, CA: Presidio Press, 1988. ISBN 0-89141-292-1 (v. 4).

Farwell, Byron. *Mr. Kipling's Army*. New York: W. W. Norton & Co., 1981. ISBN 0-393-30444-2

Farwell, Byron. *Queen Victoria's Little Wars*. New York: W. W. Norton & Co., 1972. ISBN 0-393-30235-0.

Funcken, Liliane and Fred. *L'uniforne et les armes des soldats du XIXe siecle*. Casterman, 1982. ISBN 2-202-14325-8.

Harman, Nicholas. *Bwana Stokesi and his African Conquests*. London: Jonathan Cape, 1986. ISBN 0-224-01998-8.

Hart, Lieutenant General H. G. *Hart's Annual Army List 1889*. London: John Murray, 1889.

Haythornthwaite, Philip J. *Victorian Colonial Wars*. London: Arms and Armour Press, 1988. ISBN 0-85368-869-9.

Hopkins, J. Castell and Murat Halstead. *South Africa and the Boer-British War.* Toronto, Canada: The Bradley-Garretson Company, 1900.

Johnson, Doug, "The Franco-Malagasy War of 1895," *Savage & Soldier.*

Knight, Ian. *Queen Victoria's Enemies (I): Southern Africa*. London: Osprey, 1989. ISBN 0-85045-901-X.

Knötel, Richard, Herbert Knötel, and Herbert Sieg. *Uniforms of the World*. New York: Charles Scribner's Sons, 1980. ISBN 0-684-16304-7.

Koerner, Alfred. *The Hotchkiss Revolving Cannon*. Paris: Hotchkiss & Co., 1879.

Laffin, John. *The Australian Army at War, 1899-1975*. London: Osprey, 1982. ISBN 0-85045-418-2.

Novak, Greg. *And Continually Wear the Blue*. Champaign, IL: Ulster Imports, 1988.

Schreier Jr., Konrad F., ed. *1880's American Arms*. Santa Monica, CA: Quail Ranch Books, 1981.

Stanley, Henry M. *In Darkest Africa: Quest, Rescue, and Retreat of Emin Governor of Equatoria*. New York: Charles Scribner's Sons, 1890 (two volumes).

Vaughan, Ron, "The Dahomean Army." *Savage & Soldier.* Vol XX, No. 4 (1989).

Whitehouse, Howard. *Battles in Africa, 1874-1914*. Mansfield, England: Field Books, 1987. ISBN 1-869871-01-4.

Flag Coloration Key

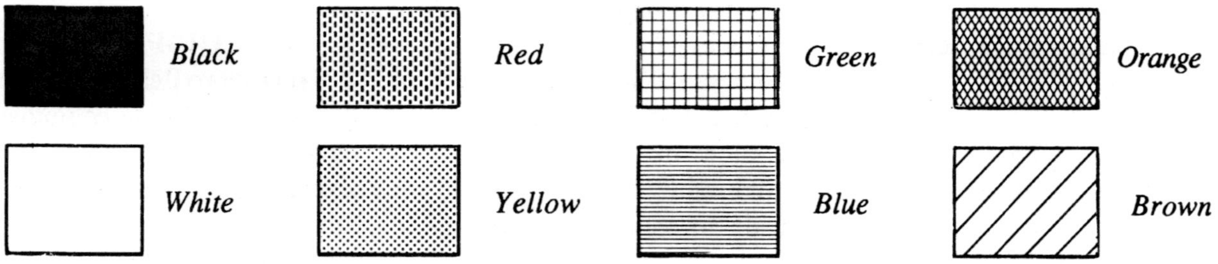

Designer's Notes

MY INTENT in designing these rules was fairly simple. I wanted a good, workmanlike set of colonial, 19th-century rules to which the science-fiction aspect of **Space: 1889** could be grafted. That particular order of things is important. The colonial rules come first, not the weird science. A number of our playtest games were fought with no mechanical conveyances at all, and one was even a Northwest Frontier battle between Brits and Pathans.

Having said that, it should also be obvious that the rough framework upon which the game was built was **Sky Galleons of Mars**. These rules are almost 100-percent compatible with that boardgame, and it is a very simple matter to use Geohex terrain tiles for the miniatures terrain and treat those 12" hexes as equivalent to a single hex on the **Sky Galleons** map. If you want, you can even use this mega-grid to move and turn your ships; it produces the same results as the miniatures game movement rules.

My next goal was to remain as faithful to the 19th century as possible. The sidebar quotations from articles are not invented; all are authentic. All units mentioned in this book (with the obvious exception of those raised on Mars, Venus, or the Moon) are real, to the best of my ability to ascertain. Even that unlikely unit of "Amazonians," Company A, 62nd St. John Fusiliers of New Brunswick, Canada was a genuine militia unit, and for a photograph of the company in uniform (including the male company commander in the regiment's mess jacket) see plate 127 of Haythornthwaite's *Victorian Colonial Wars*.

Likewise, all British commanders of army units mentioned in the various orders of battle, along with their military records, are authentic, with the obvious exception, again, of service on Mars or Venus. The parenthetical comments on their characters and abilities are, however, completely fabricated, and some have been made "plodders" for game interest rather than as a result of their actual abilities or performances. In that sense, this does not pretend to be history, and no criticism of men who served with unblemished records is intended.

Players interested in additional readings in this era are directed to the bibliography on page 167. I am certain that I have neglected several books consulted along the way, but the majority of sources are there.

There are several mechanics worth discussing briefly. One, of course, is figure scale. Since we have small companies in the game and only four companies per battalion instead of eight or more, it's obvious we've scaled things down a bit. There is no precise figure scale, but there end up being about 80 men to a battalion that usually fielded upward of 800, so 10:1 is as good a rule of thumb as any. Where I have specified the size of various native armies in Africa, it is based on this 10:1 rule.

One rating that I am quite happy with is the Fieldcraft skill, which I originally encountered in a set of rules by Greg Novak on German colonial warfare in southwest Africa. Although I have played around a bit with how it is used, the basic concept was his, and I think that it's a good one and is very useful in differentiating troop types and capabilities.

One important mechanic in the game is the use of hits as a modifier to morale instead of casualties, an idea I first saw used by Hal Thinglum in his very entertaining Rourke's Drift miniatures game. This rule, along with the saving throw rule on small arms fire, enabled me to put together a game where there could be a lot of firing and a lot of game results (checks, shaken morale, and so forth) but relatively few casualties. Of course, there can be a lot of casualties if you are formed in the open, but in a skirmish through broken ground the effects of firepower will be more morale-centered than casualty-centered.

My playtesters made me promise to include some advice on how to play irregulars. It isn't easy in this game, as regulars have numerous advantages. I can make a few suggestions, however.

First, take a look at how the actual irregular armies fought and whether or not they were successful. The Zulus had a very useful technique, for instance. They would have their reserve troops in a battle sit down on the ground with their backs to the enemy. If they could not see the course of the battle, they would not become frenzied and carry out a premature charge. This is a useful way of avoiding the witness-to-victory morale test. In the game this can be accomplished by judicious placement of troops.

Second, getting the intiative can be a real problem. Try to leave yourself with a means to seize the initiative at a critical moment, which is to say, try to keep at least one unit hidden but in a position where it can see the enemy. If in such a position, it can launch a charge from hiding and guarantee you the initiative for one turn.

Next, regular human troops tend to have tremendous firepower, particularly if armed with bolt-action rifles, so don't give them targets just for the heck of it. In one game a small village had a few regulars defending it who were spread around the village's perimeter. When the natives charged, they did so from every side, thus guaranteeing that every defender was able to fire. It is better to hit the defenses from one side with all of your strength.

If you have a good Fieldcraft, use it. Keep in open order in cover and snipe at the nice redcoats standing there in close order formation.

Let me close with a piece of general advice to players and referees alike. Miniatures gaming is a form of entertainment, and these rules are intended to provide you with the means of putting on an entertaining game. It is foolish, then, to let the printed rules stand in the way of your enjoyment. The bulk of this book should serve as testimony to the effort put into making it as complete as it can be, but a set of rules is sterile without an active set of players. If you disagree with anything in these rules, please feel free to modify it to suit your own tastes. Just don't argue about it while the game is being played. During the game, the referee's word is absolute law, above even the printed words of the rules.

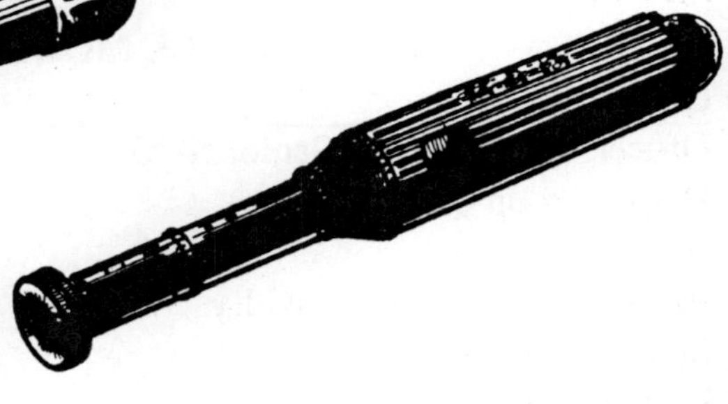

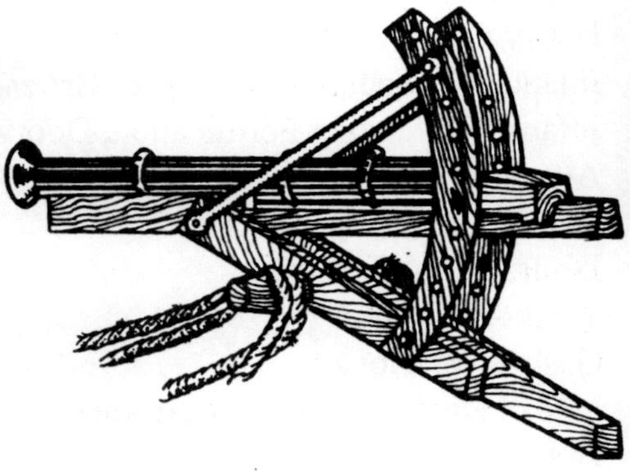

MOVEMENT CHART

Infantry	*Formation*	*Move*	*Charge*
Regular	Column	18"	30"
	Line, Open Order, Disorder	12"	20"
	Square	6"	*
Irregular	All	3D"	5D"

*A square may not charge. One or more sides of the square may charge, however, and do so as lines.

Cavalry	*Formation*	*Move*	*Charge*
Regular Light	Column	24"	48"
	Line, Open Order, Disorder	18"	42"
Regular Heavy	Column	24"	42"
	Line, Open Order, Disorder	18"	36"
Irregular	All	4D"	8D"

ARTILLERY MOVEMENT

Type	*Limber*	*Move*	*Unlimber*	*Move*
Light	1/2	24"	Free	8"
Medium	1/2	24"	1/2	6"
Heavy	1/2	18"	Full	4"
Very Heavy	Full	18"	Full	2"
Siege	2 turns	12"	2 turns	—

Horse-drawn vehicles (including wagons and carts) move as siege artillery.

MELEE MODIFIERS

Condition	*Modifier*
Officer, Leader, Chief, Senior NCO	+1
Higher Troop Quality	+ Difference
British in Square	+1
Infantry in Square vs. Cavalry	+1
Lancers Charging	+1
Light Horse	+1
Light Cavalry (And Irregulars)	+2
Heavy Cavalry	+3
Infantry Defending from Higher Ground	+1
Infantry Defending Fortification, Doorway, or Barricade	+1
Attacking from Flank	+1
Checked Adversary	+1
Disordered Adversary	+1
Weak Adversary*	+1
Gashant vs. Horse	+1 (for gashant)

*Includes Moon Men, Lizard-men, Selenites, and firearm-equipped irregulars.

SMALL ARMS FIRING TABLES

Pistols

Weapon	*Dice*	*Range*
Single Shot	1/2	2/4
Light Multibarrel	1	1/2
Heavy Multibarrel	1	3/6
Revolver	1-2	2/4

Rifles

Weapon	*Dice*	*Range*
Bolt Action	2:1	16/32
Lever Action	1-2	10/20
Breechloader	1	12/24
Rifle Musket	1/2	10/20
Smoothbore Musket	1/2	6/12
Hunting Rifle	1/2	24/48

Carbines

Weapon	*Dice*	*Range*
Bolt Action	2:1	12/24
Lever Action	1-2	6/12
Breechloader	1	8/16
Rifle Musket	1/2	6/12
Smoothbore	1/2	4/8

Miscellaneous

Weapon	*Dice*	*Range*
Shotgun**	1-2	4/—
Scattergun**	1-2	2/—
Spear*	1/2	2/4
Bow	1	4/8
Shield Gun***	1	2/—

*A unit may only throw spears twice. **May not fire at long range. ***Shield guns fire as scatterguns.

Machineguns

Weapon	*Dice*	*Range*
0.5" Gatling	3 (5)	24/48
Mitrailleuse	3	24/48
Nordenfelt 1-B LMG	2	12/24
Nordenfelt 3-B	3	24/48
Nordenfelt 5-B	5	24/48
Gardner	2 (3)	24/48
Maxim	6	24/48

SMALL ARMS HIT NUMBER MODIFIERS

Made to the required number, not the roll itself.

Basic Hit Number: 6

TARGET

Condition	*Modifier*
Column, Mass, or Disorder	1
Enfiladed Line	–1
Green Troops	–1
Charging	–1
Open Order	+1
Light Cover	+1
Medium Cover	+2
Hard Cover	+3
Skirmishing	+Fieldcraft
Shield vs. Spear	+1
Shield vs. Bow	+2
Martian Shield Gunner	+1

FIRING UNIT

Condition	*Modifier*
Scattergun, 1/2 Range	–2
Shotgun, 1/2 Range	–1
Green Troops	+1
Mounted	+2
Long Range	+2
Volley Fire	+2

INITIATIVE TABLE

Condition	*Modifier*
Better Leader	+1
Regulars vs. Irregulars	+1
Frenzied Troops	+1
Isolated Leader	–1

MORALE NUMBERS

Morale Level	*Number*
Green	7
Trained	8
Experienced	9
Veteran	10
Elite	12

TERRAIN TYPES

Terrain	*Infantry*		*Cavalry*		
Type	*Open*	*Formed*	*Open*	*Formed*	*Artillery*
Clear	Open	Open	Open	Open	Open
Field	Open	Open	Open	Open	Open
Vinyard	Open	Diff	Diff	Diff	Diff
Orchard	Open	Diff	Diff	Imp	Open
Woods	Diff	Imp	Diff	Imp	Diff
Forest	Diff	Imp	Imp	imp	Imp
Swamp	Diff	Imp	Diff	ImpImp	Imp
Brush	Open	Diff	Open	Diff	Diff
Boulder Field	Diff	Imp	Imp	Imp	Imp
Barrier					
Gentle Slope	Open	Open	Open	Open	Diff
Steep Slope	Diff	Imp	Diff	Imp	Imp
Ford	Diff	Diff	Diff	Diff	Diff
Low Wall	Open	Diff	Open	Open	Imp

Abbreviations: *Diff:* Difficult *Imp:* Impassable.

MORALE MODIFIERS

Condition	*Modifier*
Under Cover	+2
Attacked (by Melee or Fire) from Flank or Rear	–2
Fired at by Volley Fire	–2
Charging in Open Order	–2
Firearm Irregulars Charging or Charged	–2
Banner, Flag, or Musician Advancing in Sight	+1
Banner, Flag, or Musician Retiring in Sight	–1
Frenzied	+2
Checked	–1
Shaken	–2
Demoralized	–3
Superior Officer Present	+Leadership rating
No Officer Present (Regulars Only)	–1
Own (Regular) Wounded Left to Irregular Enemy	–2
Testing for Witness to Victory	–2
Fired at by Friendly Troops	–2
Defending at Night	–2
Cavalry Charging Steady Infantry in Square	–2

RIFLED FIELD ARTILLERY

Weapon	*Weight*	*Pen*	*DV*	*ROF*	*Crew*	*Range*
7" gun	Sg	4/2	7	(2)	6	5/10
7" hwtzr	Sg	1	7	(1)	4	10
6" long gun	Sg	5/3	6	(1)	4	5/10
6" short gun	Sg	4/2	6	(1)	4	4/8
6" hwtzr	Sg	1	6	(1)	4	8
5" gun	Sg	4/2	4	(1)	4	5/10
5" hwtzr	VH	1	4	1	4	8
4" gun	VH	3/2	2	1	4	4/8
40-pdr gun	VH	3/1	3	1	4	4/8
20-pdr gun	Hv	2/1	2	1	4	3/6
15-pdr gun	Md	2/1	1	1	4	3/6
12-pdr gun	Md	1/1	1	1	4	3/6
9-pdr gun	Lt	1/0	1	1	4	3/6
7-pdr hwtzr	Lt	0	1	2	4	6
6-pdr gun	Lt	0/0	1	1	4	2/4
6-pdr HRC	Md	1/0	1*	3	2	3/6
3-pdr HRC	Lt	1/0	1*	3	2	2/4
2-pdr gun	Lt	0/0	1*	1	4	2/4
1-pdr HRC	Lt	0/0	1*	3	2	2/4
1-pdr PP	Lt	0/0	1*	4	2	2/4
1" Gatling	Lt	0/0	1*	3/4	2	1/2

*Only fires shell; cannot fire shrapnel.

Abbreviations: *PP:* Pom-Pom *HRC:* Hotchkiss Revolving Cannon *Pdr:* Pounder *QF:* Quick-Firing *Hwtzr:* Howitzer.

SMOOTHBORE FIELD ARTILLERY

Weapon	*Weight*	*Pen*	*DV*	*ROF*	*Crew*	*Range*
13" mortar	Sg	2	10	(3)	8	7
11" gun	Sg	3/1	5	(2)	6	3/6
10" gun	Sg	2/1	4	(2)	6	2/4
68-pdr gun	Sg	2/1	3	(1)	4	3/6
10" mortar	Sg	1	8	(2)	6	6
9" gun	Sg	1/1	3	(1)	4	2/4
8" mortar	Sg	0	6	(2)	4	5
5.5" mortar	Sg	0	4	(1)	4	4
32-pdr gun	Sg	1/1	2	(1)	4	3/6
32-pdr hwtzr	VH	0	3	1	4	4
24-pdr gun	VH	1/0	2	1	4	2/4
24-pdr hwtzr	Hv	0	2	1	4	3
12-pdr gun	Hv	1/0	1	1	4	2/4
12-pdr hwtzr	Md	0	1	1	4	3
9-pdr gun	Md	0/0	1	1	4	2/3
6-pdr gun	Lt	0/0	1	1	4	1/2

Abbreviations: *Pdr:* Pounder *Hwtzr:* Howitzer.

ARTILLERY BASE HIT NUMBERS

Condition	*Modifier*
Gun, Short Range	3-6
Gun, Long Range	5-6
Rifled Howitzer, Any Range	5-6
Smoothbore Mortar, Howitzer, Lob Gun, Any Range	6

WEAPON CHARACTERISTICS: EXOTIC AERIAL WEAPONS

	Naval Mount			
Gun	*Pen*	*DV*	*ROF*	*Range*
Liquid Fire	—	F	D6	—
Spike Drop	—	P	D6	—
Rocket	0	1	D6	4
Bomb	1	2	D6	—

ARMOR VALUES OF COVER

Cover Type	*Armor Value*
Hut or Wood Frame House	0 (medium cover)
Adobe or Brick House, 12" Thick	1
Low Stone Wall, 24" Thick	2
Hasty Earthwork, 48" Thick	2
Prepared Earthwork, 6' Thick	3
City Wall, 3' Thick	3
Fortress Wall, 4' Thick	4

CASUALTIES CAUSED BY ARTILLERY

Ammunition	*Open*	*Column/Mass*	*Enfiladed Line*	*Other*	*Medium Cover*	*Hard Cover*
Shot	1/2DV	DV	DV	1/2DV	NE	Pen
Shell	1/2DV	2DV	DV	DV	NE	Pen
Grape	1/2D6	D6	D6	D6	1/2	No Fire
Shrapnel	1/2D6	D6	D6	D6	1/2	No Fire

MARTIAN FIELD ARTILLERY

Weapon	*Weight*	*Pen*	*DV*	*ROF*	*Crew*	*Range*
Lob Gun	Sg	2	4	(2)	6	6
Rogue	Sg	2/1	3	(2)	6	3/6
Heavy Gun	VH	1/0	2	1	4	2/4
Rod Gun	Hv	2/1	1	(1)	4	3/6
Light Gun	Md	0/0	1	1	4	1/2
Sweeper	Lt	P	1*	1	2	0/1

*Only fires grapeshot. Range of 1' (12") is the actual grapeshot range for the gun.

Abbreviations: *Pdr:* Pounder *SB:* Smoothbore *Mort:* Mortar.

MODERN BREECH-LOADING GUNS AND MACHINE CANNONS

Weapon	*Weight*	*Pen*	*DV*	*ROF*	*Crew*	*Range*
18”	3400	18/9	20	(4)	8	14/28
17”	2800	17/9	18	(3)	7	13/26
16”	2250	16/8	16	(2)	6	10/20
14”	1300	14/7	14	(1)	6	9/18
12”	900	12/6	12	(1)	5	8/16
10”	600	10/5	10	(1)	4	7/14
8”	300	9/5	8	(1)	3	6/12
6”	100	5/3	6	1	2	5/10
5”	80	4/2	4	1	2	5/10
4.7” QF	100	4/2	3	2	2	4/8
4” (long)	40	3/2	2	1	2	4/8
3” (15-pdr)	25	2/1	1	1	2	3/6
6-pdr HRC	15	1/0	1*	3	1	3/6
3-pdr HRC	10	1/0	1*	3	1	2/4
2-pdr gun	5	0/0	1*	1	2	2/4
1-pdr HRC	10	0/0	1*	3	1	2/4
1-pdr PP	10	0/0	1*	4	1	2/4
1” Gatling	5	0/0	1*	3/4	1	1/2

*Only fires shell; cannot fire shrapnel.

Abbreviations: *QF:* Quick-Firing *HRC:* Hotchkiss Revolving Cannon *PP:* Pom-Pom.

LOW-POWERED RIFLED GUNS AND HOWITZERS

Weapon	*Weight*	*Pen*	*DV*	*ROF*	*Crew*	*Range*
18”	2000	14/7	18	(4)	8	9/18
16”	1600	12/6	16	(3)	6	8/16
14”	1000	10/5	14	(2)	6	7/14
13”	750	9/4	13	(1)	6	6/12
12”	500	8/4	12	(1)	5	6/12
10”	400	7/3	10	(1)	4	6/12
9”	250	6/3	9	(1)	3	5/10
8”	200	5/2	8	(1)	3	5/10
7”	140	4/2	7	(1)	3	5/10
7” hwtzr	100	1	7	1	2	10
6”	80	4/2	6	(1)	2	4/8
6” hwtzr	70	1	6	1	2	8
5” hwtzr	60	1	4	1	2	8
4.7” (40-pdr)	50	3/1	3	1	2	4/8
4” (20-pdr)	30	2/1	2	1	2	3/6
3” (12-pdr)	20	1/1	1	1	2	3/6
9-pdr	10	1/0	1	1	2	3/6
7-pdr MH	15	0	1	2	2	6
6-pdr	10	0/0	1	1	2	2/4

Abbreviations: *Hwtzr:* Howitzer *MH:* Mountain Howitzer *Pdr:* Pounder.

MARTIAN AND OLD EARTH SMOOTHBORE WEAPONS

Weapon	*Weight*	*Pen*	*DV*	*ROF*	*Crew*	*Range*
15"	300	4/2	7	(2)	4	4/8
Lob gun	200	2	4	(1)	3	6
13" mortar	150	2	10	(2)	4	7
11"	150	3/1	5	(1)	3	3/6
10"	80	2/1	4	(1)	3	2/4
10" mortar	90	1	8	(1)	3	6
Rogue	60	2/1	3	(1)	3	3/6
68-pdr	80	2/1	3	1	2	3/6
9"	60	1/1	3	1	2	2/4
8" mortar	60	0	6	(1)	2	5
32-pdr	60	1/1	2	1	2	3/6
32-pdr hwtzr	40	0	3	1	2	4
5.5" mortar	40	0	4	1	2	4
Heavy gun	40	1/0	2	1	2	2/4
24-pdr	40	1/0	2	1	2	2/4
24-pdr hwtzr	30	0	2	1	2	3
Rod mun	30	2/1	1	(1)	2	3/6
12-pdr	30	1/0	1	1	2	2/4
12-pdr hwtzr	20	0	1	1	2	3
9-pdr	25	0/0	1	1	2	2/3
Light gun	20	0/0	1	1	2	1/2
6-pdr	20	0/0	1	1	2	1/2
Sweeper	10	P	—	1	1	0/1

Abbreviations: *Hwtzr:* Howitzer *Pdr:* Pounder *P:* Personnel (Crew) Only.

CRITICAL HIT

Die Roll	*Vehicle Result*	*Ship Result*	*Flyer Result*
2	Magazine	Magazine	Magazine
3	Bridge	Fire/Boiler	Bridge
4	Fire/Boiler	Rudder Right	Fire/Boiler
5	Running Gear	Rudder	Loss of Trim
6	Steering	Flooding	Rudder
7	Fire	Fire	Fire
8	Throttle	Bridge	Lifters
9	Armor	Screw	Screw
10	Magazine	Rudder Left	Magazine
11	Bridge	Magazine	Bridge
12	Fire/Boiler	Fire/Boiler	Fire/Boiler

CONVEYANCE HIT LOCATION

Die	*Location*
1	Hull/Running Gear
2	Hull/Running Gear
3	Crew
4	Crew
5	Gun
6	Critical

FLOODING ROLL MODIFIERS

Condition	*Modifier*
Rammer 3 or more times the size of the rammed ship	+2
Rammer twice the size of the rammed ship	+1
Rammed ship twice the size of the rammer	–1
Rammed ship four times the size of the rammer	–2

HIT MODIFICATIONS

Condition	*Modifier*
To Hit Tall City/Fortress Walls	+2
To Hit a Building	+1
To Hit Abatis	–1
To Hit Trench	–2

MINE ACCURACY

Die	*Result*
1	On Target
2	On Target
3	Right
4	Left
5	Long
6	Short

Roll 2D6 for deviation in inches.

ARMOR VALUE OF 1

Inches	*Material*
2	Steel
3	Iron
12	Brick or Stone
24	Earthworks
48	Wood

STRUCTURES

Structures	*AV*	*Damage*
Hut	0	5
Wood House	0	10
Brick House	1	40
Stone Wall	2	40
City Wall	3	60
Fortress Wall	4	80
Wooden Gate	1	40
Iron Gate	4	80

SIEGE WORKS

Siege Works	*AV*	*Damage*	*Shifts*
Rifle Pit	1	80	1
Trench	2	80	2 (Rifle pit+1)
Ditch	2	80	4 (Trench+2)
Breastwork	2	80	3 (Trench+1)
Redoubt	3	80	4 (Breastwork+1)
Gallery	4	40	4 (Trench+2)
Abatis	0	40	1
Barbed Wire	0	80	1/4
Rubble Wall	2	30	1
Barricade	0	5	1/8
Mine Opening	—	—	1
Mine Section	—	—	1
Log Stockade	1	40	1+1*

*One shift to gather enough logs for one section, one shift to build the stockade section.

BRIDGES

Bridges	*AV*	*Damage*	*Shifts*	*Load (tons)*
Pontoon Bridge	0	10	1	10
Footbridge	0	3	1	Men
Wooden Bridge	0	20	4	10
Stone Bridge	1	40	8	20
Heavy Bridge	2	80	16	40

Ship Record Form

Name: *Trafalgar*

Type/Class: *Battleship*

Nationality: *Great Britain*

HS	24
Length	7
Ram	N
Move	3

ARMOR

Blt:	9
Bty:	9
Blk.	9
Trt.	9
Dck.	3

Crew

Bridge

Deck

Maneuver

Armament

4 X 14"
6 X 4.7" QF
8 X 6# HRC*
9 X 3# HRC*
BT-1*
ST-1*
MT-1*

*Not shown on plan

No gunners shown on plan (Total of 53)

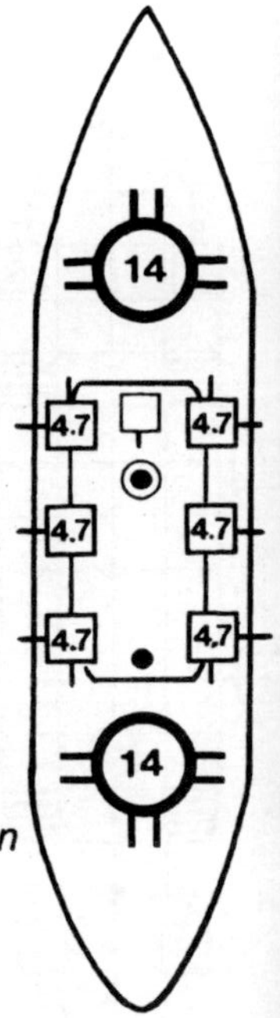

Hull:

(Not to scale with other ships)

Ship Record Form

Name: *Cyclops*

Type/Class: *Coast Defense Monitor*

Nationality: *Great Britain*

HS	7
Length	4
Ram	N
Move	2

ARMOR

Blt:	4
Bty:	–
Blk.	–
Trt.	5
Dck.	1

Crew

Bridge

Deck

Maneuver

Armament

4 X 10" LP

No gunners shown on plan (Total of 16)

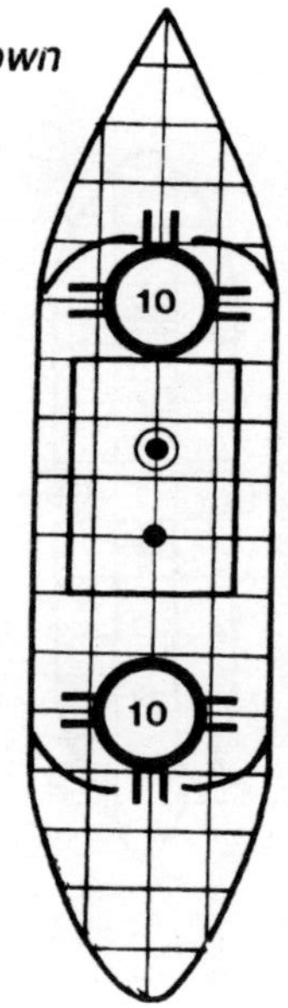

Hull:

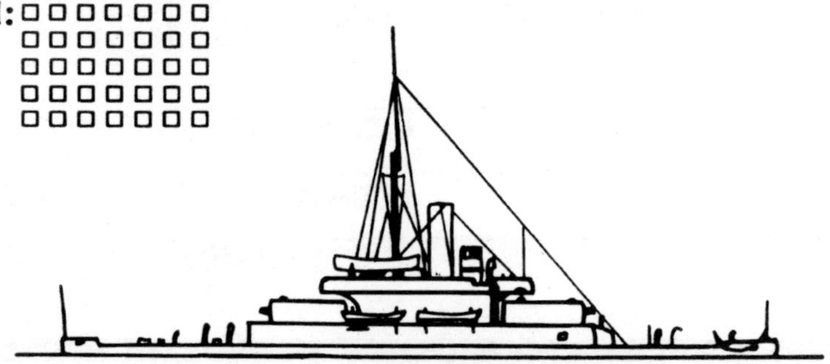

Ship Record Form

Name: *Beagle*

Type/Class: *Sloop*

Nationality: *Great Britain*

HS	2
Length	4
Ram	N
Move	2

Crew

Bridge ☐☐☐☐

Deck ☐☐☐

Maneuver ☐☐☐☐☐☐☐☐

Armament

8 X 5"
8 X 5-b N.F.*

*Not shown on plan

No gunners shown on plan (total of 24)

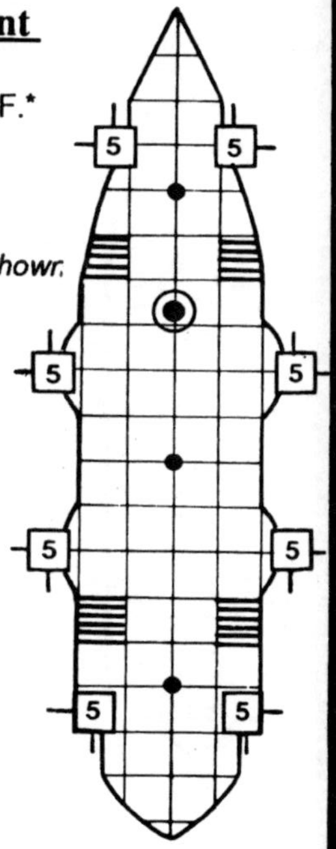

ARMOR	
Blt:	–
Bty:	–
Blk.	–
Trt.	–
Dck.	–

Hull: ☐☐☐☐☐☐☐☐☐☐

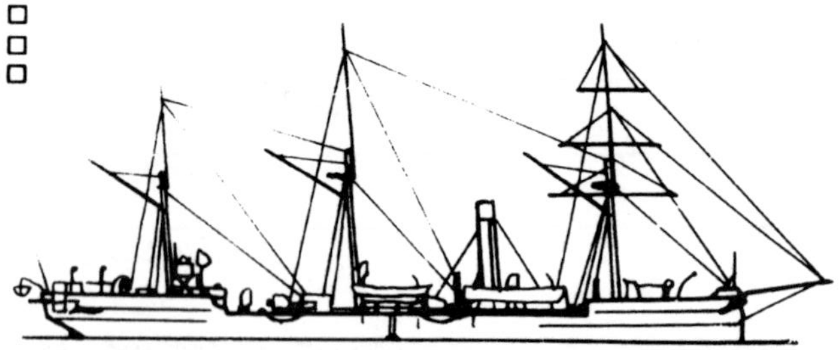

Ship Record Form

Name: *Algerine*

Type/Class: *Gun Vessel*

Nationality: *Great Britain*

HS	1
Length	3
Ram	N
Move	2

Crew

Bridge ☐☐☐☐

Deck ☐☐☐☐☐

Maneuver ☐☐☐☐

Armament

2 X 5"
2 X 6" LP

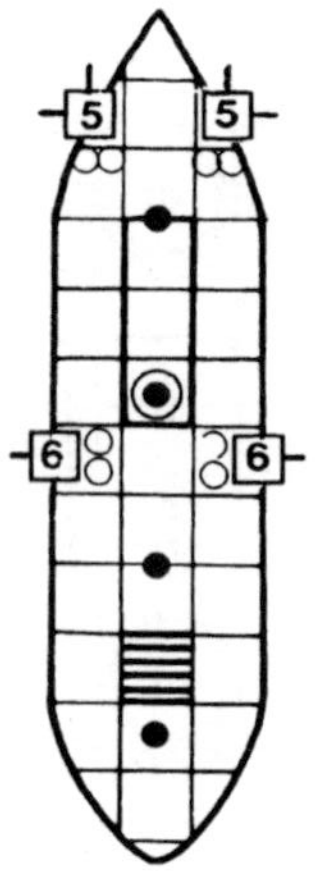

ARMOR	
Blt:	–
Bty:	–
Blk.	–
Trt.	–
Dck.	–

Hull: ☐☐☐☐☐

Ship Record Form

Name: *Yarrow-130*

Type/Class: *Torpedo Boat*

Nationality: *Great Britain*

HS	(1)
Length	3
Ram	N
Move	4

Crew

☐ Bridge ☐ Maneuver

Armament

2 X 5-b N.F.
DT-4

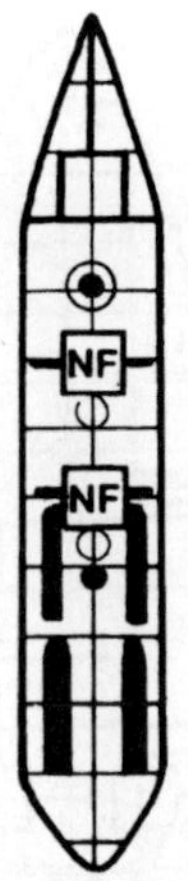

ARMOR

Blt:	–
Bty:	–
Blk.	–
Trt.	–
Dck.	–

Hull: ☐

Ship Record Form

Name: *Batum*

Type/Class: *Torpedo Boat*

Nationality: *Russia*

HS	(1)
Length	2
Ram	N
Move	4

Crew

☐ Bridge ☐ Maneuver

Armament

1 X 1-pdr. HRC
BT-2 + 2

ARMOR

Blt:	–
Bty:	–
Blk.	–
Trt.	–
Dck.	–

Hull: ☐

Ship Record Form

Name: *Acheron*

Type/Class: *Armored Gunboat*

Nationality: *France*

HS	3
Length	4
Ram	N
Move	2

Crew

Bridge ☐☐☐☐
Deck ☐☐☐☐☐☐
Maneuver ☐☐☐☐☐☐

Armament

1 X 10"
3 X 4"(Long)
4 X 1-pdr. HRC

Gun crews not shown on plan (Total of 14)

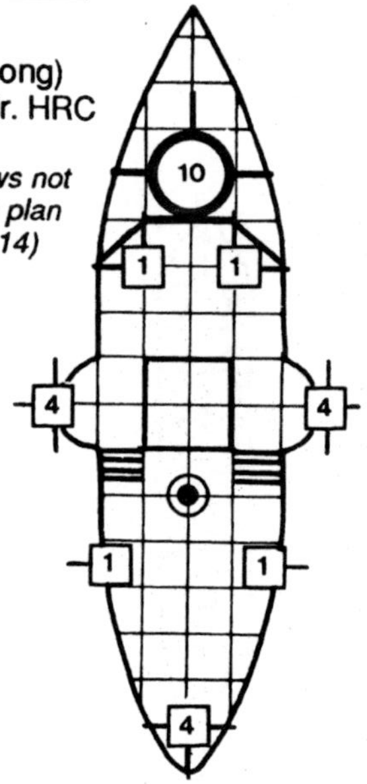

ARMOR	
Blt:	4
Bty:	–
Blk.	–
Trt.	4
Dck.	–

Hull: ☐☐☐☐☐☐☐☐☐☐☐☐☐☐☐

Ship Record Form

Name: *Comete*

Type/Class: *Gunboat*

Nationality: *France*

HS	1
Length	3
Ram	N
Move	2

Crew

Bridge ☐☐☐
Deck ☐☐☐☐
Maneuver ☐☐

Armament

2 X 5"
2 X 4"(Long)
2 X 1-pdr. HRC

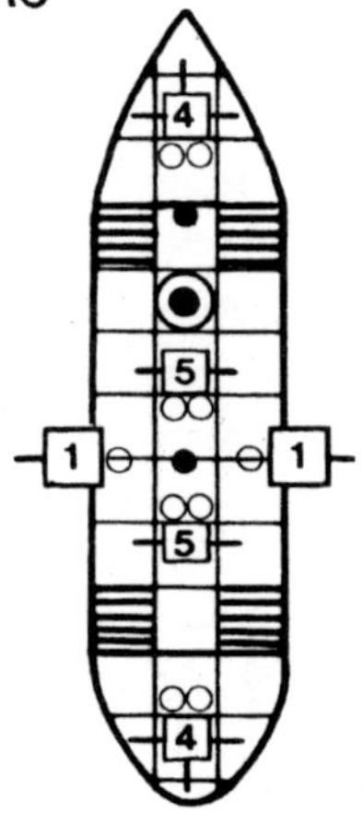

ARMOR	
Blt:	–
Bty:	–
Blk.	–
Trt.	–
Dck.	–

Hull: ☐☐☐☐☐

Ship Record Form

Name: *Eber*

Type/Class: *Gunboat*

Nationality: *Germany*

HS	1
Length	3
Ram	N
Move	2

Crew

Bridge: C H S O

Deck

Maneuver

Armament

3 X 4"(Short)
4 X 1-pdr. HRC

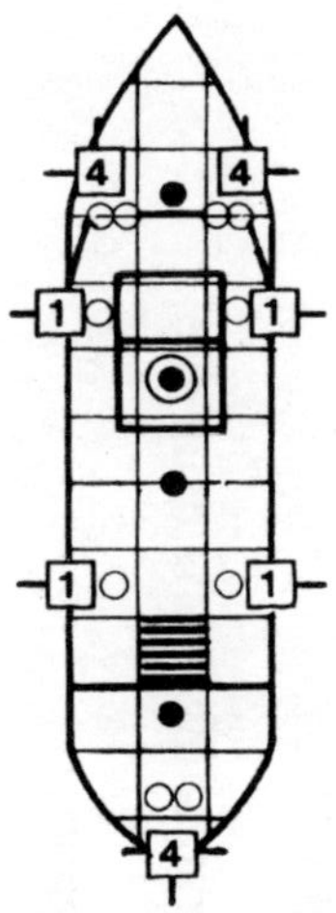

ARMOR

Blt:	–
Bty:	–
Blk.	–
Trt.	–
Dck.	–

Hull: □ □ □ □ □

Ship Record Form

Name: ______

Type/Class: ______

Nationality: ______

HS	
Length	
Ram	
Move	

Crew

Bridge

Deck

Maneuver

Armament

ARMOR

Blt:	
Bty:	
Blk.	
Trt.	
Dck.	

Small Craft

The ships and boats listed on this table represent a wide sampling of unarmed and lightly armed small craft. Rather than print a separate ship record form for each of them, we have instead summarized the important information in tabular form. If a ship record form is required, photocopy the blank form provided on page 181 and fill in the information provided below. None of these ships are armored.

					Crew				
Type	**HS**	**Len**	**Ram**	**Move**	**Bridge**	**Deck**	**Mnvr**	**Gnrs**	**Armament**
Skiff	(1)	1	No	2	1	--	2	--	--
Small Sail Boat	(1)	1	No	D6/2	1	_	1	_	_
Large Sail Boat	(1)	2	No	D6/2	1	1	2	_	_
Steam Launch	(1)	1	No	2	1	_	1	_	_
River Steamer	1	3	No	2	2	3	3	_	_
Hydrofoil	1	2	No	R x 2	1	_	1	_	1 Maxim
Submarine	1	3	Yes	1	2	2	2	_	BT-2
Deep Diving Sub	1	3	Yes	1	2	2	2	_	BT-2 +2
Canal Barge	2	4	No	1	2	2	6	_	_
Small Sailing Ship	1	3	No	D6/2	2	2	6	_	_
War Galley	1	3	Yes	2	3	3	12	2	1 Heavy Gun (Martian)
Lunar Submarine	1	3	Yes	3	2	_	2	_	_
Lunar Motor Boat	(1)	1	No	4	1	_	_	2	1 20-pdr catapult

Key to the Armament Displays

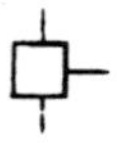 gun showing fields of fire

 gunner

 rocket battery angled up

 rocket battery angled down

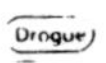 drogue torpedo

 spike dropper

 tether mine

 Smutts torpedo

 bomb rack

 Martian Fire rack

A heavy line or box around a gun and its gunners indicates that they are protected by armor.

Description

Type: *Juggernaut*

Nationality: *Britain*

ID: *H.M.L. Truculent*

Weight: *30 Tons*

Price: *£4,640*

Fuel Weight: *1 Ton Coal*

Fuel Consumption: *1 Ton*

Hull Size: 1

Movement: 2

Armor H 3

Armor RG 1

Crew

Command C D

Engineering ☐ ☐

Armament Display

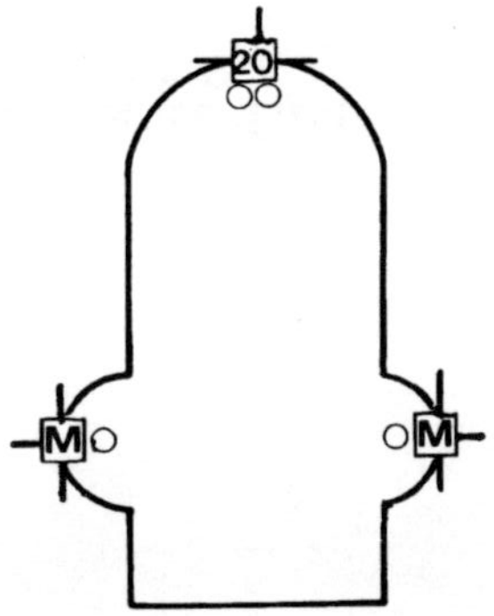

Notes:

Running Gear Hits

2 ☐ ☐
1 ☐ ☐

Armament List

Bow: 1 20-pdr. gun
Wing Sponsons:
2 Maxim guns

Description

Type: *Combat Tripod*

Nationality: *German*

ID: *P2Kpfd Storch*

Weight: *2 Tons*

Price: *£1,210*

Fuel Weight: *1/2 Ton Coal*

Fuel Consumption: *1/2 Ton*

Hull Size: 1

Movement: 5

Armor H 1

Armor RG 0

Crew

Command C

Engineering

Armament Display

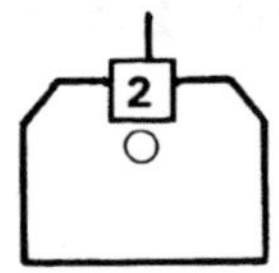

Notes:

Running Gear Hits

5 ☐
4 ☐
3 ☐
2 ☐
1 ☐

Armament List

1 2-pounder gun, bow

Description

Type: *Tractor*

Nationality: ______

ID: ______

Weight: ______

Price: *£500*

Fuel Weight: *1/2 Ton Coal*

Fuel Consumption: *1/2 Ton*

Hull Size: 1

Movement: 2

Armor H –

Armor RG 1

Crew

Command ☐

Engineering

Armament Display

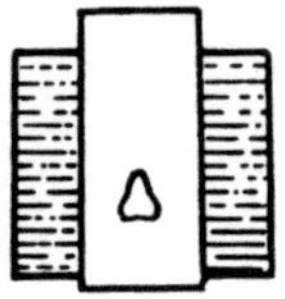

Notes:

Running Gear Hits

2 ☐ ☐

1 ☐ ☐

Armament List

None

Description

Type: *Machinegun Quad.*

Nationality: ______

ID: ______

Weight: ______

Price: ______

Fuel Weight: ______

Fuel Consumption: ______

Hull Size: 1

Movement: 4

Armor H –

Armor RG –

Crew

Armament Display

Notes:

Running Gear Hits

5

4 ☐

3 ☐

2 ☐

1 ☐

Armament List

Bow: Maxim gun

Description

Type: *Armored Train*

Nationality: ______

ID: ______

Weight: *100+ Tons*

Price: *£ 5,000*

Fuel Weight: *4 Tons Coal*

Fuel Consumption: *1 Ton*

Hull Size: 4

Movement: 40"

Armor H 1

Armor RG 1

Crew

Command D C

Engineering ☐ ☐

Armament Display

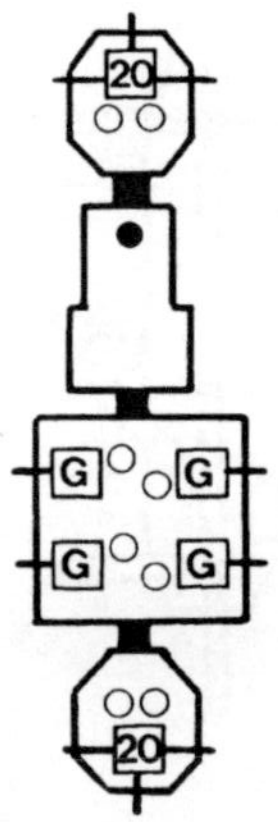

Notes:

Running Gear Hits

4 ☐
3 ☐
2 ☐
1 ☐

Armament List

Fore and Aft Turrets:
1 20-pdr. gun each
Broadsides:
4 .50-col. Gatlings

Description

Type: ______

Nationality: ______

ID: ______

Weight: ______

Price: ______

Fuel Weight: ______

Fuel Consumption: ______

Hull Size: ☐

Movement: ☐

Armor H ☐

Armor RG ☐

Crew

Command ☐ ☐

Engineering ☐ ☐ ☐ ☐ ☐

Armament Display

Notes:

Running Gear Hits

5 ☐ ☐ ☐ ☐ ☐ ☐
4 ☐ ☐ ☐ ☐ ☐ ☐
3 ☐ ☐ ☐ ☐ ☐ ☐
2 ☐ ☐ ☐ ☐ ☐ ☐
1 ☐ ☐ ☐ ☐ ☐ ☐

Armament List

Great Britain

APHID

⬡2 £ 23,220

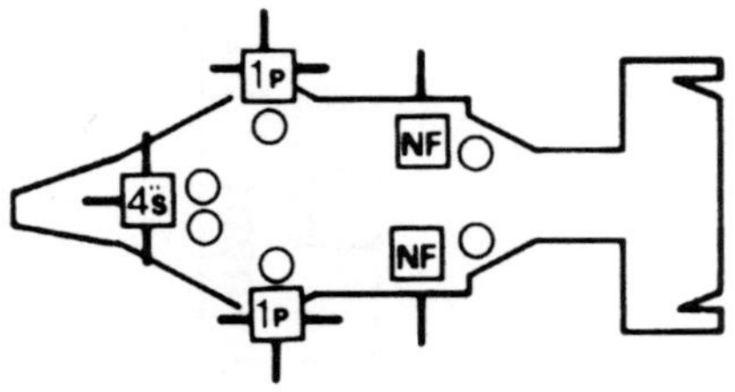

2 **Boiler=2** 160 TONS 6

Bridge C H T S

Deck

Maneuver

Screw 6 5 4 3 2 1

Hull Hits VH H M L VL

AUTOGYRO

⬡0 £ 1,700

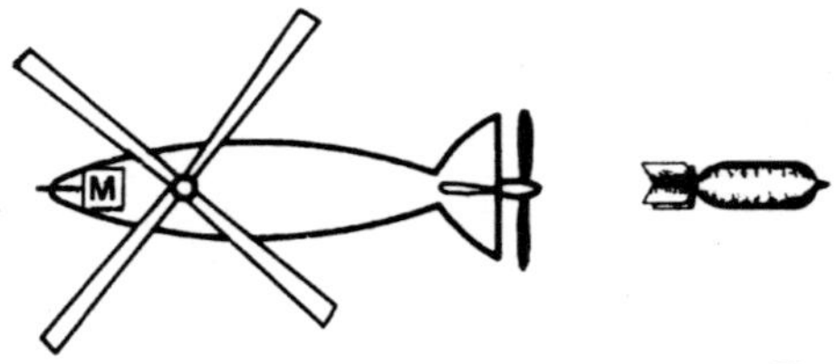

1 1 TON R+5

Bridge C

Screw

Rotor Hits VH H M L VL

AEROPLANE

⬡0 £ 3,400

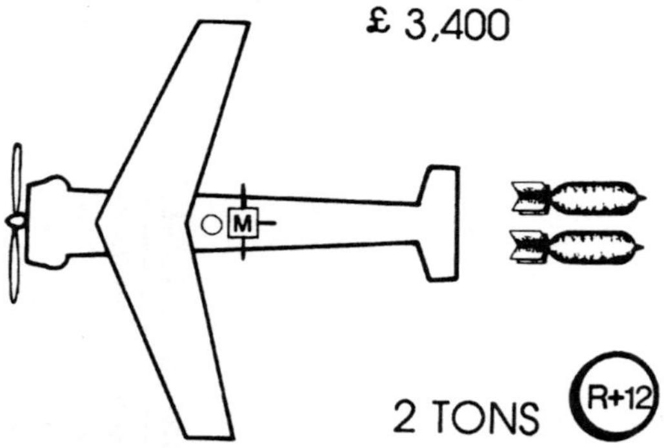

1 2 TONS R+12

Bridge C

Screw

Wing Hits VH H M L VL

HELICOPTER

⬡0 £ 4,500

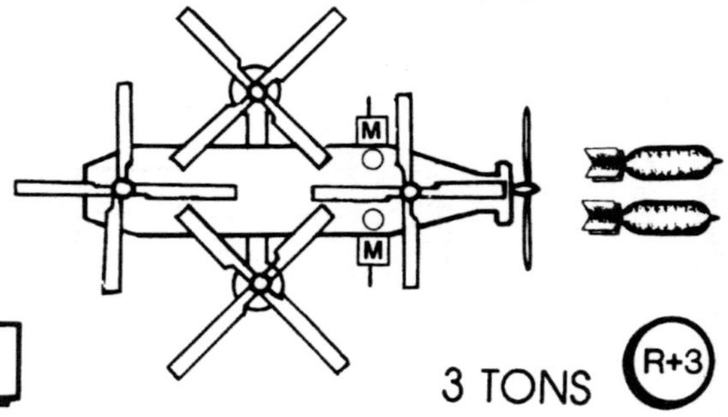

1 3 TONS R+3

Bridge C H

Rotor Hits VH H M L VL

Marines

Great Britain — *RELIANT*

2

£ 92,040

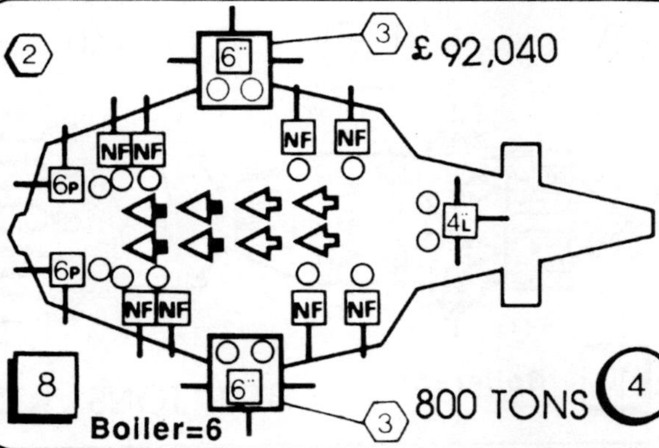

8

Boiler=6

800 TONS

4

Bridge C H T S O O

Deck P P P

Maneuver

Screw 4 3 2 1

Hull Hits H M L VL

Marines 0

GLIDER

0

£ 300

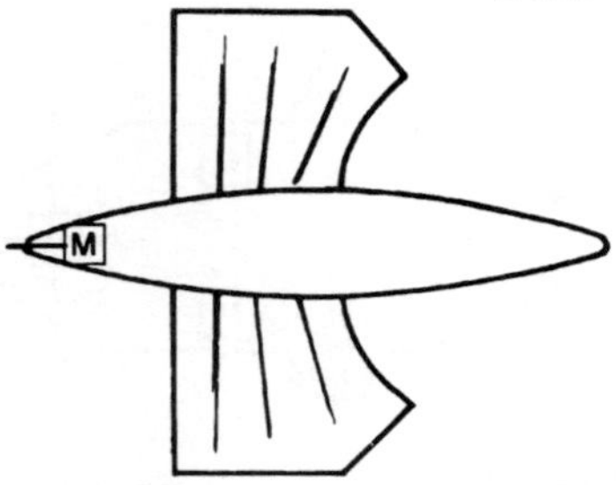

1

1 TON

12

Bridge C

Wing Hits VH H M L VL

Great Britain — *TRIUMPH*

3

£ 138,400

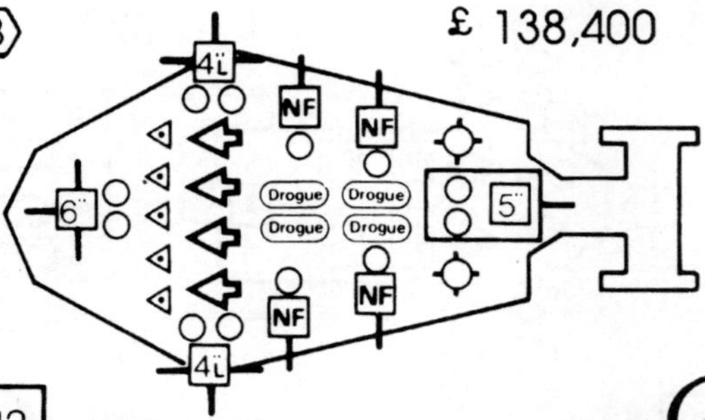

12

Boiler=10

1,200 TONS

4

Bridge C H T S O O

Deck P P P P

Maneuver

Screw 4 3 2 1

Hull Hits H M L VL

Marines 0

Great Britain — *INTREPID*

3

£ 194,540

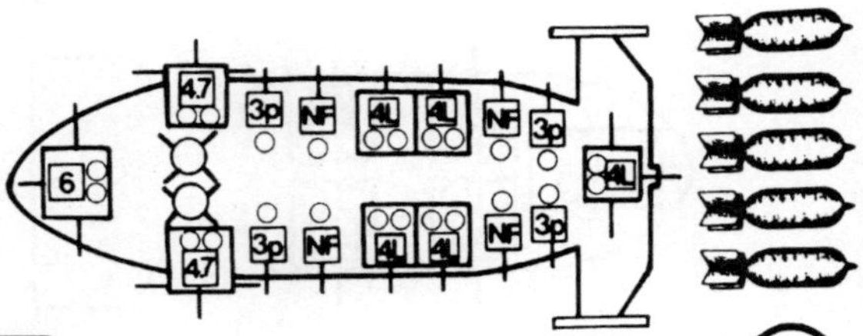

16

Boiler=11

1,600 TONS

4

Bridge C H T S O O

Deck P P P P P

Maneuver

4 3 2 1

Hull Hits H M L VL

Marines 0 0

France ***HARPON***

⟨2⟩ £ 37,880

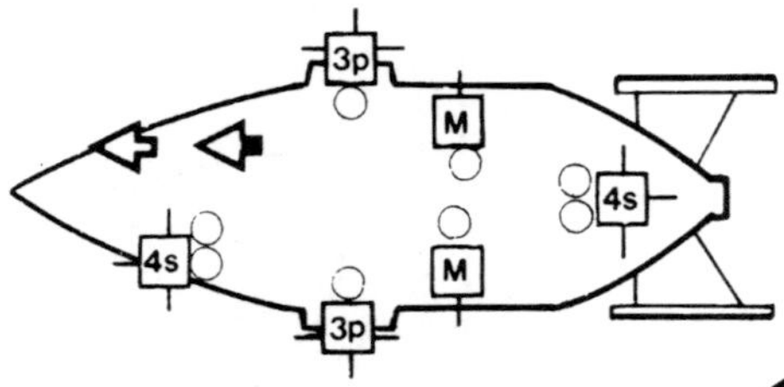

3 **Boiler=3** 250 TONS 6

Bridge C H T S O

Deck P

Maneuver

6 5 4 3 2 1

Hull Hits

VH
H
M
L
VL

France ***GLOIRE***

⟨4⟩ £ 112,760

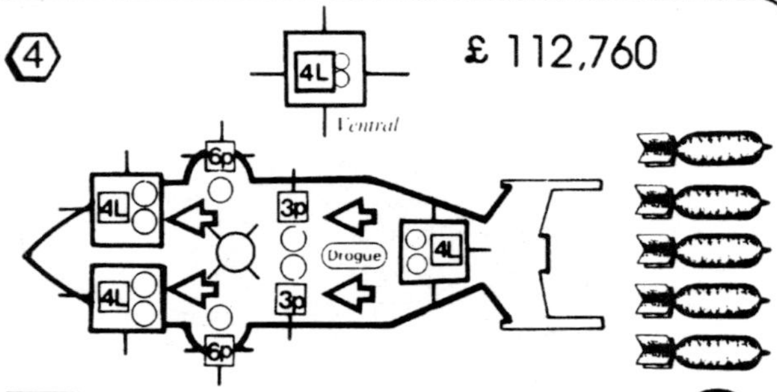

10 **Boiler=5** 1001 TONS 3

Bridge C H T S O O

Deck P P P

Maneuver

Screw 3 2 1

Hull Hits

H
M
L
VL

Marines 0

Germany ***HAMBURG***

⟨3⟩ £ 69,400

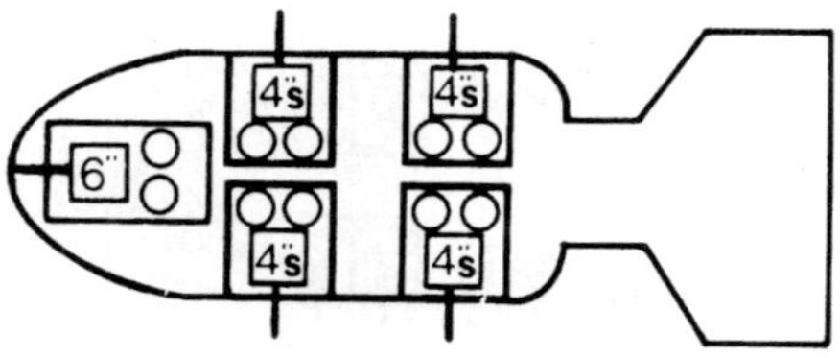

6 **Boiler=5** 600 TONS 5

Bridge C H T S O O

Deck P P

Maneuver

Screw 5 4 3 2 1

Hull Hits

H
M
L
VL

Marines 0 0

USA ***EAGLE***

⟨2⟩ £ 67,870

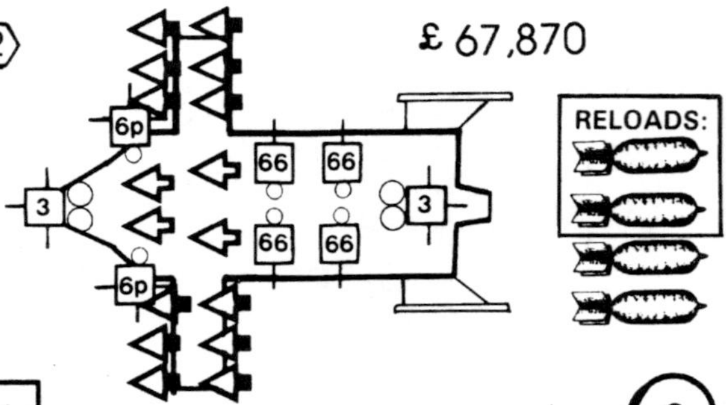

4 **Boiler=4** 400 TONS 6

Bridge C H T S O

Deck P P

Maneuver

Screw 6 5 4 3 2 1

Hull Hits

H
M
L
VL

Marines 0 0

USA *RANGER*

⬡0 £ 23,600

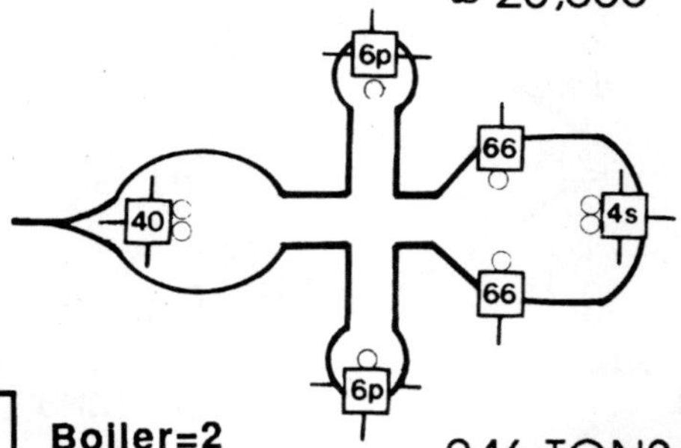

3 **Boiler=2** 246 TONS 4

Bridge C H T S O

Deck P

Maneuver

Screw 4 3 2 1

Hull Hits VH H M L VL

Marines 0 0

Belgium *LEOPOLD*

⬡2 £ 69,080

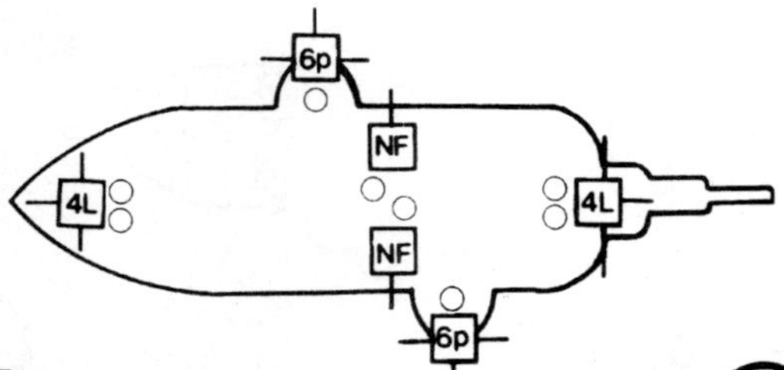

6 **Boiler=6** 320 TONS 6

Bridge C H T S O

Deck P P

Maneuver

Screw 6 5 4 3 2 1

Hull Hits VH H M L VL

Belgium *LIEGE*

⬡0 £ 113,000

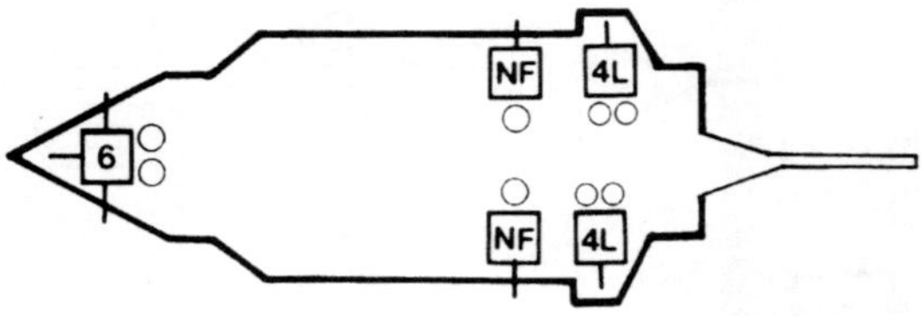

12 **Boiler=10** 940 TONS 5

Bridge C H T S O O

Deck P P P

Maneuver

Screw 5 4 3 2 1

Hull Hits VH H M L VL

Marines 0 0

Belgium *DUC DE BRABANT*

⬡2 £ 69,400

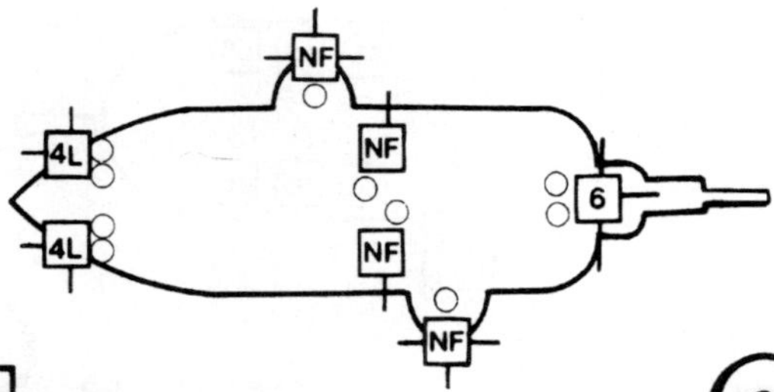

6 **Boiler=6** 400 TONS 6

Bridge C H T S O

Deck P P

Maneuver

Screw 6 5 4 3 2 1

Hull Hits VH H M L VL

Russia — *CZARINA*

3

£ 46,000

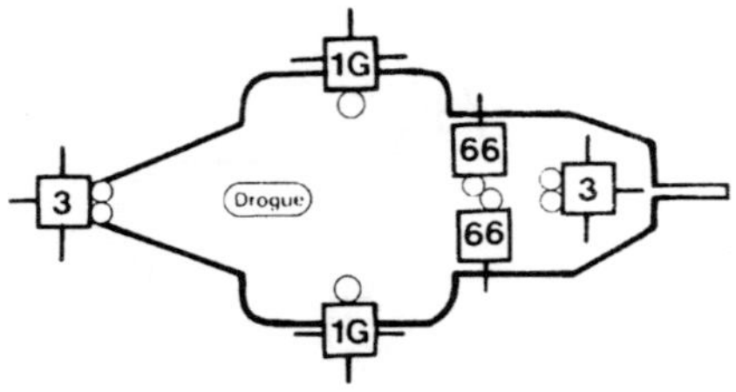

4 Boiler=4

330 TONS

6

Bridge: C H T S O

Deck: P

Maneuver

Screw: 6 5 4 3 2 1

Hull Hits: VH, H, M, L, VL

Japan — *MIKASA*

0

£ 17,780

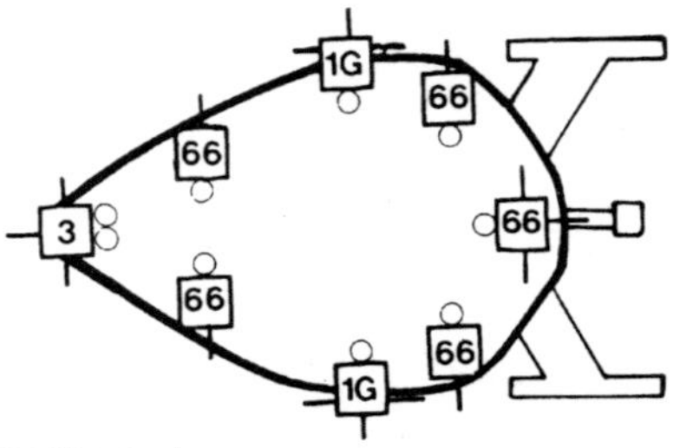

2 Boiler=1

200 TONS

3

Bridge: C H T S O

Deck: P

Maneuver

Screw: 3 2 1

Hull Hits: H, M, L, VL

Troops: 0 0 0 0 0

Japan — *YASHIMA*

2

£ 34,100

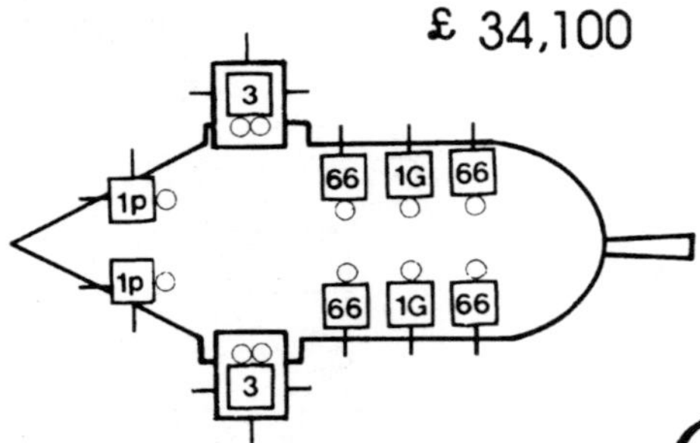

3 Boiler=2

250 TONS

4

Bridge: C H T S O

Deck: P P

Maneuver

Screw: 4 3 2 1

Hull Hits: VH, H, M, L, VL

SWIFTWOOD

0

£ 20,140

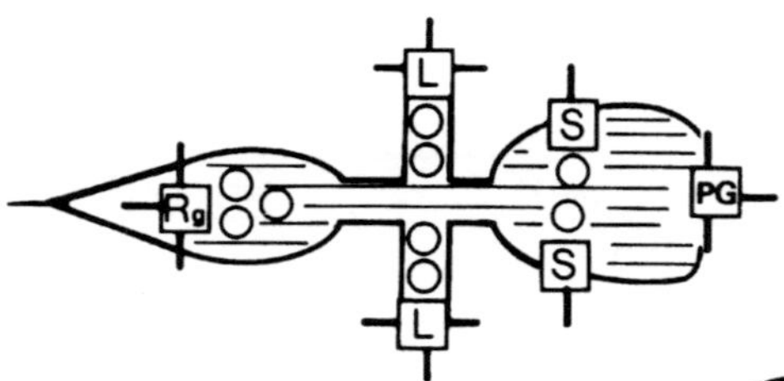

3

250 TONS

K

Bridge: C H T S O

Deck

Maneuver

Screw: -1 -2 -3 -4 -5 -6

Hull Hits: VH, H, M, L, VL

Marines: 0 0

SMALL BIRD

0

£ 13,000

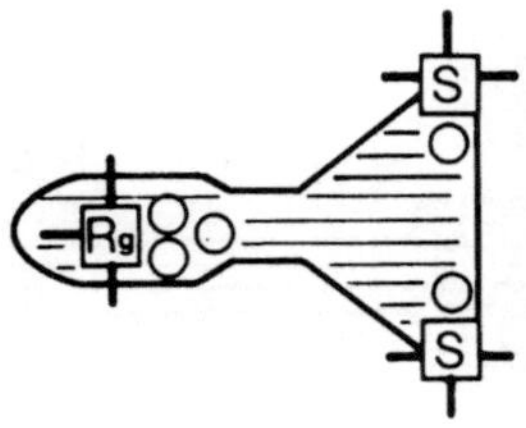

2

140 TONS

3

Bridge C H T S

Deck

Maneuver

Screw 3 2 1

Hull Hits VH H M L VL

Marines

FLEETFOOT

0

£ 6,000

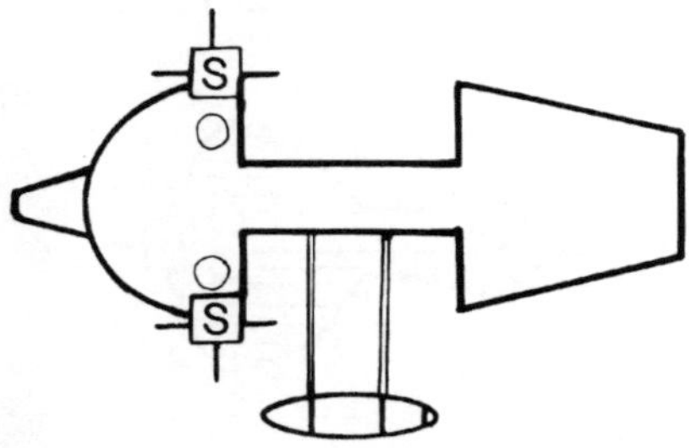

1

80 TONS

5

Bridge C H T S

Deck

Maneuver

Screw 5 4 3 2 1

Hull Hits VH H M L VL

Marines

AERIAL STEAM LAUNCH

0

£ 4,840

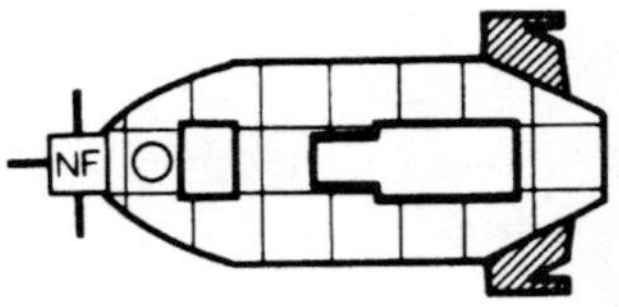

1

50 TONS

5

Bridge C H T

Deck

Maneuver

Screw 5 4 3 2 1

Hull Hits VH H M L VL

Passengers

SKY RUNNER

0

£ 25,600

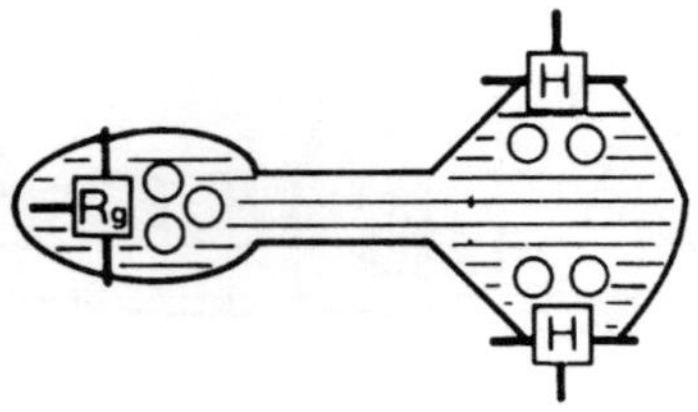

4

300 TONS

4

Bridge C H T S O

Deck

Maneuver

Screw 4 3 2 1

Hull Hits VH H M L VL

Marines

BLOODRUNNER

(0) £ 7,600

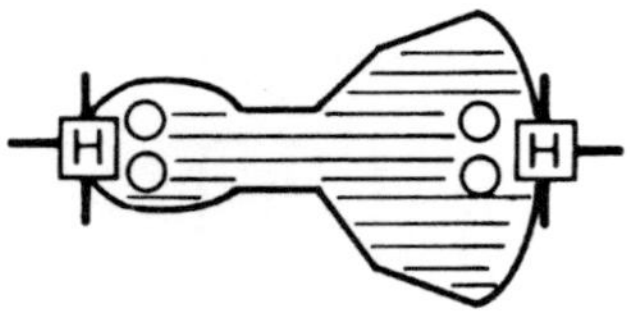

1 — 100 TONS — K

Bridge C H T S

Deck

Maneuver

Masts -1 -2 -3 -4 -5 -6

Hull Hits H M L VL

HULLCUTTER

(0) £ 46,800

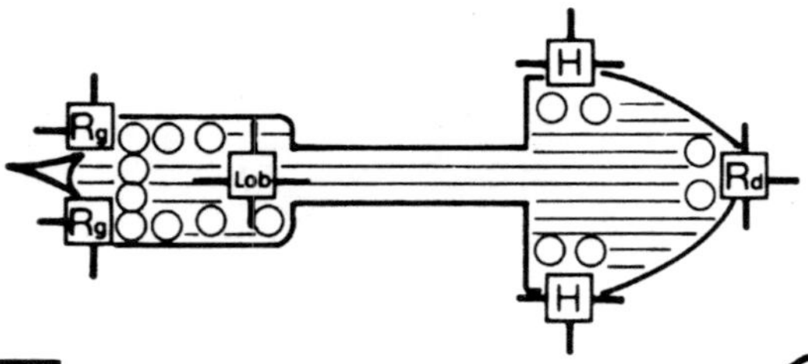

7 — 695 TONS — 3

Bridge C H T S O O O

Deck

Maneuver

Screw 3 2 1

Hull Hits H M L VL

Marines 0

ZEPPELIN

(0) £ 20,000

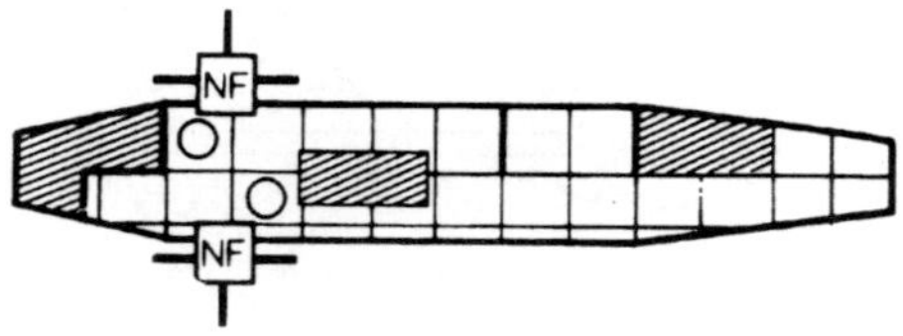

2 — 200 TONS — 6

Bridge C H T S

Deck

Maneuver

Screw 6 5 4 3 2 1

Hull Hits VH H M L VL

Passengers

£

TONS

Bridge C H T S O O

Deck

Maneuver

Hull Hits VH H M L VL

Marines

Lightning Source UK Ltd.
Milton Keynes UK
22 October 2009

145313UK00002B/9/P